CHRISTIANITY IN JAPAN

A Bibliography of Japanese and Chinese Sources

Christianity in Japan

A Bibliography of Japanese and Chinese Sources

PART I

(1543—1858)

Compiled by

Arimichi Ebisawa

Committee on Asian Cultural Studies
International Christian University

TOKYO 1960

This book has been compiled by the Committee on Asian Cultural
Studies of International Christian University
Copyright in Japan, 1960, by International Christian University

All rights reserved

First edition, 1960

Manufactured in Japan for International Christian University by
the Charles E. Tuttle Company

Preface

THE PRIMARY concern of the Committee on Asian Cultural Studies at the International Christian University at this initial stage is a study of the historical impact of Christianity on Asian culture, past and present. Needless to say, this is a multifacetted research project and requires interdisciplinary cooperation and integrated interpretation. As a basic research tool, a comprehensive bibliography on Christianity in Asia is both desirable and necessary. Therefore the Committee has decided to prepare such a bibliography in connection with the present research project. Fortunately, we have a most competent Japanese scholar for this purpose in the person of Prof. Arimichi Ebisawa, who is a research member of the Committee. Building on his former publications, Prof. Ebisawa has now completed a bibliography covering the period between 1543 and 1858, that is, from the time of first introduction of Christianity to Japan by the Roman Catholic missionaries to the year preceding the arrival of the first Protestant missionaries. The Committee is now working on bibliographies covering the later periods.

It is hoped that this present volume will be found convenient to scholars both in the East and in the West, since it was so prepared as to make it usable to western investigators who are able to deal with the original materials directly. Now that the West is rediscovering the East, so to speak, the Committee felt it opportune to start publishing a series of bibliographies relevant to our studies. It may be pointed out that the publication of this bibliography at this time is also opportune because Japanese Protestant Christians are now celebrating the Centennial anniversary of the arrival of first missionaries in 1859, the beginning of the Protestant churches in Japan.

The Committee wish .... sincere appreciation to Dr. Edwin O. Reischauer, Director of the Harvar .... and publication of this ....

Errata

page	col.	no.	line	errata	read
xxi	r		11 from top	SAKURAI TADASU	SAKURAI MASASHI
7	1	97		1951 (昭和 26)	1950 (昭和 25)
16	1		7 from top	(1567–1512)	(1567–1612)
19	r	478	13 from top	478	477
20	1	493		Zesshō Dōbunki Shūyō	Zesshō Dōbunki Shuyō
95	r	2727		Satū Nobuhiro	Satō Nobuhiro
96	r	2754		塩谷　宏陰	塩谷　宕陰
96	r	2755		○咶唎紀略	嘆咶唎紀略
102	1	2891		塩谷　宏陰	塩谷　宕陰
104	1	2948		c. Jishu	c. Jinshu
104	r		36 from top	1869	1859
112	r	3168		塩谷　宏陰	塩谷　宕陰
158	1		16 from top	Yüeh-li Li-chih	Yüeh-li Li-chih
158	1		16 from bottom	1286, 1787	1286, 1789
165	r		30 from bottom	Sakurai Tadasu	Sakurai Masashi
166	r		15 from top	xv, xiii	xv, xviii
168	r		14 from bottom	Mesuration	Mensuration

Foreword

THE YEAR 1959 is of particular importance for the Christian world as the centenary of the reopening of the Roman Catholic mission and the beginning of the Protestant mission to Japan. I am very glad to present this bibliography at this time to historians to be used as a basic tool for research.

The dates of publications listed here cover the three centuries from the year 1549 when Christianity was introduced to 1858. During the first forty years many spiritual books were compiled but not published, for the Jesuits did not have available to them the techniques of printing with wooden blocks which had been long used in Japan. In 1590 Alessandro Valignano, S.J. introduced printing with moveable type from Europe, after which time the Roman Church in Japan gradually began to publish books. The total number of publications grew until according to some reports about one hundred and fifty books had been published in the twenty years before 1610. However, because of subsequent persecution only thirty printed books and about fifty manuscripts now remain from that period.

By the end of the seventeenth century, stringent enforcement of the laws against Christianity had succeeded in stamping it out, at least on the surface. The persecution was very harsh because certain ideas that had been brought by Christianity were against the policy of the Tokugawa Government to build up and support a centralized feudal state. The feudal rulers feared Christian views of mankind and the world, the universal character of the Church, the scientific techniques and the scientific thinking itself that the Christians had introduced into Japan. In 1630 the government prohibited the importation of any books, including scientific ones, connected with Christianity. It also spread abroad the idea that the priests were sorcerers and that Christianity was dangerous for Japan. But even this oppression could not kill the seeds of Truth once they had been sown. During more than two centuries of oppression, Christians handed down their faith in family groups, and in 1865 when a Roman Catholic chapel was built at Ōura in Nagasaki, about fifty thousand people came forth to confess that they were Christians, members of such families who had kept the faith.

On the other hand, scientific books written by the Jesuits in China which were imported secretly into Japan helped advance the new techniques which had been introduced with Christianity. Throughout the whole Edo Period there was hardly any scholar who studied even a little science, or who tried to solve pressing contemporary problems who did not read some of these prohibited books or was otherwise influenced by Christianity. Ideas from the Christian world presented through Chinese Roman Catholic books were almost entirely responsible for the advancement of medicine, mathematics, astronomy, calendar science, navigation, mensuration and geography. The *Rangaku* or Dutch learning, which developed with the introduction of Protestant ideas through Nagasaki in the last half of the eighteenth century, built upon this foundation of Western scientific ideas. As Protestant missions developed in China in the nineteenth century increasing numbers of their books were brought into Japan. These books not only brought new knowledge but gradually led to the development of views about the world which ultimately brought about the opening of the country and the relaxation of the prohibition against Christianity. Thus these

Christian cultural traditions played an important part in the formation of modern Japan.

The books listed here include those both directly and indirectly related to Christianity, even though among them there are some which at first sight may appear to be unrelated.

Even the Shintō books listed here show definite influences of Christianity.

To attempt to cover all the materials in so wide a field is to set oneself a great task, a task which I am afraid is beyond my ability. There are many books with which I am not yet familiar enough, and there are probably many more of which I am unaware. I hope that this bibliography will be used by those sharing my interest to increase our knowledge of Christian history, and that they will pass along any suggestions to me which may be used in preparing future revision.

In closing, I wish to express my thanks to the persons in the scores of libraries I visited gathering materials, and to my friends and assistants for their co-operation.

Tokyo
July, 1959

ARIMICHI EBISAWA

Contents

Explanatory Notes

1. THIS CATALOGUE lists books and manuscripts connected with Christianity which were written in Japan and China and in Japanese and Chinese between 1543 and 1858. It was compiled from catalogues of the libraries mentioned in the "List of Libraries"; from notes included in works mentioned in the "List of Sources"; and from my own personal observation.

2. Historical documents such as government regulations which were not published as books are omitted as a rule except when they appear in collectanea (*Sōsho*) or were very important to the history of Christianity in Japan.

3. Books are arranged in chronological order of publication. In case this date is unknown, the volume is arranged according to the date of the author's death. In case both the date of publication and the date of the author's death are unknown, books are arranged with those covering similar topics.

4. If a book has more than one author or more than one publisher, the most representative among them are listed. When the author is unknown, the book is listed under its title.

5. Translations of the Scriptures are listed under the translator's name.

6. Titles are listed in *rōmaji* followed by *kanji* and *kana* which is in turn followed by an English title. This is intended to give some idea of the contents and is enclosed in parentheses.

7. Titles in Japanese or Chinese are translated into English but those in other European languages are not always translated.

8. Dates of publication are shown according to the Western calendar followed by the Chinese or Japanese reign name and the year of the reign. In cases where the month of publication is known and there is some possibility that by the Western calendar the publication may in fact have been early the following year, the reign name, year of the reign and month are given.

9. Manuscript copies of any given work often differ in the number of volumes and the number and size of the pages. Where this is not the case, the number of volumes and other information are given. Where it is the case such facts are not included.

10. Owners are indicated either by the name of the owner if an individual, or when the owner is a library or a large collection, a code word which is indexed in the "List of Libraries." The word which follows the code word joined by a hyphen shows the special collection of that library. The book mentioned in 0005, for example, is in the "Bunka Branch" of the Kyūshū University Library.

11. In the case of reprints, only those published as independent books are mentioned in detail, while for those which are contained in collectanea, only the name of the collectanea and the volume number are mentioned.

12. Asterisks (*) indicate entries having the same contents as those of the immediately preceding book under different titles.

13. Entries beginning with a line followed by parentheses indicate that the work mentioned above is a part of a collectanea.

14. "Abridged" indicates that portions of the work mentioned above have been included in this work.
15. "Construed" refers to the Japanese practise of adding *kunten* (marks for guidance in rendering Chinese into Japanese) to Chinese texts.
16. Romanization of Japanese is according to the Hepburn system except where the original is in another system it is preserved. Romanization of Chinese book title and personal names is in both Japanese and Chinese pronunciation. Place names follow the "Manual of Chinese-Manchuria Personal and Place Names" compiled by the Japan Times Press, Tokyo 1939.
17. Words taken from Western languages and listed in titles in *kana* are presented here in their original form and not as literal transcriptions of the *kana*. For instance, "Xavier" is presented as "Xavier," and not "Sabieru," "Shabieru," etc.
18. Brackets ([ ]) enclosing material indicate
    1) pages not numbered in the volume itself;
    2) information not mentioned in the volume itself but obtained from other sources.
19. Entries following "cf." refer to the "List of Sources."
20. Entries following "c." or "ms." refer to the "List of Libraries."

Abbreviations

c.	copy		nos.	numbers
cb.	Chinese binding		n.p.	no place
cf.	confer		orig.	original
cm.	centimeter		p.	page
col.	column		phot.	photograph
ed.	edition		pl.	plate
f.	leaf		pr.	print(ed)
facs.	facsimile		repr.	reprint(ed)
Jap.	Japanese		roto.	rotograph
jb.	Japanese binding		tr.	translated
lib.	library		v.	volume
mimeogr.	mimeographed ed.		vols.	volumes
ms.	manuscript		univ.	university
n.	number		wb.	western binding
n.d.	no date			

List of Libraries

Akioka Private Collection of Prof. Akioka Takejirō 秋岡武次郎, Setagaya-ku, Tokyo.

Akita Akita Prefectural Lib. 秋田縣立圖書館, Akita.

Amagasaki Amagasaki Municipal Lib. 尼崎市立圖書館, Amagasaki-shi, Hyōgo Pref.

Aoi Aoi Bunko 葵文庫, Shizuoka Prefectural Lib., Shizuoka.

Aoyama Aoyama Gakuin Univ. Lib. 青山學院大學間島記念圖書館, Shibuya-ku, Tokyo.

Ayuzawa Private Collection of Dr. Ayuzawa Shintarō 鮎澤信太郎, Fussa, Tokyo.

Chiba Chiba Prefectural Lib. 千葉縣立圖書館, Chiba.

Daitokyu Dai-tōkyū Ki'nen Bunko 大東急記念文庫, Meguro-ku, Tokyo.

Doi Private Collection of Dr. Doi Tadao 土井忠生, Hiroshima.

Doshisha Dōshisha Univ. Lib. 同志社大學圖書館, Kamigyō-ku, Kyoto.

Ebisawa Private Collection of Prof. Ebisawa Arimichi 海老澤有道, Nerima-ku, Tokyo.

Fujinami Fujinami Bunko 藤浪文庫, Higashi-ku, Osaka.

Fukuoka Fukuoka Prefectural Lib. 福岡縣立圖書館, Fukuoka.

Gakushiin Gakushiin (Academy of Japan) Lib. 學士院圖書館, Daitō-ku, Tokyo.

Gakushuin Gakushūin Univ. Lib. 學習院大學圖書館, Toshima-ku, Tokyo.

Hakodate Hakodate Municipal Lib. 函館市立圖書館, Hokkaido.

Hatano Private Collection of Mr. Hatano Kazuo 波多野和夫, Chōfu-shi, Tokyo.

Hazama Hazama Bunko 羽間文庫, Osaka.

Hibiya Hibiya Public Lib. 東京都立日比谷圖書館, Chiyoda-ku, Tokyo.

Hikone Hikone Municipal Lib. 彦根市立圖書館, Hikone-shi, Shiga Pref.

Hokudai Hokkaidō Univ. Lib. 北海道大學附屬圖書館, Sapporo-shi, Hokkaidō.

Hokugaku Hokkaidō Gakugei Univ. Lib. 北海道學藝大學圖書館, Sapporo-shi, Hokkaido.

ICU Kokusai Kirisutokyō (International Christian) Univ. Lib. 國際基督教大學圖書館, Mitaka-shi, Tokyo.

Imoto Imoto Bunko 井本文庫, Kobe.

Ishida Private Collection of Prof. Ishida Mikinosuke 石田幹之助, Minato-ku, Tokyo.

Ishin Ishin Shiryō Hensanjo 維新史料編纂所, Bunkyō-ku, Tokyo.

Iwase Iwase Bunko 岩瀬文庫 in Nishio Municipal Lib. 西尾市立圖書館, Aichi Pref.

Iwate Iwate Univ. Lib. 岩手大學圖書館, Morioka-shi, Iwate Pref.

JBS Nippon Seisho Kyōkai (Japan Bible Society) 日本聖書協会, Chūō-ku, Tokyo.

Jingu Jingū Bunko 神宮文庫, Ise-shi, Mie Pref.

Jinshu Jinshū Bunko 神習文庫, Shinjuku-ku, Tokyo.

Junshin Junshin Joshi Junior College Lib. 純心女子短期大學圖書館, Nagasaki.

Kagoshima Kagoshima Prefectural Lib. 鹿兒島縣立圖書館, Kagoshima.

Kamakura Kamakura Municipal Lib. 鎌倉市立圖書館, Kanagawa Pref.

Kanazawa Kanazawa Municipal Lib. 金澤市立圖書館, Kanazawa-shi, Ishikawa Pref.

Kanezawa Kanezawa Bunko 金澤文庫, Kanezawa-ku, Yokohama.

Kansei Kansei-gakuin Univ. Lib. 關西學院大學圖書館, Nishinomiya-shi, Hyogo

Pref.

Kariya   Kariya Municipal Lib. 刈谷市立圖書館, Kariya-shi, Aichi Pref.

Kawasaki   Kawasaki Municipal Lib. 川崎市立圖書館, Kawasaki-shi, Kanagawa Pref.

Keio   Keiō-gijuku Univ. Lib. 慶應義塾大學圖書館, Minato-ku, Tokyo.

Kichu   Kirisutokyō Chūō (Christian Central) Lib. 基督教中央圖書館, Chiyoda-ku, Tokyo.

Kobedai   Kōbe Univ. Lib. 神戸大學圖書館, Nada-ku, Kobe.

Kobejo   Kōbe Jogakuin Univ. Lib. 神戸女學院大學圖書館,   Nishinomiya-shi, Hyōgo Pref.

Kobeshi   Kōbe Municipal Lib. 神戸市立圖書館, Ikuta-ku, Kobe.

Kochi   Kōchi Prefectural Lib. 高知縣立圖書館, Kōchi.

Kokugakuin   Kokugakuin Univ. Lib. 国學院大學圖書館, Shibuya-ku, Tokyo.

Kompira   Kompira-gū Lib. 金比羅宮圖書館, Kotohira-machi, Kagawa Pref.

Kurita   Private Collection of Dr. Kurita Genji 栗田元次 (destroyed).

Kyodai   Kyōto Univ. Lib. 京都大學附屬圖書館, Sakyōku, Kyoto.

Kyoto   Kyōto Prefectural Lib. 京都府立圖書館, Sakyō-ku, Kyoto.

Kyudai   Kyūshū Univ. Lib. 九州大學附屬圖書館, Fukuoka.

Matsura   Matsūra Archive 松浦史料館, Hirado-shi, Nagasaki Pref.

Meiji   Meiji Gakuin Univ. Lib. 明治學院大學圖書館, Minato-ku, Tokyo.

Miyagi   Miyagi Prefectural Lib. 宮城縣立圖書館, Sendai-shi, Miyagi Pref.

Naikaku   Naikaku (Cabinet) Bunko 内閣文庫, Chiyoda-ku, Tokyo.

Nagasaki   Nagasaki Prefectural Lib. 縣立長崎圖書館, Nagasaki.

Nagasakishi   Nagasaki Municipal Lib. 長崎市立圖書館, Nagasaki.

Nakatani   Private Collection of Mr. Nakatani Shigezō 中谷繁藏, Takatsuki-shi, Osaka Pref.

Nanzan   Nanzan Univ. Lib. 南山大學圖書館, Shōwa-ku, Nagoya-shi, Aichi Pref.

Narita   Narita Lib. 成田圖書館, Narita-shi, Chiba Pref.

ND   Kokuritsu Kokkai (National Diet) Lib. 國立國會圖書館, Minato-ku, Tokyo.

Nichidai   Nihon Univ. Lib. 日本大學圖書館, Chiyoda-ku, Tokyo.

Oda   Oda Bunko 織田文庫, Shinjuku-ku, Tokyo.

Odawara   Odawara Municipal Lib. 小田原市立圖書館, Odawara-shi, Kanagawa Pref.

Okayama   Okayama Prefectural Lib. 岡山縣立圖書館, Okayama.

Okinawa   Okinawa Prefectural Lib. 沖繩縣立圖書館, Naha-shi, Loochoo (destroyed).

Osaka   Ōsaka Prefectural Lib. 大阪府立圖書館, Kita-ku, Osaka.

Otani   Ōtani Univ. Lib. 大谷大學圖書館, Kita-ku, Kyoto.

Oura   Ōura Cathedral 大浦天主堂, Nagasaki.

Rikkyo   Rikkyō (St. Paul's) Univ. Lib. 立教大學圖書館, Toshima-ku, Tokyo.

Ryukoku   Ryūkoku Univ. Lib. 龍谷大學圖書館, Shimogyō-ku, Kyoto.

Saba   Saba Bunko 佐波文庫 in Tokyo Women's Christian College 東京女子大學, Suginami-ku, Tokyo.

Sakai   Sakai Municipal Lib. 堺市立圖書館, Sakai-shi, Osaka Pref.

Seikado   Seikadō Bunko 静嘉堂文庫, Setagaya-ku, Tokyo.

Seisakudo   Seisakudō Bunko 成簣堂文庫, Ota-ku, Tokyo.

Seishin   Seishin Joshi Univ. (Univ. of the Sacred Heart) Lib. 聖心女子大學圖書館, Shibuya-ku, Tokyo.

Shimazu   Shimazu Archive 島津家史料館, Kagoshima.

Shimmura   Private Collection of Dr. Shimmura Izuru 新村出, Kita-ku, Kyoto.

Shinken   Shinken Bunko 眞軒文庫, Shinjuku-ku, Tokyo.

Shiryo   Shiryō Hensanjo 史料編纂所 of Tokyo Univ., Bunkyō-ku, Tokyo.

Shokokan   Shōkōkan 彰考館, Mito-shi, Ibaraki Pref.

Shoryobu   Shoryōbu 書陵部 of the Imperial Household, Chiyoda-ku, Tokyo.

Sophia   Jōchi (Sophia) Univ. Lib. 上智大學

圖書館, Chiyoda-ku, Tokyo.

Sonkeikaku Private Collection of the Maeda Family 前田家, Meguro-ku, Tokyo.

Sukeno Private Collection of Mr. Sukeno Kentarō 助野健太郎, Minami-ku, Yokohama.

Tagita Private Collection of Prof. Tagita Kōya 田北耕也, Shōwa-ku, Nagoya.

Taisho Taishō Univ. Lib. 大正大學圖書館, Toshima-ku, Tokyo.

Takagi Takagi Bunko 高木文庫, Tokyo.

Tenri Tenri Chūō (Tenri Central) Lib. 天理中央圖書館, Tenri-shi, Nara Pref.

Todai Tokyo Univ. Lib. 東京大學附屬圖書館, Bunkyō-ku, Tokyo.

Tohoku Tōhoku Univ. Lib. 東北大學附屬圖書館, Sendai-shi, Miyagi Pref.

Tokugawa Private Collection of Mr. Tokugawa Kuniyori 徳川圀順, Tokyo.

Tokyoiku Tokyo Kyōiku Univ. Lib. 東京教育大學圖書館, Bunkyō-ku, Tokyo.

Tokyoshin Tōkyō Shingaku (Theological) Univ. Lib. 東京神學大學圖書館, Mitaka-shi, Tokyo.

Toyo Tōyō Bunko (Oriental Lib.) 東洋文庫, Bunkyō-ku, Tokyo.

Toyodai Tōyō Univ. Lib. 東洋大學圖書館, Bunkyō-ku, Tokyo.

Tsuruoka Tsuruoka Municipal Lib. 鶴岡市立圖書館, Tsuruoka-shi, Yamagata Pref.

Tsushima Tsushima Municipal Lib. 市立津島圖書館, Tsushima-shi, Aichi Pref.

Ueda Private Collection of Mr. Ueda Teijirō 上田貞治郎, Osaka, (destroyed).

Ueno Ueno Lib. 上野圖書館 of the National Diet Lib., Daitō-ku, Tokyo.

Waseda Waseda Univ. Lib. 早稻田大學附屬圖書館, Shinjuku-ku, Tokyo.

Yanagiya Private Collection of Prof. Yanagiya Takeo 柳谷武夫, Kamakura, Kanagawa Pref.

Yasaka Yasaka Jinja Bunko 八坂神社文庫, Higashiyama-ku, Kyoto.

Yasuda Yasuda Bunko 安田文庫 in Ōhashi Lib. 大橋圖書館, Nerima-ku, Tokyo.

Yokohama Yokohama Municipal Lib. 橫濱市立圖書館, Nishi-ku, Yokohama.

Yokohamashidai Yokohama Municipal Univ. Lib. 橫濱市立大學圖書館, Kanezawa-ku, Yokohama.

Yoshida Private Collection of Mr. Yoshida Tora 吉田寅, Nerima-ku, Tokyo.

List of Sources

1. This list contains the names of books, catalogues, dictionaries and other literatures rich in bibliographical notes concerning Christian history to which the author referred in making this catalogue. They are listed with the names of authors and compilers in alphabetical order.
2. Printed catalogues of libraries except for those of particular value to this study are omitted.
3. Also omitted are the names of annotated texts, collectanea and periodical articles.

ANESAKI-BUNGAKU Anesaki Masaharu 姉崎正治; Kirishitan Shūkyō Bungaku 切支丹宗教文學, Tokyo 1932.

ANESAKI-HAKUGAI —Kirishitan Shūmon no Hakugai to Sempuku 切支丹宗門の迫害と潜伏, Tokyo 1926.

ANESAKI-JIMBUTSU —Kirishitan Hakugaishichū no Jimbutsu Jiseki 切支丹迫害史中の人物事蹟, Tokyo 1930.

ANESAKI-KINZEI —Kirishitan Kinzei no Shūmatsu 切支丹禁制の終末, Tokyo 1926.

ANESAKI-MARTYRDOM —Writings on Martyrdom in Kirishitan Literature, Tokyo 1931.

ANESAKI MASAHARU; A Concordance to the Kirishitan Missions, Tokyo 1930.

AOYAMA GAKUIN MAJIMA KI'NEN TOSHOKAN 青山學院間島記念圖書館; Meijiki Kirisutokyō kankei Tosho Mokuroku 明治期基督教關係圖書目録, Tokyo 1954.

— Meijishoki Kirisutokyō kankei Tosho Tenran Mokuroku 明治初期基督教關係圖書展覧目録, Tokyo 1955.

ARAKI-EIGOGAKU Araki Ibyōe 荒木伊兵衛; Nippon Eigogaku Shoshi 日本英語學書誌, Tokyo 1931.

ARAKI KŌTARŌ 荒木幸太郎; Bunka Inyū ni kansuru Kosho Tenrankai Mokuroku 文化移入に關する古書展覧會目録, Osaka 1925.

ASAHI Asahi Shimbunsha 朝日新聞社;

Kaikoku Bunka Shiryō Taikan 開國文化史料大觀, Osaka 1929.

AUREL, J. C.; Seisho Wayaku no Rekishi to Seisho Kyōkai 聖書和譯の歴史と聖書協會, Tokyo 1926.

AYUZAWA-RICCI Ayuzawa Shintarō 鮎澤信太郎; Mateo Ricci no Sekaizu ni kansuru Shiteki Kenkyū マテオリッチの世界圖に關する史的研究, Yokohama 1953.

AYUZAWA-SEKAI — Sakokujidai no Sekai Chirigaku 鎖國時代の世界地理學, Tokyo 1943.

AYUZAWA SHINTARŌ; Chirigakushi no Kenkyū 地理學史の研究, Tokyo 1948.

AYUZAWA-TOYO — Tōyō Chiri Shisōshi Kenkyū 東洋地理思想史研究, Tokyo 1940.

BESSHO UMENOSUKE 別所梅之助; Kaitei Sambika Monogatari 改訂讃美歌物語, Tokyo 1933.

BOXER-COMPAGNIE C. R. Boxer; Jan Compagnie in Japan, 1600–1850, The Hague, revised ed., 1950.

BOXER, C. R.; Bibliotheca Boxeriana, Macao 1937.

BRITISH BIBLE SOCIETY; Historical Catalogue of the Printed Editions of Holy Scripture in the Library of the British and Foreign Bible Society compiled by T. H. Darlow and H. F. Moule, London 1911. 2 vols.

BRITISH MUSEUM; Catalogue of Chinese printed Books, Manuscripts and Drawings in the Library of the British Museum by Robert K. Douglas, London 1877–92. 2 vols.

CORDIER, HENRI; Essai d'une bibliographie des ouvrages publiée en Chine par les Européens au XVIIe et XVIIIe siècle, Paris 1883.

CORDIER-JAPONICA — Bibliotheca Japonica, Paris 1912 (Tokyo 1931).

CORDIER-SINICA — Bibliotheca Sinica, Paris 1904 (Shanghai 1938). 5 vols.

DEUTSCHES FORSCHUNGSINSTITUT; Bibliographischer Alt-Japan-Katalog 1542–1853, Kyōto 1940.

DOI Doi Tadao 土井忠生; Kirishitan Gogaku no Kenkyū 吉利支丹語學の研究, Tokyo 1942.

DŌSHISHA DAIGAKU TOSHOKAN 同志社大學圖書館; Niishima-kyūtei Bunko Shozō Mokuroku 新島舊邸文庫所藏目録, Kyoto 1958.

EBISAWA ARIMICHI 海老澤有道; (Kubota Yukio 窪田幸夫) Kirishitan Bungaku Nōto 吉利支丹文學ノート, Tokyo 1952.

— Kirishitanshi Bunken Kaidai キリシタン史文献解題 by Ebisawa Arimichi and Sukeno Kentarō 助野健太郎, Yokohama 1955.

— Kirishitanshi no Kenkyū 切支丹史の研究, Tokyo 1942.

— Kirishitanshi Tenrankai Kaisetsu Mokuroku キリシタン史展覧會解說目録, Yokohama 1955.

— Meiji-shoki no Katorikku Shuppan 明治初期のカトリック出版, Tokyo 1950.

— Nippon Kirisutokyō-shi kankei Wakanjo Mokuroku 日本基督教史關係和漢書目録, Tokyo 1954.

— Nippon no Sambika 日本の讃美歌, Tokyo 1947.

— Nippon Shoki Seiyō Kirisutokyōshi kankei Bunken Kaisetsu Mokuroku 日本初期西洋基督教史關係文献解說目録, Yokohama 1952.

— Seishin Joshi Daigaku Toshokan Shozō Wakanjo Kaidai 聖心女子大學圖書館所藏和漢書解題, Tokyo 1954–55. 4 vols.

EBISAWA-MATSUMURA Catalogue of Printed Books relating to the Early Catholic Missions in Japan, compiled by Ebisawa Arimichi and Matsumura Tamiko 松村多美子, Tokyo 1958.

EBISAWA-NAMBAN — Namban-gakutō no Kenkyū 南蠻學統の研究, Tokyo 1958.

EBISAWA-TENSEKI — Kirishitan Tenseki Sōkō 切支丹典籍叢考, Tokyo 1943.

FREITAS, JOÃO; Shoki Yasokyōto Henjutsu Nippon Gogakusho Kenkyū 初期耶蘇教徒編述日本語學書研究, tr. by Okamoto Yoshitomo 岡本良知, Tokyo 1929.

GAKUSHIIN 學士院; Wasansho Mokuroku 和算書目録, Tokyo 1932.

GUILHERMY, E. DE; Ménologe de la Compagnie de Jésus, Poitiers 1867.

HEIBONSHA 平凡社; Dai Jimmei Jiten 大人名事典, Tokyo 1953–54. 9 vols.

HIBIYA TOSHOKAN 日比谷圖書館; Arai Hakuseki Kankei Bunken Sōran 新井白石關係文献綜覧, Tokyo 1926.

— A Short List of Books and Pamphlets relating to European Intercourse with Japan (Private Collection of Prof. S. Kōda) Exhibited at the Mitsukoshi, Tokyo 1930.

— Kondō Ki'nen Kaiji Zaidan Bunko Tosho Mokuroku 近藤記念海事財團文庫圖書目録, Tokyo 1937.

HIIRAGI GEN'ICHI 柊源一 and Shimmura Izuru 新村出; Kirishitan Bungakushū 吉利支丹文學集, v. I. (Nippon Koten Zensho 日本古典全書), Tokyo, 1957.

HIROSE BIN 廣瀬敏; Zōtei Nippon Sōsho Sakuin 增訂日本叢書索引, Tokyo 1957.

HOTEI SHUJIN 穂亭主人; Seiyō-Gakuka Yakujitsu Mokuroku 西洋學家譯述目録 Edo (Tokyo) 1852.

HUMBERTCLAUDE, PIERRE; Recherches sur Deux Catalogues de Macao (1616 and 1632), Tokyo 1942.

ISHIDA MIKINOSUKE 石田幹之助; Ōjin no Shina Kenkyū 歐人の支那研究, Tokyo 1932.

ISHII HARUMI 石井晴美; Kirisutokyō Dendō Shōsasshiten Mokuroku 基督教傳道小冊子展目録, Tokyo 1942.

ISHIKAWAKENRITSU TOSHOKAN 石川縣立圖書館; Seiyō Bunka Inyū ni kansuru

Tosho Tenrankai Mokuroku 西洋文化移入に關する圖書展覽會目錄, Kanazawa 1928.

ITAZAWA Itazawa Takeo 板澤武雄; Nichiran Bunka Kōshōshi no Kenkyū 日蘭文化交渉史の研究, Tokyo 1959.

IWANAMI SHOTEN 岩波書店; Iwanami Seiyō Jimmei Jiten 岩波西洋人名辭典 revised, Tokyo 1956.

Jo Jo Sōtaku 徐宗澤 *Hsü Tsung-tse*; Min-Shin-kan Yasokaishi Yakucho Teiyō 明清間耶蘇會士譯著提要 *Ming-Ching-chien Yeh-su-hui-shih Yi-chu T'i-yao*, revised, Taipei 1958.

JŌCHI DAIGAKU 上智大學; Katorikku Dai-Jiten カトリック大辭典, Tokyo 1940–60. 5 vols.

JŌCHI DAIGAKU Catholic Information; Nippon Katorikku Tosho Mokuroku 日本カトリック圖書目錄, Tokyo 1933.

JŌCHI DAIGAKU Shigaku Kenkyūshitsu 上智大學史學研究室; Han-Kirishitan Shiryō Tenrankai Mokuroku 反キリシタン史料展覽會目錄, Tokyo 1952.

— Jōchi Daigaku Shozō Meiji Ishin Kirisutokyōsho 上智大學所藏明治維新キリスト教書, Tokyo 1954.

JŪJIYA 十字屋; Kirisutokyō Shoseki Mokuroku 基督教書籍目錄, Tokyo [1892?]·

KADOWAKI Kadowaki Kiyoshi 門脇清; Seisho Tenrankai Mokuroku, fu, Seisho Wayakushi no Gaikan 聖書展覽會目錄, 附, 聖書和譯史の概觀, Numazu 1939.

KAIKOKU Kaikoku Hyakunen Bunka Jigyokai 開國百年記念文化事業會; Sakoku-jidai Nippon-Jin no Kaigai Chishiki 鎖國時代日本人の海外知識, Tokyo 1953.

KAMEDA JIRO 龜田次郎; Taiseijin Nippon-go Kenkyūsho Tenkan Shomoku 泰西人日本語研究書展觀書目, Kyoto 1937.

KATAKOZAWA CHIYOMATSU 片子澤千代松; Hepburn-yaku Shinyaku Seisho, Seisho Wayaku no Rekishi ヘボン譯新約聖書, 聖書和譯の歴史, Tokyo 1952.

— Nippon Shinkyōshi no Kenkyū 日本新教史の研究, Tokyo 1957.

KAWADE SHOBŌ SHINSHA 河出書房新社; Nippon Rekishi Dai-Jiten 日本歷史大辭典, Tokyo 1956–60. 20 vols.

KAWASE Kawase Kazuma 川瀬一馬; Ko-Katusjiban no Kenkyū 古活字版の研究, Tokyo 1937.

KINDAI CHUGOKU KENKYU IINKAI 近代中國研究委員會; Chūgoku Bunkashi Nippon-go Bunken Mokuroku, Kyōiku-Kirisutokyō 中國文化史日本語文献目録, 教育・キリスト教, Tokyo 1955.

KIRISUTOKYŌ CHUŌ TOSHOKAN 基督教中央圖書館; Nippon Shuppan Kirisutokyō Bunken Kari-Mokuroku 日本出版基督教文献假目録, Tokyo 1938.

KIRISUTOKYŌ KYŌGIKAI BUNGAKUBU 基督教協議會文學部; Zenkoku Kirisutokyō Kyōgikai Bungakubu Chōsa Hōkoku 全國基督教協議會文學部調査報告, Tokyo 1926.

KŌBE JOGAKUIN TOSHOKAN 神戸女學院圖書館; Alchin-shi Shūshū Nippon Sambi-kashi Shiryō Mokuroku オルチン氏蒐集日本讚美歌史資料目録, Nishinomiya 1956.

KŌDA SHIGETOMO 幸田成友; Oranda Yawa 和蘭夜話, Tokyo 1931.

— Shiwa Higashi to Nishi 史話東と西, Tokyo 1940.

— Shiwa Minami to Kita 史話南と北, Tokyo 1948.

— Tokushi Yoroku 讀史餘録, Tokyo 1928.

KOKURITSU KOKKAI TOSHOKAN 國立國會圖書館; Nichi-ō Bunka Kōshō Bunken Mokuroku 日歐文化交渉文献目録, Tokyo 1949.

— Shiryō Tenjikai, Meiji no Minshū to Bunka, Mokuroku to Kaisetsu 資料展示會, 明治の民衆と文化, 目録と解說, Tokyo 1956.

KOKUSHI Endō Motoo 遠藤元男 and Shimomura Fujio 下村富士男; Kokushi Bunken Kaidai 國史文献解題, Tokyo 1957.

KONDŌ JUZŌ 近藤重藏; Kōsho Koji 好書故事 (Kondō Seisai Zenshū, v. III), Tokyo 1906.

KUYAMA Kō 久山康; Kindai Nippon to Kirisutokyō, Meijihen 近代日本とキリスト教, 明治篇, Nishinomiya 1956.

KYŌTO DAIGAKU BUNGAKUBU 京都大學文學部; Kirishitan Ibutsu no Kenkyū 吉利支丹遺物の研究 (Kyōto Teikoku Daigaku Kōkogaku Kenkyū Hōkoku 京都

帝國大學考古學研究報告, v. VII), Kyoto 1926.

KYOTO UNIV. LIBRARY; Annual Letters of the Early Christian Missions from Japan, China, etc. (1544–1649), Kyoto 1920.

LAURES, Johannes Laures; Kirishitan Bunko, revised and enlarged, Tokyo 1957.

MAGGS & BROS; Bibliotheca Asiatica, London 1924–29.

— Printed Books and Manuscripts on Japan, London 1926.

MAGNINO, LEO; Bibliotheca Missionalis, Pontificia Nipponica, Romae 1947–48.

MARUZEN 丸善; Tenshō Shisetsu To-ō 350 nen Ki'nen Chinseki Tenrankai Mokuroku 天正使節渡歐三百五十年記念珍籍展覧會目録, Tokyo 1932.

— Shin-kaishū Kirishitan-ban o chūshin to shita Nippon oyobi Tōyō Kankei Ko-bunken-ten Mokuroku 新回收きりしたん版を中心とした日本及東洋關係古文献展目録, Tokyo 1952.

MAYER, P.S.; The Japan Christian Year Book 1943: Supplement, General Index, List of Missionaries, Tokyo 1943.

MEIJI BUNKA KENKYŪKAI 明治文化研究會; Meiji Bunka Tenrankai Shuppin Mokuroku 明治文化展覧會出品目録, Tokyo 1927.

(SOCIÉTÉ DES) MISSIONS-ETRANGÈRES DE PARIS; Nécrologe de la Société des Missions Etrangères de Paris 1659–1930, Hongkong 1932.

MIYAZAKI Miyazaki Michio 宮崎道生; Arai Hakuseki no Kenkyū 新井白石の研究, Tokyo 1958.

MOMBUSHŌ 文部省; Ishin Shiryō Hensanjo Jimukyoku Shozō Tosho Mokuroku 維新史料編纂所事務局所藏圖書目録, Tokyo [n. d.]

MURAOKA-BUNGAKU, Muraoka Tsunetsugu 村岡典嗣; Kirishitan Bungaku-shō 吉利支丹文學抄, Tokyo 1926.

MURAOKA-SHISO — Nippon Shisōshi Kenkyū 日本思想史研究, Tokyo 1930.

NAGASAKI KENRITSU TOSHOKAN 長崎縣立圖書館; Nagasaki Kyōdoshi Mokuroku 長崎郷土誌目録, Nagasaki 1954.

NAGAYAMA TOKIHIDE 永山時英; Kirishitan Shiryō-shū 吉利支丹史料集, Nagasaki 1926.

NAIKAKU BUNKO 内閣文庫; Kanseki Bunrui Mokuroku 漢籍分類目録, Tokyo 1956.

NANASOJIKAI 七十路會; Kirisutokyō Kobunken Tenraikai Shuppin Mokuroku 基督敎古文献展覧會出品目録, Tokyo 1927.

NIPPON SEIKŌKAI 日本聖公會; Soshiki Seiritsu 50 nen Ki'nen Taikai Tenrankai Shuppin Mokuroku 組織成立五十年記念大會展覧會出品目録, Tokyo 1937.

NIPPON SHINGAKKŌ 日本神學校; Kirisutokyō Bunken Kari-mokuroku 基督敎文献假目録, Tokyo 1932.

— Meiji-jidai Kirisutokyō Bunken 明治時代基督敎文献, Tokyo 1932.

OKAMOTO YOSHITOMO 岡本良知; Porutogaru o tazuneru ポルトガルを訪ねる, Tokyo 1930.

OKANO TAKEO 岡野他家夫; Meiji Bungaku Kenkyū Bunken Sōran 明治文學研究文献總覧, Tokyo 1944.

OKUNO Okuno Hikoroku 奥野彦六; Edo-jidai no Ko-hanbon 江戸時代の古版本, Tokyo 1944.

ŌMORI SHIRŌ 大森志朗; Kirishitan Bunken Mokuroku 吉利支丹文献目録, Sendai 1929.

ŌSAKA KIRISHITAN KENKYŪKAI 大阪吉利支丹研究會; Kirishitan Tenrankai Mokuroku 吉利支丹展覧會目録, Osaka 1927.

OSATAKE Osatake Takeshi 尾佐竹猛; Kinsei Nippon no Kokusai Kannen no Hattatsu 近世日本の國際觀念の發達, Tokyo 1932.

ŌTA MASAO 太田正雄; Nippon Kirishitan-shi-shō 日本吉利支丹史抄, Tokyo 1943.

— (Kinoshita Mokutarō 木下杢太郎); Esupania Porutsugaru-ki えすはにあほるつがる記, Tokyo 1929.

— Kinoshita Mokutarō Zenshū 木下杢太郎全集, v. VI, Tokyo 1950.

ŌTSUKI NYODEN 大槻如電; Shinsen Yōgaku Nenpyō 新撰洋學年表, Tokyo 1927.

OZAWA Ozawa Saburō 小澤三郎; Bakumatsu Meiji Yasokyōshi Kenkyū 幕末明治耶蘇敎史研究, Tokyo 1944.

PAGÉS, LÉON; Bibliothèque Japonaise, Paris 1899.

— Bibliographie Japonaise, Paris 1859 (Kyoto 1927).

PAPINOT, E; Liste des Ouvrages publiés par les Missionnaires des Missions Etrangères au Japon, Paris 1917.

PFISTER Louis Pfister; Notices Biographiques et Bibliographiques sur les Jésuites de l'ancienne mission de Chine, 1552–1773, Shanghai 1932–34. 2 vols.

— Nyūka Yasokaishi Retsuden 入華耶蘇會士列傳 *Ju-hua Yeh-su-hui-shih Lieh-chuan*, tr. by Hyō Shōkin 馮承鈞 *Feng Ch'eng-chün*, Shanghai 1938.

PROFILLET; Le Martyrologe de l'église du Japon, 1549–1649, Paris 1895–97. 3 vols.

RANGAKU Rangaku Shiryō Kenkyūkai 蘭學資料研究會; Yōgaku Kotohajimeten 洋學事始展, Tokyo 1954.

RETANA, W. E.; Orígenes de la Imprenta Filipina, Madrid 1911.

RIBADENEIRA, M. and LEGISIMA, J. DE; Evangelización de Filipinas y del Japón, Madrid 1947.

RIVIERE, E. M.; Corrections et additions à la Bibliothèque de la Compagnie de Jésus, Supplément au "De Backer-Sommervogel," Toulouse 1911.

ROBERTSON, J. A.; Bibliography of Early Spanish Japanese Relations, Tokyo 1915.

SABA WATARU 佐波亘; Uemura Masahisa to sono Jidai 植村正久と其時代, Tokyo 1937–38. 5 vols.

SAEKI-SHINA Saeki Yoshirō 佐伯好郎; Shina Kirisutokyō no Kenkyū 支那基督教の研究, v. III, Tokyo 1944.

SAEKI-SHINCHO — Shinchō Kirisutokyō no Kenkyū 清朝基督教の研究, Tokyo 1949.

SAEKI-SHINTO Saeki Yūgi 佐伯有義; Shintō Bunrui Sō-Mokuroku 神道分類總目錄 Appendix, Tokyo 1937.

SAEKI YOSHIRŌ 佐伯好郎; Keikyō Bunken oyobi Ibutsu Mokuroku 景教文献及遺物目録, Tokyo 1950.

SAITŌ KIYOSHI 齋藤潔; Meiji Kirisutokyō Bungaku Zassō 明治基督教文學雜藁, Tokyo 1938.

— Nippon Kirisutokyō Bungaku Tenran-kai Shutchin Shomoku Sōran 日本基督教文學展覽會出陳書目綜覽, Tokyo 1939.

SAITŌ SEIKEN 齋藤正謙; Tekkensai Yūken Shomoku 鐵研齋猶軒書目 (Bummei Genryū Sōsho, v. III), Tokyo 1914.

SAITŌ TAKESHI 齋藤勇; Eigo Sambika 英語讚美歌, Tokyo 1941.

SAKAKIBARA YŪJI 榊原悠二; Nippon Kirishitan no Rekishiteki Yakuwari 日本切支丹の歴史的役割, Tokyo 1948.

SAKURAI TADASU 櫻井匡; Yasokyō Haigeki Shiryō-kō 耶蘇教排擊史料考, (Bukkyō Daigaku Kōza), Tokyo 1934.

SAMURA Samura Hachirō 佐村八郎; Kaitei Kokusho Kaidai 改訂國書解題, Tokyo 1931. 2 vols.

SATOW Ernest M. Satow; The Jesuit Mission Press in Japan, 1591–1610, London 1888 (Tokyo 1926).

SENDA MASAO 仙田正雄; Kanyaku Kammei Seiyō Jimmei Jiten 漢譯漢名西洋人名字典 (準備版), Tenri 1957.

SENKYŌ HYAKUNEN KINEN TAIKAI TENRAN-KAI IINKAI 宣教百年記念大會展覽會委員會; Nippon Kirisutokyō senkyō Hyakunen Ki'nen Tenrankai Kaisetsu Mokuroku 日本キリスト教宣教百年記念展覽會解説目録, Tokyo 1959.

SERRURIER, L.; Bibliothèque Japonaise. Catalogue raisonné des livres et des manuscrits Japonais, Leyden 1896.

SHIGEHISA TOKUTARŌ 重久篤太郎; A List of Foreigners who contributed toward the Culture of Japan during the Meiji Era, Kyoto 1939.

— Nippon Kinsei Eigakushi 日本近世英學史, Kyoto 1941.

— Seiyōgo to Kokugo 西洋語と國語 (Kokugo Kagaku Kōza, v. XXVI), Tokyo 1935.

SHIMMURA-ISOHO Shimmura Izuru 新村出; Bunroku Kyūyaku Amakusabon Isoho Monogatari 文禄舊譯天草本伊曾保物語, Tokyo 1928.

SHIMMURA IZURU; Kirishitan Kenkyū Yoroku 吉利支丹研究餘録, Tokyo 1948.

— Nichi-ei kankei Tosho Tenkan-shi 日英關係圖書展觀志, Kyoto 1922.

— Nippon Kirishitan Bunkashi 日本吉利支丹文化史, Tokyo 1941.

— Satō-sensei Keikōroku 薩道先生景仰録, Tokyo 1929.

— Tenseki Sango 典籍散語, Tokyo 1934.

SHIMMURA-NAMBAN — Shimmura Izuru Senshū, Namban-hen 新村出選集南蠻篇, Kyoto and Tambaichi, 1943–45. 2 vols.

SOMMERVOGEL, C.; Bibliothèque de la Compagnie de Jésus, Paris 1890–1922. 11 vols.

STREIT R. Streit & J. Dindinger; Bibliotheca Missionum, Bde. IV–VI, X., Münster 1928–38.

SUGIURA KYŪEN 杉浦丘園; Oranda oyobi Gaikoku kankei Tosho narabini Buppin Mokuroku 和蘭及外國關係圖書並物品目録 Tokyo 1921. 2 vols.

SUZUKI JIRŌ 鈴木二郎; Nisshi Kirisutokyō Bunka Tenrankai Mokuroku 日支基督教文化展覽會目録, Tokyo 1940.

TAGITA Tagita Kōya 田北耕也; Shōwajidai no Sempuku Kirishitan 昭和時代の潜伏キリシタン, Tokyo 1954.

TAKAGI JINTARŌ 高木壬太郎; Kirisutokyō Daijiten 基督教大辭典, Tokyo 1911.

TAKECHI YOSHIO 高市慶雄; Meiji Bunken Mokuroku 明治文献目録, Tokyo 1932.

TANAKA TOYOJIRŌ 田中豊次郎; Seisho Seichō-shiwa 聖書成長史話, Tokyo 1935.

TENRI CENTRAL LIB.; Catalogue of Special Books on Christian Missions, Tambaichi (Tenri), 1930–55. 2 vols.

— Catalogue of the Rare Books of the Tenri Central Library Books (other than Japanese and Chinese), Tambaichi (Tenri), 1941–57. 3 vols.

— Photo Series, v. II., The Jesuit Mission Press in Japan, Tenri 1953.

— Photo Series, v. X., Early Western Works on Japan, Tenri 1957.

TENRI-JAP. — Catalogue of the Rare Books of the Tenri Central Library (Japanese and Chinese Books), Tambaichi (Tenri), 1940–51. 2 vols.

TŌHŌ BUNKA KENKYŪJO 東方文化研究所; Kanseki Bunrui Mokuroku 漢籍分類目録, Tokyo [n.d.].

TOHOKUGAKUIN DAIGAKU REKISHIGAKU KENKYUKAI 東北學院大學歷史學研究會; Tōhokugakuin Daigaku-zō Kirisuto-kyō kankei Wa-ei Bunken Mokuroku 東北學院大學藏基督教關係和英文献目録, Sendai 1959.

TOKUSHIGE ASAKICHI 徳重浅吉; Ishin Seiji Shūkyōshi Kenkyū 維新政治宗教史研究, Tokyo 1935.

TOKUSHIGE-SEISHIN — Ishin Seishinshi Kenkyū 維新精神史研究, Kyoto 1934.

TOKYO JOSHI DAIGAKU HIKAKU BUNKA KENKYŪJO 東京女子大學比較文化研究所; Uemura-Ki'nen Saba Bunko Kari-Mokuroku 植村記念佐波文庫假目録 v. I., Tokyo 1959.

TOKYO KAGAKU HAKUBUTSUKAN 東京科學博物館; Edojidai no Kagaku 江戸時代の科學, Tokyo 1934.

TOKYO KOKURITSU HAKUBUTSUKAN 東京國立博物館; Kaei-izen Seiyō Yu'nyūhin oyobi Sankōhin Mokuroku 嘉永以前西洋輸入品及參考品目録, Tokyo 1906.

— Nippon Shoki Seiyō Bunkashi-ten Kaisetsu 日本初期西洋文化史展解說, Tokyo 1949.

— Tokyo Teishitsu Hakubutsukan Rekishibu Dai 4-ku Mokuroku 東京帝室博物館歷史部第四區目録, Tokyo 1919.

TOYO BUNKO 東洋文庫; (Oriental Library), Catalogue of the Asiatic Library of Dr. G. E. Morrison, Tokyo 1924. 2 vols.

— Tōyō Bunko Tenkan Shomoku 東洋文庫展觀書目, Tokyo 1924. 2 vols.

TOYOTA-EIGAKU Toyota Minoru 豊田實; Nippon Eigakushi no Kenkyū 日本英學史の研究, Tokyo 1939.

TOYOTA MINORU; Bible Hōyaku no Yūrai バイブル邦譯の由來, Fukuoka 1946.

UCHIDA KAKICHI 内田嘉吉; Uchida Kakichi Bunko Kikōsho Mokuroku 内田嘉吉文庫稀覯書目録, Tokyo 1937.

UEDA TEIJIRŌ 上田貞治郎; Kirisutokyō Shorui Sakuin 基督教書類索引, Osaka 1928.

— Kirisutokyō Koten Tosho Mokuroku 基督教古典圖書目録, Osaka 1940.

UENO TOSHOKAN 上野圖書館; Honzō Kankei Tosho Mokuroku 本草關係圖書目録, Tokyo 1952. 2 vols.

URAKAWA WASABURŌ 浦川和三郎; Kirishitan no Fukkatsu 切支丹の復活, Tokyo 1928. 2 vols.

VINDEL, P.; Catálogo de la Librería de P. Vindel, v. IV., Biblioteca Oriental, Madrid 1911.

WADA-KOKATSUJI Wada Mankichi 和田萬吉; Ko-Katsujibon Kenkyū Shiryō 古活字本研究資料, Kyoto 1944.

WADA MANKICHI; Nippon Shoshigaku Gaisetsu 日本書誌学概說, Tokyo 1944.

WASEDA DAIGAKU TOSHOKAN 早稲田大學圖書館; Kaikoku Hyaku'nen Ki'nen Yō-gaku Tenrankai Mokuroku 開國百年記念洋學展覧會目録, Tokyo 1953.

—— Ogura Bunko Mokuroku 小倉文庫目録, Tokyo 1957.

WENCKSTERN, FRANZ VON; A Bibliography of the Japanese Empire, London 1895–1907. 2 vols.

WYLIE Alexander Wylie; Memorials of Protestant Missionaries to the Chinese, Shanghai 1867.

YABE RYŌSAKU 矢部良策; Kirisutokyō Shiryō Tenrankai Mokuroku 基督教史料展覧會目録, Osaka 1926.

YOSHIDA TORA 吉田寅; Tōyō Kirisutokyōshi Kenkyū Ronbun Mokuroku-kō 東洋基督教史研究論文目録稿, Tokyo 1955.

YOSHINO SAKUZŌ 吉野作造; Arai Hakuseki to Johan Sidotti (Yowan Shirōte) 新井白石とヨワンシローテ, Tokyo 1924.

Abbreviations

for

Missions Functioning in Japan and China

ABC American Board of Commissioners for Foreign Missions.

ABF American Baptist Foreign Missionary Society.

BME Baptist Missionary Society in England.

CE Church of England.

DR Board of Foreign Missions of the Dutch Reformed Church in USA.

ERC Evangelical and Reformed Church.

FMA General Missionary Board of the Free Methodist Church of North America.

GO Greek Orthodox Church.

LEF Lutheran Evangelical Association of Finland.

LM London Missionary Society.

LNM Loochoo Naval Mission.

MEC Board of Foreign Missions of the Methodist Episcopal Church.

MEP Société des Missions Etrangères de Paris.

MES Board of Foreign Missions of the Episcopal Church, South.

MPC Board of Foreign Missions of the Methodist Protestant Church.

OFM Ordo Fratorum Minorum (Franciscan Order).

OP Ordo Praedicatorum (Dominican Order).

PCC General Board of Missions, Presbyterian Church in Canada.

PCE Foreign Mission Board of the Presbyterian Church in England.

PE Domestic and Foreign Missionary Society of the Protestant Episcopal Church.

PN Board of Foreign Missions of the Presbyterian Church in USA.

RCA Reformed Church in America.

RM Rheinische Missions Gesellschaft.

SA Salvation Army.

SBC Foreign Mission Board of the Southern Baptist Convention.

SJ Societas Jesu (Society of Jesus).

ULC Board of Foreign Missions of the United Lutheran Church in America.

UN Unitarian.

UPS United Presbyterian Church of Scotland.

WU Women's Union Missionary Society of America.

YMCA Young Men's Christian Association.

YWCA Young Women's Christian Association.

Table of Japanese and Chinese Era Names

Year	(Japan)		(Ming 明)		(Ch'ing 清)	
1532	Tembun 天文	1	Chia Ching 嘉靖	11		
1555	Kōji 弘治	1		34		
1558	Eiroku 永禄	1		37		
1567		10	Lung Ch'ing 隆慶	1		
1570	Genki 元龜	1		4		
1573	Tenshō 天正	1	Wan Li 萬曆	1		
1592	Bunroku 文禄	1		20		
1596	Keichō 慶長	1		24		
1615	Genwa 元和	1		43		
1616		2		44	T'ien Ming 天命	1
1620		6	T'ai Ch'ang 泰昌	1		5
1621		7	T'ien Chi 天啓	1		6
1624	Kan'ei 寛永	1		4		9
1627		4		7	T'ien Ts'ung 天聡	1
1628		5	Ch'ung Chen 崇禎	1		2
1636		13		9	Ch'ung Teh 崇徳	1
1644	Shōho 正保	1		17	Shun Chih 順治	1
1648	Keian 慶安	1				5
1652	Shōō 承應	1				9
1658	Manji 萬治	1				12
1661	Kambun 寛文	1				15
1662		2			K'ang Hsi 康熙	1
1673	Empō 延寶	1				12
1681	Tenwa 天和	1				20
1684	Jōkyō 貞享	1				23
1688	Genroku 元禄	1				27
1704	Hōei 寶永	1				43
1711	Shōtoku 正徳	1				50
1716	Kyōhō 享保	1				55
1723		8			Yung Cheng 雍正	1
1736	Gembun 元文	1			Ch'ien Lung 乾隆	1
1741	Kanpō 寛保	1				6
1744	Enkyō 延享	1				9
1748	Kan'en 寛延	1				13
1751	Hōreki 寶曆	1				16
1764	Meiwa 明和	1				29
1772	An'ei 安永	1				37
1781	Temmei 天明	1				46
1789	Kansei 寛政	1				54
1796		8			Chia Ch'ing 嘉慶	1

1801	Kyōwa 享和	1			6
1804	Bunka 文化	1			9
1818	Bunsei 文政	1			23
1821		4		Tao Kuang 道光	1
1830	Tempō 天保	1			10
1844	Kōka 弘化	1			24
1848	Kaei 嘉永	1			28
1851		4		Hsien Feng 咸豐	1
1854	Ansei 安政	1			4
1860	Man'en 萬延	1			10
1861	Bunkyū 文久	1			11
1862		2		T'ung Chih 同治	1
1864	Ganji 元治	1			3
1865	Keiō 慶應	1			4
1868	Meiji 明治	1			7
1875		8	(The Republic of	Kuang Hsü 光緒	1
1909		42	China 中華民國)	Hsüan T'ung 宣統	1
1912	Taishō 大正	1	1		4
1926	Shōwa 昭和	1	15		
1959		34	48		

Part   I

(1543—1858)

The Arrival of the Portuguese and Introduction of Guns into Japan, 1543.

0001 Nampo Bunshi 南浦文之
Teppōki 鐵炮記 (Introduction of Guns).
jb. 1 v.
cf. Kokushi, p. 212.
0002 —— (Nampo Bunshū, v. I).
0003 —— repr. and annotated by Hora Tomio 洞富雄, in *Teppō Denraiki*, Tokyo 1939 (昭和 14), pp. 269-273.

0004 Kihō Hiyaku no Maki, Teppō Nippon e hajimete wataru Shidai no Koto 奇方秘薬之巻, 鐵炮日本ヘ初テ渡ル次第ノ事 (Strange and Secret Powder, First Arrival of Guns into Japan). jb. 1 v.
ms. Nagasaki.

0005 Teppō Genshi 鐵炮原始 (The Origin of Guns). jb. 1 v.
ms. Kyudai-Bunka.

0006 Teppō Yuraiki 鐵炮由来記 (History of Guns), [n.p.], [n.d.]. jb. 3 vols., 28cm.
c. Ueno.

1552

0007 Ōuchi Yoshinaga 大内義長 (– 1557)
Daidōji Saikyojō 大道寺裁許狀 (License to the Daidōji, a Catholic Church in Yamaguchi giving it Permission to evangelize), 1552 (天文 21).
note : The original is not extant.
0008 —— facs. pr. and tr. into Portuguese in *Cartas do Jappão*, v. I., Evora 1598.
0009 —— facs. pr. by Murakami Naojirō 村上直次郎, in *Zoku Ikoku Sōsho*, v. I., Tokyo 1936 (昭和 11).
0010 —— facs. pr. by Luis Norton, in *Os Portugueses no Jappão*, Lisboa 1952.

0011 Ōuchi Yoshitaka 大内義隆記, or Tatara Seisuiki 多々良盛衰記 (Story of Ouchi Yoshitaka), 1552 (天文 21). jb. 1 v.
note : Contains material on St. Francis Xavier in 1551 in Yamaguchi. For documents relating to St. Xavier, see also Ebisawa Arimichi, "Xavier kankei no Nippon Shiryō" (*Shigaku*, v. XXIV, n. 1), Tokyo 1949.
cf. Kokushi, p. 33.
ms. Naikaku.
0012 —— (Ōshuku Zakki).
0013 —— (Gunsho Ruijū, v. CCCXCIV).

1560

0014 Muromachike Gonaisho-an, 室町家御内書案, or Kyōto Shōgunke Kōjo 京都將軍家古狀 (Draft Regulations of the Muromachi Government). jb. 2 vols.
note : Contains the license to P. Gaspar Villela, S.J., in 1560.
ms. Shokokan, Toyo-Iwasaki.
0015 —— (Kaitei Shiseki Shūran, v. XXVII).

1568

0016 Kirishitan Ōrai 貴理師端往来 (Alphabetum, Iaponicum, et Exemplare). wb. 1 v., 34f., 27cm.
note : An elementary school text book from Gotō, Kyūshū, which was copied in manuscript by Alessandro Vallaregio, S.J. in 1568 (永禄 11).
cf. Laures, n. 39.
phot. Doi, Sophia.
0017 —— facs. pr. and annotated by Doi Tadao 土井忠生, in " Kirishitan Ōrai ni tsuite " (*Kirishitan Kenkyū*, v. V), Tokyo 1959 (昭和 34).

1569

0018 Ashikaga Kiseiki 足利季世記 (History of the Fall of the Ashikagas). jb. 8 vols.
cf. Kokushi, p. 6.
ms. Naikaku, Tenri.
0019 —— (Shiseki Shūran).
0020 —— (Kaitei Shiseki Shūran, v. XIII).

1582

0021 Tenshō Nenkan Ken'ō Shisetsu kankei Monjo 天正年間遣歐使節關係文書 (Documents concerned the Mission to Europe during the Tenshō Era).
orig. ms. Kyodai-Kokushi.
0021b —— (Dai-Nippon Shiryō, Series XI, Supplement, v. I–II).
0022 —— facs. pr. and annotated by Shimmura Izuru 新村出, Kyoto 1929 (昭和 4).
0023 —— pr. and annotated by Hamada Kōsaku 濱田耕作, in *Tenshō Shisetsu Kōki*, Tokyo 1931 (昭和 6).

1583

0024 Sappan Kyūki Zatsuroku 薩藩舊記雜錄 (Miscellaneous Documents of the Satsuma Clan).
note : Contains some documents on Br. Almeida's mission to Satsuma in 1583 (天正 11).
orig. ms. Shimazu.
0025 —— abridged (Dai-Nippon Shiryō, Series XI, v. III).

3

1584

0026 Ōtomo Sōrin 大友宗麟 (1530–1587)
Ōsakajōnai Kembunroku 大坂城内見聞錄 (Record of a Visit to Ōsaka Castle).
cf. Kokushi, p. 35 ; Okamoto Yoshitomo, *Tenshō 14-nen Ōsakajō Ekkenki*, Tokyo 1942.
0027 —— (Ōsaka Shiryō, v. II).

1585

0028 Valignano, Alessandro, SJ. 范禮安 (1538–1606)
Rakan Goshū 羅漢語集 *Lo-han Yü-Chi* (A Latin-Chinese Vocabulary), Macao, 1585. cb. 1 v.
cf. Laures, n. 1.
phot. Sophia.

1586

0029 Uwai Kakuken 上井覺兼 (1545–)
Uwai Kakuken Nitchō 上井覺兼日帳 (Dairy of Uwai Kakuken, 1573–1586). jb. 27 vols.
orig. ms. Shiryo.
0030 —— (Dai-Nippon Kokiroku).

1587

0031 Bateren Tsuihōrei 伴天連追放令 (Edict of Banishment of the Jesuits). 1f.
cf. Ebisawa Arimichi, "Kirishitan Bateren Tsuihō-rei" (*Rekishi Kyōiku*, v. III, n. 9), Tokyo 1955; ditto, *Kirishitanshi no Kenkyū*, pp. 128–184.
ms. Matsura.
0032 —— (Kyūshū Shōunki).
0033 —— (Nagasaki-shi).
0034 —— (Sokkyohen, v. I).
0035 —— facs. pr. (Kirishitan Shiryō-shū).
0036 —— tr. into Italian in *Lettera Annale del Giapone*, 1588, Rome 1590, pp. 61–62.
0037 —— tr. into Portuguese in *Cartas do Jappão*, Euora 1598, v. II., f. 209.
0038 —— tr. into Spanish by Luís de Guzmán, SJ., in *Historia de las missiones que han hecho los Religiosos de la Compañia de Iesus, para Predicar el Santo Evangelio en la India Oriental, y en los Reynos de la China y Japon*, Bilbao 1891, p. 495.
0039 —— tr. into Italian by Daniello Bartoli, SJ., in *Dell'Istoria della Compagnia di Giesv, Il Giappone*, Rome 1660, v. I., pp. 303–304.
0040 —— tr. into French, by Jean Crasset, SJ., in *Histoire de l'église du Japon*, Paris 1689, v. I., pp. 539–540.
0041 —— tr. into English by C. R. Boxer, in *The Christian Century in Japan*, Berkeley 1951, p. 148.

0042 Goshuin-shishiki Kokaku 御朱印師職古格 (Examples of the Vermillion Stamped Laws). jb. 1 v.
note: Contains the 1587 edict of Toyotomi Hideyoshi 豊臣秀吉 prohibiting Christianity.
ms. Jingu.
0043 —— pr. and annotated by Watanabe Yosuke 渡邊世祐, in "Waga Shiryō yori mitaru Sengoku-jidai Tōzai Kōshōshi" (*Tōzai Kōshōshiron*, v. I), Tokyo 1939, pp. 462–463.
0044 —— pr. and annotated by Ebisawa Arimichi 海老澤有道, in *Kirishitanshi no Kenkyū*, Tokyo 1942, pp. 158–161, 185–188.

0045 Kyūshū Godōzaki 九州御動座記 (Record of the Expedition of Toyotomi Hideyoshi to Kyūshū). jb. 1 v.
ms. Naikaku.

Documents relating to Ōmura Bartholomeo Sumitada 大村純忠 (1533–1587)

0046 Ōmurake Hiroku 大村家秘録 (Secret Record of the Ōmuras). jb. 1 v.
0047 —— (Shiseki Zassan, v. I).

0048 Ōmurake Oboegaki 大村家覺書 (Memorials of the Ōmuras). jb. 4 vols.
ms. Nagasaki.

0049 Ōmuraki 大村記 (History of the Ōmuras). jb. 1 v.
0050 —— (Shiseki Zassan, v. I).

Documents relating to Ōtomo Francisco Sōrin 大友宗麟 (1530–1587)

0051 Kyūshū Ōtomoki 九州大友記 (History of the Ōtomos in Kyūshū). jb. 1 v.
ms. Todai-Nanki.

0052 Ōtomoki 大友記, or Kyūshū Chiranki 九州治亂記 (History of the Ōtomos, or the Record of Peace and War in Kyūshū).
cf. Kokushi, pp. 35–36.
ms. Jingu, Naikaku, Sonkeikaku, Ueno.
0053 —— (Ōshuku Zakki).
0054 —— (Gunsho Ruijū, v. CCCXC-VII).
0055 —— (Ōitaken Kyōdoshiryō shūsei).

0056 Ōtomo Kōhaiki 大友興廢記 (Rise and Fall of the Ōtomos). jb. 22 vols.
cf. Kokushi, p. 36.
ms. Kanazawa-Kado, Naikaku, Sonkeikaku, Todai-Nanki, Ueno.

0057 —— (Ōitaken Kyōdoshiryō Shūsei).

0058 Ōtomokō On'ie Oboegaki 大友公御家覺書 (Memorandum of the Otomos).
0059 —— (Kokushi Sōsho).

0060 Ōtomo Yoshimune Kashin Isamegusa 大友義統家臣諫草 (Remonstrances of Ōtomo Yoshimune's Retainers).
ms. Sonkeikaku.

0061 Toyotomi Chinzei Gunki 豊臣鎭西軍記 (Military Record of the Expedition of Toyotomi Hideyoshi to Kyūshū).
0062 —— (Tsūzoku Nippon Zenshi, v. XX).

1588

0063 Gokinai Kirishitan Daihyō Hōshojō 五畿内キリシタン代表奉書狀 (Letter from Christians in Gokinai to the General of the Society of Jesus).
0064 —— pr. and annotated by Matsuda Kiichi 松田毅一, "Jesusukai Sōchō ate Gokinai Kirisitan Daihyō Hōshojō to sono Shomei'nin ni tsuite" *Shigaku Zasshi*, v. LXVII, n. 9), Tokyo 1958.

1589

0065 Shikike Kyūki 志岐家舊記 (History of the Shiki Family).
0066 —— (Amakusagun Shiryō, v. II).
note: Documents related to Shiki João Shigetsune 志岐鎭經 (–1589).

1591

0067 [Oratio-shō おらしよ抄], (A Fragment of Prayers) [Kazusa 加津佐], [1591?]. 2f., 33cm.
cf. Laures, n. 7.
c. Sophia.

0068 Sanctos no Gosagveono vchi Nvqigaqi, Fiienno Cvni Taccacvno Gvn Iesvsno Companhiano Collegio Cazzusa ni voite Superiores no von yuruxi uo còmuri core uo fan to nasu mono nari. Goxuxxe irai MDLXXXI (Compendium of the Acts of the Saints, Printed by permission of the Superiors at the College of the Society of Jesus at Kazusa in the District of Takaku, Province of Hizen, in 1591. A.D.). wb. 2 vols., 8°.
cf. Cordier-Japonica, col. 76; Laures, n. 9; Satow, pp. 1–12; Streit IV, p. 515.
c. Bodleian Lib. (Oxford).
roto. Tōdai.
phot. Sophia, Tenri.
0069 —— mimeogr. repr. by Takaba Gorō 高羽五郎, Kanazawa 1949–52 (昭和

24–27). wb. 6 vols.
0070 —— abridged transcription into Jap. characters, Aneseki-Bungaku, pp. 599-709.
0071 —— abridged transcription into Jap. characters. Muraoka-Bungaku, pp. 3–109.

0072 Tomiokake Monjo 富岡家文書 (Documents of the Tomioka Family).
note: A letter of the Kampaku 關白 Toyotomi Hideyoshi 豊臣秀吉, to the Vice-king of Portuguese India in Tenshō 天正 19 nen, 7 gatsu, 25 nichi (Sep. 12th, 1591) and others.
ms. Tomioka (Kyoto)
0072b —— (Kokushi Shiryōshū, v. III).
0073 —— (Ikoku Sōsho, Ikoku Ōfuku Shokanshū).

0074 Vatican Monjo ヴァチカン文書 (Documents of the Vatican Lib., codex Reg. Lat. 459), compiled by Manoel Barreto, SJ., 1591. wb. 1 v., [5], 382, [4]f., 17cm.
Contents:
1. Report on the Miraculous Cross which was discovered at Obama (in *Rōmaji*).
2. Book of Gospels.
   a) Gospels of the Sundays.
   b) Gospels of the Fridays in Lent and the Passion of Christ.
   c) Gospels of the Feasts of Saints.
3. The Acts of the Saints.
cf. Josef F. Schütte, SJ., "Christliche japanische Literatur, Bilder und Druck-blätter in unbekannten vatikanischen Codex aus dem Jahre 1591" (*Archivum Historicum Societatis Iesu*, v. IX), Rome 1940, pp. 226–280; Laures, n. 41.
0075 —— transcription with notes of Pt. 2,a, by Murakami Naojirō 村上直次郎, in "Dominika no Sekkyō ni tsuite", (*Kirishitan Kenkyū*, v. II), Tokyo 1944 (昭和 19), pp. 1–26.
note: A Jap. ms., see n. 2048.

1592

0076 Luís de Granada, OP. (1504–1588)
Fides No Doxi to xite P. F. Luís de Granada amaretaru xono riacu, Core Companhia no Superiores no go saicacu vomotte Nippon no cotoba ni vasu. Iesvs No Companhia No Collegio Amacusa ni voite Superiores no go menqio toxite core uo fan ni qizamu mono nari. Go xuxxe yori M.D.C.XXXXII. (Summary of a book composed by Father Luís de Granada as a guide to Faith, translated into Japanese by arrangement and with the permission of the Superiors of the Society of Jesus. A.D. 1592). wb. lv., 8°, [12], 619, [32]p.

note: This book is also entitled *"Xiniinrocu"* 信心録 (Treatise of Faith). It is an abridged and adopted translation of Luís de Granada's *Introduccion del Symbolo de la Fe,* Salamanca 1588. The translation was arranged by Father Pero Ramon, SJ.
cf. Laures, n. 11; Satow, pp. 20–25; Streit IV, p. 514.
c. Lib. of the Univ. of Leyden.
roto. Toyo.
phot. Sophia, Tenri.

0077 —— transcribed into Jap. characters and pr., in Anesaki-Bungaku, pp. 269–582.

0078 * Fidesno Qvio ひですの經, Nagasaqvi Ex Officina Goto Thomæ Soin Typographi Societatis Iesv. 1611. wb. 1 v., 95f., 27cm.
cf. Laures, n. 33.
note: An abridged Jap. ed. of the *Fides no Dōxi.*

0079 Nifon No Cotoba To Historia uo narai xiran to Fossvrv Fito no Tame ni Xeva Ni Yavaragvetaru Feiqve no Monogatari. Iesvs No Companhia No Collegio Amacusa ni voite Superiores no go menqio to xite core uo fan ni qizamu mono nari. Go xuxxe yori M.D.L. XXXXII. (Heike Monogatari explained in colloquial Japanese for the use of persons desiring to study the language and history of Japan, Printed by permission of the Superiors at the Amakusa College of the Society of Jesus, AD. 1592). wb. 1 v., 8°, [4], 408, [6]p.
cf. Satow, pp. 12–20; Streit IV, p. 515; Laures, n. 13.
c. British Museum.
roto. Tōyō.
phot. Sophia, Tenri.

0080 —— mimeogr. repr. by Inoue Akira 井上彰, *Amakusabon Heike Monogatari,* Sendai 1954–56 (昭和 29–31).

0081 —— mimeogr. repr. by the Kokugo Kenkyūshitsu of Kokugakuin Univ. 國學院大學國語研究室. Tokyo 1954 (昭和 29).

0082 —— transcribed repr. in Jap. characters by Kamei Takayoshi 龜井高孝, Tokyo 1927 (昭和 2).

0083 Nippon No Iesvs no Companhia no Superior yori Christan ni Sōtō no cotouari uo tagaino mondō no gotoqu xidai uo vacachi tamō Doctrina. Iesvs No Companhia No Collegio Amacusa ni voite Superiores no von yuruxi uo cŏmuri, core uo fan to nasu mono nari, Toqini go xuxxe no Nenqi 1592. (Cathechism composed by the Superior of the Society of Jesus in Japan in which matters important to a Christian are arranged in the form of questions and answers. Printed in the Amakusa College of the Society of Jesus with permission of the Superiors, A.D. 1592). 8°, [4], 114p.
cf. Streit X, p. 161; Laures, n. 10.
c. Tōyō.

0084 —— facs. repr. and transcribed into Jap. by Hashimoto Shinkichi 橋本進吉, *Bunroku Gannen Amakusaban Kirishitan Kyōgi no Kenkyū* (Tōyō Bunko Ronsō, v. XI), Tokyo 1928.

0085 * Doctrina Christam [どちりなきりしたん] (Christian Cathechism), [Amakusa 1592]. jb. 1 v., [2], 78f. 27cm.
cf. Streit IV, pp. 514–515; Satow, pp. 38–42; Laures, n. 8.
ms. Nakatani.
phot. Sophia.

0086 —— facs. repr. of Nakatani's manuscript (Kirishitan Sōsho).

0087 Doctrina Christan. (A Christian Doctrine). In Collegio Iaponico Societatis Iesv. Cum facultate Oridinarij, & Superiorum. Anno 1600. [Nagasaki]. 8°, 58p.
cr. Kokushi, p. 230; Laures, n. 22; Streit X, pp. 151, 161, 499.
c. Tokugawa.

0088 —— facs. repr. (Kirishitan Sōsho).

0089 —— repr. by Ernest Satow, "The Jesuit Mission Press in Japan" (*Transactions of the Asiatic Society of Japan,* v. XXVII, n. 1), Tokyo 1899.

0090 * Doctrina Christam. どちりなきりしたん Nagasaqvi Ex Officina Gotō Thome Sōin typographi Societatis Iesv. Cum Facultate Ordinarij, & Superiorum. Anno. 1600. (慶長 5). jb. 1 v., 55f., 27cm.
cf. Laures, n. 23; Satow, pp. 44–45; Streit IV, p. 514.
c. Biblioteca Casanatense, Rome.
roto. Keiō-Koda, Tōyō.
phot. Sophia.

0091 —— (Namban Bunshū).

0092 —— repr. and annotated by Ebisawa Arimichi 海老澤有道 (Iwanami Bunko), Tokyo 1949 (昭和 24).

0093 —— repr. and annotated by Hiiragi Gen'ichi 柊源一 (*Kirishitan Bungakushū,* v, II), Tokyo 1960.

0094 Sanctissimo Sacramento no Ladainhas さんちいしもさからめんとのらたにやす (Litany of the Most Holy Sacrament), copied in manuscript by Paul Hitomi はうろ人見, 1592 (文禄 1). 1 fold.
orig. ms. Sawada.

1593

0095 Bautismo no Sazukeyō to Byōja ni Penitencia o susumuru Kyōke no Koto ばうちずもの授けやうとびやうじやにへにてんしやをすすむるけうけの事 (Salutary advice on the Method of administering

Baptism and exhorting the sick to receive the Sacrament of Penitence), [n. p.]. [1593?]. jb. 1 v., [1], 25, [3]f. 26cm.

cf. Streit X, p. 161; Laures, n. 12.
c. Tenri.
phot. Sophia.

0096 Esopo No Fabvlas, Latinuo vaxite Nippon no cuchito nasu mono nari. Iesvs No Companhia No Collegio Amacusani voite Superiores no gomenqio toxite coreuo fanni qizamu mono nari. Goxuxxe yori M.D.L.XXXXIII. (Esop's Fables, translated from Latin into Japanese Language. Printed by permission of the Superiors at the Amakusa College of the Society of Jesus, A.D. 1593). wb. 1 v, 8°, (bounds as pp. 409–506 of n. 79).

cf. Satow, pp. 12–20; Laures, n. 13; Cordier-Japonica, col. 76–77, 126; Streit IV, p. 515.
c. British Museum.
roto. Tōyō.
phot. Kyodai, Sophia.

0097 —— mimeogr. repr. by Takaba Gorō 高羽五郎, *Esopo No Fabvlas*, Kanazawa 1951 (昭和 26).

0098 —— transcribed into Jap. characters by Shimmura Izuru 新村出, *Bu nroku Kyūyaku Amakusabon Isoho Monogatari,* Tokyo 1911 (大正 10).

0099 —— ditto, Shimmura-Isoho.

0100 —— ditto, *Amakusaban Isoho Monogatari* (Iwanami Bunko), Tokyo 1939 (昭和 14).

0101 —— (Namban Bunshū).

0102 —— repr. and annotated by Hiiragi Gen'ichi 柊源一 (*Kirishitan Bungakushū*, v. II), Tokyo 1960.

0103 —— changed into modern Jap. by Shimmura Izuru 新村出, *Isoppu Monogatari,* Tokyo 1947 (昭和 22).

See also, nos. 582–592.

0104 [Quincuxu 金句集], Xixo, xixxo nadono vchiyori nuqi idaxi, quincuxŭto nasu mono nari. (A Collection of Proverbs extracted from the Four Books and the Seven Books). Amacusa 1593. wb. 1 v., 8°. (bound as pp. 507–553 of n. 79).

cf. Laures, n. 13.
c. British Museum.
roto. Tōyō.
phot. Sophia.

0105 —— facs. repr. and transcribed into Jap. characters by Yoshida Sumio 吉田澄夫, *Kinkūshū no Kenkyū* (Tōyō Bunko Ronsō, v. XXIV), Tokyo 1938 (昭和 15).

0106 —— transcribed into Jap. characters by Yoshida Sumio 吉田澄夫, "Amakusaban Kinkushū" (*Kokugo Kyōiku,* v. XVIII, nos.

5–10), Tokyo 1932 (昭和 9).

1594

0107 Takatsuki Hakken Kirishitan Monjo 高槻發見切支丹文書 (Kirishitan Documents found at Takatsuki). 1 fold.

Contents:
1. A Church Calendar with Paul Hitomi's Notes, 1594 (文禄 3). 1 fold (27,5,6f.) 16cm.
2. A Convenant signed by Paul Hitomi to the Fathers of Society of Jesus, Dec. 3rd., 1595. 1f., 37 × 20cm.

cf. Laures, n.48.
orig. ms. Osaka Asahi Shimbunsha.

0108 —— facs. pr. and noted by Sakurai Yasuji 櫻井安二, *Takatsuki Hakken Kirishitan Monjo*, Tokyo 1933 (昭和 8).

1595

0109 Dictionarivm LatinoLvsitanicvm, Ac Iaponicvm, Ex Ambrosii Calepini volumine depromptum: in quo omissis nominibus proprijs tam locorum, quàm hominum, ac quibusdam alijs minùs vsitatis, omnes vocabuloru significationes, elegantioresq; dicendi modi apponuntur: in vsum, & gratiam Iaponicae iuuentutis, quae Latino idiomati operam nauat, nec non Europaeorũ, qui Iaponicũ sermonem addiscunt. In Amacvsa In Collegio Iaponico Societatis Iesv cum facultate Superiorum. Anno M.D.XCV. 4°, [4], 908p.

cf. Streit IV, p. 514; Laures, n. 15.
c. Bodleian Lib., Oxford, and etc.
phot. Sophia, Tōyō.

0110 —— facs. repr. by Toyo Bunko, Tokyo 1953 (昭和 28).

0111 * Lexicon Latino-Iaponicum Depromptum Ex Opere Cui Titulus Dictionarium Latino-Lusitanicum ac Iaponicum typis primum mandatum in Amacusa In Collegio Iaponico Societatis Iesu anno Domini M.D.XCV. Nunc Denuo Emendatum Atque Auctum A Vicario Apostolico Iaponiae Romae Typis S.C. De Propaganda Fide Socio Eq. Petro Marietti Admin. MDCCCLXX. 4°, [6], 749p., 26cm.

note: repr. with the omission of the Portuguese words.
cf. Streit IV, p. 514, X, p. 107; Laures, n. 71.
c. Ebisawa, Junshin, Nagasaki, Sophia, Tōdai.

0112 —— facs. repr. by Miyagoshi Shin'ichirō 宮越信一郎, Tokyo 1945 (昭和 20).

0113 Gamō Ujisato-ki 蒲生氏郷記, or Ujisato-ki 氏郷記. (Life of Gamō Ujisato). jb. 1 v.

note: Gamō Leão Ujisato (1556–1595).

cf. Kokushi, p. 21.
ms. Naikaku.

0114 —— (Gunsho Ruijū, v. CCCL-XXXIX).

0115 —— (Buhen Sōsho).

0116 —— (Ōshuku Zakki).

0117 —— (Shiseki Shūran).

0118 —— (Kaitei Shiseki Shūran, v. XIV).

0119 —— (Kokushi Sōsho).

0120 Ricci, Matteo, SJ. 利西泰 (1552–1610)

Kōyūron 交友論 *Chiao-yu Lun* (On Friendship), Nanchang 1595 (萬曆 23). cb. 1v.
cf. Pfister, p. 35; Jo, pp. 343–345; Cordier-Sinica, col. 1091; Saeki-Shina, pp. 201–203.
ms. Jinshu, Tohoku-Kano.

0121 —— Nanking 1599 (萬曆 27). cb. 1 v.

0122 —— Peking 1604 (萬曆 32). cb. 1 v.

0123 —— (Tengaku Shokan).

0124 —— (Kō Hyakusen Gakukai).

0125 —— (Zoku Seppu).

0126 —— (Rekidai Shōsetsu Ihen).

0127 —— (Kōhikyū).

0128 —— (Sanrin Keizaiseki).

0129 —— (Hōgandō Hikyū).

0130 —— (Rokumeikan Sōsho).

0131 —— repr. by Ono Tadashige 小野忠重, *Mateo Ricci to Shina Kagaku,* Tokyo 1944 (昭和 19).

0132 Ricci, Matteo, SJ. 利瑪竇 (1552–1610)

Tengaku Jitsugi 天學實義 *T'ien-hsüeh Shih-i,* (The True Doctrine of Catholicism), Nanchao 1595 (萬曆 23). cb. 2 vols.
note: See also n. 0193.

1596

0133 Thomas á Kempis (1380–1471)
Comtemptvs Mvndi jenbu. Core Yo Vo Itoi, Iesv Christono gocoxeqiuo manabi tatematçuru michiuo voxiyuru qio. Nippon Iesvsno Companhia no Collegio nite Superiores no goguegiuo motte coreuo fanni firaqu mono nari. Toqini goxuxxeno nenqi. 1596. (Comtemptus Mundi, complete. This is a book which teaches the way to despise the world and to imitate the conduct of Jesus Christ. Printed by order of the Superiors at the College of the Society of Jesus in Japan, A.D. 1596). wb. 1 v., 8°, [1], 432, [26]p.
cf. Satow, pp. 28–31; Streit IV, p. 513; Laures, n. 16.
roto. Todai, Tōyō·
phot. Sophia, Tenri.

0134 —— transcribed into Japanese characters, Anesaki-Bungaku, pp. 57–582.

0135 —— mimeogr. repr. by Takaba Gōrō 高羽五郎, Kanazawa 1955–1956 (昭和 30–31).

0136 * Contemptvs Mundi. こんてむつすむん地, Miaci Ex Officina Farada Antonii, 1610 (慶長 15). jb. 1 v., [1], [4], 79, [1]f., 27cm.
cf. Laures, n. 32.
c. Tenri.
phot. Sophia.

0137 —— repr. and noted by Hiiragi Gen'ichi 柊源一 (Kirishitan Bungakushū, v. I).

0138 —— facs. repr. of the title, contents and three example pages by Hayashi Wakakichi 林若吉, Tokyo 1921 (大正 10).

The Account of Spanish Ship, S. Felipe, 1596

0139 San Felipe-gō Kōkaizu Utsushi サンフェリーペ號航海圖寫 (A Copy of the Chart of the S. Felipe). 1f., 31×48cm.
ms. Kōchi.

0140 —— facs. pr. and annotated by Matsuda Kiichi, 松田毅一 "San Felipe-gō ni yurai suru Sekaizu" (*Kirisutokyō Shigaku,* v. IV), Yokohama 1953 (昭和 28)

0141 —— [ditto], *Kirishitan Kenkyū Shikokuhen,* Osaka 1953 (昭和 28), pp. 129–135.

0142 Shikoku Gunki 四國軍記 (War Records of the Shikoku Expedition), jb. 12 vols.

0143 —— (Kokushi Sōsho).

0144 —— (Tsūzoku Nippon Zenshi, v. XV).

0145 Tosa Monogatari 土佐物語 (Tales of Tosa Province). jb. 20 vols.

0146 —— (Kokushi Sōsho).
See also, nos. 666–667.

1598

0147 Oyudono no Ue no Nikki 御湯殿上日記 (Diary of the Imperial House).
cf. Kokushi, p. 41.
orig. ms. Shoryobu-Higashiyama.

0148 —— (Zoku Gunsho Ruijū, Hoi 補遺). wb. 10 vols.

0149 —— abridged (Dai-Nippon Shiryō, Series X–XII.)

0150 Keichō Sannen-ki 慶長三年記 (Gunsho Ruijū, v. CDLVII).

0151 Racvyoxu 落葉集 (Dictionary of Chinese Characters) in Collegio Iaponico Societatis Iesv. [Nagasaki] M.D.XCVIII.

jb. 1 v., [109]f., 27cm.
cf. Satow, p. 35; Streit IV, p. 515; Laures, n. 20.
c. British Museum, Leyden Univ. Lib., Bibliothèque
Nationale, Paris.
roto. Doi, Tōdai.
phot. Sophia.

0152 —— mimeogr. repr. by Takaba Gorō 高羽五郎, Kanazawa 1951 (昭和 26).

0153 Salvator Mundi (Manual of the Forgiveness of Sin), Confessionarivm In Collegio Iaponico Societatis Iesv. Cum facultate Superiorum, [Nagasaki], Anno M.D.XLVIII. jb. 1 v., 30f., 22cm.
cf. Ebisawa-Tenseki, pp. 59–70; Satow, pp. 36–38;
Laures, n. 19; Streit IV, p. 515.
c. Biblioteca Casanatense, Rome.
roto. Keiō-Koda, Tōyō.
phot. Sophia, Tenri, Tōdai.
ms. Ebisawa.

0154 —— (Namban Bunshū).

0155 * Kōsei Saikoku Toganozoki Kisoku 校正再刻科除規則 (A Rule of Forgiveness of Sin, revised ed.), compiled by Bishop Bernard T. Petitjean, MEP., Nagasaki 1869 (明治 2). jb. 1 v., [1], 24f., 22cm.
cf. Laures, n. 69; Tenri-Jap. II, p. 86.
c. Junshin, Nagasaki, Seishin, Sophia, Tenri, Ueno.

0156 —— (Kaihyō Sōsho, v. I).

0157 —— (Meiji Bunka Zenshū, v. XI).

0158 —— (Namban Bunshū).

0159 * Tenshu Kyūkyō Kokkaishiki 天主舊教告解式 (Manual of the Confession), compiled by Abe Shinzō 阿部眞造, 1872 (明治 5). jb. 1 v., 43f., 23cm.
note: This is changed into modern Jap. language
with Chinese terminology.
ms. Jinshu.
phot. Ebisawa, Seishin.

1599

0160 Luís de Granada, OP. (1504–1588)
Gvia Do Pecador ぎやどぺかどる, In Collegio Iaponico Societatis Iesv, Nagasaki, 1599 (慶長 4). jb. 2 vols., 26cm.
cf. Kokushi, p. 65; Laures, n. 21; Satow, pp. 43–44;
Streit IV, p. 514; ditto X, pp. 161–162.
c. Tenri (v. II only).
phot. Sophia, Tōdai.

0161 —— repr. by Muraoka Tsunetsugu 村岡典嗣 (Nippon Koten Zenshū).

0162 —— (Namban Bunshū).

0163 *—— ms. of v. II.
ms. Nakatani.

0164 —— facs. repr. of title, preface and contents pages (Kirishitan Sōsho).

1600

0165 Oratio no Honyaku, tsuketari Christão Oshie no Jōjō おらしよの翻譯, 付

きりしたん教の條々 Doctrinae Christanae, cum alijs pijs Orationibus, (Translation of the Daily Prayers), Nagasaqvi ex Officina Goto Thome Soin Typographi Societatis Iesv, 1600. wb. 1 v., 26f., 21cm.
cf. Anesaki-Hakugai, p. 47.
c. Tenri.
phot. Sophia.

0166 —— (Yasokyō Sōsho).

0167 —— abridged repr. and annotated by Kōda Shigetomo 幸田成友, *Sekai Ippon Oratio no Honyaku no Shutsugen,* Tokyo 1941 (昭和 16).

0168 —— [ditto], *Shiwa Minami to Kita,* Tokyo 1948 (昭和 23), pp. 135–157.

0169 Ōta Gyūichi 太田牛一 (1527–)
Nobunagakō-ki 信長公記, or Azuchi-ki 安土記 (Record of Nobunaga or Azuchi), jb. 15 vols.
cf. Kokushi, p. 250.

0170 —— [Kyoto], 1644 (正保 1). jb. 3 vols.
c. Tōdai-Nanki.

0171 —— Tokyo 我自刊我, 1881 (明治 14). jb. 3 vols., 24cm.
c. Tōyō-Iwasaki, Nichidai-Mukasa, Ueno, Waseda.

0172 —— (Kaitei Shiseki Shūran, v. XIX).

0173 Ricci, Matteo, SJ. 利瑪竇 (1552–1610)
Seikin Kyokui 西琴曲意 *Hsi-ch'in-ch'ü-i* (Eight Airs on Western Organs).
cf. Pfister, p. 36; Jo, p. 149.
note: Appendix to the *Kijin Jippen.* (n. 303).

0174 Rōyei. Zafit [朗詠雑筆], In Collegio Iaponico Societatis Iesv. [Nagasaki] 1600 (慶長 5). jb. 1 v., 17, 2, 5, 1, 3f., 27cm.
contents: Wakan Rōeishū, v. I. 倭漢朗詠集巻之上
Kuzōka narabini Jo 九相歌並序
Mujō 無常
Zappitsushō 雑筆抄
Jitsugokyō 實語教
cf. Streit X, pp. 161–162; Laures, n. 25.
c. Biblioteca S. Lorenzo, Spain
phot. Doi, Sophia.

Death of Donna Gratia Hosokawa (1563–1600)

0175 Hosokawa Tadaoki-ki 細川忠興記 (Life of Hosokawa Tadaoki). jb. 1 v.
ms. Naikaku.

0176 Ikushima Sōshiku 生島宗竹 (1482–1573)
Hosokawa Ryōkaki 細川兩家記 or Nisen Bunryūki 二川分流記, (History of the Two Hosokawas). jb. 1 v.

cf. Kokushi, pp. 238–239.
ms. Naikaku.

0177 —— (Gunsho Ruijū, v. CCCL-XXX).

0178 Kosuga Oboegaki 小須賀覺書 (Memorials of Kosuga). jb. 1 v.
0179 —— pr. by Yamamoto Hideteru 山本秀煌, *Tadaoki-fujin no Shinkō Bidan,* Osaka 1930 (昭和 5), pp. 30–32.

0180 Shimo 霜 (–1657)
Shūrin'insama Onhate nasaresoro Shidai no Koto しうりんゐん様御はて被成候次第の事 (Last Moment of Donna Gratia Hosokawa Shūrin'in), 1648 (正保 5). jb. 1 v.
0181 —— pr. by Yamamoto Hideteru 山本秀煌, in *Tadaoki-fujin no Shinkō Bidan,* Osaka 1930 (昭和 5), pp. 25–30.

0182 Takagi Shimei 高木紫溟
Gindai Iji 銀臺遺事 (Life of Hosokawa Shigekata). jb. 1 v.
ms. Jingu.
0183 —— Tokyo, 1909 (明治 42). wb. 1 v., 2, 146, [1]p., 23cm.
c. Hibiya-Ichimura.
0184 —— (Chūko Sōsho).
0185 —— (Ōshuku Zakki).
0186 —— (Higo Bunken Sōsho, v. I).
0187 —— (Dai-Nippon Fūkyō Sōsho, v. XI-XII).
0188 —— (Nippon Ijin Genkō Shiryō, v. XI).
0189 —— (Shūyō Bunko, Kentetsuden).

1601

0190 Hyō Ōkei 馮應京 *Feng Ying-ching*
Getsurei Kōgi 月令廣義 *Yüeh-ling Kuang-i* (The Seasons, fully explained), Peking 麟瑞堂, 1601 (萬曆 29). cb. 16 vols., 27cm.
c. Kyoto-Bungakubu, Naikaku, Ueno.
0191 —— Peking 1691 (康熙 30). cb. 12 vols.
c. Imoto, Naikaku, Seikado, Toyo-Odagiri.
0192 —— (Ekisai Hitsuroku).

0193 Ricci, Matteo, SJ. 利瑪竇 (1552–1610)
Tenshu Jitsugi 天主實義 *T'ien-chu Shih-i,* De Deo veta ratio (The Truth concerning God), Peking 燕貽堂, 1601 (萬曆 29). cb. 2 vols.
cf. Pfister, p. 34; Jo, pp. 142–148; Cordier-Sinica, col. 1092.
note: Revised version of the Tengaku Jitsugi (n. 0132). Specifically outlawed in 1630 in Japan.
0194 —— Peking 1604 (萬曆 32). 欽一堂 cb. 2 vols.

c. Naikaku, Tōhoku.
ms. ICU, Seishin-Sankocho.
0195 —— Hangchaw [1605?]. cb. 2 vols.
0196 —— Hangchaw 1630 (崇禎 3). cb. 2 vols.
0197 —— Shanghai, 1868 (同治 7). cb. 2 vols., 27cm.
c. Ebisawa, Jinshu, Nagasaki, Tenri, Tōhoku-Kano, Waseda.
0198 —— Shanghai 土山灣印書館, 1930 (民國 19). wb. 1 v., [6], [12], 164p., 19cm.
c. Seishin, Tōhoku.
0199 —— (Tengaku Shokan).
0200 —— construed from Chinese into Jap. by Kojima Junji 小島準治, Tokyo 開世堂, 1885 (明治 18). wb. 1 v., 130, 38p., 19cm.
c. Sophia, Tenri, Ueno.
0201 —— abridged translation into Jap., Saeki-Shina pp. 217–320.

0202 Pantoja, Didaco de, SJ. 龐廸我 (1571–1618)
Jitsugi Zokuhen 實義續篇 *Shih-i Hsü-p'ien* (Supplement to Tenshu Jitsugi), Peking [n.d.]. cb. 1 v.
cf. Pfister, p. 72.
note: Specifically outlawed in 1630.

1602

0203 Longobardi, Nicolas, SJ. 龍華民 (1559–1654)
Seikyō Nikka 聖敎日課 *Sheng-chiao Jih-k'o* (Daily Prayers), Shao-chou 1602 (萬曆 30). cb. 1 v.
cf. Pfister, p. 64; Jo, pp. 33–34.
note: There are many Prayer books in the Chinese language. See also n. 3190.

0204 Ricci, Matteo, SJ. 利瑪竇 (1552–1610)
Kon'yo Bankoku Zenzu 坤輿萬國全圖 *K'un-yü Wan-kuo Ch'üan-t'u* (World Map), Peking, 1602 (萬曆 30). 3rd ed., 1 fold.
note: No copies of the first, second and fourth editions.
cf. Ayuzawa-Ricci; Jo, pp. 317–318; Pfister, p. 39.
c. Kyōdai, Miyagi.
0205 —— repr. and annotated by P. M. D'Elia, SJ., *Il Mappamondo cinese del P. Matteo Ricci,* Rome 1938.
0206 —— facs. repr. by the Ukō Gakukai 禹貢學會 *Yü-kung Hsüeh-hui,* Peking 1936 (民國 25).
0206b —— repr. and annotated by Ayuzawa Shintarō 鮎沢信太郎, *Nippon Bunkashijō ni okeru Ricci no Sekai-chizu,* Tokyo 1941 (昭和 16) pp. 1–54.
0207 * Bankoku Shūsetsu 萬國集說 by

Arai Hakuseki 新井白石. jb. 1 v.
cf. Miyazaki, p. 740.
orig. ms. Shoryobu.

0208 * Bankoku Zushaku 萬國圖釋, jb.
1 v.
ms. Akioka.

0209 * Chikyū Betsuroku 地球別録. jb.
1 v.
ms. Okayama

0210 * Kon'yo Zen-zusetsu 坤輿全圖說
by Inagaki Shishin 稻垣子戩, 1802 (享和 2).
jb. 1 v., 43f., 26cm.
cf. Kaikoku, p. 135.
c. Ayuzawa, Tōhōku-Kano, Tōkyōiku.

0211 * Sankai Yochi Zen-zusetsu 山海
輿地全圖說. jb. 1 v.
ms. Akioka, Okayama, Shoryobu.

1603

0212 Contrição no Riyaku こんちりさん
のりやく (On Contrition), Nagasaki, 1603
(慶長 8). jb. 1 v.
cf. Laures, n. 36–15; Tenri-Jap. II, p. 84.
c. None known.
ms. Ōura, Tenri.
phot. Sophia.

0213 —— pr. by Urakawa Wasaburō 浦川
和三郎, *Kirishitan no Fukkatsu,* v. II, Tokyo
1928 (昭和 3), pp. 861–876.

0214 * Contriçam no Ryaku 胡无血利佐
無の略, Nagasaki, 1869 (明治 2). jb. 1 v., [1],
2, 14f., 24c.m.
note: Revised ed. of n. 212.
c. Junshin, Nagasaki, Seishin, Sophia, Tagita.
ms. Ebisawa.

0215 —— (Kaihyō Sōsho, v. I).
0216 —— (Namban Bunshū).
0217 —— (Meiji Bunka Zenshū, v. XI).
0218 —— changed into modern Jap. by
Emile Raguet, MEP., *Kanzen naru Tsukai*
完全なる痛悔, Fukuoka 1902 (明治 35).
cf. Ebisawa Arimichi, "Kirishitan Tenseki Kenkyū
    Yoroku" (*Seishin Studies,* v. III), Tokyo 1953.
c. Seishin-Iwashita, Sophia.

Disputation with the Hokke
Bonzes, 1603

0219 Nichiō 日奥
Bandai Kikyōroku 萬代亀鏡録, compiled
by Nisshō 日正. jb. 8 vols.
0220 —— Kyoto 妙覺寺, 1890 (明治 23).
jb. 8 vols.
0221 —— abridged (Dai-Nippon Shiryō,
Series XII, v. I).
0222 Sekijōshi 石城志 (Notes of Sekijō).
0223 —— abridged (Dai-Nippon Shiryō,
Series XII, v. I).

0224 Ricci, Matteo, SJ. 利瑪竇 (1552–
1610)
Ryōgi Genranzu 兩儀玄覽圖 *Liang-i Hsüan-
lan T'u* (World Map), Peking, 1603 (萬曆
31). 8f., 203 × 59cm.
phot. Ayuzawa.

0225 —— facs. repr. by Ayuzawa Shintarō, 鮎澤信太郎 "Mateo Ricci no Ryōgi
Genranzu ni tsuite" (*Chirigakushi Kenkyū,*
v. I), Tokyo 1957 (昭和 32).

0226 Takenaka Jūmon 竹中重門 (1573–
1631)
Toyokagami 豐鑑 (Life of Toyotomi
Hideyoshi), [1603?]. jb. 1 v.
cf. Kokushi, p. 231–232.
ms. Shoryobu, Tōdai-Nanki.

1604

0227 Ikoku Raikan Mitome 異國來翰認
(Copy of Letters from Foreign Countries).
0228 —— abridged pr. and annotated by
Murakami Naojirō 村上直次郎 (Ikoku Sōsho,
Ikoku Ōfukushokanshū).

0229 Itasaka Bokusai 板坂卜齋 (1578–
1655)
Keichō-nenjū Bokusaiki, 慶長年中卜齋記,
or Itasaka Bokusai Oboegaki 板坂卜齋覺書
(Bokusai's Chronicle from 1598 to 1604).
jb. 3 vols.
cf. Kokushi, p. 82.
ms. Daitokyu, Keiō, Naikaku, Ueno, Waseda.
0230 —— Tokyo 古書保存書屋, 1882 (明治
15). jb. 1 v., 2,5,32, [1]f., 24cm.
c. Dōshisha, Ebisawa, Gakushiin, Nichidai-Mukasa,
    Tōyō-Iwasaki, Waseda.
0231 —— (Bunhen Sōsho).
0232 —— (Shiseki Shūran).
0233 —— (Kaitei Shiseki Shūran,
v. XXVI).
0234 * Bokusai Nikki 卜齋日記 (Dairy
of Bokusai). jb. 1 v.
ms. Naikaku.

0235 Ricci, Matteo, SJ. 利瑪竇 (1552–
1610)
Nijūgogen 二十五言 *Erh-shih-wu Yen*
(Twenty-five Moral Maxims), Peking 1604
(萬曆 32). cb. 1 v.
cf. Pfister, pp. 35–36; Jo, pp. 327–330; Saeki-Shina,
    pp. 230–205.
ms. Ebisawa, Naikaku, Seikado, Shokokan, Waseda.
0236 —— (Tengaku Shokan).
0237 —— (Tenkyō Goten).
0238 —— (Yōkyō Shichishu).
0239 Rodriguez Tçuzu, João, SJ.
(1561?–1634)
Arte Da Lingoa De Iapam, Nangasaqui

1604–08. wb. 1 v., 4°, [5], 239, [1]f.

cf. Satow, pp. 46–47; Streit V, p. 379; Laures, n. 28.
c. Bodleian Lib.
phot. Sophia.
roto. Doi, Tenri, Toyo.
ms. by L. Pagés; P. Humbertclaude, Rome.

0240 —— tr. into Jap. by Doi Tadao 土井忠生, *Rodriguez Nippon Dai-Bunten,* Tokyo 1955 (昭和 30).

0241 * Arte Breve Da Lingoa Iapoa Tirada Da Arte Granda Da Mesma lingoa, Amacao M. DC.XX., 4°, [4], 96f.

cf. Satow, p. 47; Streit V, p. 379; Laures, n. 35.
note: Abridged ed. of the above.
c. Marsden Lib. of King's College, Biblioteca da Ajuda.
phot. Sophia.
roto. Doi, Tenri.

0242 Santa Quaranta Monjo サンタクワランタ文書 (Document of the Franciscan Convent in Santa Quaranta, Italy).

note: A petition by Jap. Christians requesting canonization of the twenty-six martyrs.

0243 —— pr. by Kimura Tarō 木村太郎, in *Nihon Nijūroku Seijin Junkyōki,* Tokyo 1931 (昭和 6), pp. 275–283.

0244 —— pr. by Ebisawa Arimichi 海老澤有道, in "Nijūroku Seijin kankei Nippon Shiryō" (*Bōrō,,* v. II, n. 1), Tokyo 1947 (昭和 22).

0245 Vocabvlario Da Lingoa De Iapam com adeclaração em Portugues, feito por Algvns Padres, E Irmaõs Da Companhia De Iesv. Com Licença Do Ordinario, & Superiores em Nangasaqui no Collegio de Iapam Da Companhia De Iesvs. Anno M.D.CIII, Supplemento Deste Vocabulario impresso no mesmo Collegio da Cõpanhia De Iesv Com a sobredita licença & approuação. Anno. 1604. 4°, wb. 1 v., [2], 402f.

cf. Satow, pp. 45–46; Streit V, p. 378; Laures, n. 27.
c. Bibliothèque Nationale Française, Bodleian Lib., Biblioteca Publica da Evora, Convento de S. Domingo de Manila.
phot. Sophia.
roto. Tōyō.

0246 * [tr. into Spanish], Vocabvlario De Iapon Declarado Primero En Portvgves Por Los Padres De La Compañia de Iesvs de aquel reyno, y agora en Castellano en el Colegio de Santo Thomas de Manila. Con Licencia En Manila Por Tomas Pinpin, y Iacinto Magaurlua. Año de 1630. 4°, wb. 1 v., [315], [301]f.

cf. Satow, p. 46; Streit V, p. 580; Laures, n. 53.
c. Tenri, Tōyō, Sophia.

0247 * Dictionnaire Japonais-Fran-

çais, tr. into French by Léon Pagés, Paris 1868. wb. 1 v., [4], 933p. 27cm.

cf. Satow, pp. 45–46; Streit X, pp. 67–68; Laures, n. 786.
c. Ebisawa, Keio-Koda, Kyōdai, Nagasaki, Sophia, Tōdai, Shiryō.

0248 —— facs. repr. with notes by Doi Tadao 土井忠生, Tokyo 1952 (昭和 27).

1605

0249 Cerqueira, Luis de, SJ. (1552–1614)

Sacramento To Sono Foca xinajinano guini tçuiteno voxiye (Instructions on the Sacraments and various other matters), Nangasaqvii. In Collegio Societatis Iesv. Anno M.DCV. wb. 1 v., 33p. 24cm.

cf. Laures, n. 29.
note: This is an appendix to the Latin Litual book, *Manvale ad Sacramenta Ecclesiae Ministranda,* Nangasaqvii 1605.
c. Toulouse Public Lib.
phot. Doi, Keio-Koda, Sophia, Toyo.

0250 —— repr. and annotated by Johannes Laures, SJ. and Kobayashi Yoshio 小林珍雄, "Aratani Hakken seraretaru Nagasaki Sacramenta Furoku no Hōbun Tekisuto" (*Kirishitan Kenkyū,* v. I), Tokyo 1942 (昭和 17).

0251 —— [ditto] *Japanische Ansprachen und Gebete aus einem alten Rituale, gedruckt zu Nagasaki 1605* (Monumenta Nipponica Monograph, v. VII), Tokyo 1941.

0252 Fabian Fucan, SJ. 不干ハビアン (1565?–)

Myōtei Mondō 妙貞問答 (Dialogue of Myōshū and Yūtei), [Nagasaki], 1605 (慶長 10), jb. 3 vols.

cf. Laures, n. 43; Kokushi, p. 301.
note: No copies of the first edition or of the first volume available.
ms. Jingu, Sophia, Tenri.

0253 —— (Nippon Koten Zenshū).

0254 —— (Nippon Shisō Tōsō Shiryō, v. X).

0255 —— (Nippon Tetsugaku Shisō Zensho, v. X).

0256 —— (Zuihitsu Bungaku Senshū, v. VI).

0257 —— tr. into French by Pierre Humbertclaude, SM., "Myōtei Mondō, Une apologétique chrétienne japonaise de 1605", (*Monumenta Nipponica,* v. I, n. 2–v. II, n. 1), Tokyo 1938–39.

0258 * Buppō no Shidai Ryaku Nukigaki 佛法の次第略抜書 (Summary of the Buddhist Doctrine).

cf. Laures, n. 44–8.

note: Abridged manuscript of the first volume of the *Myōtei Mondō* (n. 252).

0259 —— (Yasokyō Sōsho).

0260 —— pr. and annotated, Anesaki-Jimbutsu, pp. 481–496.

0261 Ricci, Matteo, SJ. 利瑪竇 (1552–1610)
Kika Gempon 幾何原本 *Chi-ho Yüan-pen* (Principles of Euclid's Geometry), Peking, 1605 (萬曆 33). cb. 4 vols., 27cm.
cf. Pfister, p. 37; Jo, pp. 256–262; Saeki-Shina, pp. 214–216.
c. Waseda-Ogura.
ms. Gakushiin, Seikado.

0262 —— Peking, 1611 (萬曆 39). 2nd ed.
0263 —— Peking, 1896 (光緒 22). cb. 24 vols.
c. Kyūdai-Butsuri.

0264 —— (Tengaku Shokan).
0265 —— (Sūri Seiun).
0266 —— (Kaizansenkan Sōsho, vv. XCVII–C).
0267 —— (Chūsei Sangaku Taisei, vv. I–IV).
0268 —— compiled by Alexander Wylie 偉烈亞力 LM., Nanking, 1865 (同治 4). cb. 8 vols., 30cm.
cf. Cordier-Sinica, col. 1328; Wylie, p. 173.
c. Kyōdai, Kyūdai-Butsuri, Naikaku, Seikado, Tōhoku-Kano, Ueno, Waseda-Ogura.

0269 —— (Kokon Sangaku Sōsho, vv. III–VIII).

0270 Ricci, Matteo, SJ. 利瑪竇 (1552–1610)
Rōmaji Chūon 羅馬字註音, *Lo-ma-tzu Chu-yin* (Chinese Pronunciation in Roman Letters), Peking 1605 (萬曆 33). cb. 1 v., 7, 6, [5]f., 1pl., 33cm.

0271 —— (Teishi Bokuen 程氏墨苑, *Ch'eng-shih Mo-yüan*, v. II), Peking [n.d.].

0272 —— facs. repr. by Berthold Laufer, *Christian Art in China,* Berlin 1910.

0273 —— facs. repr. by Hojin Daigaku 輔仁大學 *Fu-jen Ta-hsueh*, *Minki Ōka Bijutsu oyobi Rōmaji Chūon* 明季歐化美術及羅馬字註音, *Ming-chi Ou-hua Mei-shu Chi Lo-ma-tzu Chu-yin,* Peking 1927 (民國 16). cb. 1 v.,

0274 —— facs. repr. (Heion Moji Shiryō Sōsho).

1606

0275 Hayashi Razan 林羅山 (1583–1657)
Hai Yaso 排耶蘇 (Anti-Christian). 1606 (慶長 11). jb. 1 v.
cf. Ebisawa-Namban, pp. 60–63; Shimmura-Nam-

ban, pp. 99–104.

0275b —— (Razan Bunshū, v. LVI).
0276 —— (Sokkyohen, v. IX).
0277 —— (Nippon Shisō Tōsō Shiryō, v. X).
0278 —— (Dai-Nippon Shisō Zenshū, v. II).
0279 —— (Kirishitan Shiryō).
0280 —— repr. by Uchida Ginzo 内田銀藏, in *Nippon Kinseishi*, v. I., Tokyo 1903 (明治 36).
0281 —— tr. into German by Hans Müller, S.J. (*Monumenta Nipponica*, v. II, u. 1.). Tokyo 1939.

1607

0282 Sū Genpyō 鄒元標 *Tsou Yüan-piao* (–1624)
Gangakushū 願學集 *Yüan-hsüehchi* (Essays), 1607 (萬曆 35). cb. 12 vols.
note: Specifically outlawed subsequent to 1630.

0283 —— 1619 (萬曆 47). cb. 12 vols.
c. Naikaku.

0284 Ricci, Matteo, SJ. 利瑪竇 (1552–1610)
Kongai Tsūken Zusetsu 渾蓋通憲圖說 *Hun-kai T'ung-hsien T'u-shuo* (Illustrated Explanation on the Stereographic Projection of the Celestial Sphere), Peking 1607 (萬曆 35). cb. 2 vols., 27cm.
cf. Pfister, p. 39; Jo, pp. 263–264.
ms. Kyudai, Naikaku, Tōhoku-Kano.

0285 —— (Tengaku Shokan).
0286 —— (Shuzankaku Sōsho).

0287 Spiritval Xvgvio no tameni yerabi atçumuru xuquanno Manual. Core Iesvsno Companhia ni voite amitatçuru mono nari. Svperioresto, Ordinariono yuruxiuo cõmuri, Nagasaqi Iesvsno Collegioni voite fanni firaqu mono nari. (A Manual of Meditations chosen and collected with regard to Spiritual Exercises, composed by the Society of Jesus. Published at Nagasaki, in the College of the Society of Jesus, with permission of Superiors and Ordinary), 1607. wb. 1 v., [4], 404, [3]f., 6pl. 18cm.
cf. Ebisawa-Tenseki, pp. 71–102.
note: This contains the Meditations on the Fifteen Mysteries of the Rosary and the Passion by Gaspar Loarte SJ. (–1578), the Passion of Our Lord compiled from the four Gospels by a Jesuit, and meditations on various subjects by Pedro Gomez, SJ. (1535–1600).
c. Ōura.
phot. Nagasaki, Sophia, Tōyō.

0288 —— mimeogr. repr. by Takaba Go-ro 高羽五郎, Kanazawa 1957–60 (昭和 32–35).

0289 —— transcribed into Jap. characters by Ebisawa Arimichi 海老澤有道, (Kirishitan Bunko, B. vv. I–V.)

0290 —— ms. in Jap. characters in the Keichō 慶長 period. wb. 1 v., 15cm.

cf. Ebisawa-Tenseki, pp. 102–108.
ms. Tōyō.

0291 * Shichika Kannensho 七科觀念書 (Meditations on the Seven Sins), jb. 1 v., 13f., 16×45cm.

cf. Ebisawa Arimichi, "Shichika Kannensho no Gempon", (Kirisutokyō Shigakukai Kaihō, n. 31), Yokohama 1957; Laures, n. 45–5.
note: This is a manuscript transcription of the Spiritual Xuguio, part 3.
ms. Tokugawa.

0292 —— facs. repr. (Kirishitan Sōsho).

0293 * [Gobassho no Kotowari 御バッショノ理], (The Passion of Our Lord), [Yokohama 1873?].

cf. Laures, n. 85.
note: Ebisawa has a printed fragment of four leaves from the part of Spiritual Xuguio which contains meditations on the Passion (ff. 83–121), but we have no complete copy of the entire work.

0294 —— repr. and annotated, Ebisawa-Tenseki, pp. 87–102.

0295 * [Gobassho no Kannen 御ばっしょの觀念] (Meditations on the Passion). jb. 1 v.

cf. Ebisawa-Tenseki, pp. 81–87.
note: Partial manuscript of the Spiritual Xuguio (ff. 121–160), present whereabouts not known.

0296 —— partial pr., Anesaki-Kinzei, pp. 234–237.

0297 * Gobatsushiyo 後婆通志與 (The Passion from the Four Gospels), approved by Bishop Bernard T. Petitjean, MEP., Nagasaki 1873 (明治 6). jb. 1 v., [1], 44p., 24cm.

note: Partial reprint of the Spiritual Xuguio (ff. 161–174).
cf. Ebisawa-Tenseki, pp. 76–80; Laures, n. 79; Tenri-Jap. I, p. 84.
c. Ebisawa, Nagasaki, Oura, Sophia, Tenri.

0298 —— repr. by Ebisawa Arimichi 海老澤有道, "Kirishitan-yaku Sei-Fukuinsho no Ichirei", (Seishin Studies, v. II), Tokyo 1952 (昭和 27).

0299 * Kirishitan Yōgo Ryakuge Dankan 吉利支丹用語略解斷簡 (A Fragment of an Explanation of Christian Terminology in the Spiritual Xuguio). jb. 1 v., 4f., 16×22cm.

cf. Laures, n. 45–4.
ms. Tokugawa.

0300 —— facs. pr. (Kirishitan Sosho).

0301 —— repr. and annotated by Hiiragi Gen'ichi 柊源一, "Spiritual Shugyō to Kiri-shitan Yōgo Ryakuge", (Kokugo Kokubun, v. XXVI, n. 3), Kyoto 1957 (昭和 32).

1608

0302 Ri Takugo 李卓吾, Li Tso-wu (1527–1602)

Giyō 疑耀, I-yao, 1608 (萬曆 36). cb. 7 vols.
note: Specifically outlawed subsquent to 1630.
ms. Naikaku.

0303 Ricci, Matteo, SJ. 利瑪竇 (1552–1610)

Kijin Jippen 畸人十篇 Chi-jen Shih-p'ien (Ten Paradoxes), Peking 愼修堂, 1608 (萬曆 36). cb. 2 vols., 27cm.
cf. Pfister, p. 36; Jo, pp. 148–152; Saeki-Shina, pp. 198–201; Leon Hurvitz, Samidareshō (Monumenta Nipponica, v. IX), n. 2.
c. Naikaku.
ms. Naikaku, Shoryobu.

0304 —— Nanking 1609 (萬曆 37). 2nd ed.

0305 —— (Tengaku Shokan).

0306 —— [n.p.], [1821? 道光 1]. cb. 2 vols., 26cm.

c. Rikkyo (v. II only).

0307 —— Shanghai 1847 (道光 27). cb. 2 vols., 21cm.

c. ICU, Nagasaki, Seishin (v. II only), Tenri.
ms. Waseda,

0308 —— construed from Chinese into Jap. by Mishima Yoshitada 三島良忠, Tokyo 1886 (明治 19). wb. 1 v.

c. Sophia.

0309 Ricci, Matteo, SJ. 利瑪竇 (1552–1610)

Sokuryō Hōgi 測量法義 Ts'e-liang Fa-i (Practical Method of Mensuration), Peking, [1608?]. cb. 1 v., 24f., 29cm.
note: Specifically outlawed in 1630.
cf. Pfister. p. 38; Jo, pp. 267–269.
ms. Seikado.

0310 —— (Tengaku Shokan).

0311 —— (Kaizansenkan Sōsho).

0312 —— (Shikai).

0313 —— (Sōsho Shūsei).

0314 Jo Kōkei 徐光啓 Hsü Kuang-ch'i (1562–1633)

Sokuryō Idō 測量異同 Ts'e-liang Yi-t'ung (Analogy of Practical Geometry), compiled by Jo Kōkei and M. Ricci, SJ., [n.p.], [n.d.]. cb. 1 v., 5f., 29cm.
cf. Pfister, p. 38; Jo, p. 270.
ms. Seikado.

0315 —— (Tengaku Shokan).

0316 —— (Shikai)

0317 —— (Kaizansenkan Sōsho, v. CVI).

0318 —— (Chūsei Sangaku Shishū).

0319 —— (Sōsho Shūsei).

0320 Ricci, Matteo, SJ. 利瑪竇 (1552–1610)

Bengaku Itō 辯學遺牘 *Pien-hsüeh Yi-tu* (Disputation with Idolaters), Peking 習是齋, 1609 (萬曆 37). cb. 1 v., 26f.. 27cm.
cf. Pfister, p. 36; Jo, pp. 119–120; Saeki-Shina, pp. 212–214; Leon Hurvitz, "Samidareshō" (*Monumenta Nipponica*, v. IX), n. 4.
c. Naikaku.

0321 —— Peking 欽一堂, 1609 (萬曆 37). cb. 1v.
c. Naikaku.

0322 —— Peking 救世堂, 1880 (光緒 6). cb. 1v., 38f., 21cm.
c. Tohoku.

0323 —— Peking, 1919 (民國 8). cb. 1 v., [2], 15f., 23cm.
c. Ebisawa.

0324 —— Peking 救世堂, 1934 (民國 23). wb. 1 v., 42p., 20cm.
c. Tenri.

0325 —— (Tengaku Shokan).

0326 Rocha, João de, SJ. 羅如望 (1566–1623)

Tenshu Seizō Ryakusetsu 天主聖像略說 *T'ien-chu Sheng-hsiang Liao-shuo* (Explanations of Saintly Images), [Peking] 1609 (萬曆 37). cb. 1 v.
note: Specifically outlawed in 1630.
cf. Pfister, p. 69.
c. Naikaku.
ms. Ebisawa, Jinshu, Shoryobu, Sophia, Waseda.

0327 —— ms. by Kiyū-Dōjin 杞憂道人.
ms. Otori.

0328 —— (Yōkyō Shichishu).

0329 —— (Seihō Zatsuwa).

Destruction of the Portuguese Ship, „Madre de Deos", 1609

0330 Kuroyanagi Takehide 畔柳武英
Kurobune Hanchinki 黑船燔沈記 (Record of the Destruction of the Black Ship). jb. 1 v.
cf. Samura, p. 517.
ms. Naikaku.

0331 Bansen Kassenki Densho 蕃船合戰記傳書 (Recollections of Records of the Battle with the Foreign Ship). jb. 1 v.
ms. Hibiya-Kondo.

0332 Nagasaki Kurofune Kassenki 長崎黑船合戰記 (Record of the Combat with the Black Ship in Nagasaki). jb. 1 v.
ms. Shiryō.

0333 Ricci, Matteo, SJ. 利瑪竇 (1552–1610)
Keitengai 經天該 *Ching-t'ien Kai* (On Astronomy).
cf. Jo, p. 352.

0334 —— (Geikai Shujin).

0335 —— (Denkeidō Sōsho).

0336 —— (Seigaku Taisei, v. II.)

0337 Ricci, Matteo,. SJ. 利瑪竇 (1552–1610)
Kenkon Taigi 乾坤體義 *Ch'ien-k'ung T'i-yi* (Explanation of the Globes), Peking, [n.d.]. cb. 3 vols.
cf. Pfister, p. 40; Jo, pp. 312–313.

0338 —— (Sansho Ihen).

0339 Ricci, Matteo. SJ. 利瑪竇 (1552–1610)
Kōkōgi 勾股義 *Kou-ku-i* (Theory of the Triangle and Rectangle), compiled by M. Ricci and Jo Kōkei 徐光啓 *Hsü Kuang-ch'i,* [n.p.], [n.d.]. cb. 1v., 3, 1, 21f., 29cm.
cf. Pfister, p. 39; Jo, pp. 272–273.
ms. Seikado.

0340 —— (Tengaku Shokan).

0341 —— (Kaizansenkan Sōsho, v. CVI).

0342 —— (Shikai).

0343 —— (Chūsei Sangaku Shishu).

0344 —— (Seigaku Taisei, v. I).

0345 Shimai Sōshitsu 島井宗室 (1539–1615)
Shimai Sōshitsu Ikenjō 島井宗室異見狀 (Shimai Soshitsu's Will), 1610 (慶長 15).
cf. Kokushi, p. 130.

0346 —— pr. and annotated by Kuwata Tadachika 桑田忠親, in *Sengoku Bushō no Seikatsu,* Tokyo 1952 (昭和 27).

0347 —— abridged pr. by Ebisawa Arimichi, 海老澤有道, in *Nippon-shi Kenkyū Shiryō,* Tokyo 1958 (昭和 33).

0348 Taiheiki Nukigaki 太平記抜書 (Taifeiqui), [Nagasaki, [1610?], jb. 6 vols., 26cm.
cf. Yamada Yoshio, 山田孝雄 "Yasokai Shuppan Taiheiki" (*Geibun*, v. III, n. 3), Kyoto 1921; Laures, n. 34; Streit X, p. 161.
c. Tenri.
phot. Sophia.

0349 Ursis, Sebastian de, SJ. 熊三拔 (1575–1620)
Kampeigi-setsu 簡平儀說 *Chien-p'ing-yi-shuo* (Description of Astronomical Instrument), Peking, 1611 (萬曆 39). cb. 1 v.
note: Specifically outlawed in 1630.

cf. Pfister, p. 105; Jo, pp. 270–272.
ms. Seikado, Tōhoku-Kano.

0350 —— (Tengaku Shokan).
0351 —— (Shuzankaku Sōsho).

1612

Arima Protasio Harunobu
有馬晴信 (**1567–1512**)

0352 Arima Denki 有馬傳記 (Record of the Arimas). jb. 1 v.
cf. Samura, p. 56.
0353 —— (Shimabara-ki, v. II).
0354 —— (Buhen Sōsho, A).
0355 —— (Shiseki Shūran).

0356 Arima Harunobu-ki 有馬晴信記, or Arima Ryūzōji-ki 有馬龍造寺記 (Diary of Arima Harunobu). jb. 1 v.
cf. Kokushi, p. 9.
ms. Shiryo.
0357 —— (Kaitei Shiseki Shūran, v. XV).
0358 —— (Zoku Gunsho Ruijū, v. DCLII).

0359 Arima Ryūzōji Shimzazu Ōtomo Kassen Isetsu 有馬龍造寺島津大友合戦異説 (Different Opinions on the Battle of Arima, Ryūzōji, Shimazu and Ōtomo).
0360 —— (Ōitaken Kyōdoshiryō Shūsei, v. II).
0361 Ryūzōjiki 龍造寺記 or Ryūzōji Takanobu Jiseki 龍造寺隆信事蹟 (Life of Ryuzōji Takanobu). jb. 1 v.
ms. Naikaku.

———————

0362 Ursis, Sebastian de, SJ. 熊三拔 (1575–1620)
Taisei Suihō 泰西水法 *T'ai-hsi Shui-fa* (Hydraulic Machines of Europe), Peking, 1612 (萬暦 40). cb. 6 vols.
note: Specifically outlawed in 1630.
cf. Pfister, p. 105; Jo, pp. 307–312.
c. Naikaku, Tōhoku-Kano.
ms. Ebisawa (v. I–II only), Kyōdai-Fujikawa. Seikado, Shokokan, Tenri.
0363 —— [n. p.], 1843 (道光 23). cb. 6 vols.
c. Seikado.
0364 —— Peking, 1880 (光緒 6). cb. 6 vols.
c. Naikaku.
0365 —— (Tengaku Shokan).
0366 —— (Nōsei Zensho).
0367 —— (Juji Tsūkō),
0368 —— construed from Chinese into Japanese by Matsushita Kenrin 松下見林 Kyoto 1664 (寛文 4). jb. 2 vols.
c. Shokokan.
ms. Shokokan.

1613

Documents concerning Date Masamune's Mission to Europe.

0369 Dateke Monjo 伊達家文書 (Documents of the Date Family).
cf. Kokushi, pp. 195–196.
orig. ms. Miyagi.
0370 —— (Dai-Nippon Komonjo, Dateke Monjo).
0371 Date Narizane 伊達成實 (1568–1646)
Masamuneki 政宗記, or Date Narizaneki 伊達成實記 (Life of Date Masamune). jb. 3 vols.
cf. Samura, p. 1334.
0372 —— (Sendai Sōsho, B., v.XI).
0373 Date Teizan Chika Kiroku 伊達貞山治家記録 (Notes of Date Teizan's Management of his Household).
cf. Kokushi, p. 196.
0374 —— (Sendai Hanso Seiseki, v. V).
0375 —— abridged pr. (Dai-Nippon Shiryō, Series XII, v. XII).
0376 Nambankoku Shokan Ambun 南蠻國書翰案文 (Letters to the Western Country, Spain).
note: Letters of Date Masamune, the Lord of Ōshu, to King of Spain and Archbishop of Spain.
ms. Ebisawa, Tenri.
0377 —— (Ishimoda Monjo).
0378 —— (Dai-Nippon Shiryō, Series XII, v. XII),
0379 —— (Ikoku Sōsho, Ikoku Ōfuku Shokanshū).
0380 —— (Sendai Hanso Seiseki, v. V.).
0381 —— (Date Kashi Sōdan, v. IV).
0382 Sakuma Dōgan 佐久間洞巖 (1653–1736)
Date Masamunekyō Nempu 伊達政宗卿年譜 (Biographical Table of Date Masamune).
0383 —— (Sendai Sōsho, B., v. I).
0384 Tanabe Kibun 田辺希文 (1692–1773)
Dateke Seshinden 伊達家世臣傳 (Lives of Retainers of the Dates). jb. 3 vols.
cf. Samura, p. 1334.
0385 —— (Sendai Sōsho, A., v. II).

0386 Tenshō Keichō Dateke Kiroku 天正慶長伊達家記録 (Documents of the Date Family between the Tenshō and Keichō Eras). jb. 1 v.
ms. Todai-Nanki.

———————

0387 Ri Shisō 李之藻, *Li Chih-ts'ao* (1552–1610)

Dōbun Sanshi 同文算指 *T'ung-wen Suan-chih* (Practical Arithmetic), Peking 1614 (萬曆 42). cb. 2 vols., 27cm.
note: Specifically outlawed in 1630.
cf. Pfister, p. 38; Jo, pp. 265–267.
c. Kyūdai-Butsuri.
ms. Seikado.
0388 —— (Tengaku Shokan).
0389 —— (Kaizansenkan Sōsho, vv. CI–CV).

1614

0390 Miura Jōshin 三浦淨心 (1565–1644)

Keichō Kenmonjū 慶長見聞集 (Story of the Keicho Era), 1614 (慶長 19). jb.
cf. Kokushi, p. 82.
ms. Naikaku, Tenri, Ueno.
0391 —— (Shiseki Shūran),
0392 —— (Kaitei Shiseki Shūran, v. X).
0393 —— (Meicho Bunko, v. XXV).
0394 —— (Edo Sōsho, v. II).
0395 —— (Yūzankaku Bunko).
0396 —— (Zoku Kokumin Bunko, v. VI).

0397 Pantoja, Didaco de, SJ. 龐廸我 (1571–1618)

Shichikoku 七克 *Ch'i-k'o* (Seven Victories over the Cardinal Sins), Peking 1641 (萬曆 42). cb. 7 vols., 27cm.
note: Specifically outlawed in 1630.
cf. Pfister, p. 71; Jo, pp. 51–56.
ms. Shoryobu, Taisho
0398 —— Peking, 1643 (崇禎 16). cb. 4 vols.
c. Nagasaki.
0399 —— Peking 始胎大堂, 1798 (嘉慶 3). cb. 2 vols., 25cm.
c. ICU, Naikaku, Sophia, Tenri, Tōyō.
0400 —— Siking, 1843 (道光 23). cb. 2 vols.
0401 —— Shanghai, 1849 (道光 29). cb. 2 vols.
0402 —— Shanghai, 1873 (同治 12). cb. 4 vols.
0403 —— Peking 始胎大堂, 1898 (光緒 24). cb. 4 vols., 25cm.
c. Tōhoku-Kano.
0404 —— Shanghai 土山灣印書館 1931 (民國 20). cb. 1v., 1, 14, 2, 302p., 19cm.
c. Seishin.
0405 —— (Tengaku Shokan).
0406 * Shichikoku Shinkun 七克眞訓 *Ch'i-k'o Chen-hsün* (Explanation of Pantoja's Shichikoku) by F.X. Danicourt, OP. 沙勿略, Shanghai 1857 (咸豊 7). cb. 2 vols., 21cm.
cf. Pfister, p. 72.

c. Aoyama, Hibiya-Ichimura, ICU, Seishin, Tenri.
0407 —— Shanghai 1910 (宣統 2). wb. 2 vols., 10cm.
c. Tōhoku.
0408 —— Shanghai 1922 (民國 11). wb. 1v., 4, 4, 197p., 19cm.
c. Ebisawa.

0409 Ricci, Matteo, SJ. 利瑪竇 (1552–1610)

Kanyō Kōgi 圜容較義 *Huan-yung Chiao-yi* (On Isoperimetric Figures), by M. Ricci and Ri Shisō 李之藻, *Li Chih-ts'ao*, Peking 1614 (萬曆 42). cb. 1 v., [1] [4], [24]f., 28cm.
note: Specifically outlawed in 1630.
cf. Pfister, p. 39; Jo, pp. 274–277.
c. Kyudai-Butsuri, Waseda.
ms. Seikado.
0410 —— (Tengaku Shokan).
0411 —— (Kaizansenkan Sōsho, v. CVI).
0412 —— (Shuzankaku Sōsho).
0413 —— (Seigaku Taisei, v. I).

0414 Sūden 崇傳 (1569–1633)

Zokubun Kaitei 屬文階梯 (Manifesto Prohibiting Christianity), 1614 (慶長 18 年 12 月).
0415 —— (Ikoku Nikki).
0416 —— (Nippon Shisō Tōsō Shiryō, v. X).
0417 —— (Haja Sōsho, v. I).
0418 —— tr. into English by Ernest Satow (*Transactions of the Asiatic Society of Japan*, v. VI, n.1), Yokohama 1878.
0419 * Hai-Kirishitan 排吉利支丹 (Anti-Christian).
0420 —— (Sokkyohen, v. XV).

0421 Ursis, Sebastian de, SJ. 熊三拔 (1575–1620)

Hyōdosetsu 表度說 *Piao-tu-shuo* (On Gnomonics), Peking 1614 (萬曆 42). cb. 1 v.
note: Specifically outlawed in 1630.
cf. Pfister, p. 105; Jo, pp. 280–284.
ms. Seikado.
0422 —— (Tengaku Shokan).

1615

0423 Diaz, jr., Emmanuel, SJ. 陽瑪珞 (1574–1659)

Temmon-ryaku 天文略 *T'ien-wen Lüeh* (Short Explanation of the Celestial Sphere), Peking 1615 (萬曆 43). cb. 1 v.
note: Specifically outlawed in 1630.
cf. Pfister, p. 110; Jo, pp. 27 –279.
ms. Seikado.
0424 —— (Tengaku Shokan).
0425 —— (Geikai Shujin).
0426 —— (Sōsho Shūsei, v. I).

0427 Oze Hoan 小瀬甫庵 (1564–1640) Nobunaga 信長記 (Story of Nobunaga), revised by Oze Hoan, [Kyoto], 1615 (元和 1). jb. 8 vols., 28cm.

note: see nos. 169–172.
cf. Kawase, pp. 608–609; Kokushi, p. 250; Tenri-Jap. II, p. 97; Wada, n. 342.
c. Naikaku, Tenri, Yasuda.
ms. Seisakudo, Sonkeikaku, Ueno.

0428 —— [Kyoto], [n.d.]. jb. 12 vols., 26cm.

cf. Wada, n. 343.
c. Daitokyu. Sesson,

0429 —— [Kyoto], 1622 (元和 8). jb. 8 vols., 28cm.

c. Keio, Takagi (vv. IX–X missing), Tenri, Tōdai-Nanki.

0430 —— [n.p.], [n.d.]. jb. 3 vols.

c. Seisakudo.

0431 —— [n.p.], [n.d.]. jb. 5 vols.

c. Tōyō-Iwasaki.

0432 —— [Kyoto], 1624 (寛永 1). jb. 8 vols., 29cm.

cf. Okuno, p. 110.
c. Kanazawa-Ujiie, Naikaku.

0433 —— [Kyoto] 1632 (寛永 9). jb. 8 vols., 29cm.

cf. Okuno, p. 193.
c. Doshisha, Ueno.

0434 —— [Kyoto], 1643 (寛永 20). jb. 6 vols.

cf. Okuno, p. 303.

0435 —— Kyoto 積雲堂, 1672 (寛文 12). jb. 8 vols., 27cm.

c. Kichu, Naikaku.

0436 —— (Nippon Rekishi Bunko).

0437 —— (Kokumin Bunko).

Keichō Era, 1596–1615

0438 Bussho Shōroku 佛書抄録 (Extract from a Buddhist Book) by a Jesuit. jb. 1 v.
cf. Laures, n. 45–7.
ms. Tokugawa.

0439 —— facs. pr. (Kirishitan Sōsho).

0440 Gomisa Henjigoto 御みさへんじ事 (Responses of the Mass). jb. 1 v.
cf. Laures, n. 45–2.
ms. Tokugawa.

0441 —— facs. pr. under the title, *Ratenbun Hiraganagaki Misa Tonaebun oyobi Rentō* 羅甸文平假名書彌撒唱文及連禱 (Kirishitan Sōsho).

0442 —— pr. and annotated by Endō Hiroshi 遠藤宏, "Go-Misa Henjigoto to Misa Seisai" (*Nichi-i Bunka Kenkyū*, v. VII), Tokyo 1942 (昭和 17).

0443 Kirishitan Jikkai 吉利支丹十誡 (Ten Commandments). jb. 1 v.
cf. Laures, n. 45–3.
ms. Tokugawa.

0444 —— facs. pr. (Kirishitan Sōsho).

0445 Kirishitan Korekisho Dankan 吉利支丹古暦書斷簡 (Fragment of an old Kirishitan Calendar), 1 fold, 13cm.
cf. Laures, n. 45–10; Ebisawa-Namban, pp. 446–447, 466–469.
ms. Tokugawa.
phot. Shiryo.

0446 —— facs. repr. (Kirishitan Sōsho)

0447 Kirishitan Koyomi 吉利支丹暦 (The Church Calendar). wb. 1 v., 23f., 20cm.
ms. Tenri.

0448 —— pr. and annotated by Ebisawa Arimichi 海老澤有道, "Hayashi-shi Kyuzō Kirishitan Korekisho" (*Seishin Studies*, v. I), Tokyo 1952 (昭和 27).

0449 —— facs. pr. and annotated by Ebisawa Arimichi 海老澤有道, Tokyo 1954 (昭和 29).

0450 —— pr. and annotated, Ebisawa-Namban, pp. 444-496.

0451 Kirishitan-shō 切支丹抄 (An abridged Collection of Christian Books). jb. 1 v., 9f., 17cm.
cf. Laures, n. 47.
ms. Tenri.

0452 —— pr. and annotated by Nishimura Shinji 西村眞次, "Nippon ni okeru Rōma Kakorikku-kyōto no Shitsuyō naru Shinkō Denshō" (*Bungaku Shisō Kenkyū*, v. I), Tokyo 1925 (大正 14).

0453 —— pr. and annotated by Nishimura Shinji 西村眞次, *Nippon Bunkashi Tenbyō*, Tokyo 1937 (昭和 12).

0454 —— pr. and annotated by Ebisawa Arimichi 海老澤有道, "Tamura-shi kyūzō Kirishitan Kyōsho Shahon" (*Kirisutokyō Shigaku*, v. II), Yokohama, 1952 (昭和 27).

0455 Kirishitan Shōmono 吉利支丹抄物 (Some Collections of Kirishitan Books), wb. 1 v., 142f., 14cm.
cf. Laures, n. 46.
ms. T. Higashi.

0456 —— facs. repr. (Kirishitan Sōsho,

0457 —— abridged repr. and annotated by Shimmura Izuru 新村出, "Kirishitan Ibutsu no Kenkyū" (*Studies on the Christian relics in Japan found near (sic) Takatsuki and in Kyoto, Report on (sic) Archaeological Research in the Department of Lit.,* v. VII), Kyoto 1923.

0458 Oratio Zassan Dankan オラショ雑纂断簡 (Fragments of Various Prayers), jb. 1 v.
cf. Laures, n. 45–6; Ebisawa Arimichi, "Kirishitan Tenseki Kenkyū Yoroku". (*Seishin Studies,* v. III), Tokyo 1953.
orig. ms. Tokugawa.

0459 —— facs. pr. (Kirishitan Sōsho).

0460 Sancta Maria no Officio さんたまりやのおひしよ [Yasokyō Shakyō 耶蘇教寫經], (Office of S. Virgin Mary), [n.p.], [n.d.]. wb. 1 v., 47., 10cm.
cf. Laures, n. 49; Ebisawa-Tenseki, pp. 146–148.
ms. Tokyo National Museum.
phot. Ebisawa, Sophia, Yanagiya.

0461 —— pr. and annotated by Hiiragi Gen'ichi 柊源一, "Kokuritsu Hakubutsukan-zō Yasokyō Shakyō-kō" (*Kokugo Kokubun,* v. XXII, n. 10), Kyoto 1953 (昭和 28).

0462 Sexta-kō Sadame no Koto 勢數多講定之事 (Regulation of the Confraternity of Friday), Edo [Tokyo].
ms. Vatican Lib.

0463 —— (Dai-Nippon Shiryō, Series XII, v. XII).

0464 Shoseijin Ki'nenbi-hyō 諸聖人記念日表 (Church Calendar). 1 fold, 12cm.
cf. Ōsaki Masaji 大崎正次, "Kirishitan no Koyomi" (*Shigaku Zasshi,* v. XLIX, n. 12), Tokyo 1938; Laures, n. 45–8; Ebisawa-Namban, pp. 446–447, 466–469.
ms. Tokugawa.
phot. Shiryo.

0465 —— facs. pr. (Kirishitan Sōsho).

0466 Sumpuki 駿府記 (Diary of the Shizuoka Court). jb. 1 v.
cf. Kokushi, p. 161.
ms. Iwase, Shiryo.

0467 —— (Shiseki Zassan, v. II).

0468 Tōdaiki 當代記 (Record of the Present Age). jb. 11 vols.
cf. Kokushi, p. 220.
note: Records of the state of society in 1532–1615.
ms. Doshisha, Naikaku, Shiryo, Sonkeikaku, Todai-Nanki.

0469 —— (Shiseki Zassan, v. II).

0470 Zola, Giovanni Battista, SJ. (1575–1626)
Jesus no Kumi Reglas no Koto 世主々の組れいがらすの事 (Regulations of the Confraternity of Jesus). jb. 1 v., 9f., 27cm.
orig. ms. National Lib. (Madrid).

0471 —— pr. by Murakami Naojirō 村上直次郎, "Kirishitan Kenkyū no Kaiko" (*Kirishitan Kenkyū,* v. I), Tokyo 1942 (昭和 17).

1616

0472 Honda Masanobu 本多正信 (1538–1616)
Honsaroku 本佐録 (Historical Record by Honda Sado-no-Kami), [n.p.], 至誠堂, [n.d.]. jb. 1 v., 1, [1], 23f., 25cm.
cf. Kokushi, p. 287.
c. Hibiya-Kaga.

0473 —— (Kō Hakuseki Sōsho, v. IX).
0474 —— (Nippon Kyōiku Bunko, v. II).
0475 —— (Irō Monogatari).
0476 —— (Nippon Keizai Sōsho, v. I).
0478 —— (Nippon Keizai Taiten, v. III).

1618

0478 Chō Han 張燮 *Chang Fan*
Tōzai Yōkō 東西洋考 *Tung-hsi-yang K'ao* (On the East and West). [n.p.], 1618 (萬曆 46). cb. 4 vols., 29cm.
c. Gakushūin, Hibiya-Kondo, Keiō, Seikado, Tōkyō-iku, Waseda.
ms. Ueno-Shirai.

0479 —— (Sekiinken Sōsho).
0480 —— (Kokugaku Kihon Sōsho).

0481 Ikeda Kōun 池田好運
Genwa Kōkaisho 元和航海書 (Manual of Navigation Arts). jb. 1 v.
cf. Ebisawa-Namban, pp. 63–78.
ms. Hibiya-Kondo, Kyōdai, Tōhoku.

0482 —— (Kaihyō Sōsho, v. III).
0483 —— (Kaiji Shiryō Sōsho, v. V).
0484 —— (Dai-Nippon Shiryō, Series XII, v. XXIX).
0485 —— (Nippon Kagaku Koten Zen-sho, v. XII).
0486 * Banreki 蠻曆 (Table of Celestial Latitude). jb. 1 v.
note: Extract from the table of *Genwa Kōkaisho* (n. 481).
ms. Shokokan.
0487 —— [different ms.], jb. 2 vols.
ms. Shokokan.

Books under Influence of the Genwa Kōkaisho

0488 Anjinjutsu 按針術 (Method of Navigation). jb. 1 v.
ms. Mr. Mikami Yoshio.

0489 Kairo 海路 (Sea Routes). jb. 1 v.
0490 —— (Kaiji Shiryō Sōsho, v. V.).

0491 Pirouto 比呂宇土 (Piloting). jb. 1 v.
ms. Gakushiin.
See also n. 1297.

0492 Pantoja, Didaco, SJ. 龐廸我 (1571–1618)

Zesshō Dōbunki 絶繳同文紀 *Chüeh-chiao T'ung-wen-chi* (Collected Essays), compiled by D. Pantoja and Yō Teikin 楊廷筠 *Yang T'ing-yun,* [n.p.], [n.d.]. cb. 1 v.
c. Naikaku.

0493 * Zesshō Dōbunki Shūyō 絶繳同文紀取要 (Abridged Manuscript of the Zesshō Dobunki) by Hosoi Kōtaku 細井廣澤. jb. 1 v.
ms. Mr. Okamura Chibiki.

0494 Santo Aleixo no Gosagyō oyobi Papa Sixto Quinto no Bulla さんとあれしよの御さ行及びははしすときんとのぶうら (The Act of St. Aleixo and the Bull of Pope Sixtus V.). jb. 1 v., 30f., 22cm.
note: The Bull was translated by Fray Francisco Galves, OFM., at the Province of Shimotsuke in 1618 (元和 4).
cf. Laures, n. 45–9.
ms. Tokugawa.

0495 —— facs. pr. under the title of *Shō-seijin Gosagyōsho-shō oyobi Shūmon Shoshō* 諸聖人御作業書抄及宗門諸抄 (Kirishitan Sōsho).

0496 —— pr. and annotated by Ebisawa Arimichi 海老澤有道, "Papa Sixto V. no Kyōsho" (*Seishin Studies,* v. VIII), Tokyo 1951 (昭和 26).

1619

0497 Fujiwara Seika 藤原惺窩 (1561–1619)

Chiyomoto-gusa 千代もと草 (Essays). jb. 1 v.
cf. Sakuma, p. 1397
0498 —— (Nippon Rinri Ihen, v. VII).
0499 —— (Nippon Kyōiku Bunko, v. XI).

0500 Yamamoto Gensen 山本玄仙

Mangai Shūyō 萬外集要 (Textbook of Surgery), Kyoto 西村載文堂, 1619 (元和 5). jb. 1 v., 22, 22, 20f., 13×20cm.
c. Kyodai-Fujikawa.
ms. Jingu.
0501 —— [n.p.], 1626 (寛永 3). jb. 1 v.
cf. Okuno, p. 134.
0502 —— [n.p.] 安田十兵衛, 1642 (寛永 19). jb. 1 v.
cf. Okuno, p. 272.
0503 —— [n.p.] 1648 (慶安 1). jb. 1 v., 22, 22, 20f., 14×21cm.
c. Ebisawa.
0504 —— [n.p.], 1671 (寛文 11). jb. 1 v.

1620

0505 Aleni, Giuglio, SJ. 艾儒略 (1582–1649)

Ri-Matou Kōjitsu 利瑪竇行實 *Li Matou Hsing-shih,* (Life of Matteo Ricci), Peking 1620 (泰昌 1). cb. 1 v.
cf. Pfister, p. 133; Jo, p. 225.

0506 * Taisei Ri-Sensei Kōseki 大西利先生行跡 *To-hsia Li-hsien-sheng Hsing-chi,* revised by Ei Renshi 英斂之, *Ying Chien-chih,* Peking, 1919 (民國 8). cb, 1 v., 10f., 26cm.
cf. Cordier-Sinica, col. 1091.
c. Ebisawa.

0507 Fukan Fabian 不干ハビアン (1565?–   )

Ha-Daiusu 破提宇子 (Anti-God). [n.p.], 1620 (元和 6). jb. 1 v., 38f., 14×19cm.
cf. Asahi, p. 104; Shimmura–Namban I, p. 394; Tenri-Jap. II, p. 83; Kokushi, p. 257.
c. Kyōdai, Shokokan, Tenri.
0508 —— facs. repr. (Kirishitan Sōsho).
0509 —— (Sokkyohen, v. XV).
0510 —— rep. and annotated by Kiyū Dōjin 杞憂道人, [n.p.], 1868 (慶應 4). jb. 1 v., 3, [1], 30, [1]f., 27cm.
c. Aoyama, Ebisawa, ICU, Iwase, Kichū, Kyoto, Keiō-Koda, Nagasaki, Ōtani, Osaka, Nagasaki Museum, Seikado, Seishin, Sophia, Taishō, Tanaka, Tenri, Tōdai, Tōdai-Nanki, Tōhoku-Kano, Tōkyōiku, Ueno, Waseda.
0511 —— ditto, [n.p.], 1869 (明治 2). jb. 1 v., 32f., 26cm.
c. Tenri.
0512 —— (Zokuzoku Gunsho Ruijū, v. XII).
0513 —— (Nippon Koten Zenshū).
0514 —— (Kirishitan Bunko, v. I).
0515 —— (Kirishitan Shiryō).
0516 —— (Nippon Shisō Tōsō Shiryō, v. X).
0517 —— (Nippon Tetsugaku Shisō Zenshū, v. X).
0518 —— abridged (Haja Sōsho, v. I).

1621

0519 Barberini Monjo バルベリニ文書 (Documents of the Barberini Lib., Rome).
note: Five letters form the Jap. Catholics to Pope Paulus V., in 1620–1621.
0520 —— facs. pr. (Taigai Shiryō Hōkan).
0521 —— pr. and annotated Murakami Naojirō 村上直次郎, "Kirishitan Kenkyū no Kaiko", (*Kirishitan Kenkyū,* v. I), Tokyo 1942 (昭和 17).
0522 —— pr. and annotated, Anesaki-Jimbutsu, pp. 497–540.

0523 Giannone, Giacomo Antonio, SJ. (–1633)

Santa Maria no Confraria no Jōjō さんたまりやのこんふらりやの條々 (Regular of the Confraternity of S. Mary), Hizen Takaku, 1621 (元和 7). jb. l v.

cf. Joseph Schütte, SJ. "Santa Maria no Onkumi no Soshiki ni tsuite", (*Kirishitan Kenkyū,* v. II,) Tokyo 1944 (昭和 19).
phot. Yanagiya.

0524 —— pr. by Yanagiya Takeo 柳谷武夫 (*Kirishitan Kenkyū,* v. II), Tokyo 1944 (昭和 19), pp. 135–147.

0525 Yō Teikin 楊廷筠, *Yang T'ing-yün* Daigihen 代疑篇 *Tai-i pien* (Errors of Buddhism), Peking 1621 (天命 6). cb. l v., 3, 4, 2, 56, 12f., 21cm.

cf. Jo, pp. 157–160.
c. Aoyama, Hibiya-Ichimura.

1622

0526 Diaz, Emmanuel, jr. SJ. 陽瑪琋 (1574–1659)
Daigiron 代疑論 *Tai-i-lun* (Responses to some questions on the Passion and Salvation of Our Lord), Peking 1622 (天命 7) cb. l v.

note: Specifically outlawed in 1630.
cf. Pfister, p. 109; Jo, pp. 160–161.

0527 Juan de los Angeles, Rueda, OP.
Virgen S. Mariano Tattoqi Rosario no xuguioto, vonajiqu Iesusno minano Cofradiani ataru riacuno qirocu (A brief Account of the Holy Rosary of the blessed Virgin Mary and of the Confraternity of the Holy Name of Jesus), [Manila S. Gabriel Hospital], 1622. wb. l v., [6], 225, [6]p., 12°.

cf. Laures, n. 51; Ebisawa-Tenseki, pp. 109–128.
c. Dominican Convent, Manila.
phot. Sophia, Tōyō.

0528 —— mimeogr. repr. by Takaba Gorō 高羽五郎, *Rosario no Kyō,* Kanazawa 1952–53 (昭和 27–28). 2 vols.

0529 * Virgen S. Mariano tattoqi Rosariono Iardin tote fanazononi tatoyuru qio, Vonajiqu Iesvsno Cofradiano Regimientono Riacv. (A Book comparing the Holy Rosary of the Blessed Virgin Mary to a Flower Garden, as it were, and also a Summary of the Rules of the Confraternity of the Name of Jesus), Manila S. Gabriel Hospital, 1623. wb. lv., [17], 353, [11]p. 12°.

note: Revised and enlarged version of the above.
cf. Ebisawa-Tenseki, pp. 109–124; Laures, n. 52.
c. S. Thomas Univ., Manila .
phot. Sophia, Tōyō.

0530 —— mimeogr. repr. by Takaba Gorō 高羽五郎, *Rozario no Kyō,* Kanazawa 1954 (昭和 29). 4 vols.

0530b —— transcribed into Jap. characters by Takaba Gorō 高羽五郎, Kanazawa

1955–56 (昭和 30–31). 3 vols.

0531 * Rozario Kiroku 玫瑰花冠記録, arranged and transcribed into Japanese characters by Bernard T. Petitjean, MEP., [Nagasaki] 1869 (明治 2). wb. l v., [2], 128p., 16pl., 28cm.

cf. Ebisawa-Tenseki, pp. 109–124; Laures, n. 70.
c. Aoyama, Ebisawa, Keio, Seishin, Sophia, Tenri. Tōyō, Ueno.

0532 —— (Meiji Bunka Zenshū, v. XI).

0533 Kyōgoku Takatsugu Takatomo Denki 京極高次高知傳記 (Lives of Kyōgoku Takatsugu and Takatomo). jb. l v.

note: Kyōgoku Takatsugu (1563–1609) and his brother João Takatomo (1572–1622).

0534 —— (Seiyūdō Sōsho).

0535 Momokawa Chūbyōe 百川忠兵衛 Shokanbunbutsu 諸勘分物 (Division Textbook). jb. l v.

ms. Tōhoku-Sūgaku.

0536 —— facs. pr. by Hirayama Akira 平山諦, Sendai 1959 (昭和 34).

0537 Mōri Shigeyoshi 毛利重能
Warizansho 割算書 (Division Textbook), [n.p.], 1622 (元和 8). jb. l v., 24f., 14 × 19cm.

cf. Ebisawa-Namban, pp. 115–116; Okuno, p. 186.
c. Gakushiin, Tōhoku-Okamoto.

0538 —— [n.p.], 1631 (寛永 8). jb. l v., 24f., 14 × 19cm.

c. Gakushiin, Tōhoku-Sugaku, Waseda-Ogura.

0539 —— facs. repr. and annotated by Yamada Yoshio 山田孝雄, Hirayama Akira 平山諦 and Ebisawa Arimichi 海老澤有道, Tokyo 日本珠算連盟, 1956 (昭和 31).

0540 —— (Nippon Koten Zenshū, Kodai Sūgakushū 古代數學集 v. I).

1623

0541 Aleni, Giuglio, SJ. 艾儒略 (1582–1649)
Seigakuhan 西學凡, *Hsi-hsüeh Fan* (Outline of Western Studies), Hangchaw 1623 (天啓 3). cb. l v., 6, 3, 17, 8, 16f., 27cm.

note: Specifically outlawed in 1630.
cf. Pfister, p. 135; Jo, pp. 289–294; Saeki-Shina, pp. 194–198.
contents: Seigakuhan 西學凡, *Hsi-hsüeh Fan* by G. Aleni.
    Keikyō Ryūkō Chūgoku-hi Shō 景教流行中國碑頌, *Ching-chiao Liu-hsing Chung-kuo Pei-sung* by Keijō 景淨 *Ching-Ching.*
    Doku Keikyōhi shogo 讀景教碑書後, *Tu Ching-chiao Pei-shu Hou* by Ri Ryōan 李凉菴 *Li Liang-an.*
c. Naikaku.
ms. Kyudai-Bunka, Shoryobu, Tōhoku, Tōhoku-Kano, Waseda.

0542 —— (Tengaku Shokan).

0543 —— (Yōkyō Shichishu).

0544 —— (Kaigaki Jirui Zassan).

0545 —— (Tenkyō Goten).

0546 —— repr. by Ono Tadashige 小野忠重 in *Mateo Ricci to Shina Kagaku*, Tokyo 1944 (昭和 19), pp. 117–124.

0547 * Seigaku Ryakujutsu 西學略述, *Hsi-hsüeh Lüeh-shu*, Shanghai 1886 (光緒 12). wb. 1 v.
note: revised ed. of the *Seigakuhan* (n. 541).
c. Kyudai.

0548 Aleni, Giuglio, SJ. 艾儒略 (1582–1649)
Shokuhō Gaiki 職方外紀 *Chih-fang Wai-chi* (World Geography), Hangchaw 1623 (天啓 3). cb. 2 vols. 27cm.
note: Specifically outlawed in 1630.
cf. Pfister, p. 235; Jo, pp. 313–317.
c. Naikaku.
ms. Ayuzawa, Ebisawa, Iwase, Jingu, Kariya, Kyoto, Naikaku, Oda, Seikado, Tenri, Tōhoku-Kano, Waseda.

0549 —— (Tengaku Shokan).

0550 —— (Shuzankaku Sosho).

0551 —— (Kōchō Hanzoku Yochi Sōsho).

0552 —— (Bokkai Kinko, v. LXXII).

0553 —— (Kō-Min Shokuhō Chizu).

0554 —— (Sōsho Shūsei, v. I).

0555 —— construed from Chinese into Japanese by Ozawa Teibi 小澤廷美, 1844 (天保 15). jb. 1 v.
ms. Ebisawa (v. I only).

Documents related to Kuroda Simeão Nagamasa 黒田長政 (1568–1623)

0556 Kurodaki 黒田記 (Record of the Kurodas). jb. 3 vols.
cf. Samura, p. 516.
ms. Naikaku.

0557 Kuroda Kokyō Monogatari 黒田故郷物語 (Tales of Kuroda's Home Country). jb. 3 vols.
ms. Naikaku.

0558 —— (Kokushi Sōsho, v. XXIII).

0559 Kuroda Nagamasa-den 黒田長政傳 (Life of Kuroda Nagamasa). jb. 1 v.
ms. Tōdai-Nanki.

0560 Kuroda Nagamasa-ki 黒田長政記 (Life of Kuroda Nagamasa). jb. 1 v.
cf Kokushi, p. 79.
ms. Naikaku, Sonkeikaku, Tōdai-Nanki.

0561 —— (Koshindō Sōsho).

0562 —— (Zoku Gunsho Ruijū, v. DCL).

0563 —— (Kokushi Sōsho, v. LI).

0564 Tashiro Hikosuke 田代彦助
Kuroda Josuiki 黒田如水記 (Life of Kuroda Josui). jb. 1 v.
cf. Samura, p. 516.
ms. Naikaku, Sonkeikaku, Tōdai-Nanki.

1624

0565 Sambiaso, Francisco, SJ. 畢方濟 (1582–1649)
Reigen Reishaku 靈言蠡勺 *Ling-yen Li-chü* (On the Human Soul), Shanghai, 1624 (天啓 4). cb. 2 vols.
note: Specifically outlawed in 1630.
cf. Pfister, pp. 142–143; Jo, pp. 200–204.

0566 —— Shanghai, 1919 (民國 8). cb. 1 v., 30f, 26cm.
c. Tenri.

0567 —— Peking 公記印書局, 1921 (民國 10). cb. 1 v., 1, 1, 1, 1, 26.f., 27cm.
c. Tōhoku.

0568 —— (Tengaku Shokan).

0569 Vagnoni, Alphonso, SJ. 王泰隱 (1566–1640)
Tenshu Jikkai Geryaku 天主十誡解略 *T'ien-chu Shih-cheng Chieh-lüeh*, (Short Explanation of the Ten Commandments), Peking 欽一堂., 1624 (天啓 4). cb. 1 v.
note: Specifically outlawed in 1630.
c. Naikaku.
ms. Jinshu, Shoryobu, Waseda.

0570 —— (Seihō Zatsuwwa).

0571 * Seigaku Jikkai 西學十誡 (Ten Commandments of the Western Studies). jb. 1 v.
ms. Tōhoku.

0572 * Seigaku Jikkai Shokai 西學十誡初解 (Elementary Explanation of the Ten Commandments). jb. 1 v.
ms. Ueda (destroyed).

0573 * Tenshu Jikkai 天主十誡 (Ten Commandments of God). jb. 1 v.
ms. Tohoku-Kano.

0574 * Tenshu Jikkai Shokai 天主十誡初解 (Elementary Explanation of the Ten Commandments of God).

0575 —— (Yōkyō Shichishu).

Genwa Era (1615–1624)

0576 Baterenki 伴天連記 (Notes on the Jesuit Missionaries). jb. 1 v.
cf. Shimmura-Namban I, pp. 411–416.
ms. Tenri.

0577 —— (Zokuzoku Gunsho Ruijū, v. XII).

0578 —— (Kaihyō Sōsho, v. I).

0579 —— (Kirishitan Bunko, A., v. I).

0580 * Kirishitan Kiji Ippen 切支丹紀事逸篇 (Episode of the Christians).
note: Different manuscript of the *Baterenki* (n. 576).

0581 —— (Tangai Sōsho).

0582 Isoho Monogatari 伊曾保物語 (Esop's Fables) [n.p.], [n.d.]. jb. 3 vols., 26cm.
cf. Kawase, pp. 604–605; Okuno, pp. 55, 250; Shimmura-Namban I, pp. 297–307.
c. Kyodai, Seikado, Tōyō, Ueno.

0583 —— [n.p.], [n.d.]. jb. 3 vols.
c. Sasaki Nobutsuna, Tenri, Yasuda.

0584 —— [n.p.], 1639 (寛永 16). jb. 3 vols., 27cm.
c. Seisakudo, Shokokan, Tenri, Tokyoiku, Yasuda (v. I only).

0585 —— [n.p.], [n.d.]. jb. 3 vols., 27cm.
c. Shoryobu, Tenri.

0586 —— [n.p.], 伊藤三右衛門, 1659 (萬治 2). jb. 3 vols., 27cm.
cf. Asahi, p. 83; Tenri-Jap. II, p. 187.
c. Kyodai, Tenri, Ueno, Waseda.
ms. Jingu, Ueno.

0587 —— facs. repr. (Kisho Fukuseikai Sōsho).

0588 —— compiled by Ōkubo Tsunekichi 大久保常吉, Tokyo 春陽堂, 1886 (明治 19). wb. 1 v., 113p., 19cm.
c. Ebisawa.

0589 —— compiled by Kyūurō 舊雨楼, 百華書房, 1916 (大正 5). wb. 1 v.
c. Ebisawa.

0590 —— (Bunmei Genryū Sōsho, v. I).

0591 —— (Nippon Kyōiku Bunko, Kunkaihen).

0592 —— (Kindai Nippon Bungaku Taikei, v. I).

1625

0593 Nampo Bunshi 南浦文之
Nampo Bunshū 南浦文集 (Collected Works of Nampo), Kyoto, 1625 (寛永 2). jb. 3 vols., 28cm.
cf. Kawase, pp. 573–574; Okuno, p. 126; Wada, n. 325.
c. Seisakudō, Tōhoku, Tōyō-Iwasaki, Ueno, Yasuda.

0594 —— Kyoto, 1629 (寛永 6). jb. 3 vols.
cf. Okuno, p. 165.

0595 —— Kyoto 中野道伴, 1649 (慶安 2). jb. 3 vols., 28cm.
c. Naikaku, Ueno.

1626

0596 Oze Hoan 小瀬甫庵 (1564–1640)
Taikōki 太閤記 or Toyotomiki 豊臣記 (Life of Toyotomi Hideyoshi), [n.p.], 1626 (寛永 3). jb. 22 vols., 28cm.
cf. Okuno, pp. 134–135; Kokushi, p. 180.

c. Naikaku.
ms. Tenri.

0597 —— [n.p.], 1646 (正保 3). jb. 22 vols.
c. Hibiya.

0598 —— [n.p.], 1659 (萬治 2). jb. 22 vols.
c. Iwase, Waseda.

0599 —— [n.p.], 1661 (寛文 1). jb. 22 vols., 24cm.
c. Jingu, Naikaku.

0600 —— (Shiseki Shūran),

0601 —— (Zoku Gunsho Rujiū, v. DLXXXIV).

0602 —— ed. by Kokumin Bunko Kankōkai 國民文庫刊行會, Tokyo 1910 (明治 43).

0603 —— annotated by Kuwata Tadachika 桑田忠親 (Iwanami Bunko).

0604 * Eiri Taikōki 繪入太閤記, [n.p.], 1710 (實永 7). jb. 11 vols.
c. Naikaku, Tōdai-Nanki.

0605 Kawasumi Saburouemon 川角三郎右衛門
Kawasumi Taikōki 川角太閤記 (Life of Toyotomi Hideyoshi). jb. 5 vols.
cf. Kokushi, p. 180.
ms. Hibiya, Iwase.

0606 —— (Kaitei Shiseki Shūran, v. XIX).

0607 —— (Gajikangasho).

0608 —— (Tsūzoku Nippon Zenshi, v. XI).

0609 Trigault, Nicolas, SJ. 金尼閣 (1577–1628)
Engi 況義 *K'uang-yi* (Aesop's Fables), Si-an 1626 (天啓 6). cb. 1 v.
note: Specifically outlawed in 1630.
cf. Pfister, p. 117; Jo, pp. 294–295; Shimmura-Isoho, pp. 49–89.

0610 Trigault, Nicolas, SJ. 金尼閣 (1577–1628)
Seiju Jimokushi 西儒耳目資 *Hsi-ju Erh-mu Tsu* (Chinese Vocabulary for European Scholars), Hangchow, 1626 (天啓 6). cb. 4 vols.
cf. Pfister, p. 117; Jo, pp. 321–325; Cordier-Sinica, col. 1588.
c. Tenri.
ms. Tōyō.

0611 —— facs. repr. by Mei Kan'un 明韓雲, *Ming Han-yün*, Peking 1933 (民國 22).

0612 —— (Heion Moji Shiryō Sōsho).

0613 Vagnoni, Alphonso, SJ. 高一志 (1566–1640)
Kūsai Kakuchi 空際格致 *K'ung-chi Ke-chih* (Trait of the Composition of Universe), [n.p.], (1626). cb. 2 vols.
cf. Pfister, p. 94.

0614 —— mimeogr. repr. by Imai Itaru

今井溱, Kyoto 1959 (昭和 34).

0615 Vagnoni, Alphonso, SJ. 高一志 (1584–1640)
Kyōyō Geryaku 教要解略 or Tenshu Kyōyō Geryaku 天主教要解略 *T'ien-chu Chiao-yao Chieh-lüeh* (Short Instruction on the Catholic Doctrine), Kiangchow 1628 (天啓 6). cb. 1 v.
note; Specifically outlawed in 1630.
cf. Pfister, p. 91.
c. Naikaku.
ms. Shoryobu.

0616 —— Shanghai 1869 (同治 8). cb. 1 v., [2], 58, 33f., 27cm.
c. Seishin, Tenri.

0617 —— Shanghai, 1914 (民國 3). wb. 1 v.

1627

0618 Aleni, Giuglio, SJ. 艾儒略 (1582–1649)
Sanzanron Gakuki 三山論學紀 *San-shan-lun Hsüeh-chi* (Dialogues on the Fundamentals of the Catholic Religion), Hangchow 武林天主堂, 1627 (天啓 7). cb. 1 v., [31], [14]f., 24cm.
note: Specifically outlawed in 1630.
cf. Pfister, p. 133; Jo, pp. 152–154.
c. Naikaku.
ms. Ebisawa, Jinshu, Shokokan, Shoryobu, Ueno, Waseda.

0619 —— Peking 1694 (康熙 33). cb. 1 v.

0620 —— Shanghai 1847 (道光 27). cb. 1 v.
c. Tōyō.

0621 —— Shanghai, 土山灣印書館, 1923 (民國 12). wb. 1 v.

0622 Terrenz, Johann, SJ. 鄧玉函 (1576–1630)
Kiki Zusetsu 奇器圖說 *Ch'i-ch'i T'u-shuo* (Illustrated Explanation of the Western Instruments), tr. by Ō Chō 王徵 *Wang Cheng*, Peking 1627 (天啓 7). cb. 4 vols.
cf. Pfister, pp. 156–157; Jo, pp. 295–299.
ms. Kyūdai-Butsuri, Tenri.

0623 * Ensei Kiki Zusetsu Rokusai 遠西奇器圖說錄最 *Yüan-hsi Ch'i-ch'i T'u-shuo Lu-tsui*, Nanking 1628 (崇禎 1). cb. 2 vols.
c. Naikaku.
ms. Ueno, Waseda-Ogura.

0624 —— (Shuzankaku Sōsho).

0625 —— (Chūsei Sangaku Shūyō, v. VI).

0626 * Shinsei Shoki Zusetsu 新製諸器圖說 (Illustrations of New Instruments). jb. 6 vols.
ms. Waseda-Ogura.

1628

0627 Aleni, Giuglio, SJ. 艾儒略 (1582–1649)

Banbutsu Shingen 萬物眞源 *Wan-wu Chen-yüan* (The True Origin of all Things), Peking, 1628 (天啓 6). cb. 1 v.
cf. Jo, pp. 173–174; Pfister, pp. 132–133.
note: Specifically outlawed in 1630.

0628 —— Peking, 1694 (康熙 33). cb. 1 v.

0629 —— Peking, 1751 (乾隆 16). cb. 1 v., [1], 26f., 24cm.
c. Seishin.

0630 —— Peking, 1791 (乾隆 56). cb. 1 v.
c. Nagasaki.

0631 —— Shanghai, 1906 (光緒 32).

0632 —— Shanghai, 1924 (民國 13). wb. 1 v.

0633 —— Peking 西什庫天主堂, 1930 (民國 19). cb. 1v., 5, 24f., 18cm.
c. Tenri, Tōhoku.

0634 —— (Dōgen Seisui, v. I).
c. Tenri.

0635 —— construed from Chinese into Jap. by Mishima Yoshitada 三島良忠, Tokyo 叢書閣, 1886 (明治 19). wb. 1 v., [1] 38p., 19cm.
c. Sophia, Ueno.

0636 Furtado, Francisco, SJ. 傅汎濟 (1587–1653)
Kan Yū Sen 寰有詮 *Huan-yu-ch'üan* (The Heaven and Earth), Hangchow 1628 (崇禎 1). cb. 6 vols.
note: A translation by Furtado and Ri Shisō 李之藻 *Li Chih-tsao* of Aristotle's *De caelo et mundo*. Specifically outlawed subsqent to 1630.
cf. Pfister, p. 152; Jo, p. 370.

0637 Kirishitan Kokoroegaki 吉利支丹心得書 (Christian Doctrine), jb. 2 vols., 24cm.
cf. Laures, n. 45–1.
ms. Tokugawa.

0638 —— facs. repr. (Kirishitan Sōsho).

0639 —— repr. by Ebisawa Arimichi 海老澤有道 (Kirishitan Bunko, B., v. VI), Tokyo 1958 (昭和 33).

0640 —— repr. by Anesaki Masaharu 姉崎正治, (v. I only), Tokyo 1929 (昭和 4).

0641 Tengaku Shokan 天學初函 *T'ien-hsüeh Ch'u-han* (Fundamental Library of Divine Learning), compiled by Ri Leon Shisō 李之藻 *Li Chih-tsao*, Peking, 1628 (崇禎 1). cb. 32 vols., 27cm.
contents: Seigakuhan 西學凡 by Giuglio Aleni.
　　Kijin Jippen 畸人十篇 by Matteo Ricci.
　　Kōyūron 交友論 by Matteo Ricci.
　　Nijūgogen 二十五言 by Matteo Ricci.
　　Tenshu Jitsugi 天主實義 by Matteo Ricci.
　　Bengaku Itō 辯學遺牘 by Matteo Ricci.
　　Shichikoku 七克 by Didaco de Pantoja.
　　Reigen Reishaku 靈言蠡勺 by Francisco Sambiaso.

Shokuhō Gaiki 職方外紀 by Giuglio Aleni.
Taisei Suihō 泰西水法 by Sebastian de Ursis.
Kongai Tsūken Zusetsu 渾蓋通憲圖説 by Matteo Ricci.
Kika Gempon 幾何原本 by Matteo Ricci.
Hyōdosetsu 表度説 by Sebastian de Ursis.
Temmonryaku 天文略 by Emmanuel Diaz.
Kampeigi-setsu 簡平儀説 by Sebastian de Ursis.
Dōbun Sanshi 同文算指 by Matteo Ricci.
Sokuryō Hōgi 測量法義 by Matteo Ricci.
Kanyō Kōgi 圜容較義 by Matteo Ricci.
Kōkōgi 勾股義 by Matteo Ricci.

note: Specifically outlawed in 1630.
cf. Pfister, pp. 37–38; Jo, pp. 285–287; Saeki-Shina III, pp. 192–194; Cordier-Sinica, col. 1092.
c. Kyodai (vv. 1–8 only), Seikado, Tenri (vv. 1–22 only), Tōyō.

1629

0642 Adam Schall von Bell, Johann, SJ. 湯若望 (1591–1666)
Shusei Gunchō 主制群徵 *Chu-chih Ch'ün-chung* (Evidences of the Divine Order), Kiangchow [1629?]. cb. 2 vols.
cf. Pfister, p. 178; Jo, p. 154.
0643 —— [n.p.], 1915 (民國 4). cb. 1 v., 1, 3, 13, 12, 8, 2f., 26cm.
c. Tōhoku.

0644 Aleni, Giuglio, SJ. 艾儒略 (1582–1649)
Misa Saigi 彌撒祭儀 *Mi-sa Chi-yi* (Explanation of the Mass), Hangchow 1629 (崇禎 2). cb. 1 v.
cf. Pfister, p. 132.
note: Specifically outlawed in 1630.
0645 —— Shanghai 1849 (道光 29) cb. 37f., 22cm.
c. Ebisawa, Kyudai-Bunka, Seishin, Tenri.
0646 —— Shanghai 1905 (光緒 31). wb. 1 v.

0647 Vagnoni, Alphonso, SJ. 王豊肅 (1566–1640)
Seijin Kōjitsu 聖人行實 *Sheng-jen Hsing-shih* (Acts of the Saints), Kiangchaw, 1629 (崇禎 2). cb. 7 vols.
cf. Pfister, p. 92.
0648 * Shūto no Seiden 宗徒之聖傳 (Acts of the Apostles).
ms. Seikado.
0649 * Shūto Retsuden 宗徒列傳 *Tsung-t'u Lieh-chuan* (Acts of the Apostles), abridged and revised by Laurent 李問漁 (Dōgen Seisui, v. VII).

1630

0650 Adam Schall von Bell, Johann, SJ. 湯若望 (1591–1666)
Enkyōsetsu 遠鏡説 *Yüan-ching-shuo* (On Telescopes), Peking 1630 (崇禎 3). cb. 1 v., 21f., 27cm.
cf. Pfister, p. 180; Jo, pp. 294–295.
c. Fujita, Hibiya-Kondo, Naikaku.
ms. Imoto, Kyodai, Kyudai-Butsuri, Tōhoku-Hayashi, Waseda.
0651 —— (Seiyō Shimpō Rekisho, v. C).
0652 —— (Geikai Shujin).
0653 —— (Sōsho Shūsei).

Law Prohibiting Importation of Chinese Christian Books, 1630

0654 Gokinsho Mokuroku 御禁書目録 (List of Prohibited Books), in the Chūko Sōsho 中古叢書.

0655 Gokokukin Yaso Shomoku 御國禁耶蘇書目 (List of Prohibited Christian Books).
orig. printing wood-block, B. Kada.

0656 Kinsho Moku 禁書目 (List of the Prohibited Books) in the Chōfu Irin.

0657 Shomotsu Aratame Ikken 書物改一件 (Document on the Examination of Books to be Imported, jb. 1 v.
ms. T. Fukuda.

0658 Yaso Kinzei Shomoku 耶蘇禁制書目 (List of the Prohibited Christian Books). jb. 1 v.
ms. Shokokan.
See also nos. 1913, 2709.

1631

0659 Aleni, Giuglio, SJ. 艾儒略 (1582–1649)
Kika Yōhō 幾何要法 *Chi-ho Yao-fa* (Principles of Geometry), [n.p.], 1631. cb. 4 vols.
cf. Pfister, p. 135.
0660 —— (Seiyō Shimpō Rekisho, vv. LXXXVI–LXXXVII).
c. Waseda-Ogura.

0661 Furtado, Francisco, SJ. 傅汎濟 (1587–1653)
Meiritan 名理探 *Ming-li-t'an* (Logic), Hangchaw 1631 (崇禎 4). cb. 10 vols.
note: Taken from a lecture of Coimbra University, 1611.
cf. Pfister, p. 153; Jo, pp. 193–197.
0662 —— annotated by Jo Sōtaku, S.J. 徐宗澤 *Hsü Tsung-tse*, Shanghai 光啓社, 1932 (民國 21). wb. 1 v.

0663 Jo Kōkei 徐光啓 *Hsü Kuang-ch'i* (1562–1633)

Katsuen Hassen Gokyūhō 割圓八線互求法 *Ke-yüan Pa-hsien Hu-ch'in-fa* (Method of Trigonometrical Functions), Peking 1631.
ms. Naikaku, Shokokan.

0664 —— (Seiyō Shimpō Rekisho).

0665 * Katsuen Hassen-hyō Yōhō 割圓八線表用法 *Ke-yüan Pa-hsien-piao Yung-fa* (Method of Using a Table of Trigonometrical Functions). cb. 1 v.
c. Waseda-Ogura.
ms. Waseda-Ogura.

0666 Takashima Jūzen 高嶋重漸
Chōsokabe Motochika-ki 長曾我部元親記 (Life of Chōsokabe Motochika) 1631 (寬永 8). jb. 2 vols.
note: Documents concerning a Spanish ship, S. Felipe, in 1596.
cf. Kokushi, p. 205.

0667 —— (Zoku Gunsho Ruijū, v. DCXLVI).

0668 Vagnoni, Alphonso, SJ. 高一志 (1566–1640)
Seibo Kōjitsu 聖母行實 *Sheng-mu Hsieng-shih* (Life of Virgin Mary), Kiangchow 1631 (崇禎 4).cb. 1 v.
cf. Pfister, p. 91; Jo, pp. 41–42.

0669 —— Peking 1798 (嘉慶 3). cb. 1v., 4, 53f., 26cm.
c. Aoyama, Hibiya-Ichimura, Kyūdai-Bunka, Nagasaki.

0670 —— [n.p.], [n.d.], cb. 1 v., 110f., 25cm.
c. Tenri.

1632

0671 Collado, Diego, OP. (–1638)
Ars Grammaticae Iaponicae Lingvae, Romae, Typis & impensis Sac. Congr. de Propag. Fide. MDCXXXII. wb. 1 v., 4°, 75p.
cf. Streit V, p. 536; Laures, n. 54.
c Kyōdai, Ōura, Sophia, Tenri, Tōdai, Tōyō, Ueno.

0672 —— facs. repr., Roma [1935?]. wb. 1 v., 75p., 22.5cm.
c. Seishin.

0673 —— facs. repr. and tr. into Jap. by Otsuka Takanobu 大塚高信, *Koiyādo Nippongo Bunten*, Tokyo 1934 (昭和 9).

0674 Collado, Diego, OP. (–1638)
Dictionarium Sive Thesavri lingvae Iaponicae Compendivm Compositum, & Sacrae Propaganda Fide Congregationi dicatum à Patre Didaco Collado Ord. Praedicatorum Romae anno 1632. Romae, Typis & imprensis Sacr. Congr. de Prop. Fide. MDCXXXII. 4°, 355p.
cf. Streit, V, pp. 336–337; Laures, n. 56.
c. Kyōdai, Terni, Tōdai, Tōyō, Ueno.

phot. Sophia.

0675 Collado, Diego, OP. (–1638)
Niffon No Cotoba Ni Yô Confesion, Vo mósu yôdai to màta Confessor yori gòxensàcu mesarúru tàme nò canyônaru giôgiô no coto. (Practical Method for Confession), Romae, Typis & Imprensis Sacr. Congreg. de Propag. Fide. MDCXXXII. 4°, 66p.
cf. Laures, n. 55; Streit V., p 536.
c. Kyōdai, Sophia, Tenri, Tōdai.

0676 —— facs. repr. and transcribed into Jap. characters by Otsuka Mitsunobu 大塚光信, *Collado Zangeroku*, Tokyo 1957 (昭和 32).

0677 —— transcribed into Jap. characters (Namban Bunshū).

0678 —— transcribed into Jap. characters, Anesaki-Jimbutsu, pp. 549–584.

0679 —— repr., Laine et Havard, Paris 1866. 12°, 91, [1]p.
cf. Laures, n. 59.
c. Junshin, Nagasaki, Sophia, Tenri.
phot. Tenri.

0680 Rho, Giacomo SJ. 羅雅各 (1593–1638)
Getsuri Rekishi 月離曆指 *Yüeh-li Li-chih* (Theory of the Moon) compiled by J. Adam Schall. SJ. 湯若望, Peking 1632 (崇禎 5). cb. 4 vols.
cf. Pfister, p. 191.
ms. Tōhoku-Kano.

0681 —— (Seiyō Shimpō Rekisho, vv. XXX–XXXII).

0682 Rho, Giacomo, SJ. 羅雅各 (1593–1638)
Seiki Hyakugen 聖記百言 *Sheng-chi Pai-yen* (Hundred Spiritual Admonitions of St. Theresa), compiled by Giacomo Rho, Peking 1632 (崇禎 5). cb. 1 v.
note: Specifically outlawed subsqent to 1630.
cf. Pfister, p. 190; Jo, pp. 330–333.

0683 —— Shanghai, 慈母堂 1873 (同治 12). cb. 1 v., 2, 2, 21f., 27cm.
c. Aoyama, Hibiya-Ichimura, Nagasaki, Tenri, Waseda.

1633

0684 Jo Kōkei 徐光啓 *Hsü Kuang-ch'i* (1562–1633)
Byakumō 闢妄 *P'i-wang* or Shakushi Shomō 釋氏諸妄 *Shih-shih Chu-wang* (Critics of Buddhism), [Peking, 1689, 康熙 28]. cb 1 v., 16f., 23cm.
cf. Jo, pp. 106–110.
c. Ebisawa, Seishin, Sophia, Tōhoku-Kano.

0685 Jo Kōkei 徐光啓 *Hsü Kuang-ch'i* (1562–1633)

Kenshō Zusetsu 乾象圖說 *Ch'ien-hsiang T'u-shuo* (Illutrated Universe).
ms. Naikaku, Tōhoku-Kano.

0686 Sakokurei 鎖國令 (Edict of Closing the Country), 1633 (寛永 10).

0687 —— (Tokugawa Kinreikō, v. VI).

0688 —— annotated by Ebisawa Arimichi 海老澤有道, "Kan'ei Sakokurei" (*Rekishi Kyōiku*, v. V., n. 11), Tokyo 1957 (昭和 32).

0689 —— tr. into English by C. R. Boxer, *Christian Century in Japan*, 1549–1650, Berkeley 1931, pp. 439–440.

0690 *—— revised in 1635 (寛永 12).

0691 —— noted by Kōda Shigetomo 幸田成友, *Oranda Zatsuwa*, Tokyo 1934 (昭和 9). pp. 105–116.

0692 —— tr. into Dutch by François Valentyn, *Oud en Nieuw Oost Indien, v. V. Beschryvinge Van Den Handel en Vaart der Nederlanderen op Japan*, Dordrecht and Amsterdam, 1726, pp. 98–99.

0693 —— tr. into French by Léon Pagés, *Histoire de la Religion Chrétienne au Japon*, Annexes, Paris, 1870., pp. 395–397.

0694 —— tr. into German by Oskar Nachod, *Die Beziehungen der Niederländischen Ostindischen Kompagnie zu Japan im siebzehnten Jahrhundert*, Leipzig 1897. Beilage 42., pp. 134–136.

0695 Sūden 崇傳 (1569–1633)
Honkō Kokushi Nikki 本光國師日記 (Diary of Sūden, 1610–1633). jb. 46 vols.
cf. Kokushi, p. 287.

0696 —— (Dai Nippon Bukkyō Zensho, vv. CXXXVIII–CXLII). 5 vols.

0697 Sūden 崇傳 (1569–1633)
Ikoku Nikki 異國日記 (Diary of Foreign Affairs). jb. 2 vols.
cf. Kokushi, p. 11.
orig. ms. Nanzenji (Kyoto).
ms. Ishin, Iwase.

0698 —— repr. by Tsuji Zennosuke 辻善之助 (*Shien*, vv. I–VIII) Tokyo 1928–34 (昭和 3–9).

0699 —— abridged repr. by Murakami Naojirō 村上直次郎, *Zōtei Ikoku Nikki-shō* (Ikoku Sōsho), Tokyo 1929 (昭和 4).

0700 Ikoku e Tsūshō Goshuin no Utsushi 異國へ通商御朱印寫 (Copies of the Letters of Credit for Foreign Countries).

0601 —— (Shiseki Shūran, Shiryō Sōsho, v. IV).

0702 —— (Kaiten Shiseki Shūran, v. XVI).

0703 Ikoku Shukkei 異國出契 (Letters of Credit for Foreign Countries).
ms. Naikaku.

0704 Ikoku Tokai Goshuinchō 異國渡海御朱印帳 (Letters of Credit for Foreign Countries). jb. 11v.
cf. Asahi, p. 31.
orig. ms. Shōgokuji (Kyoto).

0705 —— (Ikoku Sōsho, Zōtei Ikoku Nikkishō).

0706 Ikoku Tokai Goshuinchō 異國渡海御朱印帳 (Letters of Credit for Foreign Countries). jb. 1 v.
ms. Naikaku.

1634

0707 Adam Schall von Bell, Johan, SJ. 湯若望 (1591–1661)
Kōshoku Rekishi 交食暦指 *Chiao-shih Li-chih* (Table for Predicting Eclipses) compiled by G. Rho, S.J. 羅雅各, Peking 1634 (崇禎 7). cb. 3 vols.
cf. Pfister, p. 180.
ms. Tōhoku-Kano.

0708 —— (Seiyō Shimpō Rekisho, vv. XXXIII–XXXIX).

0709 [Bastian Koyomi バスチャン暦] (A Church Calendar of the Crypt-Catholics compiled by Bastian). jb. 1 v.
cf. Taigita, pp. 165–222.
ms. Oura, Tenri.

0710 —— pr. by Koga Jūjirō 古賀十二郎, *Nagasaki Shishi, Fūzokuhen*, Nagasaki 1925 (大正 14).

0711 —— pr. by Urakawa Wasaburō 浦川和三郎, *Kirishitan no Fukkatsu*, v. II, Tokyo 1928 (昭和 3).

0712 [Domiigo Ikusuke Koyomi と見い古幾助暦] (A Church Calendar in 1643, written by hand by Domingo Ikusuke). jb. 1 v.
cf. Laures, n. 44–2.

0713 —— (Yasokyō Sōsho).

0714 —— pr. Anesaki-Hakugai, pp. 308–319.

0715 —— pr. by Murakami Naojirō 村上直次郎, "Kirishitan Kenkyū no Kaiko" (*Kirishitan Kenkyū*, v. I), Tokyo 1942 (昭和 17), pp. 37–42.

0716 —— tr. into English by Murakami Naojirō, "An old Church Calendar in Japan" (*Monumenta Nipponica*, v. V., n. 1), Tokyo 1942, pp. 220–224.

0717 Rho, Giacomo, SJ. 羅雅各 (1593–1638)

Goihyō 五緯表 *Wu-wei-piao* (Table of the Five Planets), Peking, 1634 (崇禎 7). cb. 11 vols.

cf. Pfister, p. 191.
ms. Kyōdai-Butsuri.

0718 —— (Seiyō Shimpō Rekisho, vv. LXIII–LXXII).

0719 Rho, Giacomo, SJ. 羅雅各 (1593–1638)

Goi Rekishi 五緯暦指 *Wu-wei Li-chih* (Manual for Predicting the Movements of the Five Planets), Peking, 1634 (崇禎 7). cb. 9 vols.

cf. Pfister, p. 191.
ms. Tōhoku-Kano, Tenri.

0720 —— (Seiyō Shimpō Rekisho, vv. XL–XLVIII).

0721 Terrenz, Johann, SJ. 鄧玉函 (1576–1630)

Katsuen Kōkō Hassenhyō 割圓勾股八線表 *Ke-yüan Kou-ku Pa-hsien Piao* (Table of Trigonometric Functions), Peking 1634. cb. 1 v.

c. Naikaku.

0722 —— (Seiyō Shimpō Rekisho, vv. LXXXIII–LXXXIV).

1635

0723 Aleni, Giuglio, SJ. 艾思及 (1582–1649)

Kōtaku Nisshō 口鐸日鈔 *K'ou-to Jih-ch'ao* (Letters of Fathers Aleni and Rudomina), 1635 (崇禎 8). cb. 8 vols.

cf. Pfister, pp. 136, 193; Jo, pp. 98–92.

0724 —— Shanghai 慈母堂, 1872. cb. 4 vols., 24cm.

c. Tenri.

0725 —— Shanghai 1887 (光緒 13). cb. 4 vlols.

c. Nagasaki.

0726 ——Shanghai 1922 (民國 11). cb. 2 vols.

0727 Hō Hōnen 方逢年 *Fang Feng-nien*

Teikyō Keibutsu-ryaku 帝京景物略 *Ti-ching Ching-wu-lüeh* (Guide to Peking) revised by Ryū Dō 劉侗 *Liu T'ung*, Peking 1635 (崇禎 8). cb. 4 vols.

note: Specifically outlawed subsquent to 1630.
c. ICU, Naikaku.
ms. Ueno, Waseda.

0728 —— [Peking], 1766 (乾隆 31). cb. 6 vols.

c. Waseda.

0729 —— (Zoku Seppu, v. XXVIII).

1636

0730 Adam Schall von Bell, Johann,

SJ. 湯若望 (1591–1666)

Kontengi-setsu 渾天儀說 *Hun-t'ien-yi-shou* (Manual of the Celestial Globe) compiled by G. Rho, S.J. 羅雅各, Peking 1636 (崇禎 9). cb. 5 vols.

cf. Pfister, p. 179.
c. Naikaku.
ms. Tōhoku-Kano.

0731 —— (Seiyō Shimpō Rekisho, v. I–V).

0732 Diaz, Emmanuel, jr., SJ. 陽瑪琯 (1574–1659)

Tenshu Kōsei Seikei Chokkai 天主降生聖經直解 *T'ien-chu Chiang-sheng Sheng-ching Chih-chieh* (Interpretations of the Holy Bible), Peking 始胎大堂, 1636 (崇禎 9). cb. 14 vols.

cf. Pfister, p. 109; Jo, pp. 32–25.
c. Nagasaki, Naikaku, (vv. 13–14 only).

0733 —— Peking 1642 (崇禎 15).

0734 —— Peking 始胎大堂, 1790 (康熙 55). cb. 8 vols. 28cm.

c. Tenri, Sophia (vv. 1–3 only).

0735 —— Shanghai 1842 (道光 22).

0736 —— Shanghai 1866 (同治 5). cb. 8vols.

0737 —— Shanghai 1915 (民國 4). cb. 2vols.

0738 * Wayaku Seikei Chokkai, Dai 1 Kan 和譯聖經直解第一卷 (Jap. translation of the Tenshu Kōsei Seikei Chokkai, v. I), tr. by Augustin Mishima 三島奥斯定, Tokyo 1887 (明治 20). wb. 1 v., 203p., 19cm.

c. Aoyama, Sophia, Ueno.

0739 Sawano Chūan 澤野忠庵, ex-SJ. Christovão Ferreira (1580–1650)

Kengiroku 顯偽録 (Notes of Revealing Falsehood). jb. 1 v.

cf. Shimmura-Namban I, pp. 90–91.
ms. Nagasaki,

0740 —— annotated by Shimmura-Izuru 新村出 (Nippon Koten Zenshū), Tokyo 1927 (昭和 2).

1638

0741 Rho, Giacomo, SJ. 羅雅各 (1593–1638)

Hirei Kikai 比例規解 *Pi-li Kuei-chieh* (Explanation of the Rules of Proposition). Peking, 1630 (崇禎 3). cb. 1 v.

cf. Pfister, p. 191.
ms. Waseda-Ogura.

0742 —— (Seiyō Shimpō Rekisho, v. XCI).

0743 Rho, Giacomo, SJ. 羅雅各 (1593–1638)

Nitten Rekishi 日纏曆指 *Jih-ts'ang Li-chih* (Theory of the Sun), Peking 1645 (崇禎 18). cb. 1 v.

cf. Pfister, p. 191.
c. Tōhoku-Kano.

0744 —— (Seiyō Shimpō Rekisho, v. XXIII).

0745 Rho, Giacomo, SJ. 羅雅各 (1593–1683)

Sokuryō Zengi 測量全義 *Ts'e-liang Ch'üan-i* (Practical Method of Mensuration), Peking 1645 (順治 2). cb. 10 vols, 27cm.

cf. Pfister, p. 190.
c. Hazama.
ms. Kyōdai, Tenri, Tōhoku-Kano, Tōhoku-Sugaku, Waseda-Ogura.

0746 —— (Seiyō Shimpō Rekisho, vv. LXXIII–LXXXII).

0747 —— repr. by Tai Shin 戴震 *Tai Chen*, Chūzan 籌算 *Ch'ou-suan,* 1744 (乾隆 9).

0748 —— mimeogr. repr., 1936 (昭和 11).

c. Waseda-Ogura.

Shimabara-Amakusa Rebellion (1637–1638)

0749 Amakusa Arima Hara Oboegaki 尼草有馬原覺書 (Notes on Amakusa, Hara in Arima). jb. 1 v.

cf. Samura, p 46.

0750 Amakusa Dozoku Jōchū no Hanashi 天草土賊城中之話 (Story of a Rebel in the Amakusa Castle).
0751 —— (Buhen Sōsho).
0752 —— (Shiseki Shūran).
0753 —— (Kaitei Shiseki Shūran, v. XVI).
0754 —— (Kirishitan Bunko, v. III).

0755 Amakusa Gunki Hiroku 天草軍記秘録 (Secret Story of the Amakusa Battle). jb. 1 v.

ms. Shiryō.

0756 Amakusa Ikki Hatsu Saisho no Kikigaki 天草一揆發最初之聞書 (First Recollection of the Origin of the Amakusa Rebellion).
0757 —— (Ōkōchike Kiroku).

0758 Amakusa Ikki Kakiagechō 天草一揆書上帳 (Document on the Amakusa Rebellion). jb. 1 v.

ms. Naikaku.

0759 Amakusa Ikki Shimatsu 天草一揆始末 (Outcome of the Amakusa Rebellion). jb. 1 v.

ms. Dōshisha.

0760 Amakusa Jindate no Zu 天草陣立之圖 (Map of the Amakusa Rebellion). 1 sheet, 56×40 cm.

ms. Tenri.

0761 Amakusajin Gunki 天草陣軍記 (War Record of the Amakusa Rebellion). jb. 1 v.

ms. Ebisawa.

0762 Amakusajin Ryakuki 天草陣略記 (Short Description of the Amakusa Rebellion). jb. 1 v.

ms. Ebisawa.

0763 Amakusajin Zakki 天草陣雜記 (Notes of the Amakusa Rebellion). jb. 1 v.

ms. Shiryō.

0764 Amakusa Kajōshi 天草家乘誌 (History of the Amakusa).
0765 —— (Amakusagun Shiryō, v. II).

0766 Amakusaki 天草記 (An Account of Amakusa). jb. 1 v.

ms. Kyudai.

0767 Amakusa no Ran Senzu 天草亂戰圖 (Map of the Amakusa Rebellion), 1637 (寛永 14). 2 folds.

ch. Okuno, p. 239.
c. J. Sakakibara.

0768 Amakusa Oboegaki 天草覺書 (Memorandum on Amakusa). jb. 1 v.

cf. Samura, p. 46.

0769 —— (Kembun Zakki, v. XI).

0770 Amakusa Oboegaki 天草覺書 or Matsudaira Kachū Amakusa Jūgun Nikki 松平家中天草從軍日記 (Diary of Events at Amakusa by a Soldier of the Matsudairas). jb. 1 v.

cf. Samura, p. 46.

0771 Amakusa Yuraiki 天草由來記 (History of the Amakusa Rebellion). jb. 1 v.

ms. Shiryō.

0772 Arima Harajō Sōzeme no Toki Yosete Shoka no Shishōsha Shimei 有馬原城惣責之時寄手諸家之死傷者氏名 (List of Dead and Wounded Soldiers at the General Attack on Hara Castle in Arima).
0773 —— (Ōkōchike Kiroku).

0774 Arimajinki-shū 有馬陣記集 (Stories of the Arima Rebellion), jb. 1 v.

ms. Nagasaki.

0775 * Arimajinki Shūsho 有馬陣記集書 jb. 1 v.

ms. Nagasaki.

0776 Arimake Harajō Shoki 有馬家原城諸記 (Notes on the Hara Castle of the Arimas). jb. 1 v.
ms. Shiryō.

0777 Arima Kiroku Shōroku 有馬記録抄録 (Abridged Record of the Arima Rebellion). jb. 1 v.
ms. Nagasaki.

0778 Genkan Nikki 元寛日記 (Diary of the Genwa-Kan'ei Period). jb. 12 vols.
cf. Samura, p. 607.
note: Diary covering the period 1615–1643, mostly refers the Shimabara Rebellion.
ms. Dōshisha, Tōyō-Iwasaki, Kyoto, Tenri, Tōdai-Nanki, Ueno.

0779 Harada Iyo Amakusa Arima nite Kakugo no Oboe 原田伊豫天草有馬ニ而覺悟之覺 (Harada Iyo's Memoirs of Arima, Amakusa District).
0780 —— (Ōshuku Zakki).

0781 Hara Gokokyo Shujō Shoshō Semeiri no Zu 原五古壚守城諸將攻入圖 (Illustrated Map showing the Hara Castle). jb. 1 v.
ms. Sonkeikaku.

0782 Hara no Jin Onkoroku 原陣温故録 (Record of the Hara Siege). jb. 1 v.
ms. Nagasaki.

0783 Hayashi Razan 林羅山 (1583–1657)
Sōzoku Zenki 草賊前記 and Kōki 後記 (The Amakusa Rebels: Part I and II) by Royōshi 路陽子.
0784 —— (Seiyūdō Sōsho).
0785 —— (Shōsho).

0786 Hizen Arima Kirishitan Ikki Kongen 肥前有馬切支丹一揆根源 (Origin of the Christian Riot at Arima, in Hizen Province). jb. 1 v.
ms. Kyudai.

0787 Hizen no Kuni Arima Senki 肥前國有馬戰記 (Record of the Arima Battle at Hizen Province). jb. 3 vols.
ms. Jingu, Nagasaki.

0788 Hizen no Kuni Shimabara Amakusa Gunki 肥前國島原天草軍記 (Record of the War of Shimabara-Amakusa in Hizen Province). jb. 1 v.
ms. Ebisawa.

0789 Hizen no Kuni Shimabara Ikki Shimatsuki 肥前國島原一揆始末記 or Mogi

Takaharu Kikigaki 茂木隆春聞書 (Outcome of the Shimabara Rebellion or Recollections of Mogi Takaharu).
0790 —— (Ōshuku Zakki).

0791 Hizen no Kuni Shimabara Kirishitan Ichiran Shijū 肥前國島原切支丹一亂始終 (History of the Shimabara Catholic Rebellion in Hizen Province). jb. 1 v.
ms. Nagasaki.

0792 Hizen no Kuni Takaku-gōri Hara no Shiro Chirizu 肥前國高來郡原ノ城地理圖 (Map of the Hara Castle, Takaku District, Hizen Province). 60×61cm.
ms. Ueno-Shirai.

0793 Hizen Shimabara Arima Ikki no Hōki 肥前島原有馬一揆ノ蜂起 (Outbreak of the Riot at Arima, in Shimabara, Hizen Province). jb. 1 v.
ms. Sophia.

0794 Hizen Shimabara Ikki no Koto 肥前島原一揆事 (Account of the Shimabara Rebellion in the Province of Hizen).
0795 —— (Okinagusa).

0796 Hizen Shimabara Ikki Oboegaki 肥前島原一揆覺書 (Memorandum on the Shimabara Rebellion in the Province of Hizen). jb. 1 v.
ms. Naikaku.

0797 Hizen Shimabara Yaso Seibatsu Jintorizu 肥前島原耶蘇征伐陳取圖 (Map of the Shimabara Front of the Christian Rebellion at Hizen Province).
ms. Sonkeikaku.

0798 Hizen Shimabara Youchi Chushin narabini Kii Yorinobukyō Eichi no Koto 肥前島原夜討注進並紀伊賴宣卿英智事 (Report on the Night Attack at Shimabara and the Brilliant Achievements of Yorinobu-Kyō of Kii).
0799 —— (Okinagusa).

0800 Hosokawa Tadaoki 細川忠興 (1563–1605)
Hosokawake Oboegaki 細川家覺書, or Sesshū Ōsaka Hizen Harajō Oboegaki 攝州大坂肥前原城覺書 (Memorandam of the Hosokawa Merits at the Hara in Hizen and Osaka Castle in Settsu). jb. 1 v.
cf. Samura, p. 1799.

0801 Hosokawake Amakusajin no Toki Gunzei Kōgi yori kudasaresoro Onfuchikata Uketorian 細川家天草陣時軍勢從公儀被下候御扶持方受取案 (Plan for Receiving

Support from the Bakufu for the Soldiers of the Hosokawa Clan at the Amakusa Battle Front). jb. 1 v.

0802 —— (Buhen Sōsho, v. V).

0803 —— (Shiseki Shōran).

0804 Hosokawake Shimabara Gunki 細川家島原軍記 (War Report of the Hosokawas at the Shimabara Rebellion). jb. 1 v.
cf. Samura, p. 1799.
ms. Naikaku.

0805 Ikeda Kachū Bōshi Shimabarajin Oboegaki 池田家中某氏島原陣覺書 (Notes of the Shimbara Rebellion by a Samurai of the Ikeda Clan).

0806 —— (Kibi Gunsho Shūsei, v. V).

0807 Kan'ei Chijutsu 寛永治述 (On the Rulings of the Kan'ei Era). jb. 13 vols.
ms. Daitokyu, Waseda.

0808 Kan'ei Zokubatsu Ōrai Shoshō 寛永賊罰往來諸章 (Several Records on the Rebellion in the Kan'ei Era). jb. 1 v.
ms. Sonkeikaku.

0809 Kirishitan Hōki Chūshin 吉里支丹蜂起注進 (Report on the Christian Rebellion). jb. 1 v.
ms. Daitokyu.

0810 Matsudaira Nobutsuna 松平信綱 (1596–1662)
Arima Ikki Seibatsu Nikki 有馬一揆征伐日記 (Diary of the Expedition to the Arima Rebellion). jb. 1 v.
note: See also Matsudaira Terutsuna, *Shimabara Amakusa Nikki.*
ms. Nagasaki.

0811 Matsudaira Terutsuna 松平輝綱 (1620–1671)
Shimabara Amakusa Nikki 島原天草日記 (Diary of the Expedition to Shimabara and Amakusa) 1663 (寛文 3). jb. 1 v.
ms. Ebisawa, Nagasaki, Shiryō, Tōdai-Nanki, Waseda.

0812 —— (Zokuzoku Gunsho Ruijū, v. IV), Tokyo 1907.

0813 —— (Kirishitan Bunko, v. III).

0814 * Amakusa Nikki 天草日記, jb. 1 v.
ms. Nagasaki, Naikaku, Tōyō-Iwasaki.

0815 * Amakusa Shimabara Ryō Nikki 天草島原兩日記 jb. 1 v.

0816 —— (Chintei Sōsho).

0817 * Shimabara Amakusa-jin Ōhen no Nikki 島原天草陣往返之日記. jb. 1 v.
ms. Nagasaki.

0818 * Shimabara Nikki 島原日記. jb. 1 v.

ms. Tōdai-Nanki.

0819 Nagamine Monjo 永峯文書 (Nagamine Documents). jb. 1 v.
ms. Ebisawa, Shiryō.

0820 Nagaoka Okinaga 長岡奧長
Shimabara Onjin Nagaoka Okinaga Kikigaki 島原御陣長岡奧長聞書 (Memorandum on the Shimabara Front by Nagaoka Okinaga).
ms. Waseda.

0821 * Shimabarajin no toki Hosokawake Hanshi Nagaoka-uji Kiroku Shōshutsu 島原陣之時細川家藩士長岡氏記録抄出 (Abridged Record of the Shimabara Rebellion by a Samurai of the Hosokawa Clan).

0822 —— (Buhen Sōsho. B, v. XVI).

0823 Okayama Monjo 岡山文書 (Okayama's Documents).
orig. ms. Okayama Toshiyuki 岡山敏之, Kumamoto Pref.
ms. Ebisawa, Shiryō.

0824 Sano Yashichizaemon 佐野彌七左衛門
Shimabara Jikki 島原實記 (True Story of the Shimabara Rebellion). jb. 1 v.
cf. Samura, p. 930.
ms. Naikaku, Tōdai-Nanki, Tōyō-Iwasaki.

0825 * Shimabara Jitsuroku 島原實録 (True Record of the Shimabara Rebellion).
ms. Kanazawa-Ujiie, Nagasaki, Tōhoku.

0826 * Shimabara Jitsuroku-ki 島原實録記 (True Record of the Shimabara Rebellion).
ms. Ōtani.

0827 Shimabara Amakusa Ikken Nukigaki 島原天草一件抜書 (Extracts concerning the Rebellion at Shimabara and Amakusa). jb. 1 v.
ms. Ebisawa.

0828 Shimabara Hikan 島原秘翰 (Secret Letters on Shimabara).

0829 —— (Buhen Sōsho. B, v. XXXII).

0830 Shimabara Ichiran Ryakuki 島原一亂略記 (Brief Note of the Shimabara Rebellion). jb. 1 v.
ms. Ebisawa.

0831 Shimabara Ikki 島原一揆 (The Shimabara Rebellion).

0832 —— (Okinagusa).

0833 Shimabara Ikki Matsukuraki 島原一揆松倉記. jb. 1 v.
cf. Kokushi, p. 131.

ms. Naikaku, Tōyō-Iwasaki.

0834 —— (Toriumi Sōsho).

0835 —— (Zokuzoku Gunsho Ruijū, v. IV).

0836 —— (Kirishitan Bunko. v. III.)

0837 Shimabara Ikki Monogatari Gunki 島原一揆物語軍記. jb. 1 v.
ms. Shiryō.

0838 Shimabara Ikki no Okori 島原一揆之起 (Origin of the Shimabara Rebellion).
0839 —— (Ōkōchike Kiroku).

0840 Shimabara Ikki no Shidai 島原一揆の次第 (History of the Shimabara Rebellion).
0841 —— (Okinagusa).

0842 Shimabara Ikki-ron 島原一揆論.
0843 —— (Okinagusa).

0844 Shimabara Ikki Seibatsuki 島原一揆征伐記 (Subjugation of the Shimabara Rebellion). jb. 6 vols. 28cm.
ms. Tenri.

0845 Shimabara Ikki Yōmonki 島原一揆要聞記 or Shimabara Ikki Shimatsuki 島原一揆始末記 (Recollections of the Shimabara Rebellion). jb. 1 v.
cf. Samura, p. 930.

0846 Shimabara-jin no Toki Onfure 島原陣之時御觸 (Official Notices Issued at the Time of the Shimabara Rebellion). jb. 1 v.
ms. Sophia.

0847 Shimabara-jin Oboegaki 島原陣覺書 (Notes of the Shimabara Front).
ms. Kyūdai.

0848 Shimabara Kassen Kubichō 島原合戦首帳 (List of those Beheaded at the Shimabara Battle). jb. 1 v.
contents: Bettō Mokuzaemon Oboegaki 別當杢左衛門覺書
Kumagaiuji Shimabaraki 熊谷氏島原記
Namikawa Tazaemon Oboegaki 並河太左衛門覺書
ms. Naikaku.

0849 —— (Shimabaraki, v. I).

0850 Shimabaraki 島原記 (Records of the Shimabara Rebellion). jb. 2 vols.
cf. Samura, p. 930.
contents:
v. I. Kumagaiuji Oboegaki 熊谷氏覺書
Shimabara Kassen Kubichō 島原合戦首帳
Bettō Mokuzaemon Oboegaki 別當杢左衛門覺書
Kirishitan Hōki Oboegaki 切支丹蜂起覺書
Bateren Iruman Dōjiku Hakujō no Oboe 伴天連イルマン同宿白狀の覺
II. Namikawauji Oboegaki 並河氏覺書
Arima Denki 有馬傳記

Arima Korō Monogatari 有馬古老物語
Rō'nin Kumagai Sazaemon Ryōgen Oboegaki 浪人熊谷佐左衛門良玄覺書

0851 Shimabara Monogatari 島原物語 (Story of the Shimabara Rebellion). jb. 1 v.
ms. Jingu, Naikaku.

0852 Shimabara Oboegaki 島原覺書 (Memorandam on Shimabara).
ms. Tōdai-Nanki.

0853 Shimabara Rakujō Gunki 島原落城軍記 (Story of the Fall of Shimabara Castle). jb. 1 v.
ms. Nagasaki.

0854 Shimabararan no Ki 島原亂記 (Record of the Shimabara Rebellion). jb. 1 v.

0855 —— (Ōkōchike Kiroku).

0856 Shimabara Uchijini Nikki 島原討死日記 (Reports of Death in the Battle of Shimabara). jb. 1 v.
ms. Sonkeikaku.

0857 Shimabara Yaso Batsuki 島原耶蘇罰記 (Story of Subjugation of the Christians at Shimabara). jb. 1 v.
ms. Naikaku.

0858 * Shimabara Yaso Chūbatsu Ryaki 島原耶蘇誅伐略記 (Short Description of the Subjugation of Christians at Shimabara). jb. 1 v.
ms. Tōdai-Nanki.

0859 Shimada Jūrōzaemon 島田十郎左衛門
Amakusa Ikken Oboegaki 天草一件覺書 (Notes of the Amakusa Rebellion).
0860 —— (Buhen Sōsho, B.).

0861 Tachibana Muneshige 立花宗茂 (1569–1642)
Tachibana Ryūsai Hanashi no Shidai 立花立斉咄之次第 (Narrative of Tachibana Ryūsai).
0862 —— (Toriumi Sōsho).
0863 * Tachibana Ryūsai Shimabarasen no Oboegaki 立花立齋嶋原戦之覺書 (Memorandum by Tachibana Ryūsai on the Shimabara Rebellion). jb. 1 v.
0864 —— (Shiseki Shūran).
0865 —— (Kaitei Shiseki Shūran, v. XVI).
0866 —— (Buhen Sōsho, v. X).
0867 —— (Kirishitan Bunko, A., v. III).

0868 Tachibana Tadashige 立花忠茂 (1612–1675)
Shimabara Jinki 島原陣記 (Story of the

Shimabara Rebellion). jb. 1 v.
ms. Naikaku, Shiryō.

0869 Takakunokōri Arima Kirishitan Ikki 高來郡有馬吉利支丹一揆 (Kirishitan Rebellion at Arima, Takaku Province). jb. 1 v.
ms. Nagasaki.

0870 Takakunokōri Ikki no Ki 高來郡一揆之記 (Notes on the Riot in Takaku Province). jb. 2 vols.
ms. Nagasaki, Shiryō.

0871 Temma Ibun 天馬異聞 (Strange Record of the Amakusa Rebellion).
note: Translation of a Dutch Source.
ms. Ebisawa, Iwase, Kyōdai-Fujikawa, Naikaku, Tōhoku-Kano, Ueno.
0872 —— (Bummei Genryū Sōsho, v. I).
0873 —— tr. into contemporary Jap. by Okada Akio 岡田章雄 in the *Sakoku Zenshi no Kenkyū*, Tokyo 1943 (昭和 18), pp. 392–433.

0874 Tatsuke Sadaiyu 田付左太夫
Shimabara Hara-no-jo Ranki 島原原之城 亂記 (Record of the Rebellion at the Hara Castle in Shimabara). jb. 1 v.
ms. Nagasaki.

0875 Toda Samon 戸田左門
Toda Amakusa-Jinki 戸田天草陣記 (Story of the Amakusa Rebellion by Toda). jb. 1 v.
ms. Naikaku.

0876 Totoki Sanya 十時三彌
Amakusajin no Ki 天草陣記 (Notes of the Amakusa Battle). jb. 1 v.
ms. Naikaku.
0877 * Totoki Sanya-no-suke Kakiage no Utsushi 十時三彌介書上之寫 (Copy of Totoki Sanya-no-suke's Notes). jb. 1 v.
0878 —— (Shōkai Sōsho).
0879 —— (Kaitei Shiseki Shūran, v. XVI).

0880 Tsubobe Mokuzaemon 坪部杢左衛門
Shimabara Ikki no Oboegaki 島原一揆之覺書 (Notes on the Shimabara Rebellion). jb. 1 v.
note: See also nos. 848, 850.
cf. Samura, p. 930.
ms. Naikaku.

0881 Yamada Uemosaku 山田右衛門作
Amakusa Ikki Yamada Uemosaku Kuchigaki 天草一揆山田右衛門作口書 or Yamada Uemosaku Kuchigaki 山田右衛門作口書 (Oral Record of Yamada Uemosaku at the Amakusa Rebellion). jb. 3 vols.

note: Yamada was one of the captains in the Hara Castle.
ms. Naikaku.
0882 —— (Hōro Zassho).
0883 * Yamada Uemosaku Gengo o motte no Ki 山田右衛門作以言語記 or Yamada Uemosaku Monogatari 山田右衛門作物語 (Tales of Yamada Uemosaku).
ms. Shiryō, Waseda.
0884 —— (Zoku Gunsho Ruijū, v. IV).

1639

0885 Jo Kōkei, Paul 徐光啓 *Hsü Kuang-c'hi* (1562–1633)
Nosei Zensho 農政全書 *Nung-cheng Ch'üan-shu* (Complete Works on Agriculture), Peking 1639 (崇禎 12). ob. 40 vols.
c. Kyūdai-Nogaku, Naikaku.
0886 —— Kueichow 1837 (道光 19).
0887 —— Shanghai 曙海樓, 1843 (道光 23). cb. 24 vols.
c. ICU, Naikaku, Seikado, Shinken, Ueno, Yutoku.
0888 —— Tientsin 山東書局, 1873 (同治 12). cb. 60 vols.
0889 —— [n.p.], 1897 (光緒 23). cb. 24 vols.
c. Ueno-Shirai.
0890 —— Shanghai 1909 (宣統 1).
0891 —— Peking 1956 (民国 45).
0892 —— (Banyū Bunko).

0893 Kirishitan Monogatari 吉利支丹物語 (Tales of the Christians), Kyoto 1639 (寛永16). jb. 2 vols., 28cm.
c. Tenri, Ueno, Ebisawa (v. I missing).
ms. Naikaku, Tenri.
0894 —— (Kirishitan Hakyaku Ronden, v. III).
0895 —— (Sokkyohen, v. IX).
0896 —— (Kirishitan Shiryō).
0897 —— (Kirishitan Bunko, A., v. I).
0898 —— (Nippon Shisō Tōsō Shiryō, v. X).
0899 —— (Zokuzoku Gunsho Ruijū, v. XII).
0900 —— (Edo no Omokage).
0901 * Kirishitan Taiji Monogatari 吉利支丹退治物語 (Tales of Elimination of the Christian). Kyoto 中野太郎左衛門, 1665 (寛文 5). jb. 3 vols., 26cm.
note: Second ed. of the Kirishitan Monogatari, 1639.
c. Kyōdai.
0902 —— facs. repr. (Kisho Fukuseikai Sōsho).
0903 —— (Kaihyō Sōsho, v. II).
0904 —— (Edo Monogatari).

0905 Nishinotōin Tokiyoshi 西洞院時慶 (1552–1639)

Tokiyoshi-kyō-ki 時慶卿記 (Diary of Tokiyoshi, 1591–1639). jb. 19 vols.
cf. Kokushi, p. 226.
orig. ms. Ryukoku.
ms. Naikaku.

1640

0906 Jo Shōji 徐昌治, *Hsü Ch'ang chih*
Seichō Hajashū 聖朝破邪集 *Sheng-ch'ao P'o-hsieh Chi* (Anti-Christian Works of the Sacred Dynasty), Peking 1640 (崇禎 12). cb. 8 vols., 28cm.
c. Hibiya-Ichimura.

0907 * Minchō Hajashū 明朝破邪集, edited by Tokugawa Nariaki 徳川斉昭, Edo [Tokyo], Mito-han 水戸藩, 1855 (安政 2). jb. 8 vols., 29cm.
c. Ebisawa, Gakushuin, Naikaku, Otani, Osaka, Shinken, Sophia, Taisho, Tenri, Tōhoku, Tokyoshin, Ueno, Waseda, Yoshida.
ms. Naikaku.

0908 Matsushita Shōzō 松下昌三
Irinshō 彝倫抄 (Elementary Ethics), Kyōto 1640 (寛永 17). jb. 1 v., 48, 3f., 26cm.
c. Ebisawa.

0909 Ōmagari Tōnai 大曲藤内 (1552–1640)
Ōmagari Oboegaki 大曲覺書 (Ōmagari Memorials). jb. 1 v.
note: Memorials of the Matsūra 松浦 family from Okuhide 奥榮 to Takanobu 隆信, the lord of Hirado 平戸.
cf. Samura, p. 283.
ms. Nagasaki, Shiryo.

0910 * Ōmagari-ki 大曲記 (The Ōmagari Record). jb. 1 v.
ms. Matsura, Shiryo.

0911 Tanimura Yūzan 谷村友山
Tanimura Yūzan Oboegaki 谷村友山覺書 (Memorandum of Tanimura Yūzan). jb. 1 v.
ms. Matsura, Shiryo.

0912 Shimabara-ki 島原記 (Story of the Shimabara Rebellion), [n.p.], 1640 (寛永 17). jb. 3 vols., 26cm.
cf. Kokushi. pp. 130–131; Okuno, p. 252.
c. Naikaku Sophia (v. III missing). Todai-Nanki, Ueno, Waseda.
ms. Jingu, Kanazawa-Oshima, Keio, Kyudai-Hoka, Kyudai-Bunka, Naikaku, Sonkeikaku. Tōyō-Iwasaki.
0913 —— (Irō Monogatari).
0914 —— (Gyokuchō Sōsho).
0915 —— (Sokkyohen).
0916 —— (Kaitei Shiseki Shūran, v. XXVI).
0917 —— [n.p.], 1649 (慶安 2). jb. 3 vols., 26cm.

c. Keio, Kichu, Waseda.
0918 —— [n.p.], 1704 (寶永 1). jb. 1 v.
c. Waseda.

0919 Thomas à Kempis (1380–1471)
Keisei Kinsho 輕世金書 *Ch'ing-shih Chin-shu* (Imitation of Christ), tr. by Emmanuel Diaz, jr. SJ. 陽瑪珞 (1574–1659), Peking 1640 (崇禎 13). cb. 2 vols.
note: There is another translation in Chinese, *Junshu Seihan* 遵主聖範 *Tsun-chu Sheng-fan*. See Part II.
cf. Pfister, pp. 109–110; Jo, pp. 50–51.
0920 —— Peking 1757 (乾隆 22). cb. 4 vols.
0921 —— Peking 1800 (嘉慶 5). cb. 4 vols.
0922 —— Peking 1815 (嘉慶 20). cb. 4 vols.
0923 —— Shanghai 1848 (道光 28). cb. 1 v., [2], [2], 22, [1], 13, [5], 49, [2]f., 26cm.
c. Aoyama, Hibiya-Ichimura, Seishin, Tenri.
0924 —— Shanghai 1856 (咸豊 6). cb. 4 vols.
0925 —— Shanghai 土山灣印書館 1910 (宣統 2). wb. 1 v.
0926 —— Shanghai 土山灣印書館 1923 (民國 12). wb. 1 v., 4, 14, 142p., 19cm.
c. Ebisawa.

0927 Vagnoni, Alphonso, SJ. 高一志 (1566–1640)
Jūi 十慰 *Shih-yü* (Ten Consolations), Kiang-chow [n.d.]. cb. 1 v.
note: Specifically outlawed subsquent to 1630.
cf. Pfister, p. 92; Jo, p. 69.

0928 Vagnoni, Alphonso, SJ. 高一志 (1566–1640)
Seigaku Chihei 西學治平 *Hsi-hsüeh Chih-ping* (Manual for the Administration of the State), [n.p.], [n.d.]. cb. 4 vols.
cf. Pfister, p. 93.
0929 * Minji Seigaku 民治西學 *Min-chih Hsi-hsüeh*, Peking 遣使會印書館, 1935 (民國 24). wb. 1 v., 39f., 20cm.
note: Revised ed. of the above.
c. Tenri.

1642

0930 Aleni, Giuglio, SJ. 艾儒略 (1582–1649)
Tenshu Kōsei Genkō Kiryaku 天主降生言行紀略 *T'ien-chu Chiang-sheng Yen-hsing Chi-lüeh* (Life of Our Lord), Peking, 1642 (崇禎 15). cb. 8 vols.
cf. Pfister, pp. 131–132; Jo, pp. 38–40.
0931 —— Peking, 1738 (乾隆 3).
0932 —— Peking 始胎大堂, 1796 (嘉慶 1). cb. 2 vols., 26cm.
c. Aoyama, Hibiya-Ichimura, Tōhoku-Kano.

0933 —— Shanghai 慈母堂, 1853 (咸豊 3). cb. 2 vols., 23cm.
c. Seikado, Tenri, Tōhoku-Kano.

0934 —— Shanghai, 1903 (光緒 29). wb. 1 v.

0935 —— (Dōgen Seisui, vv. II–IV).

0936 * Yaso Genkō Kiryaku 耶蘇言行紀略, tr. into Jap. by Jean Marie Marin, MEP., and Nakayama 中山, Tokyo 1880 (明治 13). jb. 4 vols., 23cm.
cf. Laures, n. 110; Streit X, pp. 80, 332.
c. Aoyama, Ebisawa, Nagasaki, Saba, Sophia, Yoshida.

0937 Aleni, Giuglio, SJ. 艾思及 (1582–1649)
Tenshu Seikyō Shiji Kyōmon 天主聖教四字經文 *T'ien-chu Sheng-chiao Szu-tzu Ching-wen* (Abridged Catechism according to the Four Syllables), Peking, 1642 (崇禎 15). cb. 1 v.
cf. Pfister, p. 124; Jo, p. 169.

0938 —— Peking, 1650 (順治 7). cb. 1 v., 5, 35f., 20cm.
c. Sophia.

0939 —— Peking, 1663 (康熙 32). cb. 1 v. 31f., 20cm.
c. Otani.

0940 —— Peking, 1798 (嘉慶 3). cb. 1 v.
0941 —— Shanghai 慈母堂, 1856 (咸豊 6). cb. 1v., 4, 31f., 20cm.
c. ICU, Sophia.

0942 —— Shanghai, 1861 (咸豊 11). cb. 1 v.

0943 —— Shanghai, 1913 (民國 2). wb. 1 v.

0944 Diaz, Emmnuel jr., SJ. 陽瑪琣 (1574–1659)
Tenshu Seikyō Jikkai Chokusen 天主聖教十誡直詮, *T'ien-chu Sheng-chiao Shih-chieh Chih-ch'üan* (Exact Explanation of the Ten Commandments), Peking 1642 (崇禎 15). cb. 2 vols.
cf. Pfister, p. 109; Jo, pp. 180–182.

0945 —— Peking 1659 (順治 16). cb. 2 vols.

0946 —— Peking 1738 (乾隆 3). cb. 2 vols.
0947 —— Peking 始胎大堂, 1798 (嘉慶 3). cb. 1 v., 5, 2, [1], 92f., 27cm.
c. Ebisawa, Nagasaki, Naikaku, Saba, Tenri, Tōyō.
ms. Kyūdai-Bunka.

0948 —— Shanghai 1915 (民國 4). wb. 1 v.
0949 —— Shanghai 1930 (民國 19). wb. 1 v., 7, 136p. 19cm.
c. Tōhoku.

0950 Tachibana Ikō 立花遺香 or Tachibana Isho 立花遺書 (Life of Tachibana

Muneshige). jb. 2 vols.
note: Tachibana Muneshige 立花宗茂 (1569–1642) was the Lord of Yanagawa, Chikugo Province. Contains records of the Shimabara-Rebellion.
cf. Samura, p. 1330.

0951 —— (Nippon Ijin Genkō Shiryō, v. XI).

1643

Foundation of the Kirishitan Jail at Edo

0952 Kirishitan Yamayashiki no zu 切支丹山屋敷圖 (Map of the Jail for Christians). 180×141cm.
cf. Nakai Nobuhiko, "Kirishitan Yamayashikizu ni tsuite" (*Shigaku,* v. XXXIV, n. 1). Tokyo 1949.
ms. Mitsui Bunko.

0953 —— [different ms.].
note: See also, n. 2273.
cf. Nakayama Kō, "Tokyo Kobinata Kirishitanzaka Meigi" (*Tōyō Gakugei Zasshi,* v. LXXXIII), Tokyo 1888.

0954 Shinsen Edoshi 新撰江戸志 (New Descriptive Geography of Edo). jb. 11 v.
note: The author is probably Kondō Gikyū 近藤義休 and it was probably compiled in the An'ei Era (1772–1781).
cf. Samura. p. 214.

0955 Namban Bateren Iruman Dōjuku Hakujō no Oboe 南蠻伴天連いるまん同宿白狀之覺 (Confession of the Catholic Fathers, Brothers and Catechists). 1643 (寛永 20). jb. 1 v.
ms. Ebisawa, Shiryo, Tenri.

0956 —— (Sokkyohen, v. I).
0957 —— (Shimabaraki, v. I).
0958 —— (Ishimoda Monjo).

0959 Nishi Luis 西類子 (–1646)
Nishi Ruisu Yuishogaki 西類子由緒書 (History of Luis Nishi). jb. 1 v.
cf. Asahi, p. 31.
orig. ms. Honjuji 本受寺 (Sakai).

Persecution in Sanuki Province, 1643–1690

0960 Eikō Jitsuroku 英公實録 (Faithful Description of Eikō). (1673?). jb. 1 v.
note: Eikō is Matsudaira Yorishige 松平頼重 (1622–1695), Daimyō of Takamatsu, Shikoku.
orig. ms. The Matsudaira (destroyed).

0961 —— pr. by Matsuda Kiichi 松田毅一, *Kirishitan Kenkyū, Shikokuhen,* Osaka 1953 (昭和 28), pp. 217–219.

0962 Okuni Yasoshū 御國耶蘇集 (Documents on the Christians in Tosa Province). jb. 1v.

note: Documents on the martyrdom of Kuwana Koan 桑名古庵 and his family in 1643–1689.
orig. ms. Yamanouchi Bunko 山内文庫, Kōchi (destroyed).

0963 —— pr. and annotated by Matsuda Kiichi 松田毅一, *Kirishitan Kenkyū, Shikokuhen,* Osaka 1953 (昭和 28), pp. 224–270.

0964 Sanuki Matsudaira-han Kirishitan Shuto Jimmeiroku 讃岐松平藩切支丹宗徒人名録 (Directory of the Christians in the Matsudaira-Clan of Sanuki Province). jb. 3 vols.

note: Covers about one hundred years beginning in 1643.
orig. ms. The Matsudairas (destroyed).

0965 —— pr. and annotated by Matsuda Kiichi 松田毅一, *Kirishitan Kenkyū, Shikokuhen,* Osaka 1953 (昭和 28), pp. 202–217, 275–286, 421–526.

1644

0966 Diaz, Emmanuel, jr. SJ. 陽瑪瑢 (1574–1659)
Keikyō Ryūkō Chūgokuhishō Seisen 景教流行中國碑頌正詮 *Ching-chiao Liu-hsing Chung-kuo Pei-sung Cheng-ch'üan* (Comments on the Monument of the Nestorian Mission), compiled by E. Diaz, G. Aleni and J. Monteiro SJ., Hangchow 1644 (崇禎 17). cb. 1 v., 8°, 68f.

cf. Pfister, pp. 109, 135; Jo, pp. 230–234; Cordier-Sinica, col. 773.

0967 —— Shanghai 慈母堂, 1878 (光緒 4). cb. 1 v., 3, 8, 5, 49, 2f., 27 cm.

c. ICU, Osaka.
note: See also n. 541.

0968 Sawano Chūan 澤野忠庵, Christovão Ferreira, ex-SJ. (1580–1650)
Temmon Biyō 天文備用 (Introduction to Astronomy), 1644 (寛永 21). jb. 2 vols.

cf. Ōya Shin'ichi 大矢眞一, "Kenkon Benzetsu no Ihon" (*Kagakushi Kenkyū,* v. XVII), Tokyo 1951; Ebisawa-Namban, pp. 97–111.
ms. Akioka.

0969 * Namban Unkiron 南蠻運氣論 (Western Astrology). jb. 1 v.
ms. Gakushiin, Kyūdai,

0970 * Namban Unkiron oyobi Zue 南蠻運氣論及圖繪 (Western Astrology and its Illustrations). jb. 3 vols.
ms. Gakushiin, The Okochis.

0971 * Temmon Sata Benkai 天文沙汰辯解 (Explanation of Astrology), tr. by Nishi Kichibyōe 西吉兵衛, |1643?]. jb. 1 v.
ms. Kyōdai.

0972 * Tenchiron 天地論 (Treatise on Heaven and Earth), handwritten by Sugi Teian 杉貞庵. jb. 1 v.
ms. Mikami Yoshio 三上義夫.

0973 * Tenchiron 天地論, or Namban Tenchiron 南蠻天地論. jb. 1 v.
ms. Tōhoku-Sugaku.

1645

0974 Schall von Bell, Johann Adam, SJ. 湯若望 (1591–1666)
Rekihō Seiden 曆法西傳 *Li-fa Hsi-ch'uan* (History of the European Calendar System), Peking 1645 (順治 2). cb. 1 v.

cf. Pfister, p. 180.
ms. Tenri, Tōhoku-Kano.

0975 —— (Seiyō Shimpō Rekisho, v. XCVI).

0976 Schall von Bell, Johann Adam, SJ. 湯若望 (1591–1666)
Shimpō Hyōi 新法表異 *Hsin-fa Piao-yi* (Tables of the New Calendar), Peking 1645 (順治 2). cb. 2 vols.

cf. Pfister, p. 180.
ms. Kyōdai-Butsuri.

0977 —— (Seiyō Shimpō Rekisho, v. XCV).

0978 —— (Shōdai Sōsho).

0979 Schall von Bell, Johann Adam, SJ. 湯若望 (1591–1666)
Shinreki Gyōsei 新曆曉成 *Hsin-li Hsiao-ch'eng* (Question and Answers on the New Calendar Science), Peking 1645 (順治 2). cb. 1 v.

0980 —— (Shōdai Sōsho).
0981 —— (Seishōdō Sōsho).

0982 Fujiwara Chinshi 藤原陳師
Sūtei Kō-Katsureki 崇禎興活曆 (Treatise on the Calendar of Emperor Sūtei). jb. 1 v.
ms. Ueno.

0983 Jo Kōkei 徐光啓 *Hsü Kuang-ch'i* (1562–1633)
Seiyō Shimpō Rekisho 西洋新法曆書 *Hsi-yang Hsin-fa Li-shu* (The New Western Calendar Book) compiled by Jō Kōkei and etc., Peking 1645. cb. 100 vols., 27cm.

cf. Pfister, pp. 179–181; Jo, pp. 239–256.
c. Gakushiin, Hazama, Naikaku, Seikado, Tōhoku-Sugaku.
ms. Naikaku, Tōhoku-Kano, Ueno, Waseda.
contents:
vv. 1– 5 Kontengisetsu 渾天儀説 by J. Adam Schall.
6–22 Sōso, Daiso 奏疏, 題疏.
23 Nitten Rekishi 日纏曆指 by G. Rho.
24–29 Kōsei Rekishi 恒星曆指, Kōsei Keii Zusetsu 恒星經緯圖説, Kōsei Keiihyō 恒星經緯表 by J. Adam Schall.
30–32 Getsuri Rekishi 月離曆指 by G. Rho.

33–39 Kōshoku Rekishi 交食曆指 by J. Adam Schall.
40–48 Goi Rekishi 五緯曆指 by G. Rho.
49–56 Kōshokuhyō 交食表 by J. Adam Schall.
57–58 Nittenhyō 日纏表 by G. Rho.
59–62 Getsurihyō 月離表 by G. Rho.
63–72 Goihyō 五緯表 by G. Rho.
73–82 Sokuryō Zengi 測量全義 by G. Rho.
83–84 Katsuen Kōkō Hassenhyō 割圓勾股八線表 by J. Terrenz.
85 Chūzan 籌算 by G. Rho.
86–87 Kika Yōhō 幾何要法 by G. Aleni.
88 Taisoku 大測 by J. Terrenz.
89 Sokuten Yakusetsu 測天約説 by J. Terrenz.
90 Seiyō Sokuryaku 西洋測略 by J. Adam Schall.
91 Hirei Kikai 比例規解 by G. Rho.
92 Kokon Kōshokuhyō 古今交食表 by J. Adam Schall.
93–94 Kōsei Shutsubotsuhyō 恒星出没表 by J. Adam Schall.
95 Shimpō Hyōi 新法表異 by J. Adam Schall.
96 Rekihō Seiden 曆法西傳 by J. Adam Schall.
97 Gakureki Shōben 學曆小辯 by J. Adam Schall.
98 Shimpō Rekiin 新法曆引 by J. Adam Schall.
99 Kyo-idohyō 距緯度表 by J. Terrenz.
100 Enkyōsetsu 遠鏡説 by J. Adam Schall.

0984 Rekiinkai 曆引解 (Explanation of the Calendar Index). jb. 1 v.
ms. Tohoku-Kano.

0985 Ri Tenkei 李天經 *Li T'ien-ching* Sūtei Rekisho Rekiin 崇禎曆書曆引 (Index of the Sūtei Rekisho), annotated by Shibukawa Kagesuke 澁川景祐, Edo [Tokyo] 渡邊枕 1855 (安政 2). jb. 3 vols., 26cm.
orig. ms. E. Ishibashi.
c. Gakushiin, Kyodai-Busturi, Kyodai-Chiri, Kyudai-Butsuri, Naikaku, Tenri, Tōhoku-Kano, Tōhoku-Sugaku, Waseda, Waseda-Ogura.
ms. Jinshu.

0986 Seiyō Rekihō Gunsho 西洋曆法群書 (Collection of Western Calendar Science). jb. 1 v.
ms. Tōhoku-Hayashi.

0987 Seiyō Shimpō Rekisho Hyō 西洋新法曆書表 (Table of the New Calendar according to the Western Method).
ms. Tōhoku-Kano.

The Namban Oath

0988 Kirishitan Korobi Kakimono no Koto 吉利支丹ころび書物之事 or Namban Seishi 南蠻誓詞 (Oath taken by Apostates approved by Chūan 中庵, the apostate Father), 1645 (正保 2). 1 sheet.
orig. ms. Saishoji.
ms. Naikaku.

0989 —— facs. pr. by Nagayama Tokihide 永山時英, in *Taigai Shiryō Bijutsu Taikan*, v. I, Nagasaki 1918 (大正 7).

0990 —— facs. pr. (Kirishitan Shiryōshū).

0991 —— pr. by Urakawa Wasaburō 浦川和三郎, in *Kirishitan no Fukkatsu*, v. I., Tokyo 1932 (昭和 7), pp. 58–61.

0992 —— pr. by Ebisawa Arimichi 海老澤有道, in *Nippon-shi Kenkyū Shiryō*, Tokyo 1958 (昭和 33), pp. 64–65.

0993 —— (Yasokyō Sōsho, n. 1).

0994 —— tr. into German by G. Voss and H. Cieslik, SJ., in *Kirishitoki und Sayō-Yoroku*, Tokyo 1940, pp. 165–166.

0995 —— tr. into English by C. R. Boxer in *Christian Century in Japan*, Berkeley 1951, pp. 441–442.

1646

0996 Aleni, Giuglio, SJ. 艾儒略 (1582–1649)
Seigaku Kakujutsu 牲學觕述 *Hsing-hsüeh Ts'u-shu* (Introduction to Psychology), Hangchow. 1646 (順治 3). cb. 8 vols.
cf. Pfister, pp. 134–135; Jo, pp. 210–214.

0997 —— Shanghai 慈母堂, 1873 (同治 12). cb. 2 vols., 25cm.
c. Aoyama, Seishin (vv. I–IV only), Tōyō.

0998 —— Shanghai 1922 (民國 11). wb. 1 v.

1647

0999 Shōho Krobune Raichōki 正保黒船來朝記 (On the Arrival of the Black-Ship during the Shōho Era). jb. 1 v.
ms. Ebisawa, the Hosokawas, Nagasaki, Naikaku.

1000 —— pr. and annotated by Mutō Chōzō 武藤長藏, "Seireki 1647 nen Nagasaki ni torai no Po-koku shisetsu ni kansuru Higo Hosokawa-ke Shozō Shōho Kurobune Raichōki" (*Shigaku*, v. XII, n. 2)., Tokyo 1933 (昭和 18), pp. 163–202.

1001 Sessō 雪窓
Jakyō Taii 邪敎大意 (Important Elements of the Evil Religion), 1647 (正保 4). jb. 1 v.

1002 —— (Nippon Shisō Yōsō Shiryō, v. X).

1003 —— pr. by Kiyū Dōjin 杞憂道人 in the *Nambanji Kōhaiki*, Appendix, Tokyo 1868 (慶應 4).
note: See n. 1011.

1004 * Taiji Jashūron 對治邪執論 (On the Elimination of the Evil Religion).
note: Chinese translation of the *Jakyō Taii* (n. 1001).
ms. Otani, Tokyoiku, Waseda.

1005 —— (Sokkyohen, v. XVI).

1006 —— (Byakuja Kankenroku).

1007 —— (Haja Sōsho, v. I).

1008 —— (Nippon Shisō Tōsō Shiryō, v. X).

1009 —— (Kirishitoki, v. II), in the possession of the Lib. of Congress, USA.
phot. Ebisawa, Seishin.

1648

1010 Nambanji Kōhaiki 南蠻寺興廢記 or Nambanji-ki 南蠻寺記 (The Rise and Fall of the Catholic Church), [1648, 正保 5]. jb. 1 v.
cf. Kokushi, p. 238; Samura, pp. 1537–1538.
ms. M. Kurokawa.

1011 —— annotated by Kiyū Dōjin 杞憂道人, [Edo], 緣山, 1868 (慶應 4). jb. 1 v. 1, 43, [1]f., 26cm.
c. Aoi, Aoyama, Dōshisha, Ebisawa, Hibiya-Kaga, ICU, Iwase, Iwasaki, Jingu, Jinshu, Keio, Keio-Koda, Kichu, Kobejo, Kyōto, Kyūdai-Bunka, Nagasaki, Ōsaka, Ōtani, Seishin, Sonkeikaku, Sophia, Sukeno, Tenri, Tōdai, Tōdai-Nanki, Tōhoku, Tōhoku-Kano, Tōyōdai, Ueno, Waseda.

1012 —— (Nippon Rekishi Bunko).
1013 —— (Shiseki Shūran).
1014 —— (Kaitei Shiseki Shūran, v. XII).
1015 —— (Kirishitan Bunko, v. II).
1016 —— (Edo no Omokage).
1017 —— (Nippon Shisō Tōsō Shiryō, v. X).
1018 —— (Kirishitan Shiryō).
1019 —— tr. into French by A. Milloud, in *Revue de l'histoire des religions,* Paris 1895.
1020 * Nambanji Kōhaiki 南蠻寺興廢記 (Rise and Fall of the Catholic Church). jb. 1 v.
note: This is a different version of the *Nambanji Kōhaiki* (n. 1010).
ms. Ebisawa.

Fiction about the Christian Mission and the Shimabara Rebellion

1021 Amakusa Gunki 天草軍記 (Story of the Amakusa Battle).
ms. Hatano, Jingu, Narita, Seikado, Ueno.
1022 * Amakusa Gunki 天草軍記, 1788 (天明 8). jb. 1 v.
ms. Hatano.
1022b * Amakusa Gunki 天草軍記, Tokyo 野村銀太郎, 1886 (明治 19). 2nd ed. wb. 1., 1, 261p., 19cm.
c. Hatano.
1023 * Amakusa Gunki, Uchiyamashū 天草軍記内山集. jb. 1 v.
ms. Sophia.
1024 * Ehon Amakusa Gunki 繪本天草軍記, Tokyo 1883 (明治 16). jb. 1 v., 20f., 18cm.
c. Hatano.
1025 * Sankō Amakusa Gunki 參考天草軍記.
ms. Jingu.

1025b —— Tokyo 由己社, 1886 (明治 19). wb. 1 v., [2], 228p., 19cm.
c. Ebisawa, Kichu.
1026 —— Tokyo 榮泉堂, 1883 (明治 16). jb. 4 vols., 22cm.
c. Ebisawa, Hatano, Sophia.
1027 * Sankō Amakusa Gunki 參考天草軍記 compiled by Shimoda Sōtarō 下田惣太郎, Tokyo 隆湊堂, 1885 (明治 18). jb. 1 v., 23f., 12cm.
c. Ebisawa, Kichu.
1028 Amakusa Sōdō 天草騷動 (The Amakusa Rebellion).
1029 —— (Kinsei Jitsuroku Zensho, v. XII).
1030 *Amakusa Sōdōki 天草騷動記 (Record of the Amakusa Rebellion). jb. 1 v.
ms. Naikaku.
1031 Banshū Seikinroku 蕃宗制禁録 (Records on the Prohibition of the Foreign Religion). jb. 2 vols.
ms. Dōshisha, Iwase, Sophia, Tenri.
1032 Edo Monogatari 江戸物語 (Tales of Edo).
1033 —— (Sokkyohen, v. XVI).
1034 Gensō Romeiden 原草露命傳 (Lives as Evanescent as the Dew in the Hara Castle). jb. 2 vols.
ms. Sophia (v. I only).
1035 Ibukiyama Mogusa-ki 伊吹山艾草記 (Mugwort of Mt. Ibuki). jb. 1 v.
ms. Jingū, Tōdai, Tōdai-Nanki.
1036 Ibukiyama Yomogi no Innenki 伊吹山艾之因縁記 (Origin of the Ibuki-Mugwort). jb. 1 v.
ms. Ueno.
1037 Ibuki Yomogi 伊吹艾 (Mugwort of Mt. Ibuki). jb. 1 v.
contents: v. I. Kirishito Raichōki 契利斯當來朝記
II. Shimabara Shimatsuki 島原始末記.
ms. Tenri.
1038 Ibuki Yomogi 伊吹蓬 (Mugwort of Mt. Ibuki). jb. 1 v.
note: Different manuscript of the *Kirishitan Shūmon Raichō Jikki* (n. 1075).
ms. Kichu, Kyōdai, Ōtani, Hikone, Ōsaka, Sukeno.
1039 —— (Kanrin Shūyō).
1040 Ibuki Yomogi Innenki 伊吹蓬因縁記 (Origin of the Ibuki-Mugwort). jb. 1 v.
ms. Ueno.
1041 Ibuki Yomogi Yurai 伊吹艾由來

(Origin of the Ibuki-Mugwort). jb. 1 v.
ms. Imoto.

1042 Ikoku Nambanji Yurai 異國南蠻寺由來 (History of the Nambanji, Catholic Church). jb. 1 v.
ms. Tōhoku.

1043 Jakyō Ryakuki 邪教略記 (Outline of the Evil Religion). jb. 1 v.
ms. Kyūdai-Bunka.

1044 Jashū Kinzeiroku narabini Kirishitan Raichō no Yurai 邪宗禁制録并ニ切支丹來朝之由來 (Record of the Prohibition of Christianity and History of the Introduction of Christianity). jb. 1 v.
ms. Tenri.

1045 Jashūmon Kikigaki 邪宗門聞書 (Recollection of the Evil Religion). jb. 1 v.
ms. Tenri.

1046 Kaisei Ibuki Yomogigusa 改正伊吹艾草 (The Ibuki-Mugwort, revised). jb. 1 v.
ms. Tōhoku.

1047 Kan'ei Nantō-hen 寛永南島變 (A Rebellion on the Southern Island in the Kan'ei Era).
ms. Sonkeikaku.

1048 Kasai Shigetomo 香西成資 (1632–)
Nankai Chiranki 南海治亂記 (War Record of the Southern Seas). jb. 17 vols.
cf. Samura, p. 1528.
ms. Naikaku.

1049 —— (Kaitei Shiseki Shūran, v. VII).

1050 Keian Taiheiki 慶安太平記 (Historical Story of the KeianRebellion). jb. 5 vols.
note: Fiction telling about Yui Shōsetsu's 由井正雪 treason in 1651 connected with the Christian Sorcerers.
cf. Samura, pp. 572–573.

1051 —— (Kinsei Jitsuroku Sōsho, v. XXII).

1052 Kinka Keiranshō 金花傾嵐抄 (Record of the Shimabara Rebellion).
ms. Ebisawa, Kyōdai, Nagasaki, Tōdai.

1053 Kirishitan 切支丹 (Christianity) in the Seiyūdō Sōsho, Zassanbu.

1054 Kirishitan Amakusa Gunki 切支丹天草軍記 (Record of the Christian Amakusa Rebellion). jb. 1 v.
ms. Ebisawa.

1055 Kirishitan Denrai Hiroku 切支丹傳來秘録 (Secret Record of the Arrival of Christianity). jb. 1 v.
ms. Dōshisha.

1056 Kirishitan Denraiki 切支丹傳來記 (Arrival of the Kirishitan Religion). jb. 1 v.
ms. Tenri.

1057 Kirishitan Guhōki 切支丹弘法記 (History of the Christian Missions). jb. 1 v.
ms. Uchida.

1058 Kirishitan Hokki 切支丹發起 (Origins of Christianity). jb. 1 v.
ms. Tōhoku-Kano.

1059 Kirishitan Jikki 切支丹實記 or Ibuki Mogusa 伊吹もぐさ (The Account of the Christianity, or Mugwort of Mt. Ibuki). jb. 1 v.
ms. Jingū, Kyūdai-Hōka, Tōdai-Nanki, Tōhoku-Kano, Sukeno.

1060 Kirishitan Jitsuroku 切支丹實録 (True Account of the Christian Religion). jb. 1 v.
ms. Kanazawa, Nagasaki.

1061 Kirishitan-ki 切支丹記 (Notes on Christians). jb. 1 v.
ms. Aoyama, Seishin.

1062 Kirishitan Metsubōki 切支丹滅亡記 (The Destruction of Christianity). jb. 1 v.
ms. Sophia.

1063 Kirishitan Raichō Jikki 切支丹來朝實記 (True Story of the Arrival of Christianity in Japan). jb. 1 v.
ms. Daitokyu.

1064 —— (Sokkyohen, v. X).

1065 Kirishitan Raichōki 切支丹來朝記, or Kirishitan Shūmon Raichōki 切支丹宗門來朝記 (Record of the Arrival of Christianity in Japan). jb. 1 v.
ms. Hatano, Kyōdai, Sophia.

1066 Kirishitan Ranshōki 切支丹濫觴記 (Origins of Christianity). jb. 1 v.
ms. Aoyama, Kichū, Naikaku.

1067 Kirishitan Seibatsuki 切支丹征伐記 (Elimination of the Christian Religion). jb. 1 v.
ms. Sophia.

1068 Kirishitan Shimatsuki 切支丹始末記 (History of the Christianity in Japan). jb. 1 v.
ms. Ebisawa, Naikaku, Shiryō.

1069 Kirishitan Shūmon Denki 切支丹宗門傳記 (Record of the Christian Religion). jb. 1 v.
ms. Kyūdai-Bunka.

1070 Kirishitan Shūmon Jikki 切支丹宗

門實記 (True Account of Christianity). jb. 1 v.

ms. Hikone, Kyūdai-Bunka.

1071 Kirishitan Shūmonki 切支丹宗門記 (History of the Christian Religion). jb. 1 v.

ms. Kyōdai.

1072 Kirishitan Shūmon Kongen Seisuiki 切支丹宗門根元盛衰記 (Rise and Fall of the Christian Religion). jb. 1 v.

ms. Kyūdai-Bunka.

1073 Kirishitan Shūmon Kotaegaki 切支丹宗門答書 (Answers to Questions about the Christian Religion). jb. 1 v.

ms. Seikado.

1074 Kirishitan Shūmon no Koto 切支丹宗門之事 (On the Christian Religion). jb. 1 v.

ms. Jingū, Tenri.

1075 Kirishitan Shūmon Raichō Jikki 切支丹宗門來朝實記 (True Account of the Arrival of Christian Religion in Japan). jb. 1 v.

cf. Ebisawa Arimichi, "Kirishitan Shūmon Raichō Jikki-kō" (*Shūkyō Kenkyū*, n. 139), Tōkyō 1954.
ms. Ebisawa, Hatano, Hibiya-Kondo, Kichu, Kyōdai, Kyūdai, Kyōto, Ōura, Seishin, Sophia, Sukeno, Taishō, Tenri, Tōdai, Ueno, Waseda.

1076 —— (Zokuzoku Gunsho Ruijū, v. XII).

1077 —— (Kirishitan Bunko, A, v. I).

1078 —— tr. into English by M. Paske-Smith, *Japanese Traditions of Christianity*, Kōbe 1930.

1079 * Kirishitan Shūmon Raichō Jitsuroku 切支丹宗門來朝實錄 (True Account of the Arrival of Christian Religion in Japan). jb. 1 v.

ms. Sophia.

1080 Kirishitan Shūmon Raiyu 切支丹宗門來由 (Origins of the Christian Religion). jb. 1 v.

ms. Sophia.

1081 Kirishitan Shūmon Ranshōki 切支丹宗門濫觴記 (Origins of the Christian Religion). jb. 1 v.

ms. Aoyama.

1082 Kirishitan Shūmon Torai Jikki 切支丹宗門渡來實記 (True Facts about the Introduction of the Christian Religion). jb. 1 v.

ms. Seikadō, Tōhoku-Kano.

1083 Kirishitan Shūmon Yurai Kikigaki 切支丹宗門由來聞書 (Recollections of the Origins of the Christian Religion). jb. 1 v.

ms. Kanazawa-Kado.

1084 Kirishitanshū Shihatsuki 切支丹宗

始發記 (Origins of the Christian Religion). jb. 1 v.

ms. Kichū.

1085 Kirishitanshū Toraiki 切支宗渡來記 (Record about the Introduction of the Christian Religion). jb. 1 v.

ms. Kyūdai-Hōka.

1086 Kirishitan Tokai Kongenki 切支丹渡海根元記 (Origins of the Christian Religion). jb. 1 v.

ms. Kichū.

1087 Kirishitan Watari 切支丹渡 (Arrival of Christianity in Japan).

1088 —— (Ōshuku Zakki, Betsuroku).

1089 Kirishitan Yurai Jikki 吉利支丹由來實記 (True Account of the Origin of Christianity). jb. 1 v.

ms. Dōshisha, Kyūdai-Hōka, Ōtani, Tōdai, Tōdai-Nanki, Tenri.

1090 —— mimeogr. pr. by the Ōtani Daigaku Kokushi Kenkyūkai 大谷大學國史研究會, Kyōto 1934 (昭和 9).

1091 * Kirishitan Yurai Jikki 切支丹由來實記 or Ibuki Yomogi 伊吹艾 (True Account of the Origin of Christianity or the Mugwort of Mt. Ibuki). jb. 1 v.

ms. Keiō.

1092 Kirishitan Yuraiki 吉利支丹由來記 (Origins of the Christianity). jb. 1 v.

ms. Gakushūin, Seikadō, Sophia, Tōdai, Tōkyōiku.

1093 —— (Sokkyohen).

1094 Kirishitan Yuraishō 切支丹由來抄 (Brief History of Christianity). jb. 1 v.

ms. Tenri.

1095 Kirishito Raichōki 契利斯當來朝記 (History of the Arrival of Christianity). jb. 1 v.

1096 —— (Ibuki Yomogi, v. I).

1097 Metsubō Namban Jikki 滅亡南蠻實記 (True Facts about the Fall of Christianity). jb. 1 v.

ms. Tōyō-Iwasaki.

1098 Namban Gunki 南蠻軍記 (Record of the Extermination of Christianity). jb. 1 v.

ms. Sukeno.

1099 Nambanji Hakyaku no Koto 南蠻寺破却之事 (Destruction of the Catholic Church). jb. 1 v.

ms. Sophia.

1100 Namban Jikki 南蠻實記 (True Account of the Christian Religion). jb. 1 v.

ms. Iwase.

1101 Nambanji Monogatari 南蠻寺物語

(Story of the Catholic Church). jb. 1 v.
ms. Ueno.

1102 —— (Bummei Genryū Sōsho, v. I).
1103 —— (Nippon Shisō Tōsō Shiryō, v. X).
1104 —— (Kirishitan Shiryō).
1105 Nambanji Yurai 南蠻寺由來 (History of the Catholic Church). jb. 1 v.
ms. Tōhoku.

1106 Namban Kirishitan Raichō Jikki 南蠻切支丹來朝實記. jb. 1 v.
ms. Tōdai.

1107 Namban Metsubōki 南蠻滅亡記 (Annihilation of Catholicism). jb. 1 v.
ms. Sophia.

1108 Namban Yōhōki 南蠻妖法記 (Story of the Western Evil Religion). jb. 1 v.
ms. Kichū, Tōdai.

1109 Nantō Henranki 南島變亂記 (Rebellion on the Southern Islands). jb. 20 vols.
1110 —— (Kokushi Sōsho).

1111 Saigoku Kirishitan Heiran no Hen 西國切支丹兵亂之變 (The Kirishitan Rebellion in the Western Districts). jb. 1 v.
ms. Hatano.

1112 Seiyōkoku Kirishitan Bateren Jitsuroku 西洋國切支丹伴天連實録 (True Account of the Catholic Fathers). jb. 1 v.
ms. Jinshū.

1113 Shimabara Kirishitan Shimatsuki 島原鬼利支丹始末記 (History of the Shimabara Christian Rebellion). jb. 13 vols.
cf. Samura, p. 930.
ms. Ueno.

1114 Shimabara Shimatsuki 島原始末記 (History of the Shimabara Rebellion). jb. 1 v.
cf. Samura, p. 931.
ms. Hatano, Ueno.
1115 —— (Irō Monogatari).
1116 —— (Ibuki Yomogi 伊吹艾, v. II).
1117 —— (Sokkyōhen, vv. XIX–XX).

1118 Yaso Jitsuroku 耶蘇實録 (True Account of Christianity). jb. 1 v.
1119 —— pr. by Chikashige Butsuan 近重物安 in the *Zenshū* 禪宗, Tokyo 1927 (昭和 2).

1120 Yaso Kimparoku 耶蘇禁破録 (Record of the Overthrow of Christianity). jb. 1 v.
ms. Iwase.

1121 Yaso Seibatsuki 耶蘇征伐記 (Record of the Extermination of Christianity). jb.

1 v.
cf. Samura, p. 1950.
ms. Dōshisha, Kichū, Naikaku.
1122 —— (Sokkyōhen, v. XVII–XVIII).
1123 * Yaso Seibatsuki 耶蘇征罰記. jb. 1 v.
cf. Samura, p. 1950.
ms. Ebisawa, Iwase, Naikaku.
1124 * Yaso Seibatsuki 耶蘇制罰記. jb. 2 vols.
ms. Ebisawa, Naikaku.

1125 Yaso Shimatsuki 耶蘇始末記 (The Beginning and the End of Christianity). jb. 1 v.
ms. Tenri.

1126 Yaso Shūmon Kōhaiki 耶蘇宗門興廢記 (Rise and Fall of Christianity). jb. 1 v.
ms. Tōdai.

1127 Yaso Shūmon Kongenki 耶蘇宗門根元記 (Origins of Christianity). jb. 1 v.
ms. Iwase.

1128 Yaso Shūmon Raichō Jikki 耶蘇宗門來朝實記 (True Account of the Arrival of Christianity in Japan). jb. 1 v.
ms. Kyūdai-Hōka, Waseda.

1129 Yaso Shūmon Raichō Kongenki 耶蘇宗門來朝根元記 (Origins of the Introduction of Christianity). jb. 1 v.
ms. Hatano, Ōsaka, Tenri.

1130 Yaso Shūmon Seikin Taizen 耶蘇宗門制禁大全 (Complete Works on the Prohibition of Christianity). jb.
ms. Ebisawa, Naikaku, Waseda.

1131 Yaso Shūmon Shimatsuki 耶蘇宗門始末記 (The Beginning and the End of Christianity). jb. 1 v.
ms. Seikadō.

1132 Yoshikawa Seishū 吉川青州 (1829–1897)
Yaso Senran Shimatsu 耶蘇煽亂始末 (Settlement of the Agitation by Christians). jb. 1 v.
ms. Ebisawa.

1133 Zokushu Raichō Jikki 賊宗來朝實記 (True Account of the Arrival of the Evil Religion). jb. 1 v.
ms. Hibiya-Kondō, Sophia.

1649

1134 Aleni, Giuglio, SJ. 艾儒略 (1582–1649)
Jōzai Seiki 滌罪正記 *Ti-tsui Cheng-chi* (Sacraments of Confession and Penitence), [n.p.], [n.d.], cb. 4 vols.
cf. Pfister, p. 132.

1135 —— [n.p.], 1849 (道光 29). cb. 1 v., 106f., 23cm.

c. Nagasaki, Tenri.

1136 Aleni, Giuglio, SJ. 艾儒略 (1582–1649)

Tenshu Kōsei Ingi 天主降生引義 *T'ien-chu chiang-sheng Yin-yi* (Introduction to the Incarnation of Our Lord), [Peking], [n.d.]. cb. 1 v., 1, 2, 22, 17f., 27cm.

cf. Pfister, p. 132.
c. Tōhoku-Kano.

1137 —— Shanghai, 1872 (同治 11). cb. 1 v., [2], 17f., 27cm.

c. Seishin.

1138 —— Shanghai, 1922 (民國 11). wb. 1 v.

1139 —— (Dōgen Seisui, v. I).

1650

1140 Brancati, Francisco, S.J. 潘國光 (1607–1671)

Tenkai 天階 *T'ien Chieh* (Steps to Heaven), Shanghai 1650. cb. 1 v.

cf. Pfister, pp. 22 –229.

1141 —— Shanghai 慈母堂, 1871 (同治 10). cb. 1 v., 12f., 16cm.

c. Tenri.

1142 —— Shanghai 1915.

1143 Brancati, Francisco, SJ. 潘國光 (1607–1671)

Tenshu Jikkai Kanron Seiseki 天主十誡勘論聖蹟 *T'ien-chu Shih-chieh Ch'üan-lun Sheng-chi* (Explanation of the Ten Commandaments), Ho-nan 1650 (順治 7). cb. 2 vols., 27cm.

cf. Pfister, p. 228; Jo, pp. 182–183.
c. Hibiya-Ichimura, Seikado.

1144 —— Shanghai 慈母堂, 1869 (同治 8). cb. 2 vols., 26cm.

c. Aoyama, Kyūdai-Bunka, Nagasaki, Seishin.

1145 —— Shanghai 土山灣印書館, 1927 (民國 16). 6th ed. wb. 1 v., 16, 154p., 19cm.

c. Ebisawa.

1146 Matsunaga Teitoku 松永貞德 (1571–1653)

Teitoku Bunshū 貞德文集 (Collection of the Letters of Teitoku), Kyōto [1650?]. jb. 2 vols., 29cm.

note: Refers to various fields of exotism.
cf. Shimmura-Namban I, pp. 455–457; Samura, p. 1427.
c. Shōkōkan, Ueno.
ms. Kyōdai.

1146b —— (Kaihyō Sōsho, v. IV).

1147 Smogolenski, Johan Nicolas, SJ. 穆尼各 (1611–1656)

Tembu Shingen Jimmeibu 天歩眞原人命部 *T'ien-pu Chen-yüan Jen-ming-pu* (Outline of Astrology).

cf. Pfister, p. 265; Jo, p. 386.

1148 —— (Shuzankaku Sōsho).

1651

1149 Mizuno Katsunari 水野勝成 (1564–1651)

Mizuno Hyūganokami Oboegaki 水野日向守覺書 (Memorandum of Mizuno Hyūganokami).

1150 —— (Buhen Sōsho, v. IV).

1151 —— (Shiseki Shūran).

1152 —— (Kaitei Shiseki Shūran, v. XVI).

1153 —— (Settsu Sōsho).

1652

1154 Fujiwara Issa 藤原一蓑

Kyūshū Shōunki 九州紹運記 or Kyūshū Heiranki 九州兵亂記 (History of Kyūshū), 1652 (慶安 5). jb. 1 v.

1155 —— (Shiseki Shūran).

1156 —— (Zoku Gunsho Ruijū, v. DC. XLVII).

1157 Lubelli, Andre Giovanni, SJ. 陸安德 (1610–1683)

Zensei Fukujū Seiro 善正福終正路 *Shan-cheng Fu-chung Cheng-Lu* (Right Way of Good Life and Death), [n p.], 1652 (順治 9). cb. 2 vols.

cf. Pfister, pp. 331–332; Jo, pp. 65–66.

1158 —— Peking 1794 (乾隆 59).

1159 —— Peking 1852 (咸豐 2). cb. 1 v., 14f., 22cm.

c. Nagasaki, Tenri.

1160 —— Shanghai 慈母堂, 1912 (民國 1). wb. 1 v.

1161 —— Peking 始胎大堂, 1927 (民國 16). cb. 1 v., 2, 73f., 15cm.

c. Tohoku.

1162 Matsunaga Teitoku 松永貞德 (1571–1653)

Nagusamegusa 慰草 (Literary Criticism of the *Tsurezuregusa*), 1652 (承應 1). jb. 8 vols

cf. Shinmura-Namban I, pp. 104–105; Samura, p. 1520.

1654

1163 Longobardi, Nicolas, SJ. 龍華民 (1559–1654)

Reikon Dōtaisetsu 靈魂道體說 *Ling-hun Tao-t'i Shuo* (Dissertation regarding the

Substance of the Soul), [n.p.], [n.d.].
cf. Pfister, p. 65; Jo, pp. 205–207.
1164 —— Shanghai 土山灣印書館, 1918 (民國 7). cb. 1 v., 1, 2, 1, 9f., 20cm.
c. Tenri.

1655

1165 Kumazawa Banzan 熊澤蕃山 (1619–1691)
Daigaku Wakumon 大學或問, or Keizaiben 經濟辯 (Argument of the Daigaku or Economics), Edo [Tokyo] 凌宵閣, 1788 (天明 8). jb. 2 vols., 27cm.
cf. Kokushi, p. 180.
c. Ebisawa, Hibiya-Kaga, Kariya, Waseda.
note: The author wrote this work in 1655 (明曆 1).
1166 —— (Chūko Sōsho).
1167 —— (Nippon Bunko, v. V.).
1168 —— (Nippon Keizai Sōsho, v. I).
1169 —— (Nippon Keizai Taiten, v. III).
1170 —— (Kinsei Shakai Keizai Gakusetsu Taikei, v. VII).
1171 —— (Nippon Shisō Tōsō Shiryō, v. VI).
1172 —— (Banzan Zenshū, v. III).
1173 —— tr. into English by Galen M. Fisher, "Daigaku Wakumon by Kumazawa Banzan" (*Transactions of the Asiatic Society of Japan, Second Series,* v. XVI), Tokyo 1938.

1656

1174 Mukai Genshō 向井元松 (1609–1677)
Kenkon Benzetsu 乾坤辯說 (Criticism of Western Astronomy), 1656 (明曆 2). jb. 4 vols.
cf. Ebisawa-Namban, pp. 90–113; Samura, p. 610.
ms. Gakushūin, Kyōdai, Shōkōkan, Tōhoku-Kano, Ueno-Shirai.
1175 —— (Bummei Genryū Sōsho, v. II).
1176 * Shidai Zensho 四大全書 (Four Elements), compiled by Nankei Dōjin 南溪道人, jb. 4 vols.
note: Abridged from *Kenkon Benzetsu* (n. 1174).
orig. ms. Kyūdai.
1177 Mukai Genshō 向井元升 (1609–1677)
Benzetsu Namban Unkisho 辯說南蠻運氣書 (Criticism of Western Astrology). jb. 4 vols.
cf. Ebisawa-Namban, p. 109.
ms. Gakushiin, the Okōchis.

1178 Smogolenski, Johan Nicolas, SJ. 穆尼閣 (1611–1656)
Tengaku Kaitsū 天學會通 *T'ien-hsüeh Hui-t'ung* (Unity of Chinese and Western Astronomy).

cf. Pfister, p. 265.
1179 * Rekigaku Kaitsū 曆學會通 *Li-hsüeh Hui-t'ung* (Unity of Calendar Science), annotated by Heki Hōso 蘗鳳祚 *Hsüeh Feng-tso*. cb. 1 v.
note: An abridged manuscript of the *Tengaku Kaitsū.*
ms. Waseda-Ogura.

1657

1180 Mukai Genshō 向井元升 (1609–1677)
Chishihen 知恥篇 (Know Shame), 1657 (明曆 3). jb. 3 vols.
note: Contains a criticism of Buddhism and Christianity.
cf. Shimmura-Namban I, pp. 406–409.
ms. Kyōdai, Shōkōkan.
1181 —— (Kaihyō Sōsho, v. I.).

Persecution at Kōri 郡 in Ōmura, 1657

1182 Ōmura ni Jashūmon Okoru Koto 大村ニ邪宗門起事 (Origin of the Evil Religion in Ōmura). jb. 1 v.
ms. Nagasaki.

1183 Ōmura Kenmonjū 大村見聞集 (Records of the Ōmuras).
1184 —— pr. and annotated by Yamaguchi Takusuke 山口宅助 in his *Ōmurahan Ko-Kirishitan Kenkyū Shiryō,* Tokyo 1937 (昭和12).

1659

1185 Gravina, Jeronimo de, SJ. 賈宜睦 (1603–1662)
Teiseihen 提正篇 *T'i-cheng-p'ien* (Catholic Doctrine), compiled by Jeronimo de Gravina and Ludovico Buglio, S.J., [n.p.], 1659 (順治 16). cb. 6 vols.
cf. Pfister, p. 245.
1186 —— Shanghai 慈母堂, 1870 (同治 9). cb. 3 vols., 26cm.
c. Nagasaki, Tenri, Waseda.

1187 Hori Seii 堀正意 (1585–1642)
Chōsen Seibatsuki 朝鮮征伐記 (Notes on the Conquest of Korea), 1659 (萬治 2). jb. 9 vols.
note: Contains Hideyoshi's Letters to the Governor of Philippine Is. in 1591.
cf. Matsuzaki Minoru 松崎實, *Nippon 26 Seijin Junkyōki,* Tokyo 1931, pp. 13–14; Murakami Naojirō 村上直次郎, *Ikoku Ōfuku Shokanshū,* Tokyo 1929, pp. 29–34; Samura, p. 1430; Kokushi, p. 204.

1661

1188 Brancati, Francisco, SJ. 潘國光 (1607–1671)

Tenshinkai-ka 天神會課 *T'ien-shen-hui-k'o* (Lesson for the Congregation of Angels), 1661 (順治 18). cb. 1 v.
cf. Pfister, p. 229.

1189 —— Shanghai 1861 (咸豐 11). cb. 1 v. 79f., 23cm.
c. Nagasaki, Seishin.

1190 —— Shanghai 1882 (光緒 8). cb. 1 v.
1191 —— Shanghai 1914 (民國 3). wb. 1 v.

1192 Inoue Masashige 井上政重 (1585–1661)
Kirishitoki 契利斯督記 (Official Records on Christianity).
cf. Tenri-Jap. II, p. 86.
ms. Kyōdai, Naikaku, Shiryō, Tenri.
phot. Cieslik, Ebisawa.

1193 —— (Zokuzoku Gunsho Ruijū, v. XII).
1194 —— (Kirishitan Bunko, v. II).
1195 —— tr. into German by G. Voss and H. Cieslik, SJ. in the *Kirishitoki und Sayō-Yoroku,* Tokyo 1940.
1196 * Tembun Batsuroku 天文末録 (Records since the Tembun Era). jb. 2 vols.
note: Different version of the *Kirishitoki.*
1197 —— (Sokkyohen, vv. XI–XII).
1198 —— abridged (Haja Sōsho, v. I).

1199 Jashūmon Sensaku no Sho 邪宗門穿鑿之書 (Examining the Evil Religion). jb. 1 v.
ms. Ōtani.

1200 Kempō Hiroku, Kirishitan Shūmon Aratame no Koto 憲法秘録, 切支丹宗門改之事 (Secret Record of Laws Inquisition of Christians). jb. 1 v.
ms. Waseda.

1201 Kirishitan Aratameyaku Densho narabini Oboegaki 切支丹改役傳書幷覺書 (Memorials of the Christian Inquisition). jb. 1 v.
ms. Akita-Higashiyama.

1202 Kirishitan Kankei Kōgi Gojōmoku 切支丹關係公儀御條目 (Decrees of the Shogunate Government regarding Christians). jb. 1 v.
ms. Ōtani.

1203 Kirishitan On'aratame Ichijō 切支丹御改一條 (Documents on the Inquisition of Christians). jb. 1 v.
ms. Byakurenji, Ebisawa, Shiryō.

1204 Kirishitan On'okite Jōjō 切支丹御掟條々 (Laws Regarding Christians). jb. 1 v.
ms. Ebisawa, Seishin.

1205 Kirishitan Shūmon Maegaki 幾利支丹宗門前書 (Preface to the Christian Examination). jb. 1 v.

ms. Kyūdai-Hōka.

1206 Kirishitan Shūmon no Mono e Fumase-ita-men narabini Oranda Kotoba 切支丹宗門之者ヘ踏せ板面並阿蘭陀詞 (The Fumie used for Discovering Christians with a Glossary of Dutch Words). jb. 1 v.
ms. Tōyō-Iwasaki.

1207 Kirishitan Shūmon On-aratame ni tsuki On-kakimono no Koto 切支丹宗門御改ニ付御書物之事 (Notes on the Inquisition of the Christian Religion). jb. 1 v.
ms. Sophia.

1208 Ofune-Bugyō Kokoroe, Shūmon Kokkoroe Fumie Gomen-an 御船奉行心得宗門心得踏繪御免案 (Plan for Abolishing the Fumie Test for Seamen). jb. 1 v.
ms. Hibiya-Kondō.

1209 Saitō Sadatsune 齋藤貞常
Shūmon-aratame Kaisonki 宗門改廻村記 (Record of an Itinerant Magistrate checking on the Suppression of Christianity).
1210 —— (Senshū Sōsho, v. V).

1211 Shūmonkata Kyūki 宗門方舊記 (Old Records of the Christian Inquisition Office). jb. 1 v.
ms. Matsūra, Shiryō.

1212 Maezono Meibu 前園鳴武
Min Shin Tōki 明清鬪記 (Report of the War between the Ming and the Ch'ing), Osaka 柏原屋, 1661 (寛文 1). jb. 10 vols., 26cm.
c. Ikeda, Naikaku, Tōdai-Nanki, Ueno.

Persecution in the Provinces of Mino and Owari (1661–1697)

1213 Binō Haguri Kemmonjū 尾濃葉栗見聞集 (Recollections of Mino and Owari Provinces). jb.
1214 —— (Mino Daishiryō Bunko, v. III).
1215 Inuyama Kujiki 犬山舊事記 (Old Record on the Arrest of Christians at Inuyama). jb. 1 v.
1216 —— mimeogr. pr. and annotated by Shibata Ryō 柴田亮, Tokyo 1958 (昭和 33).

1217 Sha Chōen 謝肇淵 *Hsieh Chao-yüan*
Gozasso 五雜組 *Wu-tsa-tsu* (Collection of Essays), [n.p.], [n. d.]. cb. 8 vols., 25cm.
cf. Tenri-Jap. II, p. 22;
c. Naikaku, Oda, Tenri, Tōhoku-Kanō.
1218 —— [n.p.], [n.d.]. cb. 12 vols., 26cm.
c. Hibiya-Ichimura, Ueno.
1219 —— Kyōto 玉枝軒, 1661 (寛文 1). jb. 16 vols., 27cm.

c. Hibiya-Kaga, Kompira, Tenri, Tōdai-Nanki, Ueno, Waseda.

1220 —— Kyōto 梅松軒, 1795 (寛政 7). jb. 8 vols., 23cm.

c. Waseda.

1221 —— Kyōto 小川庄兵衛, 1822 (文政 5). jb. 8 vol., 24cm.

c. Seishin, Tōhoku-Kanō.

1221b —— Shanghai 中華書局, 1959 (民国 48). wb. 2 vols., 19cm.

c. Rikkyo.

1662

1222 Okumura Yasuyuki 奥村保之
Jigo Keishiroku 事語繼志録 (Life of Matsudaira Nobutsuna 松平信綱, 1596–1662). jb. 2 vols.
1223 —— (Zokuzoku Gunsho Ruijū, v. III).
1224 —— (Nippon Ijin Genkō Shiryō, v. XXIII).

1225 Oshima Toyonaga 大島豊長
Nobutsunaki 信綱記 (Life of Matsudaira Nobutsuna). jb. 1 v.
cf. Kokushi, p. 250.
1226 —— (Kaitei Shiseki Shūran, v. XXVI).

1227 Suzuki Shōsan 鈴木正三 (1579–1655)
Ha-Kirishitan 破吉利支丹 (Attack against Christianity), Kyōto 小川柳枝軒, 1662 (寛文 2). jb. 1 v., 19f., 26cm.
cf. Tenri-Jap. II, p. 84; Samura, p. 1626.
c. Aoyama, Iwase, Jinshu, Jingū, Kōhejō, Ōtani, Seishin, Sophia, Shiryō, Tenri, Tōkyoiku, Tōyō-Iwasaki.
ms. Hatano.
1228 —— Kyōto 山田平左衛門, 1662 (寛文 2). jb. 1 v., 19f., 26cm.
c. Waseda.
1229 —— Kyōto 堤六左衛門, 1662 (寛文 2). jb. 1 v., 19f., 27cm.
c. Ebisawa, Taishō.
ms. Tōyōdai.
1230 —— (Sokkyohen, v. XV).
1231 —— (Nippon Shisō Tōsō Shiryō, v. X).
1232 —— (Kirishitan Shiryō).
1233 —— (Zemmon Hōgo Zenshū).
1234 * Shinkoku Ha-Kirishitan 新刻破鬼理死端 (New Edition of the Ha-Kirishitan), Kyoto 丁字屋, 1662 (寛文 2). jb. 1 v., 19f., 26cm.
c. Tōhoku-Kanō.
1235 * Kōsei Shinkoku Ha-Kirishitan 校正新刻破鬼理死端 (New and Revised Edition of the Ha-Kirishitan), Tokyo 須原屋, 1889

(明治 22). jb. 1 v., 17f., 26cm.
c. Ebisawa, Kyōto, Sophia, Tenri, Waseda.

1664

1236 Emura Sensai 江村專齋 (1565--1664)
Rōjin Zatsuwa 老人雑話 (Story of an Old Man), jb. 2 vols.
cf. Kokushi, p. 332.
ms. Dōshisha, Hibiya-Kaga, Ikeda, Iwase, Keiō, Naikaku, Ujiie, Waseda.
1237 —— (Okinagusa).
1238 —— (Koshindō Sōsho).
1239 —— (Shiseki Shūran).
1240 —— (Zuihitsu Bungaku Senshū, v. XI).
1241 —— (Zoku Kokumin Bunko).
1242 —— (Kaitei Shiseki Shūran, v. X).

1243 Hō Ichi 方以智 *Fang I-chih*
Butsuri Shōshiki 物理小識 *Wu-li Hsiao-shih* (Introduction to Physics), 宛平春音堂 [1664, 康熙 3]. cb. 6 vols., 25cm.
cf. Miyazaki, p. 740.
c. Kyōdai-Bungakubu, Kyūdai-Butsuri, Naikaku, Tōhoku-Sugaku, Ueno, Waseda.
ms. Naikaku, Shōryōbu.
1244 —— [n.p.], 1884 (光緒 10). wb. 1 v.
c. Fujita.

1245 Maki Jōdaiyu 牧丞太夫
Hosokawa Tadaoki Gunkōki 細川忠興軍功記 (Hosokawa Tadaoki's Military Merits), 1664 (寛文 4). jb.
cf. Kokushi, p. 286; Samura, p. 1800.
1246 —— (Zoku Koshindō Sōsho).
1247 —— (Shiseki Shūran).
1248 —— (Kaitei Shiseki Shūran, v. XV).
1249 —— (Zoku Gunsho Ruijū, v. DXCII).

1250 Sakuma 佐久間
Goningumichō Maegaki 五人組帳前書 (Law of Goningumi, the smallest feudal unit of Government), compiled by Sakuma, [n.p.], 1664 (寛文 4). jb. 1 v., [48]f., 30cm.
cf. Hubert Cieslik, S. J., "Die Goningumi im Dieste der Christenüberwachung" (*Monumenta Nipponica*, v. VII), Tōkyō 1951, pp. 102–155.
c. Ebisawa, Tōhoku.

1251 Goningumi Idōben 五人組異同辯 (On the Goningumi).
1252 —— (Kinsei Chihō Keizai Shiryō, v. III).

1253 Shō Shisei 鐘始聲 *Chung Shih-sheng*
Byakujashū 闢邪集 *P'i-hsieh-chi* (Collection of Anti-Christian Works), [n.p.], [n.d.], cb. 2 vols.

contents:

1254 —— construed from Chinese into Jap. by Kiyū Dōjin 杞憂道人, Edo [Tokyo] 緣山, 1861 (文久 1). jb. 2 vols., 26cm.

c. Aoyama (v. I only), Ebisawa, Hatano, Hibiya, Jinshū, Kariya, Kompira, Kyōto, Kyūdai-Bunka, Kichū, Naikaku, Nagasaki Museum, Ōkada, Osaka, Ōtani, Shōryōbu, Sophia, Taishō, Tenri, Tōdai, Tōhoku, Sukeno, Ueno, Waseda.

1255 Shō Shinshi 鐘振之 *Chung Chen-chih* Tengaku Ryōchō 天學兩徵 *T'ien-hsüeh Liang-cheng* (Criticism of Catholicism).

contains: Tengaku Shochō 天學初徵 *T'ien-hsüeh Ch'u-cheng.* Tengaku Saichō 天學再徵 *T'ien hsüeh Tsai-cheng.*

ms. Tōhoku-Sūgaku (v. I only), Tōyō-Iwasaki.

1256 —— construed from Chinese into Jap. by Akamatsu Renjō 赤松連城, Kyōto 文昌堂, 1878 (明治 11). jb. 1 v., 23f., 19cm.

c. Aoyama, Ryūkoku, Seishin.

1257 —— Kyōto 文昌堂, 1878 (明治 11). jb. 1v., [1], 21f., 23cm.

c. Waseda.

1258 —— (Byakujashū, v. I).

1259 Tsūyō 通容 *T'ung-jung* Gendō Byakujasetsu 原道闢邪説 *Yüan-tao P'i-hsieh Shuo* (Disputation against Christianity). cb. 2 vols.

ms. Tōhoku.

1260 —— (Seichō Hajashū).

1261 —— (Byakujashū, v. II).

1262 Yō Kōsen 楊光先 *Yang Kuang-hsien* Byakujaron 闢邪論 *P'i-hsieh Lun* (Against Christianity), [n.p.] 海社 [n.d.]. cb. 1 v., 19f., 26cm.

c. Tenri.

1263 —— (Futokushi).

1264 —— construed from Chinese into Jap. by Kiyū Dōjin 杞憂道人, Edo [Tokyo] 緣山, 1868 (慶應 4). jb. 1 v., 32f., 23cm.

c. Aoyama, Hatano, Kyūdai-Butsuri, ICU, Ōtani, Seishin, Sophia, Narita, Taishō, Tenri, Waseda.

1265 * Hekijaron 劈邪論 (Against Christianity).

1266 —— (Heikija Kijitsu, v. I).

1267 Yō Kōsen 楊光先 *Yang Kuang-hsien* Futokui 不得已 *Pu-te-yi* (Unsuppressable Reactions against Christianity), Peking 1664 (康熙 3). cb. 2 vols.

cf. Jo, pp. 235–236.

contents: Seichū Jakyō-jō 請誅邪教狀 *Ch'ing-chu Hsieh-*

chiao Chuang. Byakujaron 闢邪論 *P'i-hsieh-lun,* and etc.

1268 —— Peking 1929 (民國 18). cb. 2 vols., 27cm.

c. Tōhoku, Waseda.

1665

1269 Asai Ryōi 淺井了意 (1640–1709) Kyōsuzume 京雀 (Descriptive Geography of Kyoto), Kyōto 山田市郎兵衛, 1665 (寛文 5). jb. 7 vols.

cf. Kokushi, p. 68.

c. Daitokyu, Kyōto, Tōyō-Iwasaki, Ueno.

1270 —— (Kyōto Sōsho, v. VVII).

1271 —— (Kinsei Bungei Sōsho, v. I).

1272 Buglio, Ludovico, SJ. 利類思 (1606–1682) Futokui-ben 不得已辯 *Pu-te-yi Pien* (In Defense of the *Futokui*), Peking, 1665 (康熙 4). cb. 1 v.

cf. Pfister, p. 241; Jo, pp. 235–236.

1273 —— [n.p.], [n.d.]. cb. 1 v., 2 [2], 50f., 24cm.

c. Nichidai-Hayashi.

1274 —— [Shanghai?], 1847 (道光 27). cb. 1 v., 2, 2, 50, [1]f., 27cm.

c. Aoyama, Hibiya-Ichimura, Tenri.

1275 —— Shanghai, 1926 (民国 15). wb. 1 v.

1276 Matsushita Kenrin 松下見林 (1637–1703) Ron'ō Benshō 論奥辯證 (Human Geography of the West), 1665 (寛文 5). jb. 3 vols., 28cm.

cf. Kaikoku, pp. 298–299.

c. Tenri.

1666

1277 Adam Schall von Bell, Johan, SJ. 湯若望 (1591–1666) Kakō Ketsuyō 火攻挈要 *Huo-kung Ch'i-yao* (Principles of Shooting Guns).

1278 —— (Kaizansenkan Sōsho, v. XXXV).

1279 Echū 恵中 Kaijō Monogatari 海上物語 (Tales of the Sea), Kyōto 堤六左衛門 1666 (寛文 6). jb. 2 vols., 26cm.

c. Ebisawa, Kyōdai-Bunka, Naikaku.

1280 —— another ed., [Kyōto] 山本平左衛門, 1666 (寛文 6). jb. 2 vols., 26cm.

cf. Tenri-Jap. II, p. 167.

c. Tenri.

1281 —— (Kaihyō Sōsho, v. V).

1282 Oranda Jōkokubun 荷蘭上告文

(Report of the Captain of the Dutch Factory). 1666–1826 (寛文 6 – 文政 9). jb. 2 vols. ms. Gakushuin.

1283 —— pr. and annotated by Itazawa Takeo 板澤武雄, *Oranda Fūsetsugaki no Kenkyū*, Tokyo 1937 (昭和 12).

1284 Oranda Fūsetsugaki 和蘭風説書 (Report of the Captain of the Dutch Factory), 1827–1856 (文政 10–安政 3).
ms. Nagasaki.

1285 Oranda Kokumitsu 和蘭告密 (Secret Report of the Captain of the Dutch Factory), 1833–1852 (天保 4–嘉永 5). jb. 1 v.
cf. Asahi, p. 42.
ms. Yūshūkan 遊就館 (Tōkyō)

1286 Tsurunoya Kiuyemon 鶴屋喜右衛門

Amakusa no Shirō 天草の四郎, or Amakusa Monogatari あまくさ物がたり, (Shirō Amakusa or the Story of Amakusa), [n.p.], 1666 (寛文 6). jb. 1 v., 12, 10f., 9 pl., 14cm.
cf. Tenri-Jap. II, p. 148.
c. Tenri.

1668

1287 Kirishitan Shūmon no Mono Onazukechō, Hosokawa Etchū-no-kami Uchi 切支丹宗門之者御預帳細川越中守内 (List of Imprisoned in the Clan of Hosokawa Etchū-no-kami), 1668–1673 (寛文 8–13). jb. 1 v.
ms. Nagasaki.

1288 Bubun Gokyūki Ruizokubu 部分御舊記類族部 (Regulations governing the Descendants of Christians). jb.
cf. Kamizuma Hiroyuki 上妻博之, *Hosokawahan no Kirishitan*, Yatsushiro 1949.
orig. ms. The Hosokawas.

1669

1289 Buglio, Luis, SJ. 利類思 (1606–1682)
Seihō Yōki 西方要記 *Hsi-fang Yao-chi* (Geography of Europe), Peking, 1669 (康熙 8). cb. 1 v.
cf. Pfister, p. 242 ; Jo, p. 299.
ms. Jinshu, Naikaku.

1290 —— (Seishōdo Sōsho).
1291 —— (Shōdai Sōsho, v. VIII).
1292 —— (Gakukai Ruihen).
1293 —— (Shōhōkosai Yoshi Sōsho, v. LV).
1294 —— (Seihō Zatsuwa).
1295 —— repr. by Ono Tadashige 小野忠重, *Mateo Ricci to Shina Kagaku*, Tokyo 1944

(昭和 19). pp. 134–140.
1296 Seihō Zatsuwa 西邦雜話 (Chatting about Western Countries). jb.
note: Contains Vagnoni's *Tenshu Jikkai Geryaku* (n. 569) and Buglio's *Seihō Yōki* (n. 1289).
ms. Tōhoku-Kano.

1670

1297 Shimaya Sadashige 島谷定重 (– 1690)
Anjin no Hō 按針之法 (Navigation), 1670 (寛文 10). jb. 1 v.
cf. Samura, p. 61.
See also, nos. 488–491.

1298 Verbiest, Ferdinand, SJ. 南懐仁 (1623–1688)
Kyōyō Joron 敎要序論 *Chiao-yao Hsü-lun* (Introduction to Doctrine), Peking, 1670 (康熙 9). cb. 1 v., 5, 76f., 26cm.
cf. Pfister, p. 352 ; Jo, pp. 162–163.
c. Tenri.

1299 —— [different ed.], Peking, 1670 (康熙 9). cb. 1v., 2, 24f., 23cm.
c. Tohoku-Kano.

1300 —— Shanghai 慈母堂, 1867 (同治 6). cb. 1 v., 2, 5, 67f., 24cm.
c. Kyūdai-Bunka, Nagasaki, Seikadō, Seishin, Tenri.

1301 * Kyōyō Sūgen, fu, Yaso Ju'nan Kiryaku 敎要芻言, 附, 耶蘇受難紀略 *Chiao-yao Tsou-yen, fu Yeh-su Shou-nan Chi-lüeh* (Fundamental Doctrine with an Addendum on the Passion of Christ), tr. into the Mandarin language by Valentin Garnier, S.J. 倪懐綸, Shanghai, [n.d.]. cb. 1 v.
cf. Pfister, p. 352.
c. Seikadō.

1302 Verbiest, Ferdinand, SJ. 南懐仁 (1623–1688)
Zen'aku Hō Ryakusetsu 善惡報略説 *Shan-o-pao Lüeh-shuo* (Short Essay on the Retribution of Good and Evil), Peking 1670 (康熙 9). cb. 1 v.
cf. Pfister, p. 353.

1303 —— Shanghai 慈母堂, 1869 (同治 8). cb. 1 v., 13f., 24cm.
c. Tenri.

1304 Yamawaki Dōen 山脇道圓
Orandaryū Gekasho 阿蘭陀流外科書 (Surgery of the Dutch School), [Kyōto], 1670 (寛文 10). jb. 3 vols.
c. Kyōdai.
ms. Ōtsuki.

1671

1305 Kawabuchi Kyūzaemon 川淵久左衛門

47

Ruson Oboegaki 呂宋覺書 (Memorandum regarding Luzon), 1671 (寛文 11). jb. 1 v.
cf. Shimmura-Namban, pp. 477–478.
ms. Dōshisha, Ebisawa.
1306 —— (Kaihyō Sōsho, v. VI).

1672

1307 Tō Kōsei 鄧孝成 *Teng Shiao-ch'eng*
Meika Shikan Nishū 名家詩觀二集 *Ming-chia Shih-kuan Erh-chi* (Second Series in a selected Collection of Famous Poets), 1672 (康熙 11). cb. 14 vols.
note: Specifically outlawed in 1702.

1308 Tsurezuregusa Kirai Hyōban 徒然草嫌評判 (Criticism of the Contemporary Scene in the Manner of the *Tsurezuregusa*), [n p.], (1672, 寛文 12). jb. 2 vols., 29cm.
c. Ueno.

1673

1309 Lubelli, Andre Giovanni, SJ. 陸安德 (1610–1683)
Shimpuku Jikishi 眞福直指 *Chen-fu Chih-chih* (Intsruction in True Happiness), [n. p.], 1673 (康熙 12). cb. 2 vols.
cf. Pfister, p. 331; Jo, pp. 67–68.
c. Nagasaki.
1310 —— Peking 1738 (乾隆 3). cb. 2 vols.
1311 —— Shanghai 慈母堂, 1873 (同治 12). cb. 1 v., 49f., 20cm.
c. Tenri.

1312 Seikyō Kanryaku 聖教鑑略 *Sheng-chiao Chien-lüeh* (Fundamental Catholic Doctrine), [n.p.], [n.d.]. cb. 2 vols.
note: Original unknown. This seems to be a reprint of the *Seikyō Kanyō* 聖教簡要 *Sheng-chiao Chien-yao* by Louis Buglio, S. J. or the *Seikyō Ryakusetsu* 聖教略説 *Sheng-chiao Lüeh-shuo* by Andrea Giovanni Lubelli, S. J. published in Canton, 1674.
cf. Pfister pp. 241, 331.
1312b —— Shanghai 1860 (咸豊 10). cb. 2 vols. 24cm.
c. Seishin (v. II only).

1313 Suzuki Masanori 鈴木政證
Itakura Shigenori-kō Kōjōki 板倉重矩公行常記 or Shigenori Jōkōki 重矩常行記 (Life of Itakura Shigenori). jb. 1 v.
note: Itakura Shigenori (1616–1673), a famous governor of Kyōto.
ms. Naikaku.
1314 —— (Nippon Ijin Genkō Shiryō, v. XXIII).
1315 * Shigenori-kō Gogyōjōroku 重矩公御行狀録. jb. 1 v.
ms. Hibiya.

1316 Verbiest, Ferdinand, SJ. 南懷仁 (1623–1688)
Gishōzu 儀象圖 *Yi-hsiang-t'u* (Explanation of Instruments used in Astrology), Peking 1673 (康熙 12). cb. 2 vols.
cf. Pfister, p. 354.
c. Kyōdai-Kikai.

1317 Yamaga Sokō 山鹿素行 (1622–1685)
Buke Jiki 武家事紀 (Records on Military Clans), 1673 (寛文 13). jb. 58 vols.
cf. Kokushi, p. 269.
ms. Naikaku, Tōdai.
1318 —— pr. by the Sokōkai 素行會, Tokyo 1915 (大正 4). wb. 3 vols.

1319 Yamamoto Kuzaemon 山本九左衛門
Shimabara Ikusa Monogatari 島原軍物語 (Story of the Shimabara Rebellion), 1673 (寛文 13). jb. 4 vols.
ms. Iwase, Kyūdai-Bunka, Nagasaki.
1320 —— [n.p.], 1704 (寳永 1). jb. 4 vols.
c. Tōdai-Nanki.

1674

1321 Verbiest, Ferdinand, SJ. 南懷仁 (1623–1688)
Kon'yo Gaiki 坤輿外紀 *K'un-yü Wai-chi* (Outline of World Geography), Peking, [n. d.]. cb. 1 v.
cf. Pfister, p. 356.
ms. Akioka, Kyūdai, Naikaku, Nampo, Ōtsuki, Ueno-Shirai.
1322 —— (Tengaku Shokan).
1323 —— (Geien Kunka).
1324 —— (Setsurei, v. XIV).
1325 —— (Ryūi Hisho).
1326 —— (Keiho Gūhitsu).
1327 —— (Sōsho Shūsei, v. I).
1328 —— repr. by Ono Tadashige 小野忠重, *Mateo Ricci to Shina Kagaku,* Tokyo 1944 (昭和 29), pp. 125–133.
1329 —— construed from Chinese into Jap. by Matsumura Genkō 松村元綱. jb. 1 v.
ms. Miyagi.
1330 —— construed from Chinese into Jap. by Matsumura Sekō 松村世綱, jb. 1 v.
ms. Naikaku.
1331 —— construed from Chinese into Jap. by Ozawa Michishige 小澤道茂, jb. 1 v.
1332 * Kon'yo Gaiki Yakuge 坤輿外紀譯解 (Translation of the *Kon'yo Gaiki*), by Jōhoku Seikei 城北清溪, Edo [Tokyo], 1852 (嘉永 5). jb. 2 vols., 23cm.
cf. Kaikoku, pp. 154–155.
c. Akioka, Okada, Ueno-Shirai.

1333 Verbiest, Ferdinand, SJ. 南懷仁 (1623–1688)

Kon'yo Zenzu 坤輿全圖 *K'un-yü Ch'üan-t'u* (The World Map), Peking 1674 (康熙 13). 1 sheet.
cf. Pfister, p. 355; Jo, p. 318.
ms. K. Miyake.
1334 —— Seoul 1860 (咸豐 10).
c. Tokyōiku.

1335 Verbiest, Ferdinand, SJ. 南懷仁 (1623–1688)

Kon'yo Zusetsu 坤輿圖說 *K'un-yü T'u-shuo* (Explanation of the World Map), Peking 1674 (康熙 13). cb. 2 vol.
cf. Pfister, p. 355; Jo, pp. 318–321.
ms. Akioka, Naikaku, Tenri.
1336 —— (Shikai, v. XKII).

1337 Verbiest, Ferdinand, SJ. 南懷仁 (1623–1688)

Reidai Gishōshi 靈臺儀象志 *Ling-t'ai Yi-hsiang Chih* (Instruments of Astronomy), Peking 內府, 1674 (康熙 13). cb. 16 vols.
cf. Pfister, pp. 353–354; Jo, pp. 465–469.
c. Naikaku, Tenri.
ms. Ebisawa (abridged ms.), Gakushiin, Hazama, Kyōdai, Seikadō, Tōhoku-Kanō, Tenri.
1338 * Reidai Gishōshi Wage 靈臺儀象志 和解 (Japanese Translation of the *Reidai Gishōshi),* tr. by Honda Toshiaki 本多利明. jb. 1 v.
orig. ms. Naikaku.

1339 Verbiest, Ferdinand, SJ. 南懷仁 (1623–1688)

Shichiki Zusetsu 七奇圖說 *Ch'i-ch'i T'u-shuo* (Seven Wonders), Peking 1674 (康熙 13). cb. 1 v.
note: Appendix to Verbiest's *Kon'yo Zusetsu* (n. 1335).
ms. Naikaku.
1340 —— manuscripted and annotated by Matsumura Genkō 松村元綱. jb. 1 v.
ms. Miyagi.
1341 —— (Gusho Shinshi).
1342 —— (Chigaku Kyoyō).

1675

1343 Chiara, Giuseppe, SJ. 岡本三右衛門 (1602–1685)

Okamoto San'uemon Hikki 岡本三右衛門 筆記, or Okamoto San'uemon Mōshiage 岡本三右衛門申上 (Notes by Okamoto San'-uemon), 1675 (延寶 3). jb. 1 v.
contents: 1. Kirishitan susumuru Kokoro-ire no Koto 切支丹勸る心入之事.
 2. Shinajina no Gakumon no Koto 品々之 學文之事.
ms. Naikaku, Tōyōdai.
1344 —— (Kirishitoki, v. II, kept in the

Lib. of Congress, USA.).
1345 —— (Kirishitoki, v. III, kept in the Tenri Central Lib.).
1346 —— pr. and annotated by Hubert Cieslik, SJ., *Kirishitan no Gakkō ni okeru Humanism* (Daigaku to Humanism), Tokyo 1953 (昭和 28).
1347 —— pr. and annotated, Ebisawa-Namban, pp. 18–23.

1348 Couplet, Philippe, SJ. 柏應理 (1624–1692)

Shimatsu Shinron 四末眞論 *Szu-mo Chen-lun* (True Doctrine for the Four Novissimas), Peking 敬一堂, 1675 (康熙 14). cb. 1 v.
cf. Pfister, p. 310.
1349 —— Shungkiang 共樂堂, 1825 (道光 5). cb. 1 v., 36f., 24cm.
c. Aoyama, Hibiya-Ichimura, Tenri.
1350 —— Shanghai, 1925 (民國 14). wb. 1 v.

1351 Kumazawa Banzan 熊澤蕃山 (1619–1691)

Shūgi Washo 集義和書 (Political Essay), [Kyōto] 1675 (延寶 3) jb. 10 vols., 27cm.
cf. Kokushi, p. 133.
c. Ikeda, Kariya, Keiō, Kyūdai, Sonkeikaku, Tō-hoku-Kanō, Waseda.
1352 —— Kyōto 森島吉兵衛, [n.d.]. jb. 5 vols., 26cm.
c. Hibiya-Kaga.
1353 —— (Nippon Rinri Ihen, v. I).
1354 —— (Yūhōdō Bunko).
1355 —— abridged (Nippon Keizai Sō-sho, v. XXXIII).
1356 —— abridged (Bushidō Sōsho, v. I).
1357 —— abridged (Sekai Daishisō Zen-shū, v. LIV).
1358 —— abridged (Nippon Keizai Tai-ten, v. LI).
1359 —— abridged (Nippon Shisō Tōsō Shiryō, v. VI).
1360 —— (Kinsei Shakai Keizai Gaku-setsu Taikei, v. VII).
1361 —— abridged (Dai-Nippon Shisō Zenshū, v. II).
1362 —— (Banzan Zenshū, v. I).

1363 Yū Shiroku 游子六 *Yu Tze-liu.*

Tenkei Wakumon 天經或問 *T'ien-ching Huo-wen* (Introduction to Astronomy), Peking 1675 (康熙 14). cb. 4 vols.
cf. Ebisawa-Namban, pp. 125–130.
c. Naikaku, Tōhoku-Sugaku, Waseda-Ogura.
ms. Jingū, Kyōdai, Naikaku, Tenri.
1364 —— construed from Chinese into

Jap. by Nishikawa Seikyū 西川正休, Edo [Tokyo] 松葉軒, 1730 (享保 15). jb. 5 vols., 26cm.

c. Dōshisha, Ebisawa, Imoto, Iwase, Jingū, Jinshu, Kariya, Keiō, Kompira, Kyōdai, Kyūdai-Butsuri, Nagasaki, Shinken, Tenri, Tōhoku-Kanō, Tōhoku-Sugaku, Ueno.

1365 —— Edo [Tokyo], 1794 (寛政 6). jb. 5 vols.

c. Kyōdai, Kanazawa-Saikawa.

1366 —— (Joken Isho, v. X).

1367 * Kōsei Tenkei Wakumon 校正天經或問 (Tenkei Wakumon, Annotated by Shibukawa Sukekata 澁川佑賢, Edo [Tokyo] 1852 (嘉永 5). jb. 2 vols.

ms. Naikaku, Tōhoku-Kanō.

1368 Yu Shiroku 游子六 *Yu Tze-liu*
Tenkei Wakumon Kōshū 天經或問後集 *T'ien-ching Huo-wen Hou-chi* (Second Series of the Tenkei Wakumon). cb. 1 v.

note: Specifically outlawed in 1687.

1369 Jujireki Genkai, Temmon Zukai, Tenkei-Wakumon Bassui 授時暦諺解, 天文圖解, 天經或問抜萃 (Extracts from the *Jujireki Genkai, Temmon Zukai* and *Tenkei Wakumon*). jb. 1 v.

ms. Gakushiin.

1370 Shibukawa Sukekata 澁川佑賢
Kōsei Tenkei Wakumon Kokujikai 校正天經或問國字解 (Japanese Translation of *Tenkei Wakumon*). jb. 10vols.

ms. Naikaku, Tōhoku-Kanō.

1678

1371 Varo, Francisco, OP. 萬濟國
Seikyō Meichō 聖教明徴 *Sheng-chiao Ming-cheng* (Instruction on the Holy Doctrine), Peking 1677 (康熙 16). cb. 2 vols., 27cm.

c. Ebisawa, Kyūdai-Hōka, Naikaku, Nanzan, Seikadō.

1372 Verbiest, Ferdinand, SJ. 南懷仁 (1623–1688)
Kōki Ei'nen Rekihō 康熙永年暦法 *K'ang-hsi Yung-nien Li-fa* (Perpetual Calendar of the K'ang-hsi), Peking 1678 (康熙 17). cb. 32 vols.

cf. Pfister, p. 354.

c. Naikaku.

1680

1373 Hayashi Gahō 林鵞峯 (1618–1680)
Gahō Bunshū 鵞峯文集 (Essays of Gahō). jb. 120 vols.

note: Contains the preface to Hayashi Razan's Yōmei Sambi 陽明攅眉 in v. LXXXI; rejects Christianity, treating it like a theory of 王陽明 *Wang Yang-ming*.

cf. Shimmura-Namban I, p. 113; Samura, p. 387.

1374 Nagasaki Kagami 長崎鏡 (History of Nagasaki), 1680 (延寶 8). jb. 1 v.

1375 —— (Nagasaki Ikyō).

1376 Pinuela, Pedro 石鐸錄 (1649?–1704)
Shokai Mondō 初會問答 *Ch'u-hui Wen-ta* (Catechism), 1680 (康熙 19). cb. 1 v.

1377 —— [n.p.], 1822 (道光 2). cb. 1 v., 3, 37, [1]f., 25cm.

c. Aoyama, Hibiya-Ichimura, Naikaku.

1682

1378 Hizen no Kuni Arima Korō Monogatari 肥前國有馬古老物語 (Tales by an Elder of Arima in Hizen Province), [1682?]. jb. 1 v.

cf. Samura, p. 55.

1379 —— (Shimabaraki, v. II).

1380 —— (Zokuzoku Gunsho Ruijū, v. XII).

1381 Thomas Aquinas, St. (1225–1274)
Chōseigaku-yō 超性學要 *Ch'ao-hsing-hsüeh-yao* (Summa Theologica) tr. by Luis Buglio 利類思, S.J. (1606–82), [n.p.], [n.d.], cb. 34 vols.

cf. Pfister p. 239; Mutō Chōzō 武藤長藏, *Sei Thomas Gencho Summa Theologica no Kanyaku, Chōseigakuyō ni tsuite*, Nagasaki [n.d.].

1382 —— Peking 公教々育聯合會, 1930–32 (民國 19–21). wb. 9 vols., 19cm.

c. Tenri.

1684

1383 Kin Kō 金鉌 *Chin Fung*
Fukken Tsūshi 福建通志 *Fu-chien T'ung-chih* (General Description of the Topography of the Province of Fukien), [n.p.] 1684 (康熙 23). cb. 40 vols., 27cm.

note: Specifically outlawed in 1686.

c. Waseda.

1384 —— 1871 (同治 10). cb. 180 vols.

c. Waseda.

1385 —— (Jūgoshō Tsūshi, vv. XL–XLVII).

1386 Kurokawa Dōyū 黒川道祐 (–1691)
Yōshū Fushi 雍州府志 (Topography of Kyōto), 1864 (貞享 1). jb.

cf. Kokushi, p. 320.

1387 —— (Zokuzoku Gunsho Ruizū, v. VIII).

1388 —— (Kyōto Sōsho, v. XI).

1685

1389 Tōyama Nobuharu 遠山信春
Shimabara Kassenki 島原合戦記 (Story of the Shimabara Rebellion), 1685 (貞享 2). jb. 5 vols.
cf. Samura, p. 930.

1390 * Shimabara Kiroku 島原記録, or Hishū Shimabara Banzokuki 肥州嶋原蕃賊記 (Record of the Shimabara Rebellion in Hizen Province). jb. 2 vols.
cf. Kokushi, p. 131.
ms. Iwase, Naikaku, Sophia, Tenri.

1391 —— (Sokkyohen).

1686

1392 Bungo no Kuni Ōitagun, Katsuragigun Kirishitan Shūmon Shinruigaki 豊後國大分郡葛木郡切支丹宗門親類書 (List of the Families of Christians in Oita and Katsuragi Counties in Bungo), 長崎奉行所, 1686 (貞享 3). jb. 1 v.
orig. ms. Nagasaki.

1393 Bungo no Kuni Ōitagun, Kusugun Kirishitan Shūmon Shinruigaki 豊後國大分郡玖珠郡切支丹宗門親類書 (List of the Families cf Christians in Ōita and Kusu Counties in Bungo), 長崎奉行所, 1686 (貞享 3). jb. 1 v.
orig. ms. Nagasaki.

1394 Kumazawa Banzan 熊澤蕃山 (1619–1691)
Shūgi Gaisho 集義外書 (Political Essay), Kyōto 河南四郎右衛門, 1709 (實永 6). jb. 10 vols., 26cm.
cf. Kokushi, p. 133.
note: The author wrote this in 1686 (貞享 3).
c. Hibiya-Kondō, Jinshu, Keiō, Kompira, Kyūdai, Sonkeikaku, Tōhoku-Kanō, Waseda.

1395 —— Kyōto, 1791 (寛政 3). jb. 8 vols.
c. Waseda.

1396 —— (Nippon Rinri Ihen, v. II).

1397 —— (Banzan Zenshū, v. II).

1398 —— abridged (Bushidō Sōsho, v. I).

1399 —— abridged (Nippon Keizai Sōsho, v. XXXIII).

1400 —— abridged (Nippon Shisō Tōsō Shiryō, v. VI).

1401 —— abridged (Nippon Keizai Taiten, v. LI).

1402 —— abridged (Kinsei Shakai Keizai Gakusetsu Taikei, v. VII).

1403 —— abridged (Dai-Nippon Shisō Zenshū, v. II).

1404 Matsūra Mokusei 松浦黙成
Ikoku Ōraiki 異國往來記 (History of Foreign Intercourse), [n.p.] 雛林書林, 1686

(貞享 3). jb. 2 vols., 23cm.
cf. Samura, p. 79.
c. Hibiya-Kondō.

Books prohibited after 1686

1405 Chi-i 地緯 Ti-wei (Geography).
note: Specifically outlawed in 1686. It is not known to the compiler whether or not it exists.

1406 Chin Kōzan 陳耕山 Ch'en Ching-shan
Sansai Hatsuhi 三才發秘 San-ts'ai Fa-mi (Cosmology). cb. 10 vols.
note: Specifically outlawed in 1699.
c. Naikaku.

1407 Gasshōron 合掌論 Ho-chiang-lun.
note: This is not known to the compiler.

1408 Ko Keishin 胡敬信 Hu Ching-hsin
Dansetsusai-shū 檀雪齋集 T'an-hsüeh-tsai Chi (Collected Works of the T'an-hsüeh-tsai). cb. 40 vols.
note: Specifically outlawed in 1703.

1409 Ō Shiin 應嗣寅 Yin Tz'u-yin
Seiri Taichū 性理大中 Hsing-li Ta-chung, 1686 (康熙 25). cb. 28 vols.

1410 Riku Ōyō 陸應陽 Lu Ying-yang
Zōtei Kōyoki 增訂廣興記 Ts'eng-ting Kuang-yü-chi (Geography of the Empire, revised), revised by Sai Hōei 蔡方炳 Ts'ai Fang-ping, [n.p.], 1686 (康熙 25). cb. 12 vols., 26cm.
note: Specifically outlawed in 1710.
c. Hibiya-Kaga (v. II–III only), Tōyō-Fujita, Waseda.

1411 —— [n.p.], 1802 (嘉慶 7). cb. 12 vols.
c. Naikaku.

1412 Seikei Dōjin 清溪道人 Ching-ch'i Tao-jen
Zenshin Isshi 禪眞逸史 Ts'an-chen Yi-shih. cb. 2 vols.
note: Specifically outlawed in 1700.
c. Naikaku.

1413 Sō Ōsei 宋應星 Sung Ying-hsin
Tenkō Kaibutsu 天工開物 T'ien-kung K'ai-wu (Outline of Natural History). cb. 3 vols.
c. Naikaku.

1414 —— Osaka 菅生堂, 1771 (明和 8). jb. 9 vols.
c. Naikaku.

1415 —— (Keiken Sōsho).

1416 Tan Genshun 譚元春 T'an Yüan-ch'un
Tan Yūka Gasshū 譚友夏合集 T'an Yu-hsia Ho-chi (Collected Works of T'an Yu-hsia). cb. 10 vols.
note: Specifically outlawed in 1701.
c. Naikaku.

1417 Yū Dō 尤侗 *Yu-T'ung* (1618–1704)
Seidō Zenshū 西堂全集 *Hsi-t'ang Ch'üan-chi* (Complete Collection of the Hsi-t'ang), 1686 (康熙 25). cb. 61 vols.
note: Specifically outlawed in 1696.
1418 —— 1694 (康熙 33). cb. 44 vols.
c. Naikaku, Waseda-Neisai.

1688

1419 Verbiest, Ferdinand, SJ. 南懷仁 (1623–1688)
Ichimoku Ryōzen 一目了然 *Yi-mu-liao-jan* (Immediate Understanding).
1420 —— Peking 救世堂, 1930 (民國 19). wb. 1 v., [1], 30p., 16cm.
c. Tohoku.
1421 —— Peking 遣使會印書館, 1936 (民國 25). wb. 1 v., 30p., 15cm.
c. Tenri.
1422 —— [n.p.], 1939 (民國 28). 11th ed. wb. 1 v., 25p., 19cm.
c. Seishin.

1689

1423 Unshō 運敞 (1614–1693)
Jakushōdō Kokukyōshū 寂照堂谷響集 (Collected Essays of the Priest of the Jakushōdō Temple), [n.p.] 中野宗左衞門, 1689 (元禄 2). jb. 10 vols., 27cm
note: excerpts regarding Christianity from *Gozasso* (n. 1217).
c. Taishō, Waseda.
1424 —— (Dai-Nippon Bukkyō Zensho, v. CXLIX).

1690

1425 Kaku Gakuka 穫學稼 *Hu Hsüeh-chia*
Kenkoshū 堅瓠集 *Chien-hu-chi* (The Hard Calabash Collection of Tales), 1690 (康熙 29). cb. 34 vols.
note: Specifically outlawed in 1712.
c. Naikaku.
1426 —— 柏香書屋, 1926 (民國 15). cb. 15 vols.
c. Kyōdai-Bungakubu.
1427 —— (Hikki Shōsetsu Taikan, v. CXXIX–CXLVIII).

1691

1428 Asai Ryōi 淺井了意 (–1691)
Kirishitan Hakyakuron-den 鬼理至端破却論傳 (Treatise on the Defeat of Christianity). Kyōto 山田市郎兵衞, [n.d.]. jb. 2 vols.
cf. Tenri-Jap. II, p. 83.
note: v. III is the *Kirishitan Monogatari*. See n. 893.
c. Kyōdai, Tenri (v. II only).

1429 —— facs. repr. (Kisho Fukuseikai Sōsho).
1430 —— (Kaihyō Sōsho, v. I).

1431 Hizen no Kuni Sonogigōri Ōmura Rōnai On'azuke Ko-Kirishitan Zonmei narabini Shibōchō 肥前國彼杵郡大村牢内御預古切支丹存命並死亡帳 (Notes on the Christians both those alive and those who have died confined in the Ōmura Prison, Sonogi District in the Province of Hizen), 1691 (元禄 3 年 12 月). jb. 1 v.
orig. ms. The Omuras.
1432 —— mimeogr. pr. and annotated by Takamuro Kazuhiko 高室一彦, 1927 (昭和 2).
1433 —— pr. by Yamaguchi Takusuke 山口宅助 in *Ōmurahan Ko-Kirishitan Kenkyū Shiryō,* Tokyo 1937 (昭和 12)

1434 Hōjō Masafusa 北條正房 (1609–1670)
Saken Yoroku 査袄餘録 (Official Records concerning the Christian Inquisition House). jb. 1 v.
note: Though this has been often called Sayō-Yoroku 査袄餘録, Saken Yoroku is correct.
cf. Kokushi, p. 118.
ms. Naikaku.
1435 —— (Zokuzoku Gunsho Ruijū, v. XII)
1436 —— (Misonoya, v. III).
1437 —— tr. into German by Gustav Voss und Hubert Cieslik, S.J., *Kirisutoki und Sayō Yoroku, Japanische Dokumente zur Missionsgeschichte des 17. Jahrhunderts,* Tokyo 1940, pp. 110–157.

1438 Kumazawa Banzan 熊澤蕃山 (1619–1691)
Miwa Monogatari 三輪物語 (Tales of Miwa). jb.
cf. Samura, p. 1892.
ms. Nichidai-Hayashi, Sonkeikaku, Ueno.
1439 —— (Shintō Sōsetsu).
1440 —— (Banzan Zenshū, v. V).
1441 —— (Nippon Tetsugaku Zensho, v. IV).

1442 Kumazawa Banzan 熊澤蕃山 (1619–1691)
Usa Mondō 宇佐問答 (Dialogue of Usa), [n.p.], [n.d.]. jb. 3 vols.
cf. Kokushi, p. 21.
ms. Hibiya-Kaga, Ikeda, Iwase, Ueno.
1443 —— (Ōshuku Zakki).
1444 —— (Kinsei Shakai Keizai Gakusetsu Taikei, Kumazawa Banzanshū).
1445 —— (Banzan Zenshū, v. V).

1692

1446 Kirishitan Fubummeisha Hase-kura Rokuemon Shishitsuchō 切支丹不分明者支倉六右衛門死失帳 (Necrology of Hase-kura Rokuuemon, who may have been a Christian). 1692 (元禄 5). jb. 1 v.
1447 ——— (Date Kashi Sōdan, v. IV).

1448 Tamura Tomofusa 田村具房
Amakusa Gundan 天草軍談 (Story of the Amakusa Rebellion). jb.
ms. Nagasaki, Naikaku, Shokōkan.

1449 * Amakusa Seibatsuki 天草征伐記 (Story of the Subjugation of the Amakusa Rebellion), 1692 (元禄 5). jb. 18 vols.
cf. Samura, p. 46.
ms. Ebisawa, Fujimoto, Nagasaki (vv. III–VI only), Shokōkan, Tenri, Ueno.

1696

1450 Ferreira, Chiristovão, ex-SJ. 澤野忠庵 (1580–1650)
Oranda Geka Shi'nan 阿羅陀外科指南 (Introduction to Dutch Surgery), Osaka 浪華陰舎, 1696 (元禄 9). jb. 4 vols., 13×19cm.
cf. Ebisawa-Namban, pp. 497–512.
note: Ferreira's original work is lacking.
1451 ——— Kyōto 出雲寺和泉椽, 1702 (元禄 15). jb. 4 vols., 12×19cm.
c. Kyōdai.
1452 ——— Ōsaka 浪華陰舎, 1705 (寶永 2). jb. 4 vols., 13×19cm.
c. Ebisawa.
1453 * Namban Geka Hidensho 南蠻外科秘傳書 (Secret Instruction in Western Surgery). jb. 1 v.
ms. Ebisawa, Kyodai-Fujikawa.
1454 * Nambanryū Geka Shinden 南蠻流外科眞傳 (True Instruction in Western Surgery), compiled by Yoshida Seitoku 吉田成徳. jb. 2 vols.
ms. Ebisawa.

Western Surgery in the Genroku Era, 1668–1704

1455 Banden Kihōshū 蕃傳奇方集 (Strange Foreign Prescriptions). jb. 1 v.
ms. Kyōdai.

1456 Hiden Namban Kōyaku 秘傳南蠻膏藥 (Secrets of Western Ointments). jb. 1 v.
ms. Kyodai-Fujikawa.

1457 Ikeda Yajibyōe 池田彌次兵衛
Nambanryū Gekasho 南蠻流外科書 (Western Surgery). jb. 1 v.
ms. Kyōdai-Fujikawa.

1458 Kirishitan-koku Geka Ichiryū 切支丹國外科一流 (One School of Surgery in Christendom). jb. 1 v.
ms. Kyōdai-Fujikawa.

1459 Kurisaki Dōi 栗崎道意
Nambanryū Geka Jitsuyō Zensho 南蠻流外科實用全書 (Practical Works on Western Surgery).
ms. Kyōdai-Fujikawa.

1460 Nagasaki Narabayashi Namban Geka Sōden 長崎楢林南蠻外科宗傳 (Introduction to the Western Surgery of the Narabayashi School at Nagasaki). jb. 1 v.
ms. Kyōdai.

1461 Nambanguchi Wage 南蠻口和解 (Japanese Translations of European Languages). jb. 1 v.
ms. Kyōdai-Fujikawa.

1462 Namban Kurisaki-sensei ni tsutō Seiryū Geka Yakuhō no Sho 南蠻傳栗崎先生正流外科藥方之書 (Western Pharmacology of the Kurisaki Surgery School). jb. 1 v.
ms. Kyōdai-Kokushi.

1463 Nambanryū Geka Shimmeiyaku-seiron 南蠻流外科新明藥性論 (New Pharmacology of the Western Surgery).
ms. Kyōdai.

1464 Nambanryū Gekyō 南蠻流外經 or Nambanryū Gekasho 南蠻流外科書 (Western Surgery). jb. 1 v.
ms. Kyōdai-Fujikawa.

1465 Nambanryū Kinsō Geka Kikigaki 南蠻流金瘡外科聴書 (Notes on Western Surgery). jb. 1 v.
ms. Kyōdai-Fujikawa.

1466 Nambanryū Kinsō Gokui 南蠻流金瘡極意 (Secret Principles of Western Surgery). jb. 1 v.
ms. Kyōdai-Fujikawa.

1467 Nambanryū Kōhō 南蠻流膏方 (The Western Pharmacy). 1679 (延寶 7). jb. 1 v.
ms. Kyōdai.

1468 Nambanryū Meishū 南蠻流目醫集 (Western Ophthalmology). jb. 1 v.
ms. Kyōdai-Fujikawa.

1469 Nambanryū Nōdokuki 南蠻流能毒記 (The Western Pharmacy), jb. 1 v.
ms. Kyōdai.

1470 Nambanryū Rairyōji Hisho 南蠻流癩療治秘書 (Secret Book on the Western Treatment of Leprosy). jb. 1 v.
ms. Kyōdai-Fujikawa.

1471 Nambanryū Shosōkei 南蠻流諸瘡形 (Western Treatment for Boils). jb. 1 v.
ms. Kyōdai-Fujikawa.

1472 Nambanryū Yōisho 南蠻流瘍醫書 (Western Treatment for Boils). jb. 1 v.
ms. Kyodai-Fujikawa.

1473 Nambanyaku Shuji 南蠻藥主治 (Western Pharmacology). jb. 1 v.
ms. Kyōto-Fujikawa.

1474 Namban Yaso-hō no Yurai 南蠻耶蘇法之由來 (History of Catholicism). jb. 1 v.
ms. Tōdai.

1475 Nishi Gempo 西玄甫 (–1684)
Oranda Geka 阿蘭陀外科 (Dutch Surgery). jb. 1 v.
ms. Kyōdai-Fujikawa.

1476 Terauchi Shigenori 寺内重允
Oranda Kinsō Yakuhō 阿蘭陀金瘡藥方 (Dutch Pharmacy of Surgery). jb. 2 vols.
ms. Ebisawa.

1477 Tōyama Nobutake 遠山信武
Nippon Ikoku Raiōki 日本異國來往記 (Records of the Intercourse between Japan and Other Countries), Kyōto 此君堂, 1696 (元禄 9). jb. 2 vols., 23cm.
cf. Tenri-Jap. II, p. 88.
c. Tenri.
1478 —— (Kaiji Shiryō Sōsho, v. XIII).
1479 * Ikoku Ōraiki 異国往来記 (Records of Foreign Intercourse).
1480 —— (Zuihitsu Bungaku Senshū, v. III).

1697

1481 Nagasaki Kongenki 長崎根元記 (History of Nagasaki), [1697?]. 15 vols.
note: There are many books of the same kind.
cf. Shimmura-Namban I, pp. 457–458.
ms. Shimmura.
1482 —— (Kaihyō Sōsho, v. IV).

1700

1483 Chō Chō 張潮 *Chang Ch'ao*
Gusho Shinshi 虞初新誌 *Yü-ch'u Hsin-chih* (Essays), [n.p.], 1700 (康熙 39). cb. 8 vols.
c. Naikaku.
1484 —— [n.p.], 1851 (咸豊 1). cb. 20 vols., 18cm.
c. Nichidai-Mukasa, Seishin.
1485 —— [n.p.], 1877 (光緒 3). cb. 5 vols., 18cm.
c. ICU.
1486 —— (Hikki Shōsetsu Taikan, v. CXIII–XCXVIII).

1487 * Honkoku Gusho Shinshi, 飜刻虞初新誌, construed from Chinese into Jap. by Arai Renpei 荒井廉平. Ōsaka 1823 (文政 6). jb. 10 vols. 25cm.
c. Jingū, Seishin, Tōhoku-Kanō, Ueno.

1488 Shimizu Sadanori 清水貞徳 (– 1717)
Zuhō Sambushū 圖法三部集 (Three Surveying Texts) 1700 (元禄 13). jb. 1 v.
orig. ms. Tōhoku-Hayashi.

The Shimizu School

1489 Kiku Gempō 規矩元法 (Introduction to Surveying). jb. 1 v.
ms. Tōhoku-Kanō.

1490 Shimizuryū Kikujutsu Densho Zuimō 清水流規矩術傳書隨毛 (History of the Art of Surveying of the Shimizu School). jb. 2 vols.
ms. Tōhoku-Hayashi.

1491 Shimizuryū Menkyo narabini Densho 清水流免許並傳書 (Charter and Chronological List of Members of the Shimizu School). jb. 1 v.
ms. Tōhoku-Hayashi.

1492 Shimizuryū Sokuryō Zensho 清水流測量全書 (Complete Works of Surveying and Mensuration of the Shimizu School). jb. 5 vols.
ms. Tōhoku-Kanō, Ueno.

1493 Tani Shigetō 谷重遠 (1663–1718)
Shinro Memmei 新蘆面命 (Essays), 1700 (元禄 13). jb. 2 vols.
cf. Kokushi, p. 158.
ms. Tōhoku-Kanō.
1494 —— (Misonoya, v. II).

1702

1495 Arai Hakuseki 新井白石 (1657–1725)
Hankampu 藩翰譜 (Lives of the Samurai), 1702 (元禄 15). jb. 13 vols.
cf. Kokushi, pp. 259–260.
ms. Gakushiin, Hibiya.
1496 —— Tokyo 1894 (明治 27). jb. 12 vols., 23cm.
c. Kansei, Tenri, Ueno.
1497 —— (Arai Hakuseki Zenshū, v. I).

1498 Tōyama Nobuharu 遠山信春
Sōkenki 總見記, or Oda Gunki 織田軍記 (Military Record of Oda Nobunaga) 1702

(元禄 15). jb. 23 vols.
cf. Kokushi, p. 172.
1499 —— (Tsūzoku Nippon Zenshi, v. VII).
1500 —— (Shiseki Shūran).

1704

1501 Shimabara Kassenki 島原合戦記, or Amakusa Monogatari 天草物語 (Story of the Shimabara Rebellion or Story of Amakusa), Edo [Tokyo] 須原屋茂兵衛, 1704 (實永 1). jb. 3 vols., 26cm.
cf. Samura, p. 930.
c. Iwase, Naikaku, Nagasaki, Sonkeikaku, Ueno, Waseda.
ms. Nagasaki.
1502 —— [Kyōto], 1708 (實永 5). jb. 2 vols., 27cm.
c. Ebisawa, Ōsaka.

1503 Yū Dō 尤侗 *Yu T'ung* (1618–1704) Gaikoku Chikushishi 外國竹枝詞 *Wai-kuo Chu-chih-tz'u* (Miscellaneous Poems about Foreign Countries). cb. 1 v.
ms. Naikaku.
1504 —— (Seidō Zenshū).
1505 —— (Shōdai Sōsho, v. III–IV).
1506 —— (Geikai Shujin, v. XXX).
1507 —— (Ryūi Hisho, v. LXX).
1508 —— construed from Chinese into Jap. by Okuda Mototsugu 奥田元繼, Sakai 1786 (天明 6). jb. 1 v.
cf. Kaikoku, pp. 134–135.
c. Ayuzawa.

Genroku Era, 1688–1704

1509 Kokon Buke Seisuiki 古今武家盛衰記 (Rise and Fall of Military Caste, Old and New). jb. 30 vols.
note: Contains accounts of the Christian samurai.
1510 —— (Kokushi Sōsho).

1511 Sanada Zōyo 眞田増譽
Meiryō Kōhan 明良洪範 (Stories about Samurai), annotated by Yamazaki Naoyuki 山崎直行. jb. 40 vols.
cf. Kokushi, p. 309.
c. Jingū, Naikaku, Waseda.
ms. Waseda.
1512 —— repr. by the Kokusho Kankō-kai 國書刊行會, Tokyo 1912 (大正 1). wb. 1 v.

1513 Shūmon Danna Uekai no Okite 宗門檀那請合之掟 (Law for the Control of Christians). jb. 1 v.
note: A counterfeit law under the name of Tokugawa Ieyasu 徳川家康 under the date of 1613, but it seems to be of the Genroku Era.
ms. Ebisawa, Sophia, Tohoku.

1514 —— (Byakuja Kankenroku).
1515 —— tr. into English by Ernest Satow (*Transactions of the Asiatic Society of Japan*, v. VI, n. 1), Yokohama 1878.
1516 * Kirishitan Gojōmoku 切支丹御條目 (Decrees against Christians). jb. 1 v.
ms. Sophia.
1517 * Shinkunsama Gojōmoku Jūgo-kajō 神君様御條目十五ヶ條 (The Fifteen Article Law by the Holy Shōgun).
1518 —— (Renjō Sōsho).
1519 * Shūmon Jūgokajō Gojōmoku Utsushi 宗門十五箇條御條目寫 (Copy of the Fifteen Article Law on Religion). jb. 1 v.
ms. Sophia.
1520 * Tōshō Shinkun Shūmon Hikae 東照神君宗門控 (Copy of the Law by the Holy Shogun). jb. 1 v.
ms. Sophia.

1707

1521 Mori Genjuku 森儼塾 (1658–1721) Gohō Shijiron 護法資治論 (Buddhist Apology) by Fusen Koji 不染居士, Kyōto 文昌堂, 1707 (實永 4). jb. 6 vols., 26cm.
cf. Itazawa, p. 257.
c. Ōtani, Tōyōdai.
1522 —— Kyōto 文昌堂, 1766 (明和 3). jb. 6 vols., 26cm.
c. Ebisawa, Keiō, Waseda.
1523 —— Kyōto 麗澤堂, 1766 (明和 3). jb. 10 vols., 28cm.
c. Taishō.
1524 —— Kyōto 文昌堂, 1774 (安永 3). jb. 10 vols., 26cm.
c. Taisho, Waseda.
1525 —— (Nippon Shisō Tōsō Shiryō, v. II).

1708

1526 Inagaki Kōrō 稲垣光朗
Sekai Bankoku Chikyūzu 世界萬國地球圖 (World Atlas), Osaka 池田屋, 1708 (實永 5). jb. 1 v.
note: Based on the work of his teacher, Kobayashi Kentei 小林謙貞, and through that on Ricci's world atlas.
cf. Kaikoku, p. 229; Misumi Teikichi 三隅貞吉, "Bankoku Sōzu ni tsuite" (*Bungei Shunjū*, Showa 昭和 8, July), Tokyo 1933.

1527 Kobayashi Kentei Yoshinobu 小林謹貞義信 (1600–1683)
Nigi Byakusetsu 二儀略説 (Brief Explanation of the Two Globes), compiled by Ōe Ikei 大江意敬. jb. 2 vols.
note: No printed copy extant.
cf. Yajima Suketoshi 矢島祐利, "Nigi Ryakusetsu no Kenkyū" (*Kagakushi Kenkyū*, v. 10), Tokyo 1949;

Ebisawa-Namban, pp. 175–178.
ms. Naikaku.

1527b —— annotated and mimeogr. printed by Imai Itaru 今井溱, Kyōto 1958 (昭和 33).

1528 Nishikawa Joken 西川如見 (1648–1724)

Zōhō Kai Tsūshōkō 増補華夷通商考 (Treatise on the commercial intercourse between Chinese and Foreign Countries, revised), Kyoto 梅村彌右衛門, 1708 (寳永 5). jb. 5 vols., 23cm.

cf. Kaikoku, pp. 16–17; Boxer-Compagnie, p. 17; Kokushi, pp. 45–46.
c. Ebisawa, Hibiya-Kondō, Iwasaki, Iwase, Kanazawa-Kado, Kyōto, Naikaku, Okada, Tōkyō Kagaku Museum, Tenri, Ueno, Waseda.

1529 —— Kyōto 錦山樓, 1709 (寳永 6). jb. 5 vols., 23cm.

1530 —— (Joken Isho, v. IV).

1531 —— (Nippon Keizai Sōsho, v. V).

1532 —— (Nippon Keizai Taiten, v. IV).

1533 —— repr. by Iijima Tadao 飯島忠夫 and Nishikawa Tadayuki 西川忠幸 (Iwanami Bunko), Tokyo 1944 (昭和 19).

1534 —— tr. into English, Boxer-Compagnie, pp. 118–123, 173–176.

1709

1535 Arai Hakuseki 新井白石 (1657–1725)

Honchō Gunkikō 本朝軍記考 (Treatise on Guns in Japan), 1709 (寳永 6). jb. 12 vols.

cf. Miyazaki, pp. 744, 770.
orig. ms. Tōyō-Iwasaki.
ms. Naikaku, Shōryōbu, Tōdai-Nanki.

1536 —— Ōsaka 定榮堂, 1736 (元文 1). jb. 10 vols., 26cm.
c. Hibiya-Kondō.

1537 —— Kyōto 柳枝軒, 1740 (元文 5). jb. 4 vols., 27cm.
c. Tōdai, Hibiya-Kondō.

1538 —— (Shintei Kojitsu Sōsho, v. XXI).

1539 —— (Arai Hakuseki Zenshū, v. VI).

Arai Hakuseki and Father G-B. Sidotti, 1709–1715

1540 Arai Hakuseki 新井白石 (1652–1725)

Nagasaki Chūshin Rōmajin no Koto 長崎注進邏馬人事 (Report on the Romans by the Magistrate of Nagasaki). jb. 2 vols.

note: Contains reports of the magistrate of Nagasaki and Hakuseki's notes which are not contained in the Rōmajin Kanjō (See n. 1945). Not published.

cf. Miyazaki, pp. 747, 804.
orig. ms. the Arais.

1541 Arai Hakuseki 新井白石 (1657–1725)

Seigaku Kōryaku 西學考略 (Outline of Western Learning).
note: No copy extant.

1542 Arai Hakuseki 新井白石 (1657–1725)

Seigaku Suimon 西學推問 (Questions on Western Learning).
note: No copy extant.

1543 Arai Hakuseki 新井白石 (1657–1725)

Seiyō Kibun 西洋紀聞 (Reports of the Western World), [1725?]. jb. 3 vols.

cf. Cordier-Sinica, col. 2240; Kaikoku, pp. 23, 377; Kokushi, p. 165; Miyazaki, pp. 203–263, 762–763.
orig. ms. Naikaku.
ms. Ayuzawa, Ebisawa, Jingū, Seikadō, Shōryōbu, Tenri, Tōdai, Tōhoku-Kanō.

1544 —— pr. and annotated by Ōtuski Fumihiko 大槻文彦, Tokyo 白石社, 1882 (明治 15). jb. 2 vols., 23cm.

c. Ebisawa, Kichū, Kyūdai-Butsuri, Saba, Seishin, Sonkeikaku, Ueno, Waseda.

1545 —— annotated by Muraoka Tsunetsugu 村岡典嗣 (Iwanami Bunko), Tokyo 1936 (昭和 11).

1546 —— (Arai Hakuseki Zenshū, v. IV).

1547 —— (Edo Monogatari).

1548 —— (Nippon Meicho Taikei, v. III).

1549 —— (Dai-Nippon Shisō Zenshū, v. VI).

1550 —— tr. into English by Samuel R. Brown, RCA., "Sei yo kibun, or annals of the western ocean" (Jour. of the North China Branch of the Royal Asiatic Society. New Series, II–III), Shanghai, 1865–1866.

1551 —— abridged translation into English by W. B. Wright, The Capture and Captivity of P. Giovanni Battista Sidotti in Japan from 1709 to 1715 (Transactions of the Asiatic Society of Japan, v. IX), Tokyo 1881.

1552 —— condensed translation by "Anonymous," "Père Sidotti in Japan" (Chrysanthemum, v. II), Yokohama 1882.

1553 Arai Hakuseki 新井白石 (1657–1725)

Tenshukyō Taii 天主教大意 (Outline of Catholicism). jb. 1 v.

1554 —— (Seiyō Kibun, Appendix).

1555 Arai Hakuseki 新井白石 (1657–1725)

Yohan Batteisuta Monogatari ヨハンバツテイスタ物語 (Narrative of Johan Battista Sidotti). jb. l v.
cf. Miyazaki, pp. 746–747, 217–226, 771; Kaikoku, pp. 1 –21; Ebisawa-Namban, pp. 23–24.
orig. ms. Waseda.
ms. Ayuzawa.

1556 —- pr. by Ayuzawa Shintarō 鮎澤信太郎, "Arai Hakuseki no Yohan Battisuta monogatari" *(Rekishi Kyōiku,* v. III, n. 11), Tokyo 1955 (昭和 30).

1557 Kaibara Ekiken 貝原益軒 (1630–1714)
Chikuzen no Kuni Zoku Fudōki 筑前國續風土記 (The Second Series on the Topography of Chikuzen Province). 1709 (寶永 6). jb. 28 vols.
note: Contains notes about the Jesuit mission in 1643.
cf. G. Voss und H. Cieslik, SJ., *Kirishitoki und Sayō-Yoroku,* Tokyo 1940, pp. 166–168; Samura, p. 1372; Kokushi, p. 200.
1558 —— (Ōshuku Zakki).
1559 —— (Ekiken Zenshū, v. IV).

Hōei Era, 1704–1711

1560 Asakura Kagehira 朝倉景衡
Rōdan Ichigonki 老談一言記 (One Word from an Old Man). jb. 3 vols.
cf. Miyazaki, p. 776.
ms. Keiō, Naikaku, Shoryōbu, Tōhoku-Kanō, Tōyō.
1561 —— (Chōfū Irin).
1562 —— (Bizen Irō Monogatari).

1712

1563 Nishikawa Joken 西川如見 (1648–1724)
Temmon Giron 天文義論 (Discussion of Astronomy). 1712 (正徳 2). jb. 2 vols.
cf. Ebisawa-Namban, pp. 136–137.
ms. Naikaku.
1564 —— Kyōto 茨城多左衛門, [n.d.]. jb. 2 vols., 26cm.
c. Tenri, Tōhoku-Kanō.
1565 —— (Joken Isho, v. II).
1566 —— (Nippon Tetsugaku Zensho, v. VIII).

1713

1567 Arai Hakuseki 新井白石 (1657–1725)
Sairan Igen 釆覧異言 (World Geography), 1713 (正徳 3). jb. 5 vols.
cf. Miyazaki, pp. 758–759, 264–308; Kaikoku, p. 22; Kokushi, p. 114.
ms. Ayuzawa, Ebisawa, Gakushūin, Hibiya-Kondō, Iwase, Jingū, Kariya, Kyōdai, Nagasaki, Nichi-

dai-Mukasa, Shōryōbu, Tōdai-Nanki, Yūtoku.
1568 —— (Hakusekishi).
1569 —— (Hakuseki Sōsho, C., vv. XXIX–XXX).
1570 —— (Arai Hakuseki Zenshū, v. IV).
1571 —— pr. and annotated by Ōtsuki Fumihiko 大槻文彦, Tokyo 白石社, 1881 (明治 14). jb. 2 vols., 23cm.
c. Ebisawa, Hatano, Hibiya, Keiō, Kichū, Kyūdai, Nagasaki, Nichidai-Ueda, Seishin (v. I only), Sonkeikaku, Todai-Nanki, Ujiie, Ueno, Waseda.

1572 * Sairan Igen Furoku 釆覧異言附録 (Appendix of the Sairan Igen) compiled by Shimabara Sukeaki 島原佐章. jb. l v.
ms. Waseda.

1573 Pereira, Thomas, SJ. 徐日昇 (1645–1708)
Ritsuryo Seigi 律呂正義 *Lü-lü Cheng-i* (True Theory of Harmony) compiled by T. Pereira and Theodore Pedrini 徳里閣, Lazarist, Peking 1713 (康熙 52). cb. 5 vols.
cf. Pfister, pp. 384–385; Jo, pp. 325–326.
c. Seikado.
1574 —— (Ritsureki Engen).
1575 —— (Gakuritsu Zensho).

1576 Terajima Ryōan 寺島良安
Wakan Sansai Zue 倭漢三才圖繪 (Illustrated Encyclopeadia of Japan and China), Ōsaka 杏林堂, 1713 (正徳 3). jb. 105 vols.
cf. Kaikoku, pp. 22, 346; Kokushi, p. 334.
c. Hibiya-Kaga, Ueno.
1576b —— Tokyo 1901 (明治 34). wb. 6 vols.
1577 —— Tokyo 吉川弘文館, 1906 (明治 39). wb. 1 v., 14, 3, 125, 148, 1463, 8p, 16cm.
1578 —— (Nippon Zuihitsu Taisei, Bekkan).

1714

1579 Iku Son 郁蒸 *Yü Sun*
Seisei Meihen 醒世迷編 *Hsing-shih-mi-p'ien* (Criticism of Buddhism), [n.p.], 1714 (康熙 53). cb. 2 vols.
cf. Jo, pp. 115–117.
1580 —— Shanghai 慈母堂, 1873 (同治 12). cb. 1 v., 2, 2, 2, 35, 50f., 21cm.
c. ICU.

1581 Kaibara Ekiken 貝原益軒 (1630–1714)
Jigoshū 自娯集 (Essays on Pleasing Oneself), Kyōto 永田調兵衛, 1714 (正徳 4). jb. 7 vols., 27cm.
cf. Kokushi, p. 126.
c. Hibiya-Inoue, Hibiya-Kaga.
1582 —— abridged (Nippon Keizai Taiten, v. II).

1583 Nishikawa Joken 西川如見 (1648–1724)

Ryōgi Shūsetsu 兩儀集說 (Treatise on the Two Globes), [n.p.], 1714 (正德 4). jb. 8 vols.

cf. Samura, p. 2018.
ms. Naikaku, Tōyō-Iwasaki.

1584 —— (Joken Isho, v. XV–XVIII).

1715

1585 Araki Murahide 荒木村英 (1640–1718)

Kiku Gempō Chōken 規矩元法長驗 (Introduction to Surveying and Mensuration). jb. 1 v.

ms. Tōhoku-Kano.

1586 Shibukawa Shunkai 澁川春海 (1639–1715)

Meijikan Sōsho 明時館叢書 (Record of the Meijikan).

ms. Gakushiin, Imoto, Tōhoku.

1587 Shibukawa Shunsui 澁川春水

Shunkai Sensei Jikki 春海先生實記 (True Life of Shibukawa Shunkai). jb. 1 v.

ms. Jingu, Jinshū.

1588 —— (Dai-Nippon Kyōikushi Shiryō, v. IX).

1589 * Yasui Shunkai Sensei Den 保井春海先生傳. jb. 1 v.

ms. Naikaku.

1716

1590 Arai Hakuseki 新井白石 (1657–1725)

Oritaku Shiba no Ki 折たく柴の記 (Autobiography of Arai Hakuseki), 1716 (正德 6). jb. 3 vols.

cf. Kokushi, p. 42.
orig. ms. The Arais.
ms. Hibiya, Jingu, Kyoto, Naikaku, Shoryobu, Tōdai-Nanki, Ueno, Waseda.

1591 —— pr. and annotated by Takenaka Kunika 竹中邦香, Tokyo 白石社, 1881 (明治 14). jb. 3 vols., 23cm.

c. Tenri, Ueno, Waseda.

1592 —— annotated by Naitō Chisō 内藤耻叟, Tokyo 白石社, 1890 (明治 23). jb. 3 vols., 24cm.

c. Ueno, Waseda.

1593 —— annotated by Suzuki Hiroyasu 鈴木弘恭, Tokyo 青山堂, 1893–94 (明治 26–27). jb. 3 vols., 23cm.

c. Ueno.

1594 —— annotated by Hani Gorō 羽仁五郎 (Iwanami Bunko).

1595 —— (Ōshuku Zakki).

1596 —— (Kinsei Shakai Keizai Gakusetsu Taikei, v. XII).

1597 —— (Arai Hakuseki Zenshū, v. III).

1598 —— (Dai-Nippon Shisō Zenshū, v. VI).

1599 —— abridged (Sekai Dai-Shisō Zenshū, v. LIV).

1717

1600 Hosoi Kōtaku 細井廣澤 (1658–1735)

Hiden Chiiki Zuhō Daizensho 秘傳地域圖法大全書 (Secrets of Measuring and Drawing Maps), 1717 (享保 2). jb. 2 vols.

ms. Ueno, Waseda.

1601 Zoku Zenrin Kokuhōki 續善隣國寶記 (Diplomatic Records), 1717 (享保 2). jb.

note: Documents on foreign affairs, 1473–1660.
cf. Kokushi, p. 171.
ms. Jingū.

1602 —— (Kaitei Shiseki Shūran, v. XXI).

1603 —— (Zoku Gunsho Ruijū, v. DCCCLXXX).

1718

1604 Arai Hakuseki 新井白石 (1657–1725)

Hakuseki Nikki 白石日記 (Hakuseki's Diary), 1718 (享保 3). jb. 16 vols.

cf. Kokushi, p. 8.
orig. ms. Keiō.

1605 —— (Dai-Nippon Kokiroku, Arai Hakuseki Nikki).

1606 Chavagnac, Emeric de, SJ. 沙守信 (–1717)

Shindō Jishō 眞道自證 Chen-tao Tzu-cheng (Proof of Its Validity Inherent in the True Doctrine), Peking, 1718 (乾隆 57). cb. 2 vols.

cf. Jo, p. 124; Pfister, p. 570.

1607 —— Peking, 1796 (嘉慶 1). cb. 4 vols.

1608 —— Peking, 1818 (嘉慶 23). cb. 2 vols.

1609 —— Shanghai, 1858 (咸豐 8). cb. 2 vols.

1610 —— Shanghai, 1868 (同治 7). cb. 2 vols., 27cm.

c. Aoyama, Nagasaki, Saba, Seishin.

1611 —— Shanghai, 1917 (民國 6). wb. 1 v.

c. Ebisawa.

1612 —— Shanghai, 1925 (民國 14). wb. 1v.

c. Kazan.

1613 —— Chang-chia-chuang 張家莊天主

堂, 1931 (民國 20). wb. 1 v., 1, 171p., 18cm.
c. Tōhoku.

1614 —— repr. and construed from Chinese into Jap. by Mishima Yoshitada 三島良忠, Tokyo 1886 (明治 19). wb. 1 v., 22, 34, 42, 28p., 22cm.
c. Aoyama, Nagasaki, Naikaku, Sophia, Ueno, Yoshida.

1615 —— tr. into Jap., Saeki-Shinchō, pp. 241–313.

1616 Kitajima Teichō 北島定澄
Namban Geka Tōkei narabini Taii 南蠻外科統系並大意 (Chronology and Outline of European Surgery), 1718 (享保 3). jb. 1 fold.
cf. Ebisawa-Namban, p. 186.
ms. Kyōdai-Kokushi.

1617 Shimabara Gunki 島原軍記
(Story of the Shimabara Rebellion), [n.p.], 1718 (享保 3). jb. 2 vols., 19cm.
cf. Tenri-Jap. II, pp. 153–154.
c. Naikaku, Tenri (v. II only), Tōdai-Nanki.
ms. Kyūdai-Hōka, Shiryō.

1720

1618 Nishikawa Joken 西川如見 (1648–1724)
Nagasaki Yawagusa 長崎夜話草 (Twilight Tales of Nagasaki), Kyoto 柳枝軒, 1720 (享保 5). jb. 5 vols., 23cm.
cf. Boxer-Compagnie, pp. 6–9; Kokushi, p. 233.
c. Iwase, Keiō, Kyūdai-Hōka, Ōtori, Saba, Nagasaki, Tenri, Ueno, Waseda.
ms. Hibiya-Kondō, Jingū, Kichū, Waseda.

1619 —— Tokyo 1911 (明治 44). wb. 1 v.
c. Keiō.

1620 —— repr. and annotated by Iijima Tadao 飯島忠夫 and Nishikawa Tadayuki 西川忠幸 (Iwanami Bunko), Tokyo 1942 (昭和 17).

1621 —— (Joken Isho, v. VI).
1622 —— (Ōshuku Zakki).
1623 —— (Nagasaki Sōsho, A., v. I).
1624 —— (Nagasaki Sōsho, B., v. I).
1625 —— (Nambanki Bunsen).

1626 Nishikawa Joken 西川如見 (1648–1724)
Nippon Suidokō 日本水土考 (Topography of Japan), Kyoto 柳枝軒, 1720 (享保 5). jb. 1 v.
cf. Kaikoku, pp. 304–305, Kokushi, p. 243.
c. Okamura.

1627 —— (Joken Isho).
1628 —— annotated by Iijima Tadao 飯島忠夫 and Nishikawa Tadayuki 西川忠幸 (Iwanami Bunko), Tokyo 1944 (昭和 19).
1629 —— (Zoku Nippon Keizai Sōsho, v. III).

1630 Nishikawa Joken 西川如見 (1648–1724)
Shijūnikakoku Jimbutsu Zusetsu 肆拾貳國人物圖說 or Bankoku Jimbutsuzu 萬國人物圖 (Illustrated Notes on Fourty-two Countries), Edo [Tokyo] 淵梅軒, 1720 (享保 5). jb. 2 vols., 28cm.
cf. Kaikoku, pp. 335–338; Boxer-Compagnie, pp. 17–18.
c. Hibiya-Kaga, Ueno, Waseda.

1631 —— Kyōto 柳枝軒, 1843 (天保 4). jb. 2 vols.
1632 —— (Joken Isho,, v. III).

1633 Yamamura Shōei 山村昌永 (1770–1807)
Teisei Shijūnikoku Jinbutsu Zusetsu 訂正四十二國人物圖說 (Revision the Shijūnikoku Jinbutsu Zusetsu). jb. 1 v.
orig. ms. Waseda.

1721

1634 Bai Buntei 梅文鼎 *Mei Wen-ting* (1633–1721)
Hōteiron 方程論 *Fang-ch'eng-lun* (Theory of Equations). cb. 6 vols.
note: Specifically outlawed in 1701.
1635 —— Baishi Sōsho Shūyō, vv. V–VII).

1636 Bai Buntei 梅文鼎 *Mei Wen-ting* (1633–1721)
Rekigaku Gimon 曆學疑問 *Li-hsüeh I-wen* (Questions on Calendar Science). cb. 3 vols.
1637 —— (Rekizan Zensho, vv. VIII–IX).
1638 —— (Baishi Sōsho Shūyō, vv. XVII–XVIII).
1639 —— Edo [Tokyo] 須原屋, 1820 (文政 3). jb. 1 v., 4, 2, 3, 3, 4, 33, 44, 37, [1] f., 26cm.
c. Tenri, Waseda-Ogura.

1722

1640 Takebe Katahiro 建部賢弘 (1664–1739)
Fukyū Tetsujutsu 不休綴術 (Text on Progressions), 1722 (享保 7). jb. 1 v.
cf. Samura, p. 1712.
ms. Naikaku.

1641 Takebe Katahiro 建部賢弘 (1664–1739)
Enri Tetsujutsu 圓理綴術 (Text on Progressions). jb. 1 v.
cf. Samura, p. 239.
ms. Waseda-Ogura.
1642 —— (Wasan Zenshū, v. LIV).

1643 —— (Nippon Tetsugaku Zensho, v. VIII).

1723

1644 Bai Buntei 梅文鼎 *Mei Wen-ting* (1633–1721)

Rekizan Zensho 暦算全書 *Li-suan Ch'üan-shu* (Complete Works on Mathematics and Calendar Science), Peking 柏柳魏念庭 1723 (雍正 1). cb. 19 vols., 26cm.

note: Mostly based on Jesuit works. See also n. 1879
cf. Ebisawa-Namban, pp. 145–147.
c. Gakushiin, Miyagi, Naikaku, Ōsaka, Seikadō, Tōdai-Nanki, Tōhoku-Kanō, Tōhoku-Sūgaku, Tōkyo Astronomical Observatory, Waseda-Ogura.
ms. Waseda, Seishin (abridged).

1645 —— Peking 聞妙香室, 1859 (咸豊 9). cb. 32 vols., 25cm.

c. Ueno.

1646 —— Shanghai 1885 (光緒 11). cb. 23 vols.

c. Tōyō.

1647 —— annotated by Takebe Katahiro 建部賢弘, 1733 (享保 13). jb.

orig. ms. Shoryobu.

1648 Seiso 聖祖 *Sheng-chu*, Emperor of Ch'ing (1654–1722)

Sūri Seiun 数理精蘊 *Shu-li Ching-yün* (Essence of Mathematical Theories), Peking, 1723 (康熙 62). cb. 53 vols.

note: vv. 2–4 includes the *Kika Gempon* (n. 261).
c. Gakushiin, Ikeda, Kyūdai-Butsuri, Miyagi, Naikaku, Seikadō, Shinken, Tōhoku-Kanō.
ms. Tōhoku-Kanō, Ueno.

1649 —— Canton, 1882 (光緒 8). cb. 40 vols., 27cm.

c. Gakushuin, Tōhoku-Hayashi, Ueno, Waseda-Ogura.

1650 —— [Peking?], 1896 (光緒 22). cb. 24 vols., 15cm.

c. Seishin, Tohoku-Hayashi.

1651 —— (Kokugaku Kihon Sōsho). wb. 3 vols.

1652 —— (Kōnan Seizōkyoku Yakusho Ikoku).

1653 Yorozuo Tokiharu 萬尾春時

Mitatezan Kiku Buntōshū 見立算規矩分等集 (Text on Mensuration), 1723 (享保 7 年 12 月). jb. 1 v.

c. Gakushiin.

1724

1654 Arai Hakuseki 新井白石 (1657–1725)

Tokushi Yoron 讀史餘論 (History of Japan), 1724 (享保 9). jb. 3 vols.

cf. Miyazaki, pp. 509–538; 765–766; Kokushi, p.229.

ms. Jingū, Kyōdai-Kokushi, Naikaku, Shōryōbu, Tenri, Tōdai, Tōyō-Fujita.

1655 —— annotated by Hagiwara Yutaka 萩原裕, Edo [Tokyo], 1860 (萬延 1). jb. 6 vols.

c. Kansei, Naikaku, Nichidai-Mukasa, Nichidai-Ueda.

1656 —— Kōfu 温故堂, 1876 (明治 9). jb. 6 vols., 22cm.

c. Gakushiin, Hibiya, Tōyōdai.

1657 —— Tokyo 小野慶次郎, 1893 (明治 26). jb. 1 v.

1658 —— annotated by Imaizumi Teisuke 今泉定介, Tokyo 修文館, 1899 (明治 32). wb. 1 v.

1659 —— Tokyo 松榮堂, 1903 (明治 36). wb. 1 v.

1660 —— Kōfu 内藤書店, 1909 (明治 42). jb. 3 vols., 23cm.

1661 —— annotated by Hagiwara Yutaka 萩原裕, Tokyo 大同館, 1912 (明治 45). wb. 1 v.

1662 —— (Sesshūsai Sōsho). jb. 6 vols.

1663 —— (Arai Hakuseki Zenshū, v. III).

1664 —— (Yūhōdō Bunko).

1665 —— (Shinyaku Nippon Bungaku Sōsho, v. X).

1666 —— (Dai-Nippon Shisō Zenshū, v. VI).

1667 —— annotated by Muraoka Tsunetsugu 村岡典嗣 (Iwanami Bunko), Tokyo 1936 (昭和 11).

1668 * Sankō Tokushi Yoron 参考讀史餘論, annotated by Yuasa Jōzan 湯淺常山.

ms. T. Masamune.

1669 —— (Nippon Koten Zenshū).

1670 Imamura Ichibyōe 今村市兵衛

Oranda Mondō 和蘭問答 (Dailogue regarding Holland), tr. by I. Imamura etc., 1724 (享保 9). jb. 1 v.

cf. Kaikoku, pp. 23–24.
ms. Kyōdai.

1671 —— (Kaihyō Sōsho, v. II).

1725

1672 Arai Hakuseki 新井白石 (1657–1725)

Gaikoku Tsūshin Jiryaku 外國通信事略 (Outline of Correspondence with Foreign Countries). jb.

ms. Jingū, Ueno, Waseda.

1673 —— (Hakuseki Sōsho, A., v. I).

1674 —— (Chūko Sōsho).

1675 —— (Arai Hakuseki Zenshū, v. III).

1676 —— (Hakuseki-ran, v. II).

1677 Arai Hakuseki 新井白石 (1657–1725)

Gojiryaku 五事略 (Five Short Pieces). jb. 2 vols.

note: Different version of the *Kottō Zatsudan* 骨董雑談.
cf. Miyazaki, p. 758.
ms. Hibiya-Morohashi, Jingū, Naikaku, Nichidai-Hayashi, Shōryōbu, Tenri, Tōdai-Nanki.

1678 —— (Chūko Sōsho, vv. CXLII–CXLIII).
1679 —— (Hakuseki Sōsho).
1680 —— (Hakkuseki-ran).
1681 —— (Zuihitsu Shūshi , v. V).
1682 —— (Arai Hakuseki Zenshū, v. III),
1683 —— annotated by Takenaka Kunika 竹中邦香, Tokyo 白石社, 1883 (明治 16). jb. 2 vols., 23cm.

c. Hatano (v. I only), Hibiya, Jingu, Waseda

1684 —— annotated by Hagiwara Yutaka 萩原裕, Tokyo 小野慶次郎, 1893 (明治 26). jb. 6 vols. 23cm.

c. Tenri.

1685 Arai Hakuseki 新井白石 (1657–1725)
Hakuseki Ibun 白石遺文 (Essays by Hakuseki), compiled by Tatehara Suiken 立原翠軒. jb. 2vols., 18cm.

cf. Kokushi, p. 253.
c. Hibiya-Ichimura.

1686 —— (Arai Hakuseki Zenshū, v. V).
1687 —— (Kan'utei Sōsho. v. I).

1688 Arai Hakuseki 新井白石 (1657–1725)
Hakuseki Kengi 白石建議 (Memorials of Hakuseki). jb. 8 vols.

cf. Kokushi, pp. 252–253.

1689 —— (Hakuseki Sōsho).
1690 —— (Nippon Keizai Taiten, v. IV).
1691 —— (Arai Hakuseki Zenshū, v. VI).

1692 Arai Hakuseki 新井白石 (1657–1725)
Hakuseki Shukan 白石手簡 or Hakuseki Sensei Shukan 白石先生 (Hakuseki's Letters). jb. 1 v.

note: There are many kinds of collections of Hakuseki's letters. See also nos. 1709 and 1717.
cf. Miyazaki, pp. 768–769; Kokushi, p. 253.
ms. Hibiya-Inoue, Ikeda, Jingū, Naikaku, Sonkeikaku, Tōdai-Nanki.

1693 —— compiled by Arai Yoshimichi 新井義路.
ms. Kyōdai-Kokushi.

1694 —— compiled by Kudō Kyōkei 工藤鞏卿.
ms. Ueno.

1695 —— (Hakusekishi, v. IX).
1696 —— (Hakuseki Sōsho, C., v. XV).
1697 —— (Hakuseki-ran, v. IV).
1698 —— (Chūju Sōsho, v. I).

1699 —— (Arai Hakuseki Zenshū, v. V.).
1700 * Hakuseki Shokan 白石書翰 ——
(Hakuseki Sōsho,D.,v. XXXI–XXXXIII).
1701 —— annotated by Muraoka Tsunetsugu 村岡典嗣 (Iwanami Bunko 岩波文庫), Tokyo 1939 (昭和 14).
1702 —— revised ed., Tokyo 1957 (昭和 32).

1703 Arai Hakuseki 新井白石 (1657–1725)
Honsaroku-kō 本佐録考 (Impressions of the Honsaroku). jb. 1 v.

cf. Miyazaki, p. 770.

1704 —— (Chintei Sōsho, v. XIII).
1705 —— (Rinchi Sōsho, v. XIV).
1706 —— (Arai Hakuseki Zenshū, v. VI).
1707 —— (Kō Hakuseki Sōsho, v. IX).

1708 Arai Hakuseki 新井白石 (1657–1725)
Seiyo Zusetsu 西洋圖説 (Illustrated Remarks on the West).

note: no copy extant.

1709 Arai Hakuseki 新井白石 (1657–1725) Shin'an Shukan 新安手簡 (Letters between Arai Hakuseki and Asaka Tampaku 安積澹泊) compiled by Tatehara Suiken 立原翠軒. jb. 3 vols.

cf. Kaikoku, pp. 302–303; Miyazaki, p. 761.
ms. Jingū, Naikaku, Shōryōbu, Sonkeikaku, Tōdai-Nanki.

1710 —— (Hakusekishi).
1711 —— (Zoku Hakuseki Sōsho, C., vv. VIII–X).
1712 —— (Zoku Hakuseki Sōsho, D., vv. XXXVI–XL).
1713 —— (Arai Hakuseki Zenshū, v. V).
1714 —— abridged (Nippon Keizai Sōsho, v. XXIII).
1715 —— abridged (Nippon Keizai Taiten, v. LI).
1716 * Kaisei Shin'an Shukan 改正新安手簡 (Shin'an Shukan, revised), [n.p.], [n.d.]. jb. 5 vols.

note: with Kitao Mōki's 北尾孟軌 epilogue of 1787 (天明 7).
cf. Miyazaki, p. 761.
c. Jingū, Tōdai-Nanki, Waseda-Hanabusa.

1717 Arai Hakuseki 新井白石 (1657–1725)
Shinfuku Shukan 新復手簡 (Letters of Arai Hakuseki). jb. 2 vols.

cf. Miyazaki, p. 762.
ms. Naikaku, Tōdai-Nanki.

1718 —— (Hakusekishi).
1719 —— (Zoku Hakuseki Sōsho, C., vv. VI–VII).

1720 —— (Arai Hakuseki Zenshū, v. V).

1721 Arai Hakuseki 新井白石 (1657–1725)

Shinsho 紳書, or Hakuseki Shinsho 白石紳書 (Essays of Arai Hakuseki). jb. 10 vols.
cf. Miyazaki, p. 761.
orig. ms. Tōyō-Iwasaki (only 2 vols).
ms. Ikeda, Jingū, Naikaku, Shōryōbu, Tōdai-Nanki, Tōhoku-Kanō, Ueno, Waseda.

1722 —— [n.p.], 1827 (文政 10). jb. 10 vols.

1723 —— (Hakusekiran, v. XIII–XIV).

1724 —— (Hakuseki Sōsho, A., v. XVII).

1725 —— (Hakuseki Sōsho, C., v. IX).

1726 —— (Kansai Henchosho).

1727 —— (Arai Hakuseki Zenshū, v. V).

1728 —— (Kaitei Shiseki Shūran, v. XI).

1729 —— (Nippon Zuihitsu Taisei, 3rd Series, v. V).

1730 —— abridged (Shiryō Sōsho).

1726

1731 Kurisaki Seiu 栗崎正羽 (1660–1726)

Kurisakiryū Kinsō Hiketsu 栗崎流金創秘訣 (Secret Surgery of the Kurisaki School). jb. 1 v.
note: See also n. 1914.
ms. Kyōdai-Fujikawa.

The Kurisaki School

1732 Kurisakike Namban Abura Toriyō narabini Kōnō 栗崎家南蠻油取樣並効能 (Kurisaki's Method of Extracting Namban Oil and its Efficacy). jb. 1 v.
ms. Kyōdai-Fujikawa.

1733 Kurisakiryū Geka Hiden 栗崎流外科秘傳 (Secrets of the Kurisaki School). jb. 1 v.
ms. Jingū.

1734 * Kurisakiryū Geka Hiji 栗崎流外科秘事 (Secrets of Kurisaki's Surgery). jb. 1 v.
ms. Kyōdai-Fujikawa.

1735 Kurisakiryū Gekasho 栗崎流外科書 (Kurisaki's Surgery). jb. 1 v.
ms. Iwase, Tōhoku-Kanō.

1736 Kurisakiryū Geka Yakuhō 栗崎流外科藥方 (Surgical Prescriptions of the Kurisaki School). jb. 1 v.
ms. Kyōdai-Kokushi.

1737 Oranda Kurisakiryū Kahōshū 阿蘭陀栗崎流家方集 (Western Pharmacy of the Kurisaki School). jb. 1 v.
ms. Kyūdai-Ganka.

———

1738 Matsumiya Shunjō 松宮俊仍 (1686–1780)

Wakan Kibun 和漢寄文 (Documents concerning Japanese Relations with China). jb. 1 v.
ms. Iwase, Tōdai-Nanki, Ueno, Waseda.

1728

1739 Hachiya Teishō 蜂屋定章

Enri Hokki 圓理發起 (Origin of Trigonometry) 1728 (享保 13). jb. 1 v.

1740 —— (Wasan Zenshū, v. CXL).

1741 Matsumiya Shunjō 松宮俊仍 (1686–1780)

Bundo Yojutsu 分度餘術 (Mensuration Arts), 1728 (享保 13). jb. 6 vols.
cf. Samura, p. 1761.
ms. Gakushiin, Naikaku, Tōhoku-Kanō, Tōkyō Temmondai, Ueno.

1730

1742 D'Entrecolles, François Xavier, SJ. 殷弘緒 (1662–1741)

Gyakuji Chūgen 逆耳忠言 *Ni-erh Chung-yen* (Loyal Advice that Offends One's Ear), Peking 1730 (雍正 8). cb. 1 v.
cf. Pfister, p. 545; Jo, p. 405.

1743 —— Shanghai 慈母堂, 1873 (同治 12). cb. 1 v., [1], 69 f., 25cm.
c. Aoyama, ICU.

1744 Nishikawa Seikyū 西川正休 (1693–1756)

Tairyaku Tengaku Meimokushō 大略天學名目鈔 (Short Explanation of Astronomy), Edo [Tokyo] 小林新兵衛, 1730 (享保 15). jb. 1 v., 41, 3f., 26cm.
c. Tohoku-Kanō, Waseda-Ogura.

1745 —— (Tenkei Wakumon, v. V).
note: See nos. 1364–1366.

1746 —— (Joken Isho, v. XI).

1733

1747 Amano Nobukage 天野信景 (1661–1733)

Shiojiri 鹽尻 (Essays), 1733 (享保 18). jb. 100 vols.
cf. Kaikoku, p. 302; Kokushi, p. 123.
ms. Hibiya, Tōdai-Nanki, Tōhoku-Kanō, Ueno, Waseda.

1748 —— annotated by Inoue Yorikuni 井上頼圀 and Muromatsu Iwao 室松岩雄, Tokyo 帝國書院 1907 (明治 40). 2 vols.

1749 —— (Gajikangasho).

1750 —— abridged (Nippon Keizai Taiten, v. LII).
1751 —— abridged (Nippon Keizai Sōsho, v. XXXIV).
1752 —— (Nippon Zuihitsu Taisei, 3rd Series, vv. IX–X).

1753 De Mailla, Joseph François Marie Anne, SJ. 馮秉正 (1669–1748)
Seisei Sūgyō 盛世芻蕘 *Sheng-shih Ch'u-yao* (A General Discourse on Catholicism), Peking, 1773 (雍正 11). cb. 5 vols.
cf. Pfister, p. 600; Jo, pp. 82–83.
1754 —— [Peking], 1796 (嘉慶 1).
1755 —— [Peking], 1818 (嘉慶 23).
1756 —— Shanghai, 1863 (同治 2). cb. 4 vols., 23cm.
c. Aoyama, Hibiya-Ichimura, Nagasaki, Seishin, Tenri.
1757 —— Shanghai 勝世堂, 1870 (同治 9). cb. 3 vols., 22cm.
c. Tōhoku.
1758 —— Peking 遣使會印書館, 1913 (民國 2). cb. 1 v., 155f., 20cm.
c. Tenri.
1759 —— Shanghai, 1926 (民國 15). wb. 1 v.

1760 Hachisuga Jūuemon 蜂須賀重右衛門
Sampō Kiku Gempō Betsuden 算法規矩元法別傳 (A Different Method of Surveying Art), 1733 (享保 18). jb. 1 fold.
ms. Tōhoku-Kanō.

1761 Murai Masahiro 村井昌弘
Ryōchi Shi'nan 量地指南 (Introduction to Mensuration), Edo [Tokyo], 1733 (享保 18). jb. 2 vols., 27cm.
c. Tōhoku-Kanō, Waseda.

1762 Murai Masahiro 村井昌弘
Ryochi Shi'nan Kōhen 量地指南後篇 (Second Series of the *Ryōchi Shi'nan*), [Edo], 1810 (文化 7). jb. 5 vols., 27cm.
c. Tōhoku-Sūgaku.

1763 Murai Masahiro 村井昌弘
Yaso Tenchūki 耶蘇天誅記 (Heaven's Punishment on Christianity). jb. 5 vols.
ms. Kokugakuin, Nagasaki, Naikaku, Ōtani, Tenri, Ueno.

1734

1764 Shimada Dōkan 島田道桓
Kiku Gempō Chōken Bengi 規矩元法長見辯疑 (Answers to Questions on Surveying). [n.p.], 1812 (文化 9). jb. 5 vols., 23cm.
c. Kobe Art Gallery, Ueno, Waseda-Ogura.

1735

1765 Den Ōro 傳王露 *Ch'uan Wang-lu*
Seikoshi 西湖志 *Hsi-hu-chih* (Topography of the Lake *Hsi-hu*), [n.p.], 1735 (雍正 13). cb. 20 vols., 27cm.
note: Specifically outlawed in Japan.
c. Kyōdai-Bungakubu, Naikaku, Waseda.

1766 Hosoi Kōtaku 細井廣澤 (1658–1735)
Sokuryō Higen 測量秘言 (Secrets of Mensuration). jb. 1 v.
cf. Ebisawa-Namban, pp. 100–101.
orig. ms. Tōhoku-Okamoto.
ms. Kyōdai.
phot. Ebisawa.

1767 Matsunaga Ryosuke 松永良弼
Tenkei Wakumon Hakki 天經或問發揮 (Basic Explanation of the Tenkei Wakumon). jb. 1 v.
ms. Kyūdai-Butsuri, Tōhoku-Kanō.

1736

1768 Imamura Eisei 今村英生 (1671–1736)
Imamura Eisei Nikki 今村英生日記 (Diary of Imamura Eisei).
note: contains the examination of P. Sidotti.
ms. the Imamuras.
1769 —— pr. by Imamura Akitsune 今村明恒, *Rangaku no So Imamura Eisei,* Tokyo 1942 (昭和 17), pp. 324–333.

1770 Kani Yōsai 蟹養齋 (1705–1778)
Chiō Yōshi 治邦要旨 (Essentials of Ruling a Nation). jb. 3 vols.
cf. Samura, p. 13 .
1771 —— (Nippon Keizai Taiten, v. XVI).

1737

1772 Britto, Domingo de, SJ. 畢多明我 (1674–1737)
Rozario Kyō 玫瑰經 *Mei-kui-ching* (Explanation of the Rosary), [n.p.], [n.d.]. jb. 1 v.
cf. Pfister, p. 564; Jo, pp. 36–38.
c. Vatican Lib.
1773 —— Shanghai 1881 (光緒 7). cb. 1 v. 10f., 13cm.
c. Seishin.

1774 Tsuchimikado Yasukuni 土御門泰邦
Tenkei Wakumon Seigi 天經或問正義 (Criticism of the Tenkei Wakumon). jb. 1 v.
ms. Kyūdai-Butsuri, Tōhoku-Sugaku.

1775 Tsuchimikado Yasukuni 土御門泰

Yasukunikyō-ki 泰邦卿記 (Diary of Tsuchimikado Yasukuni). jb. 7 vols.
cf. Kokushi, pp. 208–209.
ms. Shōryōbu.

1738

1776 Aoki Kon'yō 青木昆陽 (1698–1769)
Sōro Zatsudan 草盧雜談 (Essays). 1738 (元文 3). jb. 2 vols.
cf. Kokushi, p. 174.
ms. Tōhoku-Kanō (2 volumes of the First Series only).
1777 —— (Nippon Keizai Sōsho, v. VII).
1778 —— (Nippon Keizai Taiten, v. XII).
1779 —— (Dai-Nippon Shisō Zenshū, v. XI).
1780 De Mailla, Joseph François Marie Anne, SJ. 馮秉正 (1669–1748)
Seikei Kōeki 聖經廣益 Sheng-ching Kuang-i (Interpretations of the Holy Bible), Peking, 1738 (乾隆 3). cb. 2 vols.
cf. Pfister, p. 600.
1781 —— Shanghai, 1859 (咸豊 9). cb. 2 vols.
1782 —— Shanghai, 1866 (同治 5). cb. 2 vols., 18cm.
c. Naikaku, Seishin, Tenri.
1783 —— [n.p.], 1875 (光緒 1). cb. 2 vols., 25cm.
c. Tōhoku.
1784 —— Shanghai, 1917 (民國 6). wb. 1 v.
1785 —— Shanghai, 1922 (民國 11). wb. 1 v.

1786 De Mailla, Joseph François Marie Anne, SJ. 馮秉正 (1669–1748)
Seinen Kōeki 聖年廣益 Sheng-nien Kuang-i (Lives of the Saints with Reflections for Every Day in the Year), Peking, 1738 (乾隆 3). cb. 24 vols., 27cm.
cf. Pfister, p. 600.
c. Tōhoku.
1787 —— Shanghai 慈母堂, 1875 (光緒 1). cb. 4 vols., 15cm.
c. Kyūdai, Nagasaki, Naikaku, Seishin (v. I lacked) Tenri.
1788 —— Shanghai, 1908 (光緒 34). wb. 1 v.

1789 Itō Baiu 伊藤梅宇 (1683–1745)
Kembun Dansō 見聞談叢 (Accounts of Personal Experience). 1738 (元文 3). jb. 6 vols.
note: v. VI contains accounts concerned Amakusa Shirō.

1790 Kitajima Kenshin 北島見信

Oranda Tenchi Nizu Zeisetsu 紅毛天地二圖贅說 (Explanation of the Dutch Celestial and Territorial Charts), 1738 (元文 3) jb. 3 vols.
cf. Kaikoku, pp. 82–83; Shimmura-Namban II, pp. 3–14.
ms. Imoto, Kyōdai (v. III lacked), Nagasaki, Tōhoku-Kanō (v. III lacked).
1791 —— Tokyo 珍書同好會 1916 (大正 5).
1792 Oyanguren de Santa Ines, Melchior, OFM. (1688–1747)
Arte De La Lengua Japona., Mexico 1738. wb. 1 v., [18], 200, [2] p., 21cm.
cf. Streit VI, p. 378; Laures, n. 57.
c. Kyōdai, Tenri, Tōyō, Ueno.
phot. Sophia.

1739

1793 Yuasa Gentei 湯淺元禎 (1708–1781)
Jōzan Kidan 常山紀談 (Tales of Jozan), 1739 (元文 4). jb. 15 vols.
cf. Kokushi, p. 141.
c. Hibiya.
ms. Iwase, Tenri.
1794 —— 1771 (明和 8). jb. 14 vols.
c. Gakushiin, Iwase.
1795 —— Osaka 宋榮堂, 1898 (明治 31). wb. 2 vols., 23cm.
c. Ebisawa, Tenri, Ueno.
1796 —— annotated by Mori Senzō 森銑三 (Iwanami Bunko).
1797 —— (Yūhōdō Bunko).
1798 —— (Zoku Kokumin Bunko).
1799 —— (Teikoku Bunko, v. XXXI).
1800 —— (Zoku Teikoku Bunko, v. V).
1801 —— abridged (Settsu Sōsho).
1802 —— tr. into Chinese by Okamatsu Ōkoku 岡松甕谷, 1916 (大正 5). jb. 11 vols.

1742

1803 Koegler, Ignatio, SJ. 戴進賢 (1680–1746)
Rekishō Kōsei Kōhen 曆象考成後篇 Li-hsiang K'ao-ch'eng Hou-p'ien (Supplement to Theories of the Astronomical Calendar), compiled by Ignatio Kögler, Andrea Perreira and Mei Anto 明安圖 Ming An-t'u, Peking 1742 (乾隆 7). cb. 10 vols.
c. Gakushiin.
cf. Pfister, pp. 647–648, 653; Ebisawa-Namban, pp. 222–233.
c. Gakushiin, Ikeda, Seikadō, Tōhoku-Sūgaku.
ms. Gakushiin, Imoto, Kyōdai-Chiri, Tōhoku-Kanō, Waseda.
1804 —— (Ritsureki Engen)
1805 —— Peking 勵志書屋, 2nd ed., 1896 (光緒 22) cb. 10 vols.

1806 Matsudaira Norimura 松平乘邑

(1686–1746)

Kujigata Osadamegaki 公事方御定書(Code of Judicial Procedure), 1742 (寛保 2). jb.
cf. Kokushi, p. 75.

1807 * Kyūbakufu Kujigata Osadamegaki 舊幕府公事方御定書 (Code of Judicial Procedure of the Shogunate Government). jb.

1808 —— (Hyakumantō).

1809 Osadamegaki Hyakkajō 御定書百箇條 (The One Hundred Laws), 1742 (寛保 2). jb.
cf. Kokushi, pp. 37–38, 75.
note: Second half of the *Kujigata Osadamegaki* (n. 1806).
ms. Hibiya.

1810 —— (Tokugawa Kinreikō, Kōshū).
1811 —— (Hyakumantō).
1812 —— (Nippon Keizai Taiten, v. I).
1813 * Kyūbakufu Osadamegaki 舊幕府御定書 (Laws of the Shogunate Government).
1814 —— (Hyakumantō).

1744

1815 Koegler, Ignatio, SJ. 戴進賢 (1696–1746)
Gishō Kōsei 儀象考成 *Yi-hsiang K'ao-ch'eng* (Examination of Astronomical Instruments), Peking 1744 (乾隆 9). cb. 32 vols.
cf. Pfister, p. 648; Jo, pp. 469–471.
c. Kyūdai-Butsuri; Tōhoku-Kanō.
ms. Gakushiin, Kyōdai, Ebisawa (vv. 1–7 only).

1816 —— Peking 1756 (乾隆 21). cb. 35 vols.
c. Hazama, Kyōdai-Butsuri, Kyōdai-Chiri, Seikadō, Tōhoku-Kanō.

1817 —— compiled by Kaneko Shōgen 金子勝現.
ms. Naikaku.

1747

1818 Dazai Shundai 太宰春臺 (1680–1747)
Shishien Mampitsu 紫芝園漫筆 (Essays). jb. 8 vols.
c. Waseda.

1819 —— (Sūbun Sōsho, Series I).
1820 —— (Ansai Sōsho).
1821 —— abridged (Nippon Keizai Sōsho, v. XXXIII).
1822 —— abridged (Nippon Keizai Taiten, v. LI).

1750

1823 Irie Shūkei 入江修敬 (–1773)
Tenkei Wakumon Chūkai 天經或問註解 (A

Commentary on the Tenkei Wakumon), Edo [Tokyo], 1750 (寛延1). jb. 3 vols., 26cm.
cf. Kaikoku, pp. 305–307.
c. Ebisawa, Gakushiin, Imoto, Keiō, Kyōdai, Shōkōkan (v. I lacked), Tōhoku-Kanō, Tōhoku-Sūgaku, Waseda-Ogura.
ms. Jingu, Kyodai.

1824 —— Osaka 1794 (寛政 6). jb. 3 vols.
c. Kyūdai-Butsuri, Tōdai-Nanki.

1825 * Irieshi Tenkei Wakumon Chūkai 入江氏天經或問註解 (Explanation of the Tenkei Wakumon Chūkai by Mr. Irie) by Nishimura Tōsato 西村遠里.
ms. Gakushiin, Kyōdai, Kyūdai-Butsuri, Naikaku, Tōhoku-Kanō.

1826 Ogura 小倉
Orandayaku Mondō 紅毛譯問答 (Dailogue on World Geography). jb. 1 v.
cf. Kaikoku, p. 24.
ms. Kyōdai.

1827 —— (Kaihyō Sōsho, v. II).

1751

1828 In Kōnin 印光任 *Yin Kuang-jen*
Ōmon Kiryaku 澳門紀略 *Ao-men Chi-lüeh* (History of Macao), by In Kōnin and Chō Jorin 張汝霖 *Chang Ju-lin*, 1751 (乾隆 16). cb. 2 vols.
note: Specifically outlawed in Japan.

1829 ——1890 (光緒 16). cb. 2 vols.
c. ICU, Tōyō-Fujita.

1754

1830 Bunyū 文雄
Hi Tenkei Wakumon 非天經或問 (Criticism of the Tenkei Wakumon), [1754?]. jb. 1 v.
ms. Gakushiin, Imoto, Jinshu.

1755

1831 Miura Baien 三浦梅園 (1723–1789)
Bungo Seki-kō 豊後跡考 (On the Remains of Bungo), 1755 (寶暦 5). jb. 1 v.

1832 —— (Baien Zenshū, v. I).

1833 Mukai Genchū 向井元仲
Hakurai Shojaku Taiigaki 舶來書籍大意書 (Compendium of Imported Books), [1755?]. jb. 1 v.
cf. Samura, p. 1633.
ms. Naikaku.

1834 Hakurai Shomoku 舶來書目 (List of Imported Books). jb. 8 vols.
ms. Ueno.

1835 * Hakusai Shomoku 舶載書目 (List of Imported Books).
ms. Shōryōbu, Ueno.

1759

1836 Hattori Nankaku 服部南郭 (1683–1759)

Bunkai Zakki 文會雜記 (Essays). jb. 3 vols.

cf. Kokushi, p. 275.

ms. Tōhoku-Kanō, Waseda.

1837 —— (Nippon Bunko, v. II).

1838 —— (Nippon Zuihitsu Taisei, v. VII).

1839 —— (Zoku Shiseki Shūran, v. XLIV).

1840 —— (Nippon Zuihitsu Zenshū, v. II).

1841 Ruizoku 類族 (Families of Christians), 1759 (實曆 9). jb. 1 v.

ms. Sophia.

1760

1842 Tanabe Mokei 田邊茂啓 (1688–1768)

Nagasaki-shi 長崎志 or Nagasaki Jitsuroku Taisei 長崎實録大成 (*History of Nagasaki*), 1760 (實曆 10). jb. 9 vols.

cf. Kokushi, p. 233; Samura, p. 1514.

ms. Iwase, Naikaku, Nagasaki, Tōdai-Nanki, Ueno, Waseda.

1843 —— pr. by Koga Jujirō 古賀十二郎, Nagasaki 1928 (昭和 3).

1844 * Nagasaki Jitsuroku 長崎實録 (True Descriptive of Nagasaki).

ms. Nagasaki, Naikaku, Sophia.

Old Records of Nagasaki

1845 Ishikawa Gibyōe 石川儀兵衛

Kiyō Bunkenroku 崎陽聞見録 (Recollections of Nagasaki). jb. 1 v.

ms. Ueno.

1846 Keiho Hikki 瓊浦筆記 (Notes on Nagasaki). jb. 1 v.

ms. Naikaku, Sonkeikaku.

1847 Keiho Kiji 瓊浦紀事 (Notes on Nagasaki). jb. 2 vols.

cf. Samura, p. 588.

ms. Naikaku.

1848 Kirishitan Nagasaki ni kansuru Utsushi 切支丹長崎ニ關スル寫 (Copies of Notes on Christianity and Nagasaki). jb. 1 v.

ms. Kyudai-Bunka.

1849 Kiyō Jitsuroku 崎陽實録 (Real History of Nagasaki). jb. 1 v.

ms. Iwase.

1850 Kiyōki 崎陽記 (History of Nagasaki). jb. 1v.

ms. Iwase, Nagasaki.

1851 Kiyō Zatsujō 崎陽雜乘 (Notes on Nagasaki). jb. 1 v.

ms. Ebisawa.

1852 Matsuura Tōkei 松浦東溪 (1752–1820)

Nagasaki Kokon Shūran 長崎古今集覧 (Outline of the History of Nagasaki). jb. 14 vols.

ms. Iwase, Nagasaki.

1853 —— (Kaishoku).

1854 Nagasaki Bugyōsho Kōgi yori aiwatashisōrō On-Kakitsukerui 長崎奉行所公儀ヨリ相渡候御書付類 (Documents from the Shogunate Government to the Nagasaki Government). jb. 1 v.

ms. Ebisawa.

1855 Nagasaki Fudoki 長崎風土記 (Geographical Record of Nagasaki). jb. 1 v.

ms. Ueno.

1856 Nagasaki Hijiki 長崎秘事記 (Secret Records of Nagasaki). jb. 1 v.

ms. Tōhoku-Kanō.

1857 * Nagasaki Hiroku 長崎秘録 (Secret Records of Nagasaki). jb. 1 v.

ms. Kariya.

1858 Nagasaki-ki 長崎記 (History of Nagasaki). jb. 1 v.

ms. Iwase, Nagasaki, Naikaku, Tōdai-Nanki, Tōhoku-Kanō.

1859 * Nagasaki Kiji 長崎紀事 (Records of Nagasaki). jb. 2vols.

cf. Samura, p. 1513.

ms. Tōdai-Nanki, Ueno.

1860 Nagasaki Kirishitan Monjo 長崎切支丹文書 (Christian Documents of Nagasaki). jb. 1 v.

ms. Ebisawa, Shiryō.

1861 Nagasaki Minato no Ki 長崎湊之記 (Notes on the Port of Nagasaki). jb. 1 v.

1862 —— (Shinobazu Sosho).

1863 Nagasakishi Kenroku 長崎志見録 (History of Nagasaki). jb. 1 v.

ms. Waseda.

1864 Nambansen Nagasaki Raishin no Koto 南蠻船長崎來津ノ事 (Arrival of the Western Ships in Nagasaki). jb. 1 v.

ms. Kyūdai-Bunka.

1865 * Nambansen Nyūshinki 南蠻船入津記 (Arrival of the Western Ships). jb.

1866 —— (Chūko Sōsho, v. LXXVII).

1867 Ōoka Bizen-no-kami 大岡備前守

Kiyō Gundan 崎陽群談 (Tales of Naga-saki). jb. 2 vols.

1868 —— (Kyūshū Shiryō Sōsho).

1869 Tanabe Mokei 田邊茂啓 (1688–1768)
Nagasaki Nenpyō Kyoyō 長崎年表擧要 (Abridged Chronological Table of Nagasaki).

1870 Tazawa Harufusa 田澤春房
Nagasaki Kibun 長崎紀聞 (Notes on Nagasaki). jb. 3 vols.
ms. Daitokyu.

1871 —— pr. by Kichō Tosho Eihon Kankōkai 貴重圖書影本刊行會, Kyoto 1930 (昭和 5). jb. 3 vols., 26cm.

1872 Tokuhō 禿法
Nagasaki Engi 長崎緣起 or Nagasaki Yuraiki 長崎由來記 (History of Nagasaki).
cf. Samura, p. 1512.
ms. Hibiya-Kondō, Iwase, Nagasaki, Shiryō.

1873 * Nagasaki Engi Ryakuki 長崎緣起略記 (Brief History of Nagasaki). jb. 1 v.
ms. Tōhoku-Kanō, Waseda.

1874 —— (Zokuzoku Gunsho Ruijū, v. VIII).

1875 —— (Kirishitan Bunko, A., v. II).

1876 * Nagasaki Hajime Yuraiki 長崎始由來記 or Nagasaki Ryakuki 長崎略記 (Origin and History of Nagasaki). jb. 1 v.
ms. Nagasaki.

1877 * Nagasaki Raiyuki 長崎來由記 (History of Nagasaki).
ms. Tōdai-Nanki.

1878 * Nagasaki Ryakuki 長崎略記 (Short History of Nagasaki). jb. 1 v.
ms. Ebisawa, Nagasaki.

1761

1879 Bai Buntei 梅文鼎 *Mei Wen-ting* (1633–1721)
Baishi Sōsho Shūyō 梅氏叢書輯要 *Mei-shih Ts'ung-shu Chi-yao* (Selected Works of Mr. Mei), [Shanghai], 1761 (道光 26). cb. 24 vols.
note: Revised ed. of n. 1644.
c. Tōhoku, Tōyō, Waseda-Ogura.

1880 —— [n.p.] 1839 (光緒 19). cb. 1 v.
c. Gakushiin.

1881 —— [n.p.], 1888 (光緒 14). cb. 6vols.
c. Seishin.

1882 Bai Kokusei 梅穀成 *Mei Ku-ch'eng*
Sekisui Ichin 赤水遺珍 *Ch'ih-shui I-chen* (Western Mathematics), [n.p.], 1761 (乾隆 26).

1883 —— (Baishi Sōsho Shūyō).

1884 Mei Anto 明安圖 *Ming An-t'u*
Katsuen Mitsuritsu Shōhō 割圓密率捷法 *Ke-yüan Mi-lü Chieh-fa* (Method of Trigonometrical Functions), 1761 (乾隆 26). cb.
note: Based on the theories of P. Pierre Jartoux, SJ.
cf. Pfister, p. 586.

1885 —— (Baishi Sōsho Shūyō).

1886 —— 1839 (道光 19). cb. 3 vols.
c. Waseda-Ogura.

1887 —— (Kangaseishitsu Ikō).

1888 —— (Kokon Sangaku Sōsho, v. XIII–XIV).

1762

1889 Arahamasen Minami-Tsūshū Hyōchaku Shimatsu 荒濱船南通州漂着始末 (Record of Shipwrecked Seamen who Drifted from Arahama to Tsushū), 1762 (寶曆 12). jb. 1 v.

1890 —— (Ikoku Hyōryū Kidanshū).

1763

1891 Aoki Kon'yō 青木昆陽 (1698–1769)
Kon'yō Manroku 昆陽漫録 (Kon'yō's Essay), 1763 (寶曆 13). jb. 1 v.
cf. Kokushi, p. 110.
ms. Gakushiin, Kariya, Tōhoku-Kano.

1892 —— (Nippon Zuihitsu Zenshū, v. X).

1893 —— (Nippon Zuihitsu Taisei, v. X).

1894 —— (Hyakka Setsurin, v. I).

1895 —— abridged (Nippon Keizai Sōsho, v. XXXIII).

1896 —— abridged (Ōshuku Zakki).

1897 —— abridged (Nippon Keizai Taiten, v. LI).

1898 —— abridged (Dai-Nippon Shisō Zenshū, v. XI).

1899 * Zoku Kon'yō Manroku 續昆陽漫録 (Second Series of the Kon'yō Manroku), 1766 (明和 3). jb. 2 vols.

1900 —— (Nippon Zuihitsu Taisei, v. X).

1901 —— (Hyakka Setsurin, v. II).

1765

1902 Gotō Rishun 後藤梨春 (1801–1875)
Oranda Banashi 紅毛談 (Tales of Holland), Edo [Tokyo] 悟陰庵, 1765 (明和 2). jb. 2 vols., 19cm.
cf. Boxer-Compagnie, pp. 130–131; Kaikoku, pp. 24–26; Kokushi, p. 41.
c. Hibiya-Kondō, Kyōdai, Ueno, Waseda.

1903 —— (Bummei Genryū Sōsho, v. I).

1767

1904 Benoist, Michel, SJ. 蔣友仁 (1715–1774)

Chikyū Zusetsu 地球圖説 *Ti-ch'iu t'u-shuo* (Illustration of the Globe), [n.p.], 1767 (乾隆 32). cb. 1 v.

1905 —— (Tazan no Ishi).
1906 —— (Bunsenrō Sōsho).
1907 —— (Sōsho Shūsei).

1908 Kaigai Hyōryū Kibun 海外漂流記聞 (Notes on drifted Seamen), 1767 (明和 4).
1909 —— (Shun'urō Sōsho).

1770

1910 Oranda Tsūshi Yuishogaki 阿蘭陀通詞由緒書 (Chronological List of the Translators from Dutch into Japanese), 1770 (明和 7). jb. 1 v.
cf. Itazawa, pp. 141–149.
ms. Nagasaki.

1771

1911 Bahr, Florian, SJ. 魏繼晋 (1706–1771).
Sei Joan Nepomucene-den 聖若望臬玻穆傳 *Sheng Jo-wang Nieh-po-mu-chuan* (Life of St. John Nepomucene) Peking, [n.p.]. cb. 1 v.
cf. Pfister, p. 750 ; Jo, p. 47.
c. Tōyō.
1912 —— Shanghai 慈母堂, 1871 (同治 10) cb. 1 v.

1913 Kinsho Mokuroku 禁書目録 (List of Prohibited Books), Kyoto 京都書林組合, 1771 (明和 8). 1f.

1914 Kurisaki Seiu 栗崎正羽 (1660–1726)
Kurisaki Geka 栗崎外科 (Surgery of the Kurisaki School). jb. 1 v.
note: copied in 1771 (明和 8). See also, n. 1731.
ms. Kyōdai-Fujikawa.

1915 Mukai Kanemi 向井兼美
Tengaku Shokan Taiigaki 天學初函大意書 (Bibliographical Notes of the Tengaku Shokan). jb. 1 v.
note: compiled in 1771. See also, n. 641.
ms. Kyūdai, Tōhoku-Kanō.

1916 Suzuki Kankei 鈴木煥卿
Rōkai Ittoku 撈海一得, Edo [Tokyo], 青黎閣, 1771 (明和 8). jb. 2 vols., 26cm.
c. Tōhoku-Kanō.
1917 —— (Nippon Zushitsu Taisei, v. VII).

1773

1918 Miura Baien 三浦梅園 (1723–1789)
Kagen 價原 (Essays on Economy), 1773 (安永 2). jb.

cf. Kokushi, p. 49.
1919 —— (Baien Zenshū, v. I).
2920 —— (Dai-Nippon Shisō Zenshū, v. VIII).
1921 —— pr. in the *Miura Baien-shū* 三浦梅園集 (Iwanami Bunko).
1922 —— abridged (Nippon Keizai Sōsho, v. XI).
1923 —— abridged (Nippon Keizai Taiten, v. XVII).
1924 —— (Kinsei Shakai Keizai Gakusetsu Taikei, v. XVII).
1925 —— (Nippon Tetsugaku Zensho, v. X).

1774

1926 Ishii Kōchi 石井光致
Kiku Gempō Myōjutsu Zukai 規矩元法妙術圖解 (Illustrated of the Mysterious Art of Surveying), 1774 (安永 3). jb. 2 vols.
ms. Waseda-Ogura.

1927 Kulmus, Johann Adam
Kaitai Shinsho 解體新書 (New Text on Anatomy), tr. by Sugita Gempaku 杉田玄白 etc., Edo [Tokyo], 1774 (安永 3). jb. 3 vols., 23cm.
note: Translation from the Dutch translation from German published in Holland under the title *Ontleedkundige Tafelen*, Amsterdam, 1731. On the front page, there is a picture of Adam and Eve.
cf. Boxer-Compagnie, pp. 48–49; Rangaku, pp. 14–15; Kokushi, p. 45.
c. Nagasaki, Otsuki, Yokohamashidai.
1928 —— (Nippon Kagaku Koten Zensho, v. VIII).
1929 —— (Dai-Nippon Shisō Zenshū, v. XII).
1930 —— (Bummei Genryū Sōsho, v. II).

1931 Nishimura Tōsato 西村遠里 (–1787)
Bankoku Yume Monogatari 萬國夢物語 (Strange Tales of Foreign Lands). (安永 3). jb. 10 vols.
cf. Kaikoku, p. 26; Kokushi, p. 260.
ms. Akioka, Ayuzawa, Nagasaki.
1932 —— (Okinagusa).

1775

1933 Nagasaki Monogatari 長崎物語 (Tales of Nagasaki), 1775 (安永 4). jb. 1 v.
ms. Ebisawa.
phot. Nagasaki.

1776

1934 Hirazawa Gengai 平澤元愷 (1733–1791)
Keiho Gūhitsu 瓊浦偶筆 (Notes on Naga-

saki), Nagasaki 1776 (安永 5). jb. 3 vols.
note: Contains Verbiest's *Kon'yo Gaiki* 坤輿外紀 *K'un-yü Wai-chi* (n. 1321).
cf. Shimmura-Namban I, pp. 474–477; Samura, pp. 588–589.
ms. Nagasaki, Shimmura, Tōyō-Iwasaki, Ueno.
1935 —— (Kaihyō Sōsho, v. VI).

1777

1936 Maeno Ryōtaku 前野良澤 (1723–1803)
Kanrei Higen 管蠡秘言 (Essays). 1777 (安永 6). jb. 1 v.
cf. Kaikoku, pp. 27, 307–308; Ebisawa-Namban, pp. 319–323.
orig. ms. Fujinami.
1937 —— pr. by Iwasaki Katsumi 岩崎克己, in his work *Maeno Ranka,* Tokyo 1938 (昭和 13), pp. 389–392.

1938 Miura Antei 三浦安貞 (1723–1789)
Kizanroku 歸山録 (Travel Home), 1777 (安永 6). jb. 2 vols.
1939 —— (Baien Zenshū, v. I).
1940 —— abridged (Dai-Nippon Shisō Zenshū, v. VIII).
1941 —— (Nippon Tetsugaku Zensho, v. VIII).

1942 Sakuma Koreaki 佐久間惟章 (– 1799)
Kirishitan Zakki 切支丹雜記 (Notes on Christians) 1777 (安永 6). jb. 1 v.
note: Contains *Rōmajin Kanjō* (n. 1945) and others.
ms. Kyōdai.

1778

1943 Ono Keitan 小野景澹
Menkō Shūroku 綿考輯録 (Records of the Hosokawas), 1778 (安永 7).
orig. ms. the Hosokawas.
1944 —— abridged pr. and annotated by Herman Heuvers, SJ., *Hosokawa Gratia Fujin,* Tokyo 1939 (昭和 14). Appendix, pp. 45–65.

1945 Sakuma Koreaki 佐久間惟章
Rōmajin Kanjō 羅媽人欵狀 (Record of Examination of the Roman), 1778 (安永 7). jb. 1 v.
note: Documents regarding to P. G.-B. Sidotti.
ms. Ebisawa, Kanazawa-Kadō, Naikaku, Ueno, Waseda.
1946 —— (Sokkyohen).
1947 —— (Shiseki Shūran).
1948 —— (Arai Hakuseki Zenshū, v. IV).
1949 —— pr. and annotated by Ōtsuki Fumihiko 大槻文彦 in *Seiyō Kibun,* Tokyo 1882 (明治 15).
1950 —— pr. and annotated by Muraoka

Tsunetsugu 村岡典嗣 in *Seiyō Kibun* (Iwanami Bunko), Tokyo 1936 (昭和 11).
1951 * Rōma Kanchō 羅媽欵帖 (Record of Examination of the Roman). jb. 1 v.
1952 —— (Hakuseiki Sōsho, D., v. XLVII).
1953 * Rōma Kanjō 羅媽欵狀 (Record of Examination of the Roman). jb. 1 v.
ms. Keiō.

1779

1954 Fukushima Denzō 福島傳藏
Sankō Shimabaraki 參考島原記 (New History of the Shimabara Rebellion), compiled by D. Fukushima and Shindō Ansei 新藤安精, 1779 (安永 8). jb. 2 vols.
ms. Tenri, Ueno.

1780

1955 D'Ollieres, Jacobe F. Marie Diendonne, SJ. 守雅各 (1722–1780)
Seiji Yōri 聖事要理 *Sheng-shih Yao-li* (Catechism), Shanghai 1780 (乾隆 45). cb. 1 v.
cf. Pfister, p. 908.
1956 —— Shanghai 1880 (光緒 6). cb. 1 v. 34f., 13cm.
c. Seishin.
1957 * [tr. into Jap.] Kyōri Mondō 教理問答 (Catechism), approved by Bishop Pierre Marie Osouf, MEP., Tokyo 1886 (明治 19). wb. 1 v., 86p., 19cm.
c. Sophia, Tenri.

1958 Matsumiya Kanzan 松宮觀山 (1686–1780)
Tenchi Kaibyaku Suiryōkōben 天地開闢推量考辯 (Criticism on the Discourse of Creation). jb.
1959 —— (Matsumiya Kanzan-shū, v. II).

1782

1960 Shitsuki Tadajirō 志筑忠次郎 (1760–1806)
Bankoku Kanki 萬國管闚 (World Geography), 1782 (天明 2). jb. 2 vols.
cf. Kaikoku, pp. 29–30.
ms. Ayuzawa, Tōyō-Iwasaki.

1783

1961 Kudō Heisuke 工藤平助 (1734–1800)
Akaezo Fūsetsukō 赤蝦夷風說考 (News on the Russians), [n.p.]. 1783 (天明 3). jb. 2 vols.

cf. Kaikoku, pp. 30–31, 386; Tenri-Jap. II, p. 151;
Kokushi, p. 4.
ms. Tenri.

1962 —— (Ōshuku Zakki).
1963 —— (Hokumon Sōsho, v. I).

1784

1964 Miura Antei 三浦安貞 (1723–1789)
Samidare-shō 五月雨抄 (Musings against
the Early Summer Rain), 1784 (天明 4). jb.
2 vols.
ms. Hibiya-Kaga, Jinshū, Kyūdai-Bunka, Naikaku,
Sophia, Tenri, Tōdai-Nanki, Tōhoku-Kanō,
Ueno.

1965 —— (Sokkyohen, v. XIV).
1966 —— (Zonsai Sōsho, v. CXXXII).
1967 —— (Baien Zenshū, v. I).
1968 —— (Kirishitan Shiryō).
1969 —— (Nippon Shisō Tōsō Shiryō,
v. X).
1970 —— compiled by Shibata Hana-
mori 柴田花守, Kagoshima 四姓堂, 1872 (明
5), jb. 2 vols., 19cm.
note: Contains *Kiyō Sawa* 崎陽茶話 and *Nagasaki
Jakyō Shimatsu* 長崎邪教始末 in v. II. See Pt. II.
cf. Samura, p. 809.
c. Ebisawa, Kichū, Kyūdai-Bunka, Nagasaki,
Naikaku, Osaka, Sophia, Sukeno, Tenri, Tōkyoiku, Ueno-Shirai.

1971 —— tr. into English and annotated
by Leon Hurvitz " Samidare-shō by Miura
Baien " (*Monumenta Nipponica*, vv. VIII–
XI), Tokyo 1952–53.

1785

1972 Hayashi Shihei 林子平 (1738–1793)
Sangoku Tsūran Zusetsu 三國通覧圖說
(General Views of Three Countries with
Maps), Edo [Tokyo], 須原屋, 1785 (天明 5).
jb. 1 v., 51f., 5maps, 27cm.
cf. Kaikoku, pp. 31–32; Boxer-Compagnie, pp. 13–
19; Kokushi, p. 120.
c. Kobe Art Gallery, Nichidai-Ueda, Tōhoku,
Tōdai, Waseda, Ueno.
ms. Jingū, Hibiya-Kondō, Kariya, Nagasaki, Tenri,
Tōdai-Nanki, Tōhoku-Kanō, Waseda.

1973 —— (Rokumusai Zensho, v. I.).
1974 —— (Hayashi Shihei Zenshū, v. II).
1975 —— (Edo Monogatari).
1976 —— (Dai-Nippon Shisō Zenshū,
v. IX).
1977 —— tr. into French by Heinrich
Julius Klaproth, *Sankokf tsou ran to sets, ou
aperçu général des trois royaumes par Rinsifée*,
Paris 1832.

1978 Hayashi Shihei 林子平 (1738–1793)
Hayashi Shihei Jōsho 林子平上書(Memorial of Hayashi Shihei).

cf. Kokushi, p. 141.
ms. Kobe Art Gallery.

1979 —— (Rokumusai Zensho, v. II).
1980 —— (Nippon Keizai Sōsho, v. XII).
1981 —— (Nippon Keizai Taiten,v. XX).

1786

1982 Blau, Johan
Shinsei Chikyū Bankoku Zusetsu 新製地
球萬國圖説 (New Illustrations of the World)
tr. by Katsuragawa Kokuzui 桂川國瑞, 1786
(天明 6). jb. 1 v.
note: Translation of Blau's *Nova Totius Terrarum
orbis Tabula*.
cf. Kaikoku, p. 88.
c. Tokyōiku.

1983 —— repr. and annotated by Ono
Tadashige 小野忠重 in the *Oranda Zatsuwa*,
Tokyo 1943 (昭和 18).

1984 Kudō Kyūkei 工藤球卿 (1734–
1800)
Sangoku Tsūran Zusetsu Hoi 三國通覧圖
說補遺, or Roshia Ryakusetsu 魯西亞略說
(Supplement to the Sangoku Tsūran
Zusetsu or State of Affairs in Russia), 1786
(天明 6). jb. 1 v.
note: Similar to the *Akaezo Fūsetsukō* (n. 1961), but
having no direct connection with Hayashi's work.
Not printed.
cf. Kaikoku, p. 31.
ms. Kyōdai.

1985 —— (Chūko Sōsho)

1986 Miura Baien 三浦梅園 (1723–1789)
Zeigo 贅語 (Essay), 1786 (天明 6). jb.
7 vols.
cf. Kokushi, p. 163.
1987 —— (Nippon Rinri Ihen, v. X).
1988 —— abridged (Nippon Keizai
Sōsho, v. XXXIII).

1989 Go Shii 呉志伊 *Wu Chih-i*
Zōho Sengaikyō Kōchū 增補山海經廣註
Tseng-pu Shan-hai-ching Kuang-chu, 1786 (乾隆
51). cb. 6 vols.
note: Specifically outlawed book in Japan.
c. Nichidai-Hayashi.

1787

1990 Morishima Nakara 森島中良(1754–
1808)
Oranda Zatsuwa 紅毛雜話 (Stories about
Holland), Edo [Tokyo] 須原屋, 1787 (天明
7). jb. 5 vols., 23cm.
cf. Kaikoku, p. 380; Boxer-Compagnie, pp. 114–115,
131.
c. Hibiya-Kondō, Iwase, Kariya, Kōbe Museum,
Kyōto, Jingū, Nagasaki-Isahaya, Naikaku, Nichi-

dai-Ueda, Tōkyō Kagaku Museum, Tōyō-Iwa-saki, Ueno-Shirai, Waseda.
ms. Waseda.

1991 —— Edo [Tokyo] 須原屋, 1796 (寛政 8). jb. 5 vols., 23cm.
c. Nagasaki-Isahaya.

1992 —— (Bummei Genryū Sōsho, v. I).

1993 —— repr. and annotated by Ono Tadashige 小野忠重, Tokyo 1943 (昭和 18).

1788

1994 Ōtsuki Bansui 大槻盤水 (1756–1827)
Rangaku Kaitei 蘭學階梯 (Steps into the Dutch Language), Edo [Tokyo] 群玉堂, 1788 (天明 8). jb. 2 vols., 23cm.
cf. Boxer-Compagnie, pp. 64–65; Asahi, p. 56; Kokushi, p. 322.
c. Hibiya-Kondō, Keiō, Ōtsuki, Ueno, Waseda.

1995 —— (Bansui Zonkyō, v. II).

1996 —— (Bummei Genryū Sōsho, v. I).

1997 Tengaku Wakumon 天學或問 (Outline of Astronomy), 1788 (天明 8). jb. 2 vols.
ms. Kompira.

1789

1998 Kuchiki Masatsuna 朽木昌綱 (1750–1802)
Taisei Yochi Zusetsu 泰西輿地圖說 (Geographical Compendium dealing with Western Countries), Edo [Tokyo] 1789 (天明 9). jb. 6 vols., 23cm.
cf. Kaikoku, pp. 88–91; Tenri-Jap. II, p. 117; Boxer-Compagnie, p. 20.
c. Ayuzawa, Okada, Tenri, Tohoku-Kano, Ueno. Waseda,

1999 —— [Edo] 1794 (寛政 6). jb. 6 vols., 23cm.
c. Waseda.

2000 —— Edo [Tokyo] 彩雲堂, 1804 (享和 4). jb. 6 vols., 23cm.
c. Ueno.

2001 Morishima Nakara 森島中良 (1754–1808)
Bankoku Shinwa 萬國新話 (New Story of the World), Edo [Tokyo] 須原屋, 1789 (寛政 1). jb. 5 vols., 23cm.
cf. Boxer-Compagnie, p. 131.
c. Kyōto.

2002 —— repr. by Ono Tadashige 小野忠重, *Kōmō Zatsuwa,* Tokyo 1943 (昭和 18).

2003 —— Osaka 藤屋, 1800 (寛政 12), 2nd ed. jb. 5 vols., 23cm.
c. Hibiya-Kondō, Keiō, Kyūdai, Waseda.

2004 Nakai Chikuzan 中井竹山 (1717–1804)
Sōbō Kigen 草茅危言 (Disputation on Social Economics), [n.p.], 1789 (寛政 1). jb. 10 vols.
cf. Kokushi, p. 173.
ms. Hibiya, Jingū, Kanazawa-Kadō, Kompira.

2005 —— Edo [Tokyo], 1868 (明治 1). jb. 5 vols.
c. Nichidai-Ueda.

2006 —— Tokyo 1942 (昭和 17). jb. 5 vols.

2007 —— (Nippon Keizai Sōsho, v. XXIV).

2008 —— (Nippon Keizai Taiten, v. XXIII).

2009 —— (Dai-Nippon Shisō Zenshū, v. VII).

2010 —— (Nippon Shisō Tōsō Shiryō, v. VI).

1791

2011 Hattori Nakatsune 服部中庸 (1756–1824)
Sandaikō 三大考 (Consideration of the Three Principles), Nagoya 1791 (寛政 3). jb. 1 v., 25f., 19cm.
c. Taishō, Tenri.

2012 Honda Toshiaki 本多利明 (1744–1821)
Sekii Dōsei 赤夷動静 (Condition of the Russians), 1791 (寛政 3). jb. 1 v.
note: not published.
cf. Kaikoku, p. 35.
ms. Kyōdai.

2013 Ōishi Hisanori 大石久敬 (1721–1794)
Jikata Hanreiroku 地方凡例録 (Model of the Reports of Local Administration), [1791, 寛政 3?]. jb.
cf. Kokushi, p. 124.
ms. Hibiya, Iwase, Jingū, Tōdai-Nanki.

2014 —— annotated by Tōjō Kō 東條耕, Edo [Tokyo] 1860 (萬延 1). jb. 20 vols.

2015 —— Chiba 大倉儀, 1866 (慶應 2). jb. 11 vols.
c. Daitokyu, Naikaku.

2016 —— revised ed., 見山樓, 1871 (明治 4). jb. 20 vols., 19cm.
c. Naikaku, Ueno.

2017 —— (Nippon Keizai Taiten, v. XLIII).

1792

2018 Kumano Seishō 熊野正紹
Nagasaki Minatogusa 長崎港草 (Notes on the Port of Nagasaki), 1792 (寛政 4). jb.
cf. Samura, p. 1515.
ms. Iwase, Nagasaki, Ueno.

2019 —— (Nagasaki Sōsho, A., v. II–IX).

Report of Daikokuya Kōdaiyu 大黒屋幸太夫 who returned to Japan with Adam Laxman, 1792

2020 Hokusa Ibun 北槎異聞 (Strange Report of Russia). jb.
2021 —— (Hokumon Sōsho, v. VI).
note: See also, nos. 2041–46.

2022 Jitsuroku Kōdaiyu Isokichi Hyōkyaku Monogatari 實録幸太夫磯吉漂客物語 (True Tales of the Shipwreck of Kōdaiyu and Isokichi). jb.
2023 —— (Hyōryūki Sōsho, v. XLIII).

2024 Kōdaiyu-bune Ikken Utsushi 幸太夫船一件寫 (Copy of the Account of the Shipwreck of Kōdaiyu). jb.
2025 —— (Hyōryūki Sōsho, v. XL).

2026 Kōdaiyu Hyōryūki 幸太夫漂流記 (Record of the Shipwrecked Sailor Kōdaiyu). jb. 1 v.
ms. Naikaku.

2027 Nakazato Chūjo 中里仲舒
Hyōmin Kōdaiyu Isokichi Kikoku Kiji 漂民幸太夫磯吉歸國記事 (Account of the Return to Japan of the Shipwrecked Sailors Kōdaiyu and Isokichi). jb. 1 v.
ms. Naikaku.

2028 Roshia Hyōryūjin Danwa Kikigaki 魯西亞漂流人談話聞書 (Report of the Shipwrecked Sailors who drifted to Russia). jb.
2029 —— (Chōfū Irin).

2030 Roshiakoku Hyōkyaku Kibun 魯西亞國漂客記聞 (Report of Sailors shipwrecked on the Coast of Russia). jb. 1 v.
ms. Hibiya-Kondō.

2031 Roshiakoku Hyōryū Ni-Jikki 魯西亞國漂流二實記 (Two authentic Records of shipwrecked Sailors who drifted to Russia). jb. 1 v.
ms. Ueno.

1793

2032 Broedelet, J.
Roshia Hongi 魯西亞本紀 (True History of Russia), tr. by Maeno Ryōtaku 前野良澤, 1793 (寛政 5). jb. 3 vols.
cf. Kaikoku, pp. 386–388.
ms. Kyōto, Naikaku, Ōtsuki, Shōkōkan, Tōdai-Nanki.

2033 Huebner, Johann (1668–1731)
Roshia-shi 魯西亞志 (Descriptive Geography of Russia), tr. by Katsuragawa Hoshū 桂川甫周, 1793 (寛政 5). jb. 1 v.
note: Abstract translation from Hübner's *Algemeene Geographie*.
cf. Kaikoku, pp. 93–94.
ms. Ayuzawa, Hibiya-Kondo, Naikaku, Shiryō, Tōkyō Museum, Waseda.

2034 Imamura Bunjūrō 今村文十郎
Imamura-ke Yuishogaki 今村家由緒書 (History of the Imamuras), 1793 (寛政 5). jb. 1 v.
note: Contains notes concerning the examination for Father Sidotti by Imamura Eisei 今村英生 (1671–1736), an official interpreter of Nagasaki.
orig. ms. Nagasaki.
2035 —— pr. by Imamura Akitsune 今村明恒, *Rangaku no So, Imamura Eisei*, Tokyo 1942 (昭和 17), pp. 10–18.

2036 Imamura Chūtarō 今村忠太郎
Imamura-ke Yuishogaki 今村家由緒書, [n.d.]. jb. 1 v.
orig. ms. Nagasaki.
2037 —— pr. by Imamura Akitsune 今村有恒, *Rangaku no So, Imamura Eisei,* Tokyo 1942 (昭和 17), pp. 18–21.

2038 Nishimura Tōsato 西村遠里 (—1784)
Tenkei Hoen Tengaku Shiyō 天經補衍天學指要 (Introduction of Astronomy, Supplement of the Tenkei Wakumon), Edo [Tokyo] 須原屋, 1793 (寛政 5). jb. 4 vols., 26cm.
c. Tenri, Waseda-Ogura.

2039 Shiba Kōkan 司馬江漢 (1738–1818)
Chikyū Zenzu Ryakusetsu 地球全圖略說 (Outline of the Globe), [Edo] 春波樓, 1793 (寛政 5). jb. 1 v., 15f., 23cm.
cf. Tenri-Jap. II, p. 124.
c. Tenri.
2040 —— [Edo] 春波樓, 1797 (寛政 9). jb. 1 v.
c. Hibiya.

2041 Yoshida Kōton 吉田篁墩 (1745–1798)
Hokusa Ryakubun 北槎略聞 (Brief Report on Russia) 1793 (寛政 5). jb. 2 vols.
cf. Kaikoku, p. 36.
ms. Ayuzawa.

1794

2042 Katsuragawa Hoshū 桂川甫周 (1751–1809)
Hokusa Bunryaku 北槎聞略 (Brief Report on Russia), 1794 (寛政 6). jb. 12 vols.
cf. Kaikoku, pp. 36, 396–397; Shimmura-Namban

II, pp. 240–261; Tenri-Jap. II, p. 117.
ms. Naikaku, Tenri, Ueno, Waseda.

2043 —— pr. and annotated by Kamei Takayoshi 龜井高孝, Tokyo 三秀舍, 1937 (昭和 12).

2044 —— pr. and annotated by Takeo Hajime 竹尾弌, Tokyo 武藏野書房, 1943 (昭和 18).

2045 * Hyōmin Gyoran no Ki 漂民御覽之記 (Record of the Shogun's Inspection of the Shipwrecked Sailors). jb.
cf. Kaikoku, p. 36; Samura, p. 1773.
ms. Hibiya-Kondō, Nagasaki-Aokata.

2046 —— (Hyōryūki Sōsho, v. XXXIII–XXXVIII).

Persecution in Urakami, 1790–1794

2047 Hizen no Kuni Sonogigōri Nagasaki Urakami-mura Kume Jirō Kakekomi Uttae Ikken 肥前國彼杵郡長崎浦上村久米次郎欠込訴一件 (Documents of Kume Jirō, Urakami), 1793 (寬政 5). jb. 1 v.
cf. Kataoka Yakichi 片岡弥吉, "Kume Jirō Sojō" (*Katorikku Kenkyū*, v. XXI, n. 1), Tōkyō 1941.
ms. Nagasaki.

2048 Yasokyō Sōsho 耶蘇敎叢書 (Collection of Catholic Books). jb.
cf. Laures, n. 44.
note: These were most probably a group of manuscripts confiscated from the Catholics of Urakami at the time of the persecution of 1790–1794.
contents: 1. Yaso Shūmon Korobi Kakimono no Koto 耶蘇宗門轉書物之事
2. Koyomi Oboegaki 曆覺書
3. Shūmonsha Shūkan ni tsuite Yūshi no Oboegaki 宗門者習慣について有司の覺書
4. Martyrio no Susume マルチリヨの勸め
5. Martyrio no Kokoroe マルチリヨの心得
6. Dominica Nukigaki ドミニカ抜書
7. Shōkoron no Issetsu 証據論の一節
8. Buppō no Shidai Ryaku Nukigaki 佛法の次第略抜書
9. Shintō no Koto 神道の事
10. Martyrio no Kagami マルチリヨの鑑
11. Oratio no Honyaku オラショの飜譯
12. Keredo けれど
13. Wammenshūshi Jikkajū ワンメンシウシ十ケ中
14. Oratio no Kuriki オラショの功力

2049 —— pr. and annotated, Anesaki-Hakugai, pp. 131–240.

2050 —— abridged translation into English, Anesaki-Martyrdom, pp. 16–50.

Manuscripts of the Crypt-Catholics

2051 Orasa no Mitsuju 歐羅沙之密呪 (Mysterious Prayers). 1 fold.
cf. Ebisawa-Namban, pp. 470–475.
ms. Ebisawa, Tenri.

2052 —— pr. and annotated by Ebisawa Arimichi 海老澤有道, "Kirishitan Tenseki Kenkyū Yoroku" (*Seishin Studies*, v. III), Tokyo 1953 (昭和 28).

2053 Senrei no Shiori 洗禮の栞 (Method of Baptism) by a crypt Christian. jb. 1 v.
ms. Sophia.

2054 Tenchi Hajimari no Koto 天地始まりの事 (Origin of the Universe). jb. 1 v.
cf. Laures, n. 50.
ms. Tenri.

2055 —— mimeogr. pr. by Tagita Kōya 田北耕也, 1931 (昭和 6).

2056 —— pr. and annotated by Tagita Kōya 田北耕也, *Shōwa-jidai no Sempuku Kirishitan,* Tokyo 1954 (昭和 29), pp. 83–163.

2057 —— tr. into German by Alfred Bohner, "Tenchi Hajimari no Koto, Wie Himmel und Erde entstanden" (*Monumenta Nipponica*, v. I., n. 2), Tokyo 1938.

1795

2058 Kanzawa Teikan 神澤貞幹 (1710–1795)
Okinagusa 翁草 (Essays). jb. 96 vols.
cf. Kokushi, p. 37.
ms. Ueno.

2059 —— abridged ed., Edo [Tokyo] 池田東籬軒, 1851 (嘉永 4). jb. 5 vols.

2060 —— annotated by Ikebe Gishō 池邊義象, Tokyo 1905 (明治 38). 21 vols.

2061 —— (Zonsai Sōsho, v. CXXXII).

2062 —— (Nippon Zuihitsu Taisei, 3rd Series, vv. XI–XIII).

2063 Sugita Gempaku 杉田玄白 (1732–1817)
Oranda Iji Mondō 和蘭醫事問答 (Dialogue on Dutch Medicine) by Takebe Seian 建部清庵 and G. Sugita, Edo [Tokyo] 紫石齋, 1795 (寬政 7). jb. 2 vols., 27cm.
cf. Asahi, p. 60; Samura, p. 288.
c. Kyodai-Fujikawa, Ueno.

2064 —— (Bummei Genryū Sōsho, v. III).

1796

2065 Shiba Kōkan 司馬江漢 (1738–1818)
Oranda Tensetsu 和蘭天說 (Dutch Astronomy), Edo [Tokyo] 春波樓, 1796 (寬政 8). jb. 1 v., 2, 26, [2]f., 25cm.
note: Another edition, jb. 1 v., 2, 6, 27, 2, [1]f., 27cm.

cf. Boxer-Compagnie, p. 67.
c. Gakushiin, Hibiya-Kondo, Imoto, Keio, Kyudai. Kobe Art Museum, Naikaku, Okada, Tenri, Tō-hoku-Sugaku, Tokyoiku, Ueno, Waseda.
ms. Waseda. Seishin (abridged).

2066 —— repr. by Nakai Sōtarō 中井宗太郎, *Shiba Kōkan,* Tokyo 1942 (昭和 17).

2067 *Rangaku Daidōhen 蘭學大道編 (A manuscripted by of the *Oranda Tensetsu*), manuscripted by Satō Nobuhiro 佐藤信淵 jb. 1 v.

2068 —— facs. repr. by the Hōkō Gikai 報効義會, Akita 1920 (大正 9).
c. Ebisawa, Waseda.

2069 Takahashi Yoshitoki 高橋至時 (1764–1804)
Seigaku Shukan 星學手簡 (Correspondence between Y. Takahashi and Hazama Shigetomi 間重富 on Astronomy), 1796 (寛政 8). jb. 3 vols.
cf. Edojidai no Kagaku, pp. 70–71.
ms. Tokyo Astronomical Observatory.

2070 —— abridged pr. and annotated by Arisaka Takamichi 有坂隆道, "Kanseiki ni okeru Asadaryū Tengakuka no Katsudō o megutte, n. 3" (*Historia,* vv. 13–14), Osaka 1955 (昭和 30).

2071 Yamamura Saisuke 山村才助 (1770–1807)
Gaiki Seigokō 外紀西語考 (Research on Place-Names in the *Shokuhō Gaiki*), 1796 (寛政 8). jb. 1 v.
cf. Kaikoku, pp. 40–41.
ms. Otsuki.
See also, nos. 548–555.

1797

2072 Hitomi Tamamura 人見璣邑 (1729–1797)
Taihei E-kotoba 太平繪詞 (Essays). jb. 1 v.
note: He criticized the *shūmon-aratame* system in it.

2073 —— (Nippon Keizai Taiten, v. XVI).

2074 Takahashi Yoshitoki 高橋至時 (1764–1804)
Kansei Rekisho 寛政暦書 (The Kansei Calendar), compiled by Y. Takahashi, Shibukawa Kagesuke 澁川景祐 and etc. 1797 (寛政 9). jb. 35 vols.
ms. Gakushiin, Tokyo Astronomical Observatory, Ueno.

2075 Takahashi Yoshitoki 高橋至時 (1764–1804)
Kansei Rekisho Zokuroku 寛政暦書續録 (Second Series of the Kansei Calendar), compiled by Shibukawa Kagesuke 澁川景祐.

jb. 5 vols.
ms. Ueno.

1798

2076 Fuji Genryō 藤元良
Oranda Sanbutsuzu-kō 和蘭産物圖考 (Illustrated Treatise on Dutch Products), [n.p.], 1798 (寛政 10). jb. 3 vols., 23cm.
cf. Kaikoku, p. 41; Boxer-Compagnie, pp. 131–132.
c. Ayuzawa, Keio, Tōyō-Iwasaki.

2077 Gotō Shōzaburō, X 後藤庄三郎, 十世
Gotō Shōzaburō Yuishogaki 後藤庄三郎由緒書 (History of Gotō Shōzaburō), 1798 (寛政 10).

2078 —— (Tokugawa-jidai Shōgyō Sōsho, v. I).

2079 Honda Toshiaki 本多利明 (1744–1821)
Saiiki Monogatari 西域物語 (Tales of the West). 1798 (寛政 10). jb. 3 vols.
cf. Kaikoku, pp. 41–42. Kokushi, p. 161.
ms. Akioka, Ayuzawa, Ebisawa (v. I only), Hosa, Kyūdai-Butsuri, Naikaku, Shokokan, Shimmura, Tōhoku-Kano, Ueno.

2080 —— Tōkyō 東京日々新聞社, 1888 (明治 21). wb. 1 v., 2, 79p., 23cm.
c. Ebisawa, Seishin.

2081 —— (Nippon Keizai Sōsho, v. XII).
2082 —— (Kaihyō Sōsho, v. II).
2083 —— (Nippon Keizai Taiten, XX).
2084 —— (Dai-Nippon Shisō Zenshū, v. XI).
2085 —— (Kinsei Shakai Keizai Taikei, Honda Toshiaki-shū).
2086 —— tr. into English by Donald Keene in *The Japanese Discovery of Europe, Honda Toshiaki and other Discoverers 1720–1798,* London 1952.

2087 Morishima Nakara 森島中良 (1754–1808)
Bangosen, tsuketari Bankoku Chimeikō 蠻語箋, 附萬國地名考 (Foreign Language, Appendix, Place Names of World), 1798 (寛政 10). jb. 1 v.
c. Waseda.

2088 Ōshima Zenbyōe 大島善兵衛
Kunitomo Teppōki 國友鐵砲記 (Record of the Guns of the Kunitomo School), 1798 (寛政 10). jb.
2089 —— pr. and annotated by Arima Seiho 有馬成甫, *Ikkansai Kunitomo Tōbyōe-den,* Tokyo 1932 (昭和 7).
2090 —— pr. and annotated by Hora

Tomio 洞富雄, *Teppō Denraiki,* Tokyo 1939 (昭和 14).

1799

2091 Chōmu Sanjin 聴夢山人
Hokuyō Jitsuroku 北洋實録, (Record on the Northern Sea) 1799 (寛政 11). jb. 5 vols.
ms. Hibiya-Kondo.

2092 Hokkai Idan 北海異談 (Strange Story of the Northern Seas). jb. 10 vols.
note: On appearances of the Russians after the Kansei Era.
cf. Asahi, p. 42.
ms. Hakodate.
2093 —— (Hyakumantō, v. V).

2094 Ōhara Sakingo 大原左金吾
Hokuchi Kigen 北地危言 (Anxiety on the Northern Border). jb. 2 vols.
cf. Samura, pp. 1793–1794.
2095 —— Tokyo 東京日々新聞社, 1888 (明治 21). wb. 1 v.
c. Hokudai.
2096 —— (Hokumon Sōsho, v. III).

2097 Oroshiiya Zatsudan 於魯志伊家雜談 (On Russia). jb. 1 v.
cf. Kaikoku, pp. 55–56.
ms. Ueno.

2098 Ōtsuki Gentaku 大槻玄澤 (1756–1827)
Hokuhen Tanji 北邊探事 (Inquiry on the Northern Border). jb. 5 vols.
cf. Samura, pp. 1794–1795.
ms. Waseda.

2099 Rokoku Enbōron 魯國遠謀論 (Russian Far-Reaching Scheme). jb. 1 v.
ms. Nagasaki.

2100 Tōyō Konsō 東洋鯤叟
Hokusui kiyū 北陲杞憂 (Concern Over the Northern Border). jb. 1 v.
ms. Naikaku.
2101 —— (Kinji Kaikoku Hitsudokusho, v. III).
2102 —— (Nippon Kaibō Shiryō Sōsho, v. II).

2103 Zōyō Rōjin 藏用老人
Hokuteki Jiryaku 北狄事略 (Russian Affairs). jb. 12 vols.
cf. Tenri-Jap. II, p. 97.
ms. Tenri.

2104 Otsuki Bansui 大槻盤水 (1756–1827)
Ransetsu Benwaku 蘭說辯惑, or Bansui Yawa 盤水夜話 (Apology for Dutch Learning), Ise 洞津幽蘭齋, 1799 (寛政 11). jb.

2 vols., 19cm.
cf. Boxer-Compagnie, p. 131;Kaikoku, pp. 33–34.
c. Hibiya-Kondo, Kanazawa-Kado, Kobeshi Museum, Tōhoku-Kano, Ueno, Waseda.
2105 —— (Bansui Zonkyō, v. I).
2106 —— (Bummei Genryū Sōsho, v. I).
2107 —— (Nambanki Bunsen).
2108 —— (Dai-Nippon Shisō Zenshū, v. XII).
2109 —— (Zuihitsu Bungaku Senshū, v. XII).

2110 Tatehara Suiken 立原翠軒 (1744–1823)
Narabaysashi Zatsuwa 楢林雜話 (Miscellaneous Stories of Narabayashi), 1799 (寛政 11). jb. 1 v.
note: Exotic stories of the Western World by Narabayashi Jubyōe Takahiro 楢林重兵衛高廣 (1750–1801), an official interpreter.
cf. Shimmura-Namban I, pp. 429–433.
2111 —— (Kaihyō Sōsho, v. II.)

1800

2112 Hirokawa Kai 廣川獬
Nagasaki Bunkenroku 長崎聞見録 (Record of Nagasaki), Osaka 1800 (寛政 12). jb. 5 vols., 27cm.
note: This is one of the principle sources on information about Deshima during the end of the eighteenth and beginning of the ninteenth centuries.
cf. Boxer-Compagnie, p. 132; Samura, p. 1515.
c. Iwase, Kariya, Kyūdai-Hoka, Kyudai-Butsuri, Waseda.
ms. Ueno-shirai, Ueno.
2113 —— Kyoto 菱屋孫兵衛 1818 (文政 1). jb. 3 vols., 26cm.
c. Tenri, Tōyō-Iwasaki, Ueno.
2114 —— Osaka 1856 (安政 3). jb. 5 vols., 26cm.
c. Ueno.

2115 Ishino Hiromichi 石野廣通 (1718–1800)
Kempō Burui 憲法部類 (Classified Laws). jb.
ms. Nagasaki-Fuji, Naikaku.

2116 Kirishitan Shiryō 切支丹史料 (Christian Documents) 1781-1800 (天明 1–寛政 12).
orig. ms. Nagasaki.

2117 Numajiri Bokusen 沼尻墨僊
Chikyū Bankoku Zusetsu 地球萬國圖説 (Illustration of the World Map), 1800 (寛政 12). jb. 1 v.
cf. Akioka Takejirō 秋岡武次郎, "Numajiri Bokusen no Chikyūgi narabini Chikyūgiyō Chizu" (*Rekishi Chiri*, v. LX, n. 5).
orig. ms. K. Nakajo.

2118 Tatehara Suiken 立原翠軒 (1744–1823)

Kirishitan Hōbuku Shokibutsu 吉利支丹法服諸器物 (Sacerdotal Robes and Vessels). 1800 (寛政 12). jb. 1 v.

orig. ms. Tokugawa.
ms. Shokokan.

2119 —— facs. repr. (Kirishitan Sōsho).
2120 —— (Sokkyohen).

2121 Yamamura Shōei 山村昌永 (1770–1807)

Kai Ichiran Zusetsu 華夷一覧圖說 (Illustrated Treatise of the World), 1800 (寛政 12). jb. 1 v.

note: Ōta Nampo's *Ichiwa Ichigen*, v. XLVII contains this treatise. See n. 2460.
cf. Kaikoku, pp. 50, 287; Ayuzawa Shintarō 鮎澤信太郎, "Yamamura Shōei no Kai Ichiranzu ni tsuite" (*Rekishi Chiri*, v. LXXXI, n. 1), Tokyo 1941.
ms. Ayuzawa, Kariya, Ueno.

1801

2122 Aizawa Seishi 會澤正志 (1782–1863)

Chishima Ibun 千島異聞 (Strange Report on the Kurile Islands), 1801 (享和 1). jb. 1 v.

cf. Tsukamoto Katsuyoshi 塚本勝義, *Aizawa Seishi no Shisō,* Tokyo 1943, p. 76.

2123 Kaempfer, Engelbert (1651–1716)

Sakokuron 鎖國論 (On the Closed Country), tr. into Japanese by Nakano Ryūho 中野柳圃, 1801 (享和 1). jb. 2 vols.

note: Abridged translation of Kaempfer's *De Beschrijving van Japan,* Amsterdam 1729, chap. 6.
cf. Itazawa, pp. 552–561.
ms. Ebisawa, Hibiya-Kondo, Jingu, Kokugakuin, Naikaku, Seikado, Tōhoku-Kano, Tōdai-Nanki, Sukeno.

2124 —— rept. by Naitō Chisō 内藤耻叟, Tokyo 博文館, 1891 (明治 24). wb. 1 v., 74p., 19cm.

c. Ebisawa.

2124b —— (Chūko Sōsho, v. LXXXIII).
2125 —— (Nippon Bunko, v. V).
2126 —— (Nippon Kokushi Zensho).

1802

2127 Sakamoto Tenzan 坂本天山 (1745–1803)

Seiyō Kakō Shinkisetsu 西洋火攻神器說 (A Secret Treasure on Fire Attack), compiled by T. Sakamoto and Ogyū Sorai 荻生徂徠, Osaka 青藜閣, 1802 (享和 2). jb. 2 vols., 26cm.

note: This was derived from a seventeenth century Sino-Jesuit translation of L. Collado's *Practica Manuale di Artiglieria,* Venice 1586. See also nos. 1277-1278.

2128 Shitsuki Tadao 志筑忠雄 (1760–1806)

Rekishō Shinsho 曆象新書 (New Book of Astronomy), 1802 (享和 2). jb. 4 vols.

cf. Shimmura-Namban I, p. 162; Kokushi, p. 330.
ms. Keio, Naikaku, Otsuki, Tōhoku-Kano, Waseda.

2129 —— (Bummei Genryū Sōsho, v. II).
2130 —— (Nippon Testsugaku Shisō Zensho, v. VI).
2131 —— (Nippon Tetsugaku Zensho, v. VIII).

2132 Ueda Senchin 上田宣珍

Amakusa Bikō 天草備考 (Topographical Sketch of Amakusa), 1802 (享和 2). jb. 3 vols.

cf. Samura, p. 46.
ms. Doshisha, Ebisawa, Naikaku, Ueno.

2133 * Amakusa Fudodi 天草風土記 (Topography of Amakusa). jb. 1 v.

ms. Daitokyu, Ueno.

2134 Ueda Senchin 上田宣珍

Amakusa Shimakagami 天草島鏡 (History of the Amakusa Islands).

cf. Kokushi, p. 8.

2135 —— Tokyo 民友社, 1913 (大正 2). wb. 1 v.

2136 —— (Amakusagun Shiryō, v. I).

2137 Uezaki Kuhachirō 植崎九八郎 (–1807)

Sensaku Zasshū 賤策雜收 (Political Memorial to the Shōgun Ienari), 1802 (享和 2). jb. 1 v.

note: refers to religious policy.
cf. Kokushi, p. 169.
ms. S. Endo.

2138 —— (Nippon Keizai Sōsho, v. XII).
2139 —— (Nippon Keizai Taiten, v. XX).

1803

2140 Maeno Ryōtaku 前野良澤 (1723–1803)

Nederuranden to Itarii ネエデルランデンとイタリイ (Netherlands and Italy), 1803 (享和 3). jb. 1 v.

ms. Otsuki.

2141 —— pr. by Iwasaki Katsumi 岩崎克己, *Maeno Ranka,* Tokyo 1938 (昭和 13). pp. 486–490.

2142 Maeno Ryōtaku 前野良澤 (1723–1803)

Roshia Sedairyaku 魯西亞世代略 (Outline of the Succession of Russian Kings). jb. 1 v.

cf. Kaikoku, p. 389; Samura, p. 2057.
ms. Naikaku.

2143 —— (Orosu Kibun).
See n. 2892.

2144 Maeno Ryōtaku 前野良澤 (1723–1803)
Roshia Taitō Ryakuki 魯西亞大統略記 (Brief Notes on Russian History). jb. 1 v.
cf. Kaikoku, pp. 388–389.
ms. Ashida Ijin 芦田伊人, Otsuki.

2145 Yamamura Shōei 山村昌永 (1770–1807)
Teisei Zōyaku Sairan Igen 訂正増譯采覧異言 (Revised compilation of the Sairan Igen), 1803 (享和 3). jb. 13 vols.
note: not published. Version of n. 1567 revised by adding references to prohibited books and Dutch books. It is rich in information regarding Christianity.
ms. Ayuzawa, Doshisha, Ebisawa, Kariya, Nagasaki, Naikaku, Seikado, Shokokan, Tōhoku-Kano, Tokyoiku, Waseda.

1804

2146 Aoki Teien 青木定遠 (1762–1812)
Tōmon Jissaku 答問十策 (Criticism of the Seclusion Policy), 1804 (文化 1). jb. 1 v.
cf. Kokushi, p. 224.
ms. Hibiya-Kondo, Hikone, Ueno.
2147 —— (Kaibō Igi, v. I).
2148 —— (Kinji Kaikoku Hitsudokusho).
2149 —— (Rinchi Sōsho).
2150 —— (Nippon Kaibō Shiryō Sōsho, v. II).
2151 —— (Nippon Keizai Sōsho, v. XII).
2152 —— (Nippon Keizai Taiten, v. XX).
2153 —— (Kōkodō Manroku, v. VI).

2154 Honda Toshiaki 本多利明 (1744–1821)
Tokai Shimpō 渡海新法 (New Art of Navigation). jb. 1 v.
cf. Kokushi, p. 225.
ms. A. Hirayama, Naikaku.
2155 —— (Kaji Shiryō Sōsho, v. VI).

2156 Kondō Morishige 近藤守重 (1771–1829)
Hen'yō Bunkaizu-kō 邊要分界圖考 (Illustrations of the Important Border Area of Hokkaidō), 1804 (文化 1). jb. 8 vols.
cf. Kokushi, p. 279.
ms. Daitokyu, Hokudai, Tenri, Tōdai, Waseda (vv. II, VI lacked).
2157 —— (Kondō Seisai Zenshū, v. I).

2158 Kōno Michinori 河野通禮
Konten Shingo 混天新語 (New Theories of Astronomy), Edo [Tokyo] 須原屋, 1804 (文化 1). jb. 2 vols., 26cm.

c. Hibiya-Kondo, Tenri.

2159 Mukai Genchū 向井元仲
Shōhaku Sairai Shomoku 商舶載來書目 (List of Books brought by Traders). jb. 1 v.
note: copied in 1804.
ms. Ueno.

2160 Nagasaki Rankanchō Ran-tsūshi Ichiran 長崎蘭館長蘭通詞一覧 (List of the Captains of the Dutch Factory and Translators in Nagasaki), 1804 (文化 1). jb. 1 v.
ms. S. Nakayama.
2161 —— pr. and annotated, Itazawa, pp. 159–168.

2162 Nagasaki Bugyō Rekidai Meibo 長崎奉行歴代名簿 (List of the Successive Governors of Nagasaki). jb. 1 v.
orig. ms. Nagasaki.

2163 Nagasaki Oranda Tsūshi Yuishogaki 長崎阿蘭陀通詞由緒書 (Chronological List of Dutch Translators of Nagasaki). jb. 1 v.
cf. Itazawa, pp. 149–159.
ms. Gakushiin, Otsuki.

2164 Nagasaki Rekidai Bugyō Kapitan Daitsūji Hikaechō 長崎歴代奉行甲比丹大通辭控帳 (Lists of the Governors, Captains and Translators of Nagasaki), 1804 (文化 1). jb. 1 v.
cf. Asahi, p. 82.
ms. T. Nakayama.

2165 Nagasaki Tsūshi Yiishogaki 長崎通詞由緒書 (Succession List of the Official Translators of Nagasaki). jb. 1 v.
ms. Gakushiin, Otsuki.

2166 Oranda Tsūshi Kishōmon 阿蘭陀通詞起請文 (A Written Oath taken by the Dutch Translators). 1 fold.
ms. Nagasaki.
2167 —— pr. and annotated, Itazawa, pp. 137–141.

2168 Sakuma Toshimori 佐久間利盛
Amakusa Gimmikata Hikae 天草吟味方扣 (Copy of the Protocol of Amakusa Law-Court), 1804 (文化 1). jb.
phot. Sophia.

2169 Tachibana Nankei 橘南谿 (1754–1806)
Hokusō Sadan 北窓瑣談 (Essays), 1804 (文化 1). jb. 2 vols.
ms. Hibiya, Tōhoku-Kano.
2170 —— Kyoto 1825 (文政 8). jb. 4 vols., 25cm.
ms. Tōhoku-Kano, Waseda.

2171 —— (Kyōrin Sōsho, v. V).
2172 —— (Yūhōdō Bunko).
2173 —— (Nippon Zuihitsu Zenshū, v. IV).
2174 —— abridged (Ōshuku Sōsho).
2175 Tachibana Nankei 橘南谿 (1754–1806)
Hokusō Sadan, Kōhen 北窻瑣談後篇 (Second Series of the Hokusō Sadan), Kyoto 三木太郎右衛門, 1829 (文政 12). jb. 4 vols., 25cm.
c. Hibiya, Jingu, Waseda.

1805

2176 Ki Min 紀昀 *Chi-Chün*
Kintei Kenryū Shiko Zensho Sōmoku 欽定乾隆四庫全書總目 *Ch'in-ting Ch'ien-lung Ssu-k'u-ch'üan-shu Tsung-mu* (General Contents of the Four Libraries of the Emperor Ch'ien-lung).

2177 —— compiled by Ōta Rōsen 太田老泉, Edo [Tokyo] 1805 (文化 2). jb. 6 vols.
c. Daitokyu, Keio, Naikaku, Todai-Nanki.
ms. Seikado.

2179 Ōta Nampo 大田南畝 (1749–1823)
Keiho Zattetsu 瓊浦雑綴 (Notes on Nagasaki), 1805 (文化 2). jb. 3 vols.
note: not printed.
2180 —— (Shin-Hyakka Setsurin, Shokuzanjin Zenshū, v. III).

2181 Shiba Kōkan 司馬江漢 (1738–1818)
Oranda Tsūhaku 和蘭通舶 (Dutch Navigation), Edo [Tokyo] 春波樓, 1805 (文化 2). jb. 2 vols., 27cm.
cf. Samura, p. 289.
c. Hibiya-Kondo, Kyodai, Tenri.
2182 —— (Zuihitsu Bungaku Senshū, v. VI).
2183 —— repr. by Nakai Sōtarō 中井宗太郎 in the *Shiba Kōkan,* Tokyo 1942 (昭和 17).

2184 Rezanov, Nikolai Petrovitch (–1807)
Hōshi Nippon Kikō 奉使日本紀行 (Voyage to Japan) tr. by Takahashi Kageyasu 高橋景保 and Aochi Ei 青地盈. jb. 13 vols.
note: Rezanov's mission to Japan in 1804–1805.
cf. Tenri-Jap. II, p. 111.
ms. Tenri.

1806

2185 Amakusa Korobi-Kirishitan narabini Ruizoku Shibōchō oyobi Butsuzō sashidasu Namaechō 天草轉切支丹並類族死亡帳及佛像差出名前帳 (Register of dead of apostate Catholics of Amakusa and their Families with the Addition of a List of their religious objects), 1806 (文化 3). jb. 1 v.
ms. Ebisawa, Nagasaki, Shiryo,

2186 Broedelet, J.
Roshia Kokushi 魯西亞國志 (History of Russia), tr. by Yamamura Shōei 山村昌永, 1806 (文化 3). jb. 1 v.
orig. title: Oude en nieuwe staat van't Russische of Moskovische Keizerryk behelzende elne uitvoerige historie van Rusland en dreszelfs groote-vorsteu, Utrecht 1744.
cf. Kaikoku, pp. 391–393.
ms. Daitokyu, Naikaku, Otsuki, Waseda.

2187 Giryō Dōjin 義了道人
Shakkyō Temmon Wadanshō 釋教天文和談鈔 (Extract of Speech on Buddhist Astronomy), 1806 (文化 3). jb. 1 v.
ms. Ueno.

2188 Habuto Seiyō 羽太正養 (–1806)
Kyūmei Kōki 休明光記 (On the Ezo District). jb. 9 vols.
cf. Tenri-Jap. II, p. 100; Kokushi, p. 66.
orig. ms. Daitokyu.
ms. Iwase, Naikaku, Sonkeikaku, Tenri, Ueno, Waseda.
2189 —— (Zokuzoku Gunsho Ruijū, v. IV).
2190 —— (Kimurake Monjo, vv. XIII–XV).

2191 Hirata Atsutane 平田篤胤 (1776–1843)
Honkyō Gaihen 本教外篇 (Apocrypha of the True Religion), 1806 (文化 3). jb. 2 vols.
note: At the beginning of the first volume there are 2 hymns by Ricci (*Seikin Kyokui,* see n. 173) and also the whole of Aleni's *Sanzanron Gakuki* (see n. 618). But Hirata changes Aleni's words into his own, for instance, he calls "God" "Ameno-minakanushi-no-kami" 天御中主之神. The second half of the first volume is almost a translation of Ricci's *Kijin Jippen* (see n. 303). In the second volume he construed Pantoja's *Shichikoku* (see n. 397) from Chinese into Jap.
cf. Ebisawa-Namban, pp. 412–418; Muraoka-Shiso, pp. 300–311.
ms. Jinshu.
2192 —— (Hirata Atsutane Zenshū, v. II).

2193 Kawahigashi Gigō 河東義剛
Matsūraki Shūsei 松浦記集成 (Collection of the Records of the Matsūras), 1806 (文化 3). jb. 5 vols.
cf. Samura, p. 1844.
ms. Matsura, Nagasaki, Shiryo.

2194 Matsūrake Oboegaki 松浦家覚書 (Memorandum of the Matsūras). jb. 1 v.
orig. ms. Matsura.
ms. Ebisawa, Shiryo.

2195 Matsūra Koji Ryakuki 松浦古事略記 (Brief Notes on the Ancient History of the Matsūras). jb. 1 v.
orig. ms. Matsura.
ms. Shiryo.

2196 Narushima Motonao 成島司直 (1778–1862)
Tokugawa Jikki 御川實紀 (True History of Tokugawa Shogunate), compiled by the Shogunate Government, 1806–49 (文化 3–嘉永 2).
cf. Kokushi, p. 227.
ms. Jingu, Naikaku.
2197 —— annotated by Naitō Chisō 内藤耻叟, Tokyo 1896 (明治 29).
2198 —— (Zoku Kokushi Taikei, v. IX–XV).
2199 —— (Shintei Zōho Kokushi Taikei, v. XXXVIII–XLVII).

2200 Shitsuki Tadao 志筑忠雄 (1760–1806)
Roshia Raireki 魯西亞來歷 (History of Russia). jb. 1 v.
cf. Kaikoku, p. 395.
ms. Otsuki.
2201 —— (Bansui Zasshō, v. XX).

2202 Tsumura Masayasu 津村正恭 (–1806)
Tankai 譚海 (Essays). jb. 15 vols.
cf. Samura, p. 1348.
ms. Hibiya-Kaga, Tōdai-Nanki, Tōhoku-Kano.
2203 —— repr. by the Kokusho Kankō-kai 國書刊行會, Tokyo 1917 (大正 6).

1807

2204 Geishū Yoshimatsu Hokubei Hyōryūtan 藝州善松北米漂流譚 (Tales of Yoshimatsu drifting to North America), 1807 (文化 4). jb. 1 v.
2205 —— (Ikoku Hyōryū Kidanshū).

2206 Hokuhen Kibun 北邊紀聞 (Notes on the Northern Border), 1807 (文化 4). jb. 9 vols.
ms. Hokudai.

2207 Huebner, Johan
Indoshi 印度志 (Topography of India), tr. by Yamamura Saisuke 山村才助, 1807 (文化 4). jb. 2 vols.
cf. Kaikoku p. 102.
note: Translation from the *Algemeene Geographie,* Amsterdam 1769, pp. 529–592.
ms. Hibiya, Kyodai, Ueno.

2208 Huebner, Johan
Ajia Shotōshi 亞細亞諸島志 (Geography of Asia), tr. into Japanese by Yamamura Saisuke 山村才助. jb. 1 v.
cf. Kaikoku, pp. 101–102.
note: Translation from the *Algemeene Geographie,* Amsterdam 1769, pp. 647–691. Not printed.
ms. Ayuzawa, Naikaku.

2209 Murase Kōtei 村瀨栲亭 (1746–1818)
Geien Nisshō 藝苑日涉 (Essays), [n.p.] 石川之聚, 1807 (文化 4). jb. 12 vols.
cf. Samura, p. 575.
c. Jingu.
2210 —— [n.p.] 1819 (文政 2). jb. 12 vols.
c. Waseda.
2211 —— [n.p.] 穀庫堂, 1857 (安政 4).
2212 —— (Nippon Zuihitsu Zenshū, v. I).
2213 —— (Hyakka Setsurin).

2214 Ōtsuki Gentaku 大槻玄澤 (1757–1827)
Kankai Ibun 環海異聞 (Strange Reports from Foreign Countries), 1807 (文化 4). jb. 15 vols.
cf. Kaikoku, pp. 50–33, 314–315; Asahi, p. 81; Kokushi, p. 57.
ms. Ayuzawa, Hibiya-Kondo, Iwase, Ishin, Hakodate, Kariya, Kyoto, Kyūdai-Butsuri, Nagasaki, Naikaku, Nichidai, Tōdai-Nanki, Tōyō-Iwasaki, Ueno, Waseda.
2215 —— (Hyōryūki Sōsho, v. LI).
2216 —— (Nambanki Bunsen).
2217 —— (Hyōryū Kidan Zenshū).
2218 —— (Hokumon Sōsho, v. IV).

2219 Sugita Gempaku 杉田玄白 (1732–1817)
Yasō Dokugo 野叟獨語 (Soliloquy of a Rustic), 1807 (文化 4). jb. 3 vols.
cf. Kokushi, p. 313.
2220 —— (Yōchō Sōsho, v. I).
2221 —— (Kaibō Igi, v. XXXI).
2222 —— (Onchi Sōsho, v. IV).
2223 —— (Nambanki Bunsen).
2224 —— (Nippon Keizai v. XIX).
2225 —— (Nippon Keizai Taiten, v. XXIX).
2226 —— (Dai-Nippon Shisō Zenshū, v. XII).

2227 Uezaki Kuhachirō 植崎九八郎 (–1807)
Uezaki Kuhachirō Jōsho 植崎九八郎上書 (A Memorial of Uezaki Kuhachirō), jb. 1 v.
cf. Kokushi, p. 19.
ms. Jingu, Ueno.

2228 —— (Ōshuku Zakki).
2229 —— (Kinji Kaikoku Hitsudokusho).
2230 —— (Nippon Keizai Sosho, v. XII).
2231 —— (Nippon Keizai Taiten, v. XX).
2232 —— (Nippon Kaibō Shiryō Sōsho, v. II).

2233 Yamamura Shōei 山村昌永 (1770–1807)
Shinyaku Tōzai Kiyū 新譯東西紀游 (Travels to the East and West) tr. by Yamamura Shōei.
ms. Otsuki.

1808

2234 Akamatsu Sokuyō 赤松則陽
Kaibōben 海防辯 (Talks on Coastal Defence), 1808 (文化 5). jb. 1 v.
ms. Tōhoku-Kano.
2235 —— (Nippon Kaibō Shiryō Sōsho, v. II).

2236 Hirose Shūhaku 廣瀬周伯
Zue Ransetsu Sansai Kikan 圖繪蘭說三才窺管 (Illustrated Glimpse of the Universe), Edo [Tokyo] 山崎金兵衛, 1808 (文化 5). jb. 3 vols., 26cm.
c. Akioka, Hibiya-Kaga, Imoto.

2237 Kaempfer, Engelbert (1651–1716)
Seikyaku Kenfuru Nihon Kiji 西客堅協鹿日本紀事 (Affairs of Japan by the Westerner, Kempfer) or Banzoku Haihin Yakusetsu 蕃賊排擯譯說, tr. into Japanese by Takahashi Kageyasu 高橋景保, 1808 (文化 5).
note: Abridged translation of Kaempfer's *De Beschrijving van Japan,* Amsterdam 1729.
cf. Rangaku, p. 33; Shimmura-Namban I, pp. 440–441.
2238 —— (Kaihyō Sōsho, v. II).
2239 * Nihon Kiji Yakushō 日本紀事譯抄 (Abridged Translation of the Nihon Kiji).
2240 —— (Heikan Issō).
2241 * Seiyōjin Nihon Kiji 西洋人日本紀事 (Notes on Japan by a Westerner).
2242 —— (Kinji Kaikoku Hitsudokusho, v. I).
2243 —— (Nippon Kaibō Shiryō Sōsho, v. II).

2244 Morishima Nakara 森島中良 (1754–1808)
Kaigai Ibun 海外異聞 (Strange Account of Foreign Countries). jb. 1 v.
ms. Kyōdai-Naikaku.

2245 Orosu Henkōroku 鄂羅斯邊寇録 (Record of the Russian Invasion), 1808 (文化 5). jb. 2 vols.
ms. Hokudai.

2246 Ōtsuki Bansui 大槻盤水 (1757–1827)
Jūhō Kigenkō 銃法起原考 (Monographs on the Origin of Gunnery). jb. 1 v.
2247 —— (Bansui Zonkyō v. I.).

2248 Shiba Kōkan 司馬江漢 (1738–1818)
Kopperu Temmon Zukai 刻白爾天文圖解 (Explanation of Kepler's Theory), Edo [Tokyo] 春波樓, 1808 (文化 5). jb. 1 v., 2, 3, 2, 3, 10, 22f., 27cm.
note: The author has mistaken Copernicus for Kepler.
cf. Boxer-Compagnie, p. 57; Kaikoku, p. 54; Ebisawa-Namban, p. 255.
orig. ms. Waseda.
c. Gakushiin, Iwase, Kobe Art Museum, Naikaku, Kyōdai-Butsuri, Tōhoku, Tōhoku-Kano, Tokyo-iku, Ueno.
2249 —— repr. by Nakai Sōtarō 中井宗太郎, *Shiba Kōkan,* Tokyo 1942 (昭和 17), pp. 161–208.

2250 Yoshio Jōzō 吉雄常三
Seisetsu Kanshōkyō 西說觀象經 (The Basic Works of Western Astronomy), [Nagoya], 1808 (文化 5). 1 fold.
cf. Asahi, p. 63; Samura, p. 1156.
c. Akioka, Tōhoku-Kano.
2251 —— [n.p.], 1878 (明治 11). 1 fold.
c. Tokyo Kagaku Museum, Tōhoku-Kano, Ueno-Oshima, Ueno-Shirai.

2252 Takahashi Yoshitoki 高橋至時 (1764–1804)
Kaichū Shūdōkō 海中舟道考 (Treatise on Navigation), annotated by Shibukawa Kagesuke 澁川景佑, 1808 (文化 15). jb. 1 v.
ms. Gakushiin, Tōhoku.

1809

2253 Furuyano Yoshiharu 古屋野意春 (1756–1812)
Bankoku Ichiranzu 萬國一覽図 (World Atlas), Kurashiki 香山樓, 1809 (文化 6). jb. 1 fold., 103 × 134cm.
cf. Kaikoku, pp. 215–217.
c. Hibiya-Kaga.

2254 Namban Hiden 南蠻秘傳 (Secret Initiation to Western Surgery), 1809 (文化 6). jb. 1 v.
ms. Kyōdai-Fujikawa.

2255 Satō Nobuhiro 佐藤信淵 (1768–1850)
Seiyō Rekkoku Shi-Ryaku 西洋列國史略 (Brief History of Western Countries), 1809

(文化 6). jb. 3 vols.

note: European history beginning with Genesis.
cf. Kaikoku, pp. 417–421.
ms. Ayuzawa, Ebisawa, Kariya, Shiryo, Tōdai-Nanki, Tōhoku-Kano.

2256 —— (Chūko Sōsho).
2257 —— (Satō Shin'en Kagaku Zenshū, v. III).

2258 Takai Ranzan 高井蘭山 (1762–1838)
Shumisen Zukai 須彌山圖解 (Illustrated View of the World according to Buddhist Interpretations), 1809 (文化 6). jb. 1 v.
ms. Itazawa.

1810

2259 Entsū 圓通 (1754–1834)
Bukkoku Rekishōhen 佛國曆象編 (Buddhist Astronomy and Calendar Science), [n.p.] 大王府, 1810 (文化 7). jb. 5 vols., 26cm.
cf. Itazawa, pp. 252–254: Samura, p. 1741.
c. Ebisawa, Hibiya-Ichimura, Itazawa, Jinshu, Kariya, Kompira, Kyūdai-Butsuri, Naikaku, Tōhoku-Sugawa, Waseda-Ogura.
2260 —— Osaka 大和屋, 1815 (文化 12). jb. 5 vols., 26cm.
c. Imoto, Narita, Shokokan, Sophia, Tenri.

2261 Bukkoku Rekishōhen Byōkan Itteki 佛國曆象編病間一適 (Impressions of the Bukkoku Rekishōhen), [n.p.], [n.d.]. jb. 1 v., 52f., 27cm.
c. Itazawa, Tenri, Tōhoku.

2262 Furuyano Yoshiharu 古屋野意春 (1756–1812)
Bankoku Ichiran Zusetsu 萬國一覽圖說 (Illustrated Geography of the World), Osaka 含章堂, 1810 (文化 7). jb. 2 vols., 26cm.
cf. Kaikoku, pp. 56–58, 316; Kokushi, p. 260.
c. Ayuzawa, Hibiya-Kaga, Okada, Kyūdai, Ueno.

2263 Inō Tadataka 伊能忠敬 (1745–1818)
Bukkoku Rekishōhen Sekihi 佛國曆象編斥非 (Criticism of the Bukkoku Rekishōhen), 1810 (文化 7). jb. 1v.
cf. Itazawa. p. 261.

2264 Matsuura Tō 松浦陶 (1752–1820)
Gaikoku Shūran 外國集覽 (World Geography), 1810 (文化 7). jb. 8 vols.
ms. Nagasaki.

2265 Takahashi Kageyasu 高橋景保 (1785–1829)
Shintei Bankoku Zenzu 新訂萬國全圖 (New World Atlas), Edo [Tokyo] 亞歐堂田善, 1810 (文化 7). 1 fold, 113×195cm.
cf. Kaikoku, p. 239.
c. Waseda.

2266 * Chikyū Bankoku Zenzu 地球萬國全圖. Copied by Aōdō Denzen 亞歐堂田善. [n.p.], [n.d.]. 1 fold.
cf. Kaikoku, pp. 283–284.
cf. Kuroda Genji.

1811

2267 Hirata Atsutane 平田篤胤 (1776–1843)
Ibuki Oroshi 氣吹魅 (Essays). [n.p.] 平田塾, [n.d.]. jb. 2 vols. 24cm.
cf. Shinto-Kaidai, p. 8; Samura, p. 142.
c. Jingu, Ueno.
2268 —— (Hirata Atsutane Zenshū, v. I).
2269 —— (Kōgaku Sōsho, v. X).
2270 —— (Nippon Kokusui Zensho).
2271 —— abridged (Sekai Daishisō Zenshū, v. LIV).
2272 —— abridged (Dai-Nippon Shisō Zenshū, v. X).

2273 Kobinatashi 小日向志 (Topography of Kobinata), 1811 (文化 8). jb.
ms. Shokokan.

2274 Ko-kirishitan Ruizoku On-aratame ni tsuki Yorozudomechō 古切支丹類族御改ニ付萬留帳 (Records of the Examination of the Families of Former Christians), 1811 (文化 8). jb. 1 v.
ms. Tōhoku.

2275 Shiba Kōkan 司馬江漢 (1738–1818)
Shumparō Hikki 春波樓筆記 (Essays at the Shumparō House), 1811 (文化 8).
cf. Ebisawa-Namban, pp. 376–406; Kokushi, p. 137.
2276 —— (Hyakka Setsurin, v. I).
2277 —— (Yūhōdō Bunko, Meika Zuihitsushū, v. II).
2278 —— (Nippon Keizai Sōsho, v. XII).
2279 —— (Nippon Zuihitsu Taisei, v. I).
2280 —— (Nippon Keizai Taiten, v. XX).
2281 —— abridged (Dai-Nippon Shisō Zenshū, v. XII).

1812

2282 Hirata Atsutane 平田篤胤 (1776–1843)
Tama no Mihashira 靈能眞柱 (Essays on Shintoism). [n.p.], 1812 (文化 9). jb. 2 vol., 27cm.
cf. Kokushi, pp. 197–198.
c. Ebisawa, Inoue, Imoto, Kansei, Kariya, Kyoto, Jingu, Kokugakuin, Naikaku, Nichidai-Ueda, Rikkyo, Sakai, Tenri, Tōhoku-Kano, Waseda, Ueno.
2283 —— (Hirata Atsutane Zenshū, v. II).

2284 —— (Yūhōdō Bunko).
2285 —— (Dai-Nippon Bunko).
2286 —— (Dai-Nippon Shisō Zenshū, v. X).
2287 —— annotated by Miyaji Naokazu 宮地直一, Tokyo 1944 (昭和 19).

2288 Hotta Masaatsu 堀田正敦 (1755–1832)
Kansei Chōshū Shokafu 寛政重修諸家譜 (Genealogical Tables, revised in the Kansei Era), 1812 (文化 9). jb. 1530 vols.
cf. Kokushi, p. 59.
ms. Ueno.
2289 —— Tokyo 榮進舍, 1917–1918 (大正 6–7). wb. 8 vols., 26cm.
2290 —— Tokyo 國民圖書株式會社, 1922 (大正 11). wb. 8 vols.
2291 —— Tokyo 國民圖書株式會社, 1926 (大正 15). wb. 8 vols.

2292 Otsuki Bansui 大槻盤水 (1757–1827)
Kinjō Hiun 金城秘韞 (Secret Record of the Golden Castle), 1812 (文化 9). jb. 2 vols.
cf. Samura, p. 484.
orig. ms. Waseda.
ms. Naikaku.
2293 —— (Bansui Zonkyō, v. I).
2294 * Kichō Tsunenaga Dōgukō-Ryaku 歸朝常長道具考略 (Short Explanation of the Instruments and tools imported by Hasekura Tsunenaga). jb. 1 v.
note: A manuscript of the second volume of *Kinjō Hiun.*
ms. Sophia.

2295 Ōtsuki Bansui 大槻盤水 (1757–1827)
Sendai Honjō Jūki Furanki-kō 仙臺本城銃器佛朗機考 (Notes on the Gun and Cannon in the Sendai-Castle), 1812 (文化 9). jb. 1 v.
note: Appendix of the *Jūhō Kigenkō* (n. 2246).
2296 —— (Bansui Zonkyō, v. I).

1813

2297 Entsū 圓通 (1754–1834)
Shumisengi-mei narabini Jo Wage 須彌山儀銘並序和解 (Japanese translation of the Epitaph of the Shumisen Globe), [n.p.]. jb. 1 v., 30f., 21cm.
ms. Doshisha-Niishima, Itazawa.

2298 Gamō Kumpei 蒲生君平 (1768–1813)
Kinsho 今書 (Essays).
cf. Kokushi, pp. 70–71.

2299 —— Edo [Tokyo] 播磨屋, 1863 (文久 3). jb. 2 vols, 26cm.
c. Ebisawa, Naikaku, Todai-Nanki, Ueno, Waseda, Yutoku.
2300 —— (Gamō Kumpei Zenshū).
2301 —— (Nippon Keizai Sōsho, v. XVII).
2302 —— (Nippon Keizai Taiten, v. XXVI).
2303 —— (Kinnō Bunko).
2304 —— (Nippon Kokusui Zensho).
2305 —— (Kokumin Dōtoku Sōsho).

1814

2306 Nakaoka Eki 中岡益
Keihotsū 瓊浦通 (Description of Nagasaki), 1814 (文化 11). jb. 6 vols.
cf. Tenri-Jap. II, p. 115.
ms. Tenri.

2307 Ogawa Kendō 小川顯道 (1737–1814)
Chirizuka-banashi 塵塚話 (Essays), 1814 (文化 11). jb. 1 v.
cf. Kokushi, p. 206.
2308 —— (Onchi Sōsho, v. IX).
2309 —— (Enseki Jusshu, v. I).

1815

2310 Chōon 潮音
Kakuretsu Jamōhen 摑裂邪網篇 (Criticism of Shintoism), [n.p.], 1815 (文化 12). jb. 2 vols,. 26cm.
c. Imoto, Kariya, Otani, Todai-Nanki, Tōhoku-Kano.
2311 —— (Shinshū Zensho, Gohōbu).
2312 —— (Nippon Shisō Tōsō Shiryō, v. II).

2313 Miyazaki Yasusada 宮崎安貞 (1623–1697)
Nōgyō Zensho 農業全書 (Complete Work on Agricultural Products), Kyoto 1815 (文化 12). jb. 11 vols., 23cm.
cf. Samura, pp. 1585–1586; Kokushi, p. 248.
c. Ueno-Shirai.
2314 —— annotated by Kaibara Rakuken 貝原樂軒, Osaka 同盟書房, 1898 (明治 31). jb. 11 v., 23cm.
2315 —— annotated by Tsuchiya Takao 土屋喬雄 (Iwanami Bunko), Tokyo 1936 (昭和 11).
2316 —— (Ekiken Zenshū, v. VIII).
2317 —— (Nippon Sangyō Shiryō Taikei, v. II).

2318 Sugita Gempaku 杉田玄白 (1733–1817)

Rangaku Kotohajime 蘭學事始 (Beginning of Dutch Learning), 1815 (文化 12). jb. 2 vols.
cf. Itazawa Takeo, *Sugita Gempaku no Rangaku Kotohajime*, Tokyo 1940; Kokushi, p. 322.

2319 —— Tokyo 天眞樓, 1869 (明治 2). jb. 2 vols.
c. Keio, Nagasaki, Otsuki, Tōdai-Nanki, Ueno, Waseda.

2320 —— Tokyo 日本醫學會, 1890 (明治 23). wb. 1 v., 23cm.
c. Keio, Naikaku, Sophia, Ueno.

2321 —— annotated by Nogami Toyoichirō 野上豊一郎, (Iwanami Bunko), Tokyo 1930 (昭和 5).

2322 —— (Bummei Genryū Sōsho, v. I).

2323 —— (Kyōrin Sōsho v. II).

2324 —— (Dai-Nippon Shisō Zenshū, v. XII).

2325 —— tr. into English by K[akichi] Mitsukuri (*Transactions of the Asiatic Society of Japan*, v. V, pt. 1), Yokohama 1877.

2326 —— tr. into English by Mōri Kōichi (*Monumenta Nipponica*, v. V), Tokyo 1942.

1816

2327 Hirayama Shiryū 平山子龍 (1759–1828)
Kaibō Mondō 海防問答 (Dialogue on Coastal Defence), 1816 (文化 13). jb. 4 vols.
cf. Samura, p. 309.

2328 —— (Nippon Kaibō Shiryō Sōsho, v. I).

2329 Inō Tadataka 伊能忠敬 (1745–1818)
Sokuryō Nikki 測量日記 (Diary of a Surveying Journey), 1816 (文化 13). jb. 28 vols.
cf. Kokushi, p. 177.
ms. Gakushiin.

2330 —— (Bōsō Bunko, vv. I–III).

2331 Katō Nantei 加藤南汀
Kakyōroku 可恐録 (Record of a Terrible Event), 1816 (文化 13). jb. 1 v.
cf. Tenri-Jap. II, p. 87.
contents: Oranda Tsūshō Raiyu 阿蘭陀通商來由
  Gaikoku Raihaku Shoshi 外國來舶諸誌
  Jashū Kakyōroku Sōkō 邪宗可恐録草稿
orig. ms. Tenri.

2332 Shiba Kōkan 司馬江漢 (1738–1818)
Tenchi Ridan 天地理談 (Essays on Natural Philosophy).
orig. ms. Nagamori.
ms. Namioka, Tenri.

2333 —— annotated by Muraoka Tsunetsugu 村岡典嗣, Tokyo 1930 (昭和 5).

2334 Shiba Kōkan 司馬江漢 (1738–1818)
Tenchi Ritan 天地理譚 (Essays on Natural Philosophy), 1816 (文化 13). jb. 2 vols.
cf. Asahi, p. 63.
orig. ms. T. Kuwaori.
ms. Kyūdai-Kogaku, Tenri.

2335 —— pr. by Nakai Sōtarō 中井宗太郎, *Shiba Kōkan,* Tokyo 1942 (昭和 17).

1817

2336 Koga Seiri 古賀精里 (1750–1817)
Kyokuron Jiji Fūji 極論時事封事 (Exhaustive Argument on Current Affairs).

2337 —— (Kaibō Igi, v. XLIV).

2338 —— (Kinji Kakoku Hitsudokusho, v. VII).

2339 —— (Nippon Kaibō Shiryō Sōsho, v. II).

2340 —— (Nippon Keizai Sōsho, v. XVII).

2341 —— (Nippon Keizai Taiten, v. XXVI).

2342 Milne, William, LM. 米憐 (1785–1822)
Yōgaku Senkai Mondō 幼學淺解問答 *Yu-hsüeh Ch'ien-chieh Wen-ta* (Easy Dialogue for Children), Malacca 1817. wb. 1 v., 37f.
note: A thorough revision of the original work, by W. C. Milne, was published with the title *Shindō Nyūmon,* Shanghai 1851. (See n. 3072).
cf. Ozawa, p. 200, Wylie, pp. 14–15.

2343 —— Ningpo 華花聖經書房, 1847 (道光 27). cb. 1 v., 27f., 13cm.
c. Otani.

2344 Nakai Riken 中井履軒 (1732–1817)
Jōseki Bōgi 攘斥茅議 (Opinion on the Exclusion Policy). jb. 1 v.
ms. Tōhoku-Kano.

2345 —— (Nippon Keizai Taiten, v. XXIII).

2346 Nakai Riken 中井履軒 (1732–1817)
Nenseiroku 年成録 (Essays). jb. 1 v.
cf. Samura, p. 1680; Kokushi, pp. 246–247.

2346b —— (Nippon Keizai Sōsho, v. XVI).

2347 —— (Nippon Keizai Taiten, v. XXIII).

2348 —— (Nippon Bunko, v. I).

2349 Sakabe Kōhan 坂部廣胖 (1759–1824)
Sampō Kairo Anshinroku 算法海路安心録 (Mathematical Method for Safe Naviga-

tion), 1817 (文化 14). jb. 1 v.
cf. Samura, p. 311.
c. Hibiya-Kondo.

2350 —— (Nippon Kagaku Koten Zen-shū, v. XII).

2351 —— (Kaiji Shiryō Sōsho, v. VI).

1818

2352 Kojima Kōken 小島好謙
Bukkoku Rekishō Benmō 佛國曆象辯妄 (Criticism of the *Bukkoku Rekishōhen*), [n.p.] 藤田貞榮, 山田道貞, 1818 (文化 15). jb. 1 v., [1], 3, 24, [1]f., 27cm.
c. Ebisawa, Gakushiin, Imoto, Jinshu, Kyōdai, Kyū-dai-Butsuri, Tenri, Waseda-Ogura.

1819

2353 Kondō Morishige 近藤守重 (1771–1829)
Gaiban Shokan 外蕃書翰 (Correspondence of Foreign Countries). jb. 1 v.
ms. Naikaku.

2354 Kondō Morishige 近藤守重 (1771–1829)
Gaiban Tsūsho 外蕃通書 (Correspondence of Foreign Countries), 1819 (文政 2). jb. 27 vols.
cf. Kaikoku, pp. 48–49; Kokushi, p. 46.
orig. ms. Tōhoku-Kano.
ms. Jingu, Naikaku, Nichidai-Mukasa, Sonkeikaku, Tenri, Ueno, Waseda.

2355 —— (Kaitei Shiseki Shūran, v. XXI).

2356 —— (Kondō Seisai Zenshū, v. I).

2357 Milne, William, LM. 米憐 (1785–1822)
Chōen Ryōyū Sōron 張遠兩友相論 *Chang-yüan Liang-yu Hsiang-lun* (Discussion on Christian Doctrine between the two Friends Chang and Yüan), Malacca 1819. cb. 1 v., 20f.
cf. Yoshida Tora, *Kirisutokyō Shigaku*, v. VI, Yoko-hama 1955; Wylie, pp. 16–17.

2358 —— Malacca 1831. cb. 1 v., 42f.

2357 —— Singapore 1836. cb. 1 v., 41f.

2360 —— revised ed., Hongkong 1844 (道光 24). cb. 1 v., 41f.

2361 —— Shanghai 1847 (道光 27). cb. 1 v., 41f.

2362 —— orig. ed., Ningpo 1847 (道光 27). cb. 1 v., 35f.

2363 —— revised by J. L. Shuck, Shang-hai 1849 (道光 29). cb. 1 v., 35f.

2364 —— revised by Wm. Charles Milne 美魏奈, Shanghai 1851 (咸豐 1). cb. 1 v., 24f.
cf. Wylie, p. 124.

2365 —— Hongkong 1851 (咸豐 1). cb. 1v., 27f.

2366 —— Ningpo 1860 (咸豐 10). cb. 1 v., 45f., 19cm.
c. Ebisawa.

2367 —— Shanghai 美華書館, 1861 (咸豐 11). cb. 1 v., 45f., 18cm.
c. Tokyoiku.

2368 —— Shanghai 美華書館, 1863 (同治 2). 9th ed. cb. 1 v., 40f., 18cm.
c. Otani.

2369 —— Shanghai 美華書館, 1868 (同治 7). cb. 1 v., 33f., 16cm.
c. Seikado, Tenri.

2370 —— Shanghai 美華書館, 1869 (同治 8). cb. 1 v., 11f., 20cm.
c. Naikaku, Saba, Taisho, Tokyoiku.

2371 —— Hongkong 英華書院, 1871 (同治 10). cb. 1 v., 32f., 16cm.
c. Kichu, Tokyoiku.

2372 —— Yang-ch'eng 小書會, 1881 (光緒 7). cb. 1 v., 30f., 23cm.
c. Tōhoku.

2373 —— tr. into Japanese by Yasukawa Kyō 安川亨, Tokyo 原胤昭, 1881 (明治 14). wb. 1 v., 66p., 19cm.
c. Doshisha-Niishima, Kichu, Tenri, Waseda.

2374 * Niyū Sōron 二友相論 *Erh-yu Hsiang-lun*, revised ed., Ningpo 1851 (咸豐 1). cb. 1 v.

2375 * Kō-otsu Niyū Ronjutsu 甲乙二友論述 *Chia-i Erh-yu Lun-shu,* revised by Alexandar Wylie 偉烈亞力 and Joseph Edkins 艾廸謹, Shanghai 1858 (咸豐 8). cb. 1 v., 22f., 21cm.
cf. Wylie, pp. 173–174.

2375b —— Shanghai 墨海書館, 1861 (咸豐 11). cb. 1 v., 22f., 21cm.
c. Otani.

2376 * Ryōyū Sōron 兩友相論 *Liang-yu Hsiang-lun* 官話, Shanghai 美華書館, 1868 (同治 7). cb. 1 v., 60f., 16cm.
c. Yoshida.

2376b —— Shanghai 美華書館, 1872 (同治 11). cb. 1 v.
c. Seikado.

2377 * Chōen Niyū Ronjutsu 張遠二友論述 *Chang-yüan Erh-yu Lun-shu,* Shanghai 1865 (同治 4). cb. 1 v., 22f., 20cm.
c. Kichu, Tōkyoiku.

2378 Ro Senri 盧千里
Semminden 先民傳 or Nagasaki Semmin-den 長崎先民傳 (Biographies of Wellknown People in Nagasaki), Edo [Tokyo] 慶文堂, 1819 (文政 2). jb. 2 vols., 27cm.
c. Hibiya-Kondo, Nagasaki, Naikaku, Seishin, Sukeno, Ueno, Waseda.

2379 —— (Chūko Sōsho).

2380 —— (Kaishoku).

2381 Satō Nobuhiro 佐藤信淵 (1769–1850)

Ame no Mihashira no Ki 天之御柱之記 or Tenchūki 天柱記 (Pillar of Heaven), 1819 (文政 2). jb. 2 vols.
cf. Shinto-Kaidai, p. 4; Samura, p. 1450; Kokushi, 213–214.

2382 —— (Hirata Atsutane Zenshū, v. II).

2383 —— (Satō Shin'en Kagaku Taikei).

2384 —— abridged (Sekai Dai-Shisō Zenshū, v. LIV).

2385 —— (Satō Shin'en Kagaku Zenshū, v. I).

2386 —— (Satō Shin'en Bugakushū, v. I).

2387 Shōnai Nigun Goningumi Okite-chō 庄内二郡五人組掟帳 (Code of Goningumi, the feudal neighbour-system). [n.p.], 1819 (文政 2). jb. 1v., 55f., 24cm.
c. Ebisawa, Iwase, Kyūdai-Hoka.

1820

2388 Yamagata Bantō 山片蟠桃 (1748–1821)

Yume no Shiro 夢の代 (A Utopia), 1820 (文政 3). jb. 12 vols.
cf. Samura, p. 1975; Kokushi, p. 319.
ms. Ueno.

2389 —— (Nippon Shisō Tōsō Shiryō, v. VI).

2390 —— (Nippon Keizai Sōsho, v. XXV).

2391 —— (Nippon Keizai Taiten, v. XXXVII).

2392 —— abridged (Nippon Shakai Keizai Gakusetsu Taikei, v. XII).

2393 * Umi no Naigai Zakki 海内外雑記 (Notes Domestic and Foreign). jb. 1 v.
note: Abridged manuscript of the *Yume no Shiro*.
ms. Yokohamashidai.

1821

2394 Gokōsatsu no Utsushi 御高札之寫 (Copies of Laws which were publicly displayed by the Tokugawa Government), 1821 (文政 4). jb. 1 v., 19cm.
c. Akita-Higashiyama.

2395 —— Edo [Tokyo], 1843 (天保 14). jb. 1 v., [14]f., 22cm.
c. Aoyama, Ebisawa, Kyūdai-Hoka, Saba, Todai-Nanki, Tohoku-Kano.

2396 —— Edo [Tokyo], 1845 (弘化 2). jb. 1 v., 14f., 18cm.

c. Ebisawa, Hibiya, Seishin, Tōdai-Hoken.

2397 Kirishitan Kōgi Onfuda no Utsushi 切支丹公儀御札之寫 (Copy of the Public Notice proscribing Christianity). jb. 1 v.
ms. Sophia.

2398 Honda Toshiaki 本多利明 (1744–1821)

Keisei Hisaku 經世秘策 (A Secret Plan for Governing the Country), [n.p.], [n.d.]. jb. 2 vols., 27cm.
note: Limited edition of only 30 copies.
cf. Kokushi, pp. 81–81.
c. Naikaku, Seishin.
ms. Naikaku, Ueno.

2399 —— (Kaibō Igi, v. XVIII).

2400 —— (Nippon Bunko, v. III).

2401 —— (Nippon Bunko, new ed., v. VIII).

2402 —— (Nippon Kaibō Shiryō Sōsho, v. II).

2403 —— (Nippon Keizai Sōsho, v. XII).

2404 —— (Nippon Keizai Taiten, v. XX).

2405 —— (Dai-Nippon Shisō Zenshū, v. XI).

2406 —— (Kinsei Shakai Keizai Gekusetsu Taikei, v. I).

2407 —— (Nippon Tetsugaku Shisō Zensho, v. IV).

2408 —— tr. into English by Donald Keene, *The Japanese Discovery of Europe, Honda Toshiaki and other Discoverers 1720–1798,* London 1952.

2409 Tsurumine Shigenobu 鶴峯戊申 (1786–1859)

Ame no Mihashira 天の眞柱 (True Pillar of Heaven), Kyoto 蛙子屋, 1821 (文政 4). jb. 1 v., [1], 2, 41f., 26cm.
cf. Saeki-Shinto, p. 4; Samura, p. 50.
c. Jinshu, Tōhoku-Kano, Waseda.

1822

2410 Entsū 圓通 (1754–1834)

Jikken Shumikai-setsu 實驗須彌界說 (Astoronomic Arguments of the Buddhist View of the World), [n.p.], 1822 (文政 5). jb. 3 vols.
cf. Itazawa, pp. 253, 258–260.
c. Itazawa.

2411 —— 1846 (弘化 3). jb. 3 vols.
c. Itazawa, Waseda-Ogura.

2412 Oranda Hōkan 和蘭寶函 (News from Dutch Magazines), tr. by the Yōsho Shirabejo 洋書調所. jb. 25 vols.
cf. Kaikoku, p. 455; Rangaku, pp. 50–51.
note: Abridged translation from the *Nederlandsch*

Magazijn ter Vverspreidung van algemeene en nuttige Kundigheden bij Gebroeders Diederichs, Amsterdam 1822–1856.
ms. Ueno.

2413 * Dojitsu Kangen 度日閑言 (Different Translation of the Oranda Hōkan), tr. by Koga Kin'ichirō 古賀謹一郎. jb. 25 vols.
orig. ms. Tōyō-Iwasaki (only 10 vols).
ms. Ueno.

2414 Satō Nobuhiro 佐藤信淵 (1789–1850)
Keizai Yōryaku 經濟要略 (Outline of Economic Policy), 1822 (文政 5). jb. 2 vols.
2415 —— (Satō Shin'en Kagaku Taiyō).
2416 —— (Satō Shin'en Kagaku Zenshū, v. I).
2417 —— (Kokugaku Taikei, v. XII).
2418 —— (Kinsei Shakai Keizai Gakusetsu Taikei, v. III).
2419 —— (Satō Shin'en Bugakushū, v. I).

1823

2420 Ikeda Hirochika 池田寛親
Funaosa Nikki 船長日記 or Tokujōmaru Senchō Nikki 督乘丸船長日記 (Diary of the Captain of Tokujōmaru), 1823 (文政 6).
cf. Kokushi, pp. 274–275.
ms. Doshisha, Hibiya-Kaga, Ishin, Kariya, Kyoto, Naikaku, Otsuki, Ueno, Waseda.
2421 —— (Ōshuku Zakki).
2422 —— (Ikoku Hyōryū Kidanshū).
2423 —— (Hyōryū Sōsho, v. LXI).
2424 —— (Kaiji Shiryō Sōsho, v. V).
2425 —— repr. by Tamai Kōsuke 玉井幸助, Tokyo 1943 (昭和 18).

2426 Medhurst, Walter Henry, CM. 向德者 (1796–1857)
Sanjikyō 三字經 *San-tzu-ching* (Three Character Classic), Batavia, 1823. cb. 1 v., 17f.
cf. Cordier-Sinica, col. 1438 ; Wylie, p. 27.
note: See also McCartee's commentary, *Shinri Sanjikyō* 眞理三字經 (n. 2901).
2427 —— Batavia, 1828. wb. 1 v.
2428 —— Malacca, 1832. wb. 1 v.
2429 —— Shingapore, 1839. wb. 1 v.
2430 —— revised ed., Hongkong, 1843 (道光 23). cb. 1 v.
2431 —— London, 1846. wb. 1v.
2432 —— new ed., Shanghai, 1845 (道光 25). cb. 1 v.
2433 —— compiled by Jehu L. Shuck, ABF. 叔士人, Shanghai, 1848 (道光 28). cb. 1 v., 19f.
cf. Wylie, p. 92.
2434 —— Ningpo, 1851 (咸豐 1). cb. 1 v.

2435 —— throughly revised ed., Shanghai, 1851 (咸豐 1). cb. 1 v.
2436 —— Hongkong, 1852 (咸豐 2). cb. 1 v.
2437 —— Amoy, 1852 (咸豐 2). cb. 1 v.
2438 —— Shanghai, 1856(咸豐 6). cb. 1 v.
2438b —— Shanghai 美華書館, 1861 (咸豐 11). cb. 1 v., 7f., 17cm.
c. Otani.
2439 —— Shanghai 美華書館, 1885 (光緒 11). cb. 1 v., 8p., 20cm.
c. Kobejo.

2440 Morrison, Robert, LM. 馬禮遜 (1782–1834)
Shinten Seisho 神天聖書 *Shen-t'ien Shengshu* (Holy Bible), tr. by R. Morrison and William Milne, LM. 米憐, [Malacca], 1823. cb. 21 vols., 17cm.
note: The first translation of the Old and New Testaments into Chinese.
cf. Muraoka-Shisō, pp. 441–465 ; Wylie, pp. 5–6, 19.
c. Ebisawa (vv. XX and XXI only), Tōhoku (vv. I–III, V–X, XIV–XVII only).

2441 Ogyū Sorai 荻生徂徠 (1666–1728)
Seidan 政談 (Discourse on Politics), [n.p.], 1823 (文政 6). jb. 4 vols., 26cm.
cf. Kokushi. p. 164.
c. Hibiya-Kaga, Inoue.
ms. Tōdai-Nanki, Yutoku.
2442 —— [Edo] 1859 (安政 6). jb. 4 vols., 26cm.
c. Hibiya-Kaga, Waseda.
2443 —— [Edo] 1868 (慶應 4). jb. 4 vols.
c. Todai-Nanki.
2444 —— (Nippon Keizai Sōsho, v. III).
2445 —— (Nippon Keizai Taiten, v. IX).
2446 —— (Nippon Shisō Tōsō Shiryō, v. VI).
2447 —— (Dai-Nippon Shisō Zenshū, v. VII).
2448 —— (Nippon Tetsugaku Shisō Zenshū, v. XVII).
2449 —— (Sesshūsai Sōsho, vv. LX-LXIII).
2450 —— (Kinsei Shakai Keizai Gakusetsu Taikei, v. XVII).

2451 Ōta Kinjō 太田錦城 (1765–1825)
Gosō Mampitsu 梧窓漫筆 (Essays), Edo [Tokyo] 山城屋玉巖堂, 1823 (文政 6). jb. 6 vols., 26cm.
cf. Samura, p. 712.
c. Hibiya-Kaga, Tōhoku-Kano, Tsuruoka.
2452 —— Edo [Tokyo] 和泉屋, 1840 (天保 11). jb. 6 vols.
c. Nichidai-Ueda.
2453 —— (Yūhōdō Bunko, Meika Zuihitsushū 名家隨筆集, v. I).

2454 —— (Nippon Zuihitsu Zenshū, v. XVII).
2455 —— (Zoku Kokumin Bunko, Zuihitsushū 随筆集).

2456 Ōta Kinjō 太田錦城 (1765–1825)
Gosō Mampitsu Shūi 梧窓漫筆拾遺 (Appendix of the Gosō Mampitsu).
2457 —— (Hyakka Setsurin, v. II).
2458 —— (Nippon Keizai Sōsho, v. XXXIII).

2459 Ōta Nampo 太田南畝 (1749–1823)
Enkai Ibun 沿海異聞 (Collection of Accounts about Drifting Ships). jb. 20 vols.
cf. Kaikoku, p. 64.
ms. Ueno.

2460 Ōta Nampo 太田南畝 (1749–1823)
Ichiwa Ichigen 一話一言 (Essays), jb. 50 vols.
cf. Kokushi, p. 15.
2461 —— annotated by Ōta Nan'yō 太田南洋, Tokyo 集成館 1883 (明治 16). jb. 50 vols., 19cm.
c. Hibiya, Ueno.
2462 —— (Shin Hyakka Setsurin, Shokuzanjin Zenshū 蜀山人全集 vv. IV–V).
2463 —— abridged (Nippon Keizai Sōsho, v. XXXIV).
2464 —— abridged (Nippon Keizai Taiten, v. LII).
2465 —— abridged (Nippon Zuihitsu Taisei, Bekkan 別巻 vv. I–II).

2466 Ōta Nampo 太田南畝 (1749–1823)
Kaden Shiryō 家傳史料 (Documents of Ōta Family).
cf. Kokushi, p. 53.
ms. Hibiya, Shiryo.
2467 —— (Shiseki Zassan, v. III).

2468 Satō Nobuhiro 佐藤信淵 (1769–1850)
Bōkaisaku 防海策 (Plans for Coastal Defense), 1823 (文政 5, 12). jb. 1 v.
cf. Kokushi, p. 280.
2469 —— (Satō Shin'en Kagaku Taiyō).
2470 —— (Satō Shin'en Kagaku Zenshū, v. III).
2471 —— (Kinji Kaikoku Hitsudokusho, v. VIII).
2472 —— (Nippon Kaibō Shiryō Sōsho, v. II).
2473 —— (Satō Shin'en Bugakushū, v. I).
2474 —— (Nippon Bugaku Taikei, v. XXI).

2475 Satō Nobuhiro 佐藤信淵 (1769–1850)

Kondō Hisaku 混同秘策 (Secret Policy for Uniting the World), 1823 (文政 6). jb. 2 vols.
cf. Kokushi, p. 110.
ms. Ueno.
2476 —— annotated by Oda Kanshi 織田完之, Tokyo 寅賓樓, 1888 (明治 21). jb. 2 vols., 23cm.
c. Naikaku, Ueno.
2477 —— Tokyo 1896 (明治 29). jb. 2 vols.
c. Naikaku.
2478 —— annotated by Kamoda Keikichi 鴨田恵吉, Tokyo 1937 (昭和 12).
2479 —— (Satō Shin'en Kagaku Taiyō).
2480 —— (Sekai Dai-Shisō Zenshū, v. LIV).
2481 —— (Nippon Kokusui Zensho, v. XIX).
2482 —— (Satō Shin'en Kagaku Zenshū, v. II).
2483 —— (Satō Shin'en Bugakushū, v. I).
2484 —— (Nippon Keizai Taiten, v. XVIII).
2485 —— (Dai-Nippon Shisō Zenshū, v. VIII).
2486 —— (Kokugaku Taikei, v. XII).
2487 —— (Kinsei Shakai Keizai Gakusetsu Taikei, v. III).

2488 Shūchin Nikka, Tenshu Seikyō Nikka 袖珍日課天主聖教日課 Hsiu-chen jih-k'e T'ien-chu Sheng-chiao jih-k'e (Daily Office of the Catholic Church), Shanghai 1823 (道光 3). cb. 3 vols., 30cm.
c. ICU.

2489 Yoshio Shunzō 吉雄俊藏
Rigaku Nyūshiki Ensei Kanshō Zusetsu 理學入式遠西觀象圖說 (Illustrated Western Astronomy), Nagoya 觀象堂, 1823 (文政 6). jb. 3 vols., 23cm.
cf. Kaikoku, p. 318.
c. Daitokyu, Doshisha, Imoto, Keio, Kyodai, Kyudai-Butsuri, Kariya, Ishin, Iwase, Hibiya-Kondo, Nagasaki, Nagasaki-Isahaya, Okada, Seishin, Tenri, Tōdai-Nanki, Tōhoku-Kano, Tōhoku-Sugaku, Tōkyoiku, Waseda.
2490 —— Osaka 加賀屋善藏 1828 (文政 11). jb. 3 vols., 23cm.

1824

2491 Aizawa Seishi 會澤正志 (1782–1863)
An-i Mondō 諳夷問答 (Dialogue on National Defense), 1824 (文政 7). jb. 1 v.
cf. Tsukamoto Ketsuyoshi 勝本勝義, *Aizawa Seishi no Shisō*, Tokyo 1943, pp. 31, 75–76.

2492 Milne, William, LM. 米憐 (1785–1822)

87

Gōkun Gojūnisoku 郷訓五十二則 *Hsiang-hsün Wu-shih-erh-tse* (Fifty-two Teachings), Malacca, 1824. cb. 1 v., 70f.

cf. Ozawa, p. 188 Wylie, pp. 18–19.

note: A thorough revision by W.C. Milne was printed under the title *Fukuin Kōkun* 福音廣訓 (see n. 3008).

2493 —— Ningpo 華花聖經書房, 1848 (道光 28). cb. 1 v., [1], 3, 51f., 18cm.

c. Otani.

2494 —— revised ed. by Medhurst, Shanghai, 1854 (咸豐 4). cb. 1 v., 49f.

2495 —— Shanghai 美華書館, 1870 (同治 9). cb. 1 v., 3, [1], 30, [2]f., 20cm.

c. ICU, Kichu, Kōbejo, Saba, Seikado, Waseda, Yoshida.

2496 —— Shanghai 美華書館, 1874 (同治 13). cb. 1 v., 3, 3, [2], 30f., 19cm.

c. Doshisha, Kichu..

2497 Watanabe Keijirō 渡邊啓次郎
Ryōchi Denshūroku 量地傳習録 (Instruction in Surveying), 1824 (文政 7). jb. 1 v.

ms. Hibiya, Ueno.

1825

2498 Golovnin, Vassilii Michaelovitch
Sōyaku Nihon Kiji 遭厄日本紀事 (Narrative of my Captivity in Japan), tr. by Baba Teiyu 馬場貞由, Sugita Seikei 杉田成卿 and Aochi Rinsō 青地林宗, 1825 (文政 8). jb. 14 vols.

note: Translation from the Dutch work by Steenbergen von Goor, *Mijne Lotgevallen in Myne Gevangenschap by de Japanners, gedurende de jaren 1812 en 1813*, Dordrecht 1817.

cf. Tenri-Jap. II, p. 111; Rangaku, pp. 34–35.

ms. Hakodate, Hibiya-Kondo, Hokudai, Nagasaki, Naikaku, Otsuki, Shiryo, Tenri, Ueno, Waseda-Hanabusa.

2499 Katō Genki 加藤玄龜
Wagakoromo 我衣 (Essays), 1825 (文政 8). jb. 1 v.

cf. Kokushi, p. 333.

2500 —— (Enseki Jisshu, v. I).

2501 —— (Kinko Bungei Onchi Sōsho, v. X).

2502 Yoshio Chūjirō 吉雄忠次郎 (– 1822)
Angeriajin Seijoshi 諳厄利亞人性情志 (On the English People), 1825 (文政 8). jb. 1 v.

note: Refers in passing to the Reformation.

cf. Kaikoku, pp. 401–402.

ms. Ayuzawa, Naikaku, Tōhoku-Kano.

2503 —— (Kinji Kaikoku Hitsudokusho, v. IV).

2504 —— (Nippon Kaibō Shiryō Sōsho, v. II).

2505 —— (Kaihyō Sōsho, v. II).

1826

2506 Huebner, Johann
Yochi Shiryaku 輿地志略 (General Geography of the World), tr. by Aochi Rinsō 青地林宗, 1826 (文政 9). jb. 8 vols.

2507 —— (Bummei Genryū Sōsho, v. I).

2508 —— tr. by Uchida Masao 内田正雄, 1874–76 (明治 7–10). jb. 10 vols.

c. Waseda.

2509 McCartee, Divie Bethune, PN. 麥嘉締 (1820–1900)
Yaso Kōsei Genkō Imbun 耶穌降生言行韻文 *Yeh-su Chiang-sheng Yen-hsing Yün-wen* (Life of Jesus in Verse), Ningpo 華花聖經書房, [n.d.]. cb. 1 v., 6f., 18cm.

cf. Wylie, p. 137.

note: revised version of D. Collie, LM., *Yaso Genkō Sōron* 耶穌言行總論 Yeh-su Yen-hsing tsung-lun, Malacca 1826 (See Wylie, p. 463.)

c. Otani.

2510 —— Shanghai 1863 (同治 2). cb. 1 v., 10f.

1827

2511 Bachiene, W. A.
Yochishi 輿地志 (General Geography), tr. by Aochi Rinsō 青地林宗, 1827 (文政 10). jb. 65 vols.

orig. title: Algemeen Geographie. Vermeerderd en met Aanteekeningen verrykt, Amsterdam 1769.

cf. Kaikoku, pp. 108–110.

ms. Ueno.

2512 Murai Ippo 邨井一甫
Kirishitan On-taijiki 切支丹御退治記 (Record of Elimination of Christianity), 1827 (文政 10). jb. 50 vols.

cf. Samura, p. 477.

ms. Naikaku, Ueno.

2513 Ōtsuki Bansui 大槻盤水 (1757–1827)
Bansui Mansō 盤水漫草 (Essays of Bansui), compiled by Hasegawa Sōsen 長谷川宗仙. jb. 2 vols.

2514 —— (Bansui Zonkyō, v. II).

2515 Ōtsuki Gentaku 大槻玄澤 (1757–1827)
Enkō Manpitsu 畹港漫筆 (Essays), jb. 8 vols.

orig. ms. Waseda.

2516 —— pr. and annotated in *Waseda Daigaku Toshokan Geppō*, nos. 18–19. Tokyo 1953–54 (昭和 28–29).

2517 Ōtsuki Bunsui 大槻盤水 (1757–1827)
Ransetsu Bensei 蘭説辯正 (Apology for

Dutch Learning). jb. 1 v.

2518 —— (Bansui Zonkyō, v. I).

2519 Ōtsuki Bansui 大槻盤水 (1757–1827)
Ranyaku Teikō 蘭譯梯航 (Textbook for Dutch Learning), jb. 2 vols.
2520 —— (Bansui Zonkyō, v. I).
2521 —— (Kyōrin Sōsho, v. I).

1828

2522 Hirata Atsutane 平田篤胤 (1776–1843)
Techū Gogakukō 天柱五嶽考 (A Shintō Cosmology). jb. 1 v.
cf. Samura, p. 1450.
ms. Naikaku, Tenri.

2523 Hirata Atsutane 平田篤胤 (1776–1843)
Tenchū Gogaku Yoron 天柱五嶽餘論 (Supplement of the *Tenchū Gogakukō*).
ms. Ueno.
2524 —— (Hirata Atsutane Zenshū, v. XIV).

2525 Medhurst, Walter Henry, LM. 麥都思 (1796–1857)
Ron Zen-aku'nin no Shi 論善惡人之死 *Lun Shan-o-jen chih szu* (On the Death of Good and Bad Persons), Batavia [1828?]. cb. 1 v. 6f.
cf. Ozawa, p. 191; Wylie, p. 31.
2526 —— Malacca 1829. cb. 1 v., 8f.
2527 —— Malacca 1835. cb. 1 v., 8f.
2528 —— Singapore 1837. cb. 1 v., 8f.
2529 —— Hongkong 1844 (道光 24). cb. 1 v., 10f. 16cm.
2530 —— London 1847. wb. 1 v.
2531 —— Shanghai 美華書館 1863 (同治 2). cb. 1 v., 10f., 16cm.
c. Otani.
2532 —— Shanghai 美華書館 1867 (同治 6). cb. 1 v., 6f., 15cm.
c. Jinshu, Saba.

2533 Uchihashi Chikuun 打橋竹雲
Nagasaki Nenreki 長崎年曆 (Chronological List of Nagasaki), 1829 (文政 11). jb. 1sheet.
note: A chronological list of all the Governors of Nagasaki 1570–1828, together with the members of Dutch and Chinese ships entering the port of Nagasaki.
cf. Boxer-Compagnie, p. 132; Samura, p. 1514.
ms. Naikaku.
2534 —— (Nanyō Sōsho).

2535 Urano Yukimitsu 浦野幸盈
Kikujutsu Betsuden 規矩術別傳 (Different Methods of Surveying), 1828 (文政 11). jb.

1 v.
ms. Tōhoku-Kano.

1829

2536 Kondō Morishige 近藤守重 (1771–1829)
Amakō-Ki Ryakusō 亞媽港紀略藁 (Short Description of Macao). jb. 2 vols.
cf. Kaikoku, p. 49.
ms. Naikaku.
2537 —— (Kondō Seisai Zenshū, v. I).

2538 Kondō Morishige 近藤守重 (1771–1829)
Annanki Ryakusō 安南紀略藁 (Short Notes on Annan), jb. 1 v., [81]f., p. 49.
cf. Kaikoku, p. 49.
c. Hibiya-Inoue.
ms. Iwase, Tōdai-Nanki, Ueno.
2539 —— (Kondō Seisai Zenshū, v. I).
2540 —— (Hyōryū Kidan Zenshū).

2541 Kondō Morishige 近藤守重 (1771–1829)
Igirisu Kiryaku 伊祇利須紀略 (Short Notes on England). jb. 1 v.
cf. Kaikoku, p. 400.
ms. Keio, Kyodai.
2542 * Igirisu Kiryaku Teiyō 伊祇利須記略提要 (Summary of the *Igirisu Kiryaku*). jb. 1 v.
ms. Kyōdai Shokokan.

2543 Kondō Morishige 近藤守重 (1771–1829)
Kenkyō Ruiten 憲敎類典 (Classified Laws of the Shogunate Government).
cf. Kokushi, p. 84.
ms. Naikaku, Ueno, Waseda.

2544 Kondō Morishige 近藤守重 (1771–1829)
Kōsho Koji 好書故事 (Bibliographical Notes in the Shogunate Library)
ms. Naikaku.
2545 —— (Kondō Seisai Zenshū, v. III).

2546 Nakayama Takenori 中山武德 (1785–1844)
Roshia Kokushi 魯西亞國史 (Russian History). tr. by T. Nakayama and Ono-dera Shōjun 小野寺將順. [1829?]. jb. 2 vols.
note: The original is unknown.
cf. Kaikoku, pp. 394–395.
ms. Otsuki (v. II only).

2547 Suzuki Hakutō 鈴木白藤
Kirishito Jikki 吉利斯督實記 (True Account of Christianity), 1829 (文政 12). jb. 1 v.
cf. Samura. p. 477.
ms. Naikaku, Ueno.

1830

2548 Ishii Kōchi 石井光致
Wakan Rekigenkō 和漢曆原考 (Treatise on the Origin of the Calendar in Japan and China). Edo [Tokyo] 須原屋, 1830 (文政 13). jb. 1 v., 1, 23f., 26cm.
c. Tenri, Waseda.

2549 Medhurst, Walter Henry, LM. 麥都思 (1786–1857)
An English and Japanese, and Japanese and English Vocabulary, Batavia 1830. wb. 1 v., 8, 1, 1, 344p., 22cm.
cf. Toyota, pp. 11, 53–57.
c. ICU, Kokkai, Kyodai, Meiji.

2550 * Yōgaku Shōkei Futsu-Ei Kumben 洋學捷徑佛英訓辯 (French and English Vocabulary), compiled by Murakami Motei 村上茂亭, Edo [Tokyo], 1855 (安政 2). jb. 1 v., 23f., 8×16cm.
note: The first French Dictionary in Japan. The compiler arranged and revised Medhurst's English Vocabulary.
cf. Toyota, p. 154.

2551 * Eigosen 英語箋, or Beigosen 米語箋 (English Vocabulary, or American Vocabulary), tr. by Inoue Shuri 井上修理, Edo [Tokyo], 1857–63 (安政 4–文久 3). jb. 7 vols., 18×26cm.
cf. Toyota, pp. 57, 155; Araki-Eigogaku, n. 9.
c. Meiji, Hibiya-Ichimura (v. I only).

Persecution in the Kansai District, 1827–1830

2552 Jashūmon Ikken Kakitome 邪宗門一件書留 (The Court Records on the Examination of Christians). jb. 2 vols.
cf. Ebisawa-Namban, pp. 334–344.
ms. Keio-Koda, Shiryo.

2553 Ōsaka Kirishitan Ikken 大坂切支丹一件 (A Protocol of the Ōsaka Law-Court on the Christians). jb. 1 v.
cf. Ebisawa Arimichi, "Bunsei Jū'nen Keihan Kirishitan Ikken" (Rekishi Chiri, v. LXXXIV, n. 2), Tokyo 1953.
ms. Seishin.

2554 Bunsei Jū'ni'nen Ushi Jū'nigatsu Ōsaka ni oite Kirishitan Oshioki Ikken 文政十二年丑十二月於大坂切支丹御仕置一件 (Execution of the Christians at Osaka in the 12th Month, 12th Year of Bunsei). jb. 1 v.
2555 —— (Ōshuku Zakki).
2556 * Jatō Ketsugi 邪徒決疑 (The Texts of Legal Decisions regarding Christians). jb. 1 v.

2557 —— (Settsu Chōsho).
2558 * Jato Ketsugoku 邪徒決獄 (The Text of Legal Decisions regarding Christians). jb. 1 v.
2559 —— (Buhen Sōsho).
2560 —— (Shiseki Shūran).
2561 —— (Shiryō Sōsho).
2562 —— (Kaitei Shiseki Shūran).
2563 * Kirishitan no Mono Oshioki no Kakitsuke 切支丹のもの御仕置の書付 (Notes on the Punishment of Christians). jb. 1 v.
ms. Jingu.

2564 * Kirishitan Shūmon Shikkōsha Zaika Shidai 切支丹宗門執行者罪科次第 (The Texts of Legal Decisions regarding Christians). jb. 1 v.
ms. Ebisawa.

2565 Toyota Mitsugi Zaian 豊田貢罪案 (Condemnation of Toyota Mitsugi). jb. 1 v.
ms. Jingu.

1832

2566 Jinryokumaru Batan Hyōryū Kuchigaki 神力丸馬丹漂流口書 (Tales of Drifting to Batan), 1832 (天保 3) jb. 1 v.
2567 —— (Ikoku Hyōryū Kidanshū).
2568 * Nangoku Kiwa 南國奇話 (Strange Stories of the Southern Countries).
cf. Shimmura-Namban I, p. 450.
ms. Kyoto.
2569 —— (Kaihyō Sōsho, v. III).
2570 * Okayama Hyōryūjin-ki 岡山漂流人記 (Record of the Shipwrecked Sailors of Okayama). jb. 1 v.
ms. Ueno.

2571 Kaempfer, Engelbert (1651–1716)
Seiyōjin Kenfuru Nihonshi 西洋人檢夫爾日本誌, tr. into Japanese by Miyake Tomonobu 三宅友信, 1832 (天保 3). jb. 1 v.
note: Abridged translation of Kaempfer's De Beschrijving van Japan, Amsterdam 1729.
cf. Rangaku, p. 33.
orig. ms. Ueno.

2572 Mortier
Chigaku Shimō 地學示蒙 (Instruction in Geography), tr. by Hōkyo Sanjin 芳滸散人. jb. 2 vols.
note: The name of the translator, Hōkyo Sanjin is a pseudonym for Aochi Rinsō 青地林宗 (1784–1833). An abridged translation from Mortier's Geographisch Zakboekje, 1820 [?].
cf. Kaikoku, pp. 166–168.
ms. Ueno.

2573 Satō Nobuhiro 佐藤信淵 (1769–1850)

Naiyō Keiiki 内洋經緯記 (On Exploration of the Inland Sea), 1833 (天保 4). jb. 1 v.
cf. Samura, p. 1511.

2574 —— (Satō Shin'en Kagaku Taiyō).

2575 —— Tokyo, 1880 (明治 13). wb. 1 v.
c. Hibiya.

2576 * Beppon Naiyō Keiiki 別本内洋經緯 (Another manuscript of the Naiyō Keiiki).

2577 —— (Satō Shin'en Kagaku Zenshū, v. II).

1834

2578 Entsū 圓通 (1754–1834)
Bonreki Sakushin 梵曆策進 (On the Indian Calendar). [n.p.], [n.d.]. jb. 1 v., 25, 4f., 26cm.
c. Ebisawa, Waseda-Ogura.

2579 —— Kyoto, [1866 慶應 2?]. jb. 1 v., 25f., 20cm.
c. Aoyama.

2580 Mitsukuri Gempo 箕作阮甫 (1799–1863)
Kon'yo Wakumon 坤輿或問 (Dialogue on World Geography), tr. by G. Mitsukuri, [n.p.], [n.d.], jb. 1 v.
cf. Kaikoku, p. 358.
orig. ms. the Mitsukuris.

2581 Morrison, Robert, LM. 馬禮遜 (1782–1834)
Gaikoku Shiryaku 外國史略 (Outline History of Foreign Countries).
note: No reference in Wylie.

2581b —— (Shōhōkosai Yoshi Sōshō).

2582 Shibukawa Rokuzō 澁川六藏 (1811–1845)
Oranda Kiryaku 和蘭紀略 (Outline of Dutch History) [1834?]. jb. 1 v.
cf. Kaikoku, pp. 380–381.
ms. Sonkeikaku.

2583 —— (Kinji Kaikoku Hitsudokusho, v. II).

2584 —— (Nippon Kaibō Shiryō Sōsho, v. III).

1835

2585 Takano Chōei 高野長英 (1804–1850)
Bunken Manroku 聞見漫録 (Recollection), 1835 (天保 6). jb.
note: Contains a brief history of Western philosophy.

2586 —— facs. pr. (Takano Chōei Zenshū, v. IV).

2587 —— pr. and annotated, Itazawa, pp. 380–385.

1836

2588 Guetzlaff, Karl Friedrich Augustus, LM. 愛漢者 (1803–1851)
Fukuin no Shinki 福音之箴規, *Fu-yin chih Chen-kui* (Gospel Precepts), Singapore 堅夏書院, 1836 (道光 16). cb. 1 v., 18f.
cf. Wylie, p. 57.
c. Tōyō.

2589 Guetzlaff, Karl Friedrich Augustus, LM. 善徳 (1803–1851)
Jōtei Bambutsu no Taishu 上帝萬物之大主, *Shang-ti wan-wu chih Ta-chu* (God, the Lord of All), Singapore 堅夏書院, 1836 (道光 16). cb. 1 v., 1, 9, 11f., 23cm.
cf. Wylie, p. 59.
c. Tohoku.

2590 Guetzlaff, Karl Friedrich Augustus, LM. 愛漢者 (1803–1851)
Kyūseishu Yaso no Seikun 救世主耶蘇之聖訓, *Chiu-shih-chu Ye-su chih Sheng-hsün* (Sacred Instruction of the Saviour Jesus), Singapore 堅夏書院, 1836 (道光 16). cb. 1 v., 1, 17f., 25cm.
cf. Wylie, p. 57.
c. Tōhoku, Tōyō.

2591 Hō Kakei 楳華谿 *Mei Hua-hsi*
Kaigai Shinsho 海外新書 *Hai-wai Hsin-shu* (New Book on Foreign Countries), [n.p.], 1836 (道光 16). cb. 3 vols., 23cm.
c. Ueno.

2592 Kamei Shōyō 龜井昭陽 (1773–1836)
Bōkai Bigen 防海微言 (Private Opinions on Coastal Defense). jb. 1 v.
cf. Samura, p. 1615.
ms. Hibiya-Kondo.

2593 —— (Kaibō Igi, v. II).

2594 —— (Nippon Kaibō Sōsho, v. II).

2595 Kōekiron 交易論 (On Trade). jb. 2 vols.
note: The author is probably Kamei Shōyō 龜井昭陽.

2596 —— (Nippon Keizai Taiten, v. XLVI).

2597 Mogami Tokunai 最上徳内 (1754–1836)
Ezo Sōshi 蝦夷草志 (Notes on Ezo).
cf. Kaikoku. p. 367; Samura, p. 205.
ms. Hokudai, Waseda.

2598 —— (Hokumon Sōsho, v. I).

2599 Takenouchi Takenobu 竹内武信
Kikujutsu Denrai no Maki Furoku 規矩術傳來之卷附録 (Appendix to the History of Surveying Art), 1836 (天保 7). jb. 1 v.
ms. Tohoku-Hayashi.

2600 Yamamoto Taizen 山本大膳
Goningumichō Maegaki 五人組帳前書 (Law of Goningumi, the feudal neighbour-control system), [Edo] 1836 (天保 7). jb. 1 v., 25f., 26cm.
c. Ebisawa, Iwase, Todai-Hoken.
2601 —— repr. by Hozumi Nobushige 穂積陳重, *Goningumi Seido*, Tokyo 1902 (明治 32).

1837

2602 Guetzlaff, Karl Friedrich Augustus, LM. 善徳 (1803–1851)
Yohane Fukuin no Den 約翰福音之傳 Yoannesuno Tayori Yorokobi ヨアンネスノタヨリヨロコビ (The Gospel according to St. John), Singapore 堅夏書院, [1837?]. cb. 1 v., 60f. 28cm.
cf. Kadowaki, pp. 2–5; Tenri-Jap. II, p. 86; Wylie. p. 63.
c. Doshisha-Shingaku, JBS, Meiji, Tenri, Tokyoshin.
2603 —— facs. repr. by Nagasaki Shoten 長崎書店, Tokyo 1941 (昭和 16). 2 vols.
2604 —— repr. and annotated by Shigehisa Tokutarō 重久篤太郎 (*Kirisutokyō Kenkyū*, v. XVI, n. 1.) Kyoto 1938 (昭和 13).
2605 —— abridged repr. by Ozawa Saburō 小澤三郎 (*Kirisutokyōshi Kenkyū*, v. I), Yokohama 1938 (昭和 13).
2606 * Yohane Fukuin no Den, Yohane Chūsho-fu 約翰福音之傳, 約翰中書附. arranged by Léon Rosny, Paris 1854. wb. 1 v., 7f., 23cm.
note: contains chap. I–II of the Gospel and the Second Epistle of St. John.
cf. Kadowaki, pp. 6–7; Wylie, p. 63.
c. JBS, Ueda (destroyed).
2607 Guetzlaff, Karl Friedrich Augustus, LM. 善徳 (1803–1851)
Yohane Jōchū-ge-sho 約翰上中下書 (Three Epistles of St. John) Singapore 堅夏書院 [1837?]. cb. 1 v., 10f.
cf. Wylie, p. 63.
2608 —— facs. repr. and annotateed by Ozawa Saburō 小澤三郎 (*Kirisutokyōshi Kenkyū*, v. IV), Yokohama 1939 (昭和 14).
2609 Kenjō Sanjin 彦城散人
Kyūshū Shoshō Gunki 九州諸將軍記 or Kyūshū Gunki 九州軍記 (War Report on Kyūshū), 1837 (天保 8).
cf. Samura, p. 421.
2610 Ōtake Shunryū 大竹春龍
Kyūshūki 九州記 (Notes on Kyūshū). jb. 18 vols.
cf. Samura, p. 421.
ms. Doshisha.
2611 —— (Amakusagun Shiryō, v. II).

2612 Ōno Gonnojō 大野權之丞 (–1841)
Buke Hikkei Taihei Nenpyō 武家必鞏泰平年表 (Chronological Table of Japanese History) compiled by Nin'oku Inshi 忍屋隠士, [n.p.], 1837 (天保 8). jb. 1 v., 121f., 18cm.
cf. Kokushi, p. 192; Samura, p. 1295.
c. Naikaku, Tenri.
ms. Gakushiin, Gakushuin, Hibiya, Naikaku, Nichidai-Mukasa, Tōyō-Iwasaki, Ueno-Shirai.

Voyage of the Ship "Morrison" and the Persecution of the Groups of "Bansha", 1837–1841

2613 Kōkaishū 江海集. jb. 1 v.
contents: Shinkiron 慎機論 by Watanabe Kazan 渡邊華山
Bojutsu Yume Monogatari 戊戌夢物語 by Takano Chōei 高野長英
Yume Monogatari Hyō 夢物語評 by Ōkura Kensuke 大倉健助
Yumeyume Monogatari 夢々物語 by Satō Nobuhiro 佐藤信淵
ms. Hibiya-Kondo.
2614 Ōkura Kensuke 大倉健助
Yume Monogatari-hyō 夢物語評 (Criticism of the *Yume Monogatari*).
2615 —— (Kaibō Igi, v. VI).
2616 —— (Kōkaishū).
2617 —— (Nippon Kaibō Shiryō Sōsho, v. II).
2618 —— (Sendai Sōsho, B., v. VII).
2619 Oranda Hōkan, Hyōmin Gosō Igirisu Morurisson-sen Ichijō Shōyaku 和蘭實函, 漂民護送 英吉利 モルリッソン船一條抄譯 (Abridged Translation from the Oranda Hōkan, An Account of the English Ship *Morrison*).
note: Translation from the *Nederlandsch Magazijn*, Amsterdam 1839. See also n. 3153.
2620 —— (Kaibō Igi, v. XLIII).
2621 * Oranda Hōkan, Nippon no Bu 和蘭實函, 日本之部 (Japanese Part of the Oranda Hōkan). jb. 1 v.
ms. Ebisawa.
2622 —— (Sokkyohen).
2623 —— (Ōen Sōsho, v. XLVI).
2624 Satō Genkai 佐藤元海 (1769–1850)
Yume Yume Monogatari 夢々物語 (Dreamy Tales). jb. 1 v.
cf. Kokushi, p. 319.
ms. Hibiya-Kondo.
2625 —— (Kaibō Igi, v. VI).
2626 —— (Kōkaishū).
2627 —— (Nippon Kaibō Shiryō Sōsho, v. II).

2628 —— (Sendai Sōsho, B., v. VII).
2629 —— (Nippon Bunko, v. II).

2630 Takano Chōei 高野長英 (1804–1850)
Bansha Sōyaku Shōki 蕃社遭厄小記 (Record of the Persecution of the Foreign Seminary). jb. 1 v.
ms. Hibiya, Naikaku.
2631 —— Tokyo, 1899 (明治 32). jb. 1 v.
c. Keio.
2632 —— (Takano Chōei Zenshū, v. IV).

2633 Takano Chōei 高野長英 (1804–1850)
Chihi Ichijo 知彼一助 (The Practical Worth of Knowing the West). jb. 1 v.
cf. Asahi, p. 52.
orig. ms. T. Kuwaori.
2634 —— (Takano Chōei Zenshū, v. IV).

2635 Takano Chōei 高野長英 (1804–1850)
Tori no Nakine 鳥の鳴音 or Wasure Katami 和壽禮加多美 (Essays), 1839 (天保 10).
2636 —— (Bummei Tōzenshi).
2637 —— (Takano Chōei Zenshū, v. IV).
2638 —— (Dai-Nippon Shisō Zenshū, v. IX).
2639 —— (Nippon Tetsugaku Shisō Zenshū, v. IV).

2640 Takano Chōei 高野長英 (1804–1850)
Yume Monogatari 夢物語, or Bojutsu Yume Monogatari 戊戌夢物語 (Narrative of a Dream). jb. 1 v.
cf. Kokushi, p. 319.
ms. Ishin, Iwase, Naikaku.
2641 —— (Heikan Issō).
2642 —— (Hōro Zasshō).
2643 —— (Kaibō Igi, v. VI).
2644 —— (Kōkaishū).
2645 —— (Reisai Sōsho).
2646 —— (Ōen Sōsho).
2647 —— (Nippon Bunko, v. II).
2648 —— (Nippon Kaibō Shiryō Sosho, v. II).
2649 —— (Takano Chōei Zenshū, v. IV).
2650 —— (Shiryō Sōsho).
2651 —— (Bummei Tōzenshi).
2652 —— (Sendai Sōsho, B., v. VII).
2653 —— (Dai-Nippon Shisō Zenshū, v. IX).
2654 —— (Gōitsu Sōsho).
2655 *Takano Chōei Yume Monogatari 高野長英諭迷物語, annotated by Kōmurō Shujin 香夢樓主人, Tokyo 1886 (明

治 19). wb. 1 v.

2656 Tempo Hachinen Rokugatsu Morison-sen Uchiharai no Shimatsu 天保八年六月モリソン船打拂之始末 (The Repulse of the Morrison), 1837 (天保 8). jb. 1 v.
ms. Naikaku.

2657 Watanabe Kazan 渡邊華山 (1793–1841)
Kaigai Jirui Zassan 海外事類雜纂 (Collection of Books on Foreign Affairs) compiled K. Watanabe. jb. 4 vols.
cf. Kaikoku, pp. 78–79.
ms. Ueno.

2658 Watanabe Kazan 渡邊華山 (1793–1841)
Ketsuzetsu Shōki 鴃舌小記 (Notes on Foreigners), [1837?]. jb. 1 v.
cf. Shimmura-Namban, II, pp. 347–348.
ms. Kyoto.
2659 —— (Hōro Zasshō).
2660 —— (Bummei Tōzenshi).
2661 —— (Nippon Bunko, v. II).
2662 —— (Kazan Zenshū, v. I).
2663 —— (Dai-Nippon Shisō Zenshū, v. IX).

2664 Watanabe Kazan 渡邊華山 (1793–1841)
Ketsuzetsu Wakumon 鴃舌或問 (Questions Regarding Foreigners). jb. 1 v.
ms. Jingu, Naikaku.
2665 —— (Nippon Bunko, v. II).
2666 —— (Zuihitsu Bungaku Senshū, v. IV).

2667 Watanabe Kazan 渡邊華山 (1793–1841)
Kuchigaki 口書 (Oral Notes), 1839 (天保 10). jb. 1 v.
cf. Kokushi, p. 335.

2668 Watanabe Kazan 渡邊華山 (1793–1841)
Seiyō Jijō Go-tōsho 西洋事情御答書 (Answers About the Western World). jb. 1 v.
2669 —— (Bummei Tōzenshi).
2670 —— (Kazan Zenshū, v. I).

2671 Watanabe Kazan 渡邊華山 (1793–1841)
Shinkiron 慎機論 (Memorial about the *Morrison*), 1838 (天保 9). jb. 1 v.
cf. Kokushi, p. 151.
ms. Keio.
2672 —— (Shinobazu Sōsho).
2673 —— (Kaibō Igi, v. VII).
2674 —— (Kōkaishū).

2675 —— (Kinji Kaikoku Hitsudokusho, v. VII).

2676 —— (Nippon Bunko, v. II).

2677 —— (Bummei Tōzenshi).

2678 —— (Dai-Nippon Shisō Zenshū, v. IX).

2679 —— (Nippon Kaibō Shiryō Sōsho, v. II).

2680 —— (Kazan Zenshū, v. I).

2681 Yume Monogatari Ruishū 夢物語類輯 (Classified Index of the *Yume Monogatari*). jb. 1 v.
ms. Iwase.

1838

2682 Bridgman, Elijah Coleman, PN. 裨治文 (1801–1861)
Shishūshi 四洲志 *Ssu-chou-chih* (Geography of the Four Continents), tr. by Rin Sokujo 林則徐 *Lin Tse-hsü*, [n.p.], 1838 (道光 18). cb. 50 vols.
cf. Kaikoku, pp. 135–139.
note: See nos. 2738–2744.

2683 Ei Yō 永瑢 *Yung Yung*
Kintei Shiko Zensho Sōmoku Teiyō 欽定四庫全書總目提要 *Ch'in-ting Ssu-k'u Chüan-shu Tsung-mu t'i-yao* (Manual of the Most Important Contents of the Four Libraries). cb. 144 vols.
note: See also no. 2176.
c. Gakushiin, Kyodai-Bungakubu, Naikaku.
ms. Naikaku.

2684 —— annotated by Ishizaka Sōtetsu 石坂宗哲, Edo [Tokyo] 1838 (天保 9). jb.
c. Naikaku (v. CIII-CV only).

2685 —— Canton 廣東書局, 1868 (同治 7). cb. 120 vols., 21cm.
c. Daitokyu, Seikado, Seishin, Tōyō-Fujita, Ueno.

2686 —— Peking 1910 (宜統 2). wb. 8 vols.
c. Kyodai-Bungakubu.

2687 Koga Dōan 古賀侗庵 (1788–1847)
Kaibō Okusoku 海防臆測 (Private Opinion on Coastal Defence), [n.p.], 1838 (天保 9). jb. 2 vols. 26cm.
cf. Kokushi, pp. 46–47.
ms. Gakushuin, Hibiya-Kondo, Iwase, Tōhoku-Kano, Waseda.

2688 —— Tokyo 彫瑛園, 1880 (明治 13). jb. 1v., 2, [2], 30, [1], 2f., 19cm.
c. Ebisawa, Jingu.

2689 —— (Heikan Issō).

2690 —— (Nippon Kaibō Shiryō Sōsho, v. V).

2691 Satō Nobuhiro 佐藤信淵 (1769–1850)
Satō Akai Nisei-gi 佐藤赤井二生議 (Memorials by Satō Nobuhiro and Akai Tōkai 赤井東海), 1838 (天保 9). jb. 1 v.

2692 —— (Kaibō Igi, v. V).

2693 —— (Nippon Kaibō Shiryō Sōsho, v. II).

2694 Utagawa Yōan 宇田川榕庵 (1798–1846)
Seiyō Ki'nenkō 西洋紀年稿 (Western Chronological Table), [1838?]. jb. 2 vols., 25cm.
note: Especially notices about intercourse between Japan and Europe.
cf. Kaikoku, pp. 429–430.
orig. ms. Fujinami.

1839

2695 Chomel, Noel (1631–1712)
Kōsei Shimpen 厚生新編 (New Encyclopaedia), tr. by the Official Institute of Western Learning, 1839 (天保 10). jb.
orig. title: *Huishoudelijk Woordenboek, door M. Noel Chomel. Tweede Druk gebeel verbetert, en meer als belste verme erdert door J.A. de Cholmet*, Leyden 1772.
cf. Itazawa, pp. 264–297; Kaikoku, pp. 105–106.
note: Not printed.
orig. ms. Aoi, Iys, Okamura.
ms. Ueno.

2696 Miyazaki Narumi 宮崎成身
Kyōrei Ruisan 敎令類纂 (Classified Laws of the Edo Period), 1839 (天保 10). jb. 232 vols.
cf. Kokushi, p. 68.
ms. Jingu, Naikaku.

2697 Sakurada Komon 櫻田虎門 (1774–1839)
Keiseidan 經世談, (Essay on Economic Policy). jb. 10 vols.
note: v. VI gives his opinion on Christianity.

2698 —— (Nippon Keizai Taiten, v. XVI).

1840

2699 Thom, Robert 羅伯淡
Ishū Yugen 意拾喻言 (Aesop's Fables), Canton, 1840 (道光 20). cb. 1 v., 4, 21, 4, 1, 4, 104, 8p.
cf. Pfister, p. 117; Shimmura-Isoho, pp. 49–89; Cordier-Sinica, col. 1683.
note: R. Thom, an English missionary in China.
c. Tōyō.
ms. Tōhoku.

2700 —— Singapore, 1843. cb. 1 v.
c. Tōyō.

2701 * Kan'yaku Isoppu-tan 漢譯伊蘇晉譚, tr. into Jap. by Abe Hirokuni 阿部弘國, Tokyo 1876 (明治 9). jb. 1 v., 30f., 22cm.
c. Aoyama.

2702 * Isabo Yugen 伊娑菩喻言, written

by hand by Masuda Mitsugi 増田貢, 1857 (安政 4). jb.
ms. Hibiya-Morohashi, K. Okazaki, Shimmura.

1841

2703 Matsūra Seizan 松浦静山 (1760–1841)
Kasshi Yawa 甲子夜話 (Essays). jb. 100 vols.
cf. Kokushi, pp. 52–53.
ms. Waseda.
2704 —— Tokyo 博聞社, 1892–1900 (明治 25–33). jb. 47 vols., 23cm.
c. Tōhoku-Kano, Waseda.
2705 —— repr. by the Kokusho Kankōkai 國書刊行會, Tokyo 1910–11 (明治 43–44). wb. 3 vols.
2706 —— abridged (Nippon Keizai Sōsho, v. XXXIV).
2707 —— abridged (Nippon Keizai Taiten, v. LII).
2708 —— (Nippon Zuihitsu Taisei, 3rd Series, w. VII–VIII).

2709 Togawa Harima-no-kami 戸川播磨守
Gokinsho Mokuroku, Gokinsho-chū Gomensho Mokuroku, Goseikin gomen Shojaku Wakegaki 御禁書目録, 御禁書中御免書目録, 御制禁御免書籍譯書 (List of Prohibited Books, List of Books released from the Prohibition and Notes), 1841 (天保 12). jb. 1 v.
cf. Ebisawa Arimichi, "Kinshorei ni kansuru Shomondai" (*Rekishi Kyōiku*, v. IV, nos. 11–12), Tokyo 1956.
ms. Nagasaki, Ebisawa.
See, nos. 654–658, 1913.

1842

2710 Aizawa Seishi 會澤正志 (1782–1863)
Tekiihen 迪彝篇 (Essays), Mito 東湖書屋, 1842 (天保 13). jb. 1 v., [3], 62f., 26cm.
cf. Kokushi, p. 211.
c. Ebisawa, Hibiya-Kaga, Gakushuin, Ishin, Kanazawa, Keio, Sonkeikaku, Ueno, Waseda, Yutoku.
ms. Iwase.
2711 —— Mito 東湖書屋, 1869 (明治 2). jb. 1v.
2712 —— (Oshie no Sono, v. I).
2713 —— (Nyofukyūsai Sōsho).
2714 —— (Kinnō Bunko, v. I).
2715 —— (Kōgaku Sōsho, v. XII).
2716 —— abridged (Nippon Keizai Sōsho, v. XXXIV).
2717 —— abridged (Nippon Keizai Taiten, v. LII).
2718 —— abridged (Haja Sōsho, v. I).

2719 —— (Mitogaku Zenshū, v. II).
2720 —— (Mitogaku Taikei, v. II).
2721 —— (Meiji Bunka Zenshū, v. XV).

2722 Ishida 石田
Tōsen Ransen Nagasaki Iribune Binran 唐船蘭船長崎入船便覧 (Handbook on the Arrival of Chinese and Dutch boats at the Port of Nagasaki), Osaka 1842 (天保 13). jb. 1 v., 17, 28f., 8×16cm.
2723 —— Osaka 1854 (嘉永 7). jb. 1 v., 17, 28f., 8×16cm.
c. Hibiya-Kondo.
2724 —— (Kaiji Shiryō Sōsho, v. XIII).

2725 Oritiz, Thomas, O. Aug. 白多瑪
Seikyō Setsuyō 聖教切要 *Sheng-chiao Ch'ieh-yao* (Catechism), [Peking?] 1842 (道光 22). cb. 1 v., [3], 62f. 22cm.
c. Aoyama, Ebisawa, Saba, Seishin, Waseda.
2726 —— [Peking?] 1842 (道光 22). cb. 1v., [3], 62f., 24cm.
c. Hibiya-Ichimura, Seishin.

2727 Satū Nobuhiro 佐藤信淵 (1769–1850)
Yōzō Kaikuron 鎔造化育論 (On the Creation), 1842 (天保 13). jb. 3 vols.
cf. Kokushi, p. 320.
orig. ms. Iwase.
ms. Kokugakuin, Kyudai, Naikaku, Tōhoku-Kano, Waseda.
2728 —— annotated by Inoue Yorikuni 井上頼圀, Tokyo 1873 (明治 6). jb. 3 vols., 27cm.
c. Ebisawa, Jingu, Jinshu, Kokugakuin, Kompira, Naikaku, Ueno, Waseda.
2729 —— (Satō Shin'en Kagaku Taiyō).
2730 —— (Satō Shin'en Kagaku Zenshū, v. I).
2731 —— (Kōgaku Sōsho, v. X).
2732 —— (Nippon Keizai Taiten, v. XVIII).
2733 —— (Hirata Atsutane Zenshū, v. II).
2734 —— (Kokugaku Taikei, v. XII).
2735 —— tr. into Jap. by Takada Yoshikazu 高田宜和, Tokyo 報徳社, 1880 (明治 13). jb. 3 vols.
2736 * Tenchi Yōzō Kaikuron 天地鎔造化育論, annotated by Oda Kanshi 織田完之, Tokyo 1881 (明治 14). jb. 3 vols.
c. Iwase, Jingu, Naikaku.

2737 Yagi Chiyuki 八木千之
Bōkai Shūsetsu 防海集説 (Opinions on Coastal Defence), 1842 (天保 13). jb. 1 v.
ms. Hibiya-Kondo.

2738 Bridgman, Elijah Coleman, PN.

稗治文 (1801–1861)

Kaikoku-Zushi 海國圖志 *Hai-kuo t'u-chih* (Illustrated Geography of Maritime Countries), compiled and revised by Gi Gen 魏源 *Wei Yuan*, Singapore 堅夏書院, 1843 (道光 23). cb. 60 vols.

note: Revised edition of the *Shishūshi* (n. 2682). Three copies were imported in 1850 into Japan, and were prohibited. In 1854, eight copies were sold.

2739 —— Chao-yang 古微堂, 1849 (道光 29). 2nd ed. cb. 24 vols., 26cm.

c. Hibiya-Ichimura.

2740 —— Chao-yang 古微堂, 1852 (咸豊 2). revised ed. cb. 24 vols., 27cm.

c. Kyoto, Naikaku, Tōhoku-Kano, Ueno.

2741 —— Chao-yang 古微堂, 1872 (同治 11). cb. 24 vols.

c. Naikaku.

2742 —— Chao-yang 古微堂, 1876 (光緒 2). cb. 24 vols., 27cm.

c. Ayuzawa, Naikaku.

2743 —— 1880 (光緒 6). cb. 28 vols.

c. Tōyō-Fujita.

2744 —— Peking 文賢閣, 1898 (光緒 24). cb.

c. Hibiya-Kondo (vv. 1–44 lacked).

Editions of the Kaikoku Zushi in Japan

2745 Amerika Sōki 亞米利加總記 (General Remarks on America), tr. by Hirose Tatsu 廣瀨達, Edo [Tokyo] 雲竹小居, 1854 (嘉永 7). jb. 5 vols.

cf. Kaikoku, pp. 143–144; Osatake, pp. 54–56.

note: This was published under the title of *Seiyō Rekkoku Shiryaku* 西洋列國史略, Tokyo 1870 (明治 3). jb. 4 vols.

c. Okada.

2746 Zoku Amerika Sōki 續亞米利加總記 (Supplement to *Amerika Sōki*), tr. by Hirose Tatsu 廣瀨達, Edo [Tokyo], 1854 (嘉永 7). jb. 2 vols.

cf. Kaikoku, p. 145.

2747 Amerika Sōki Kōhen 亞墨利加總記後篇 (Further Supplement to *Amerika Sōki*), tr. by Hirose Tatsu 廣瀨達, Edo [Tokyo], 1854 (嘉永 7). jb. 2 vols.

cf. Kaikoku, pp. 145–146.

2748 Birikakoku Sōki Wage 美理哥國總記和解 (Japanese Translation of the General Remarks on America), tr. by Masaki Atsushi 正木篤, Edo [Tokyo], 1854 (嘉永 7). jb. 3 vols.

cf. Kaikoku, pp. 148–149.

2749 Chōyaku Furansukoku Sōki 重譯

佛蘭西國總記 (General Remarks on France), tr. by Ōtsuki Tei 大槻禎, Edo [Tokyo] 蕉陰書屋, 1855 (安政 2). jb. 1 v., 37f., 27cm.

cf. Kaikoku, p. 152.

c. T. Ikeda, Keio, Waseda.

2750 Chōyaku Orosukoku Sōki 重譯織羅斯國總記 (Translation of the General Remarks on Russia), tr. by Ōtsuki Tei 大槻禎, Edo [Tokyo] 蕉陰書屋, 1854 (嘉永 7). jb. 1 v., [2], 46f., 27cm.

cf. Kaikoku, p. 149.

c. Ayuzawa, Keio, Waseda.

2751 Honkan Indokoku-bu, fu, Ijō Bisai 飜栞印度國部, 附夷情備采 (The Indian Part and Ijō Bisai Section of the *Kaikoku Zushi*), construed from Chinese into Jap. by Rai Jun 賴醇, Edo [Tokyo] 須原屋, 1857 (安政 4). jb. 3 vols., 26cm.

note: Limited edition of 300 copies.

cf. Kaikoku, pp. 143, 323.

c. Gakushuin, ICU, Keio, Seishin, Waseda.

2752 Honkan Kaikoku Zushi 飜栞海國圖志 (Translation of the *Kaikoku Zushi*), construed from Chinese into Jap. by Shionoya Kōzō 鹽谷甲藏 and Mitsukuri Gempo 箕作阮甫, Edo [Tokyo] 須原屋, 1854 (嘉永 7). jb. 2 vols., 27cm.

note: Vols. I–IV of Chinese ed., *Chūkaihen* 籌海篇 (See also n. 2760).

cf. Kaikoku, p. 140.

c. Ayuzawa, Gakushuin, Kompira, Naikaku, Narita, Osaka, Seishin, Ueno, Waseda-Hanabusa, Waseda-Ogura.

2753 Honkan Kaikoku Zushi Igirisu-koku 飜栞海國圖志英吉利國 (England Part of the *Kaikoku Zushi*), construed from Chinese into Jap. by Shionoya Kōzō 鹽谷甲藏 and Mitsukuri Gempo 箕作阮甫, Edo [Tokyo] 須原屋, 1856 (安政 3). jb. 3 vols., 27cm.

cf. Kaikoku, p. 142.

c. Ayuzawa, Keio, Okada, Seishin, Ueno, Waseda.

2754 Honkan Kaikoku-Zushi Orosu-koku 飜栞海國図志俄羅斯國 (Russian Part of the *Kaikoku Zushi*), construed from Chinese into Jap. by Shionoya Tōin 鹽谷宏陰 and Mitsukuri Hōkoku 箕作逢谷, Edo [Tokyo] 青黎閣, 1855 (安政 2). jb. 2 vols., 27cm.

cf. Kaikoku, pp. 141–142.

c. Ayuzawa, Seishin, Ueno, Waseda.

2755 Igirisiu Kiryaku ○咭唎紀略 (Brief Notes on England), construed from Chinese into Jap. by Araki Sai 荒木犻, Edo [Tokyo] 和泉屋, 1853 (嘉永 5). jb. 1 v., 13f., 23cm.

cf. Kaikoku, p. 155.

2756 Igirisu Kōjutsu 英吉利廣述 (De-

scription of England), abridged translation by Ono Gensai 小野元濟, Edo [Tokyo] 遊焉社, 1854 (嘉永 7). jb. 1 v., [2], 27f., 27cm.
c. Toyodai, Uchida, Waseda.

2757 Igirisukoku Sōki Wage 英吉利國總記和解 (Japanese Translation of the General Remarks on England), tr. by Masaki Atsushi 正木篤, Edo [Tokyo] 常惺篋, 1854 (嘉永 7). jb. 1 v., [4], 20, 8, 8f., 23cm.
cf. Kaikoku, p. 150. 147–148.
c. Ueno, Waseda.

2758 Igirisu Shinshi 英吉利新誌 (New Topography of England), tr. into Jap. by Mumonshi 無悶子, [n.p.], [n.d.]. jb. 1 v., [1], 28, [1]f., 26cm.
cf. Kaikoku, pp. 403–404.
c. Tōhoku-Kano, Waseda-Ogura.

2759 Kaikoku Zushi Ijō Bisai 海國圖志夷情備采 (The Ijō Bisai Section of the *Kaikoku Zushi*), construed from Chinese into Jap. by Ōtsuki Tei 大槻禎, Edo [Tokyo], 1854 (嘉永 7). jb. 1 v.
cf. Kaikoku, pp. 149–150.
c. Ishin.

2760 Kaikoku Zushi Chūkaihen 海國圖志籌海篇 (The Chūkai Section of the *Kakoku Zushi*), construed from Chinese into Jap. by Shionoya Sekō 鹽谷世弘 and Mitsukuri Gempo 箕作阮甫, Edo [Tokyo], 1854 (嘉永 7). jb. 1v.
c. Ayuzawa, Okada, Waseda-Hanabusa.

2761 Kaikoku Zushi Chūkaihen Yakuge 海國圖志籌海篇譯解 (Translation of the Chūkai Section of the *Kaikoku Zushi*), tr. by Nanyō Bōken 南洋榜謙, Kyoto 再思堂, 1855 (安政 2). jb. 3 vols., 26cm.
cf. Kaikoku, p. 153.
c. Ayuzawa.

2762 Kaikoku Zushi Kokuchi Sōron 海國圖志國地總論 (General Remarks on the Territory of the *Kaikoku Zushi*), construed from Chinese into Jap. by Kakurei Dōjin 鶴嶺道人, Tokyo 池上學室, 1869 (明治 2). jb. 1v., 27f., 26cm.
cf. Kaikoku, p. 153.
c. Ayuzawa, Waseda.

2763 Kaikoku Zushi Kunyaku 海國圖志訓譯 (Exposition of the *Kaikoku Zushi*), tr. by Hattori Seien 服部静遠, Edo [Tokyo], 1855 (安政 2). jb. 2 vols., 27cm.
note: Limited ed. of 300 copies. Vols. 56–58 of the original edition.
cf. Kaikoku, pp. 152–153.
c. Ayuzawa, Okada.

2764 Kaikoku Zushi Merikashū no Bu

海國圖志墨利加洲部 (American Part of the *Kaikoku Zushi*), construed from Chinese into Jap. by Nakayama Den'uemon 中山傳右衛門, Kyoto 出雲寺文次郎, 1854 (嘉永 7). jb. 8 vols., 26cm.
cf. Kaikoku, p. 139.
c. Gakushuin, ICU, Hibiya-Kondo, Seishin.

2765 Kaikoku Zushi Puroshakoku 海國図志普魯社國 (Prussian Part of the *Kaikoku Zushi*), construed from Chinese into Jap. by Shionoya Kōzō 鹽谷甲藏 and Mitsukuri Gempo 箕作阮甫, Edo [Tokyo] 須原屋, 1855 (安政 2). jb. 1 v., 1, 22f., 27cm.
cf. Kaikoku, p. 140.
c. Ayuzawa, Gakushuin, Okada, Seishiū.

2766 Merikashū Enkaku Sōsetsu Hoshū Wage 墨利加洲沿革總説補輯和解 (Jap. Translation of American History), tr. by Masaki Atsushi 正木篤, Edo [Tokyo] 常惺篋, 1854 (嘉永 7). jb. 1 v.
cf. Kaikoku, p. 146.
c. Kyudai-Bunka.

2767 Ōmon Geppō Wage 奧門月報和解 (Jap. Translation of Macao Journal), tr. by Masaki Atsushi 正木篤, [n.p.], 1854 (嘉永 7). jb. 1 v.
cf. Kaikoku, pp. 146–147.
note: The contents of this are the same as those of the "Ijō Bisai" of the *Kaikoku Zushi* (See aslo n. 2759).
c. Kyudai-Bunka.

2768 Seiyō Shimbokushi 西洋新墨志 (Descriptive Geography of America), tr. by Kōkoku Inshi 皇國隱士, Edo [Tokyo], 東洋館, 1854 (嘉永 7). jb. 2 vols.
note: Abridged translation of the Part on America in the *Kaikoku Zushi*.
cf. Kaikoku, pp. 151–152.

2769 Shinkoku-Zushi Tsūge 新國圖志通解 (Illustrated Geography of the New Country), tr. by Kōkoku Inshi 皇國隱士, Edo [Tokyo], 1854 (嘉永 7). jb. 4 vols.
note: Translation of the Part of America in the *Kaikoku Zushi*.
cf. Kaikoku, pp. 150–151.

1844

2770 Aizawa Seishi 會澤正志 (1782–1863)
Shinron 新論 (New Political Criticism), Mito 東海氏, 1844 (弘化 1). jb. 2 vols., 19cm.
cf. Kokushi, pp. 158.
c. Jingu, Todai-Nanki, Tōhoku, Ueno.
ms. Iwase.

2771 ——— Edo [Tokyo] 玉巖堂, 1857 (安政 4). jb. 2 vols., 27cm.

c. Hibiya-Ichimura, Kariya, Sonkeikaku, Taisho, Waseda-Hanabusa, Yutoku.

2772 —— Mito 東海氏, 1859 (安政 6). jb. 2 vols., 27cm.

c. Ebisawa, Waseda.

2773 —— construed from Chinese into Jap. by Kageyama Akiho 蔭山秋穂, Tokyo 1942 (昭和 17).

2774 —— (Nippon Kokusui Zensho, v. IV).

2775 —— (Meiji Bunka Zenshū, v. XV).

2776 —— (Dai-Nippon Shisō Zenshū, v. XVIII).

2777 —— (Mitogaku Zenshū, v. II).

2778 —— (Mitogaku Taikei, v. II).

2779 —— (Kokumin Dōtoku Sōsho).

2780 —— (Kōgaku Sōsho, v. XII).

2781 —— (Nippon Shisō Tōso Shiryō, v. III).

2782 Bridgman, Elijah Coleman, ABC. 稗治文 (1801–1861)
Reisei Sengen 靈生詮言 *Ling-sheng Ch'üan yen* (On Spiritual Life), [n.p.], 1844 (道光 24). cb. 1 v., 6f.
cf. Ozawa, p. 190; Wylie, pp. 70–71.

2783 —— [n.p.], 1848 (道光 28). cb. 1v.

2784 —— Shanghai 美華書館, 1863 (同治 2). cb. 1v., 13f., 16cm.

c. Otani.

2785 De Bési, Luis, 羅伯濟
Shinshi Shi'nan 愼思指南 *Shen-szu Chih-nan* (Guide on Meditations), [n.p.], 1844. (道光 24). cb. 4 vols., 23cm.

2786 —— [n.p.], 1853 (咸豊 3). cb. 4 vols., 23cm.

c. Tōhoku.

2787 —— [n.p.], 1865 (同治 4). cb. 4 vols., 22cm.

c. Nagasaki, Tenri.

2788 Kōyama Seisai 向山誠齋
Kōshin Zakki 甲辰雜記 (Notes on the Year of Kōshin), 1844 (弘化 1). jb. 1 v.

2789 Legge, James, LM. 理雅各 (1815–1897)
Yaso Sanjō Suikun 耶蘇山上垂訓 *Yeh-su Shan-shang Ch'ui-hsün* (Sermon on the Mount), Hongkong 1844 (道光 24). cb. 1 v.
cf. Wylie, p. 119.

2790 —— Hongkong 英華書院, 1865 (同治 4). cb. 1 v., 24f., 20cm.

c. Otani, Saba, Tōhoku.

2791 Naha Kigan 那波希顔
Aboku Shinwa 亞墨新話 (New Story of America), 1844 (弘化 1). jb. 1 v.

ms. Hibiya-Kaga, Ikeda.

2792 —— (Nambanki Bunsen).

2793 —— (Hyōryū Kidan Zenshū).

2794 Seiyō Shoi Ryakuhyō 西洋諸夷略表 (Chronology of Western History), 1844 (弘化 1). jb. 1 v.

ms. Ebisawa, Iwase, Jingu, Tōdai-Nanki.

2795 —— (Kinji Kaikoku Hitsudokusho, v. VI).

2796 —— (Nippon Kaibō Shiryō Sōsho, v. II).

2797 Waisui Inshi 准水隱士
Kakumō Gūgo 角毛偶語 (Essays), [n.p.], 1844 (天保 15). jb. 5 vols., 23cm.

c. Ueno.
ms. Ueno.

Arrivals of Father Forcade and the Rev. Bettelheim in the Ryūkyū, 1844–1846

2798 Furansukoku Gunkan Sanzō Torai kembun Hikki, tsuketari Orandajin Fūsetsugaki フランス國軍艦三艘渡來見聞筆記, 附和蘭人風説書 (Notes of Arrival and the Experiences of the Three French Warships with a Report by the Dutch), 1846 (弘化 3). jb. 1 v.

ms. Hibiya-Kondo.

2799 Furansu-sen Hyōchaku Nikki 佛蘭西船漂着日記 (Diary of the French Boat which drifted Ashore). 1844 (弘化 1). jb. 4 vols.

note: Documents of Father Théodore A. Forcade, MEP (1816–1885).
cf. Asahi, p. 47.
ms. Okinawa (destroyed).

2800 Furansusen Torairoku 佛朗西船渡來録 (Record of the Arrival of French Bosts), 1846 (弘化 3). jb. 1 v.

ms. Ishin.

2801 —— (Dai-Nippon Ishin Shiryō, Series I, v. 1).

2802 Futsuryū Ōfuku Bunshū 佛琉往復文集 (Diplomatic Correspondence between France and the Ryūkyū), 1844 (天保 15). jb. 1 v.

cf. Asahi, p. 49.
note: Documents relating to Father Forcade, MEP.
orig. ms. Okinawa (destroyed).
ms. Kogorō Yoshida.

2803 —— repr. and annotated by Yoshida Kogorō 吉田小五郎, "Ryūkyūgawa Shiryō yori mitaru Forcade-shi no Dōsei" (*Katorikku*

Kenkyū, v. XXI, nos. 4–5), Tokyo 1941 (昭和 16).

2804 Ikoku Nikki 異國日記 (Diary of Foreign Affairs), 1844–1856 (道光 26–咸豊 6).
note: contains many documents on Father Forcade and Rev. Bettelheim, LNM.
cf. Yoshida Kogorō, "Ryūkyū-gawa no Shiryō yori mitaru Forcade-shi no Dōsei" (*Katorikku Kenkyū* v. XXI, nos. 4–5), Tokyo 1941.
orig. ms. Okinawa (destroyed).

2805 Ji Fukkoku Yō Wakō Rin 辭佛國要和好稟 (Letters between France and the Ryūkyū Government), 1846 (弘化 3). jb. 1 v.
2806 —— (Dai-Nippon Ishin Shiryō, Series I, v. 1.)

2807 Junshō Empan Ryaku Chinjō-etsu 遵將烟帆略陳上閲 (Letters of Father T. A. Forcade, MEP., and General F. Duplan), 1844 (弘化 1). jb. 1 v.
ms. Ebisawa.
2808 —— (Kaihyō Ibun, v. LV).
2809 —— pr. and annotated by Ebisawa Arimichi 海老澤有道, Tempō 15 nen Ryū-futsu Kōshō Nippon Shiryō (*ICU Asian Cultural Studies,* v. I), Tokyo 1958 (昭和 33).

2810 Kaikei Zasshi 海警雜誌 (Notes on Coastal Defense). jb. 1 v.
ms. Doshisha.

2811 Kō Eiho 向永保
Ryūkyū-Ōchō Fuseikan Kō Eiho Shokan 琉球王廳布政官向永保書翰 (Letter of Kō Eiho, Governor of the Ryūkyū Court). jb. 1 v.
note: Document on the arrival of Rev. Bettelheim, LNM.
orig. ms. Shimazu.
2812 —— (Dai-Nippon Ishin Shiryō, Series I, v. 1)

2813 Kōka 3 Hinoe-no-toshi Ryūkyū narabini Uraga Ikokusen Torai Sho-Todoke 弘化三丙年琉球並浦賀異國船渡來諸届 (Reports on the Arrival of the Foreign Ships in the Ryūkyū and Uraga in 3rd Year of Kōka), 1846 (弘化 3). jb. 1 v.
ms. Hibiya-Kondo.

2814 * Kōka 3-nen Ihaku Torai Ikken 弘化三年異舶渡來一件 (Arrival of Foreign Ships in the 3rd Year of Kōka), 1846 (弘化 3). jb. 1 v.
ms. Ishin.

2815 Kyūyō 球陽 (Documents of Regerding the Ryūkyū). jb. 26 vols.
cf. Kokushi, p. 66.
ms. Naikaku.

2816 Nagasaki Ryūkyū e Igirisu Furansu-sen Torai Ikken 長崎琉球江英吉利佛郎西船渡來一件 (Records of the Arrival of English and French ships at Nagasaki and Ryūkyū), 1846 (弘化 3). jb. 1 v.
ms. Hibiya-Kondo.
2817 —— (Dai Nippon Ishin Shiryō, Series I, v. I.).

2818 Ryūkyū e Ikokusen Torai Jōshin-sho 琉球へ異國船渡來上申書 (Report on the Arrival of the Foreign Ships in the Ryū-kyū), 1844 (天保 15). jb. 1 v.
note: A letter from Matsudaira Ōsumi-no-kami 松平大隅守 viz. Shimazu Narioki 島津齋興.

2819 Ryūkyū Furansukoku Ōfukusho 琉球佛蘭西國往復書 (Correspondence between the Ryūkyū and France). jb. 1 v.
2820 —— (Yūsō Nenroku).
ms. Ueno.
phot. Ebisawa, Seishin.

2821 Ryūkyū Gaikoku Kankei Monjo 琉球外國關係文書 (Documents of the Ryūkyū concerning Foreign Countries).
ms. Shimazu.

2822 Ryūkyūkoku e Gaikokusen Torai Shimatsu 琉球國へ外國船渡來始末 (Notes on the Influx of French Boats to the Ryū-kyū), 1844–1846 (弘化 1–3). jb. 1 v.
ms. Hibiya-Kondo.

2823 Ryūkyūkoku e Isen Chakurai 琉球國江異船着來 (Arrival of Foreign Ships to the Ryūkyū), 1846 (弘化 3). jb. 1 v.
ms. Hibiya-Kondo.

2824 Ryūkyū Ōchō Hyōjōsho Nikki 琉球王廳評定所日記 (Diary of the Supreme Court of the Ryūkyū Royal Government), 1846 (弘化 3).
note: Contains the letters of Rev. Bettelheim and Father Le Turdu, MEP.
2825 —— (Dai-Nippon Ishin Shiryō, Series I, v. I.).

2826 Ryūkyū Ōchō Hyōjōsho Shorui 琉球王廳評定所書類 (Documents of the Supreme Court of the Ryūkyū Royal Government), 1846 (弘化 3).
note: Contains documents concerning Rev. Bettelheim and the Catholic Father Le Turdu, MEP.
2827 —— (Dai-Nippon Ishin Shiryō, Series I, v. I.).

2828 Sappan Futsujin Tsūkō o hōzuru no Sho 薩藩報佛人通好書 (Shimazu's Letter to the Shogunate Government Reporting the Arrival of French Boats), 1844 (弘化 1). jb. 1 v.

ms. Kagoshima.

2829 Shimazuke Kokuji Ōshō Shiryō 島津家國事靹掌史料 (Documents of the Political Affairs of the Shimazus, Daimyō of Satsuma).

note: Contains many documents on the arrival and stay of Rev. Bettelheim, LNM., on the departure of Father Forcade, MEP., and on the arrival of Father Le Turdu, MEP. Also contains Rev. Bettelheim's letters.
orig. ms. Shimazu.

2830 —— (Dai-Nippon Ishin Shiryō, Series I, v. 1.).

2831 Teikyū Shūsho 涕泣輯書 (Collection of a Patriot's Letters).

ms. Ishin.

2832 —— (Dai-Nippon Ishin Shiryō, Series I, v. I).

1845

2833 Dean, William, ABF. 憐爲仁 (1807–1843)

Hōkan Shinka Jimbutsuron 奉勸眞假人物論 Feng-ch'üan Chen-chia Jen-wu-lun (Exhortation to Discriminate between the True and False), Ningpo 1845 (道光 25). cb. 1 v., 6f.

cf. Wylie, pp. 86–87; Ozawa, p. 187.

2834 —— Ningpo 1847 (道光 27). cb. 1 v., 6f.

2835 —— Hongkong 1849 (道光 29). cb. 1 v., 12f.

2836 Fisscher, Johan Frederich van Overmeer (1799–   ).

Nippon Fūzoku Bikō 日本風俗備考 (Studies on Japanese Customs) tr. by Sugita Seikei 杉田成卿. jb. 22 vols.

cf. Rangaku, pp. 33, 35.
note: Selected translation of Fisscher's Bijdrage tot de kennis van het Japanische Rijk, Amsterdam 1833. S. Sugita (1817–1858) translated this in 1840–45.
ms. Tokyo Kagaku Museum, Ueno.

2837 —— (Bummei Genryū Sōsho, v. III).

2838 Ikoku Nempyō 異國年表 (Chronological Table on the History of Foreign Countries) 1845 (弘化 2). jb. 1 v.

ms. Hibiya-Kaga.

2839 Mistukuri Shōgo 箕作省吾 (1822–1847)

Kon'yo Zushiki 坤輿圖識 (Discriptive Geography of the World), Edo [Tokyo] 夢霞樓, 1845–46 (弘化 2–3). jb. 7 vols., 27cm.

cf. Kaikoku, pp. 176–177.

c. Kariya, Keio, Kyoto, Tenri, Tōdai, Tōhoku-Kano, Ueno, Waseda, Yutoku.

2840 —— Edo [Tokyo] 夢霞樓, 1847 (弘化 4). jb. 7 vols., 27cm.

c. Hibiya-Kondō, Waseda.

2841 Ōtsuki Bankei 大槻盤溪 (1801–1878)

Rusonkoku Hyōryūki 呂宋國漂流記, or Kannonmaru Ruson Hyōryūki 觀音丸呂宋漂流記 (Record of the Kannonmaru's drifting to Shore on Luzon). jb. 1 v.

ms. Hibiya-Kondō, Iwase, Jingu, Kyoto, Nagasaki, Naikaku, Sonkeikaku, Tōdai-Nanki.

2842 —— (Heikan Issō, v. VII).
2843 —— (Seikadō Sōsho).
2844 —— (Ikoku Hyōryū Kidanshū).
2845 * Ruson Hyōryūjin no Ki 呂宋漂流人之記 (Record of Shipwrecked Sailors Cast up on Luzon).
2846 —— (Chūko Sōsho).
2847 * Tempō Hyōryūki 天保漂流記 (Record of Shipwrecked Sailors Cast Ashore in the Tempo Era). jb. 1 v.

ms. Hibiya-Kondo, Nagasaki-Isahaya.

2848 Toda Tsūgen 戸田通元

Tenkei Wakumon Kōjuroku 天經或問口授錄 (Lecture on the Tenkei Wakumon), 1845 (弘化 2). jb. 1 v.

ms. Tōhoku-Sugaku.

2849 Utagawa Yōan 宇田川榕庵 (1798–1846)

Oranda Shiryaku 和蘭志略 (Outline History of Holland), 1845 (弘化 2). jb. 16 vols.

cf. Asahi, p. 26; Kaikoku, pp. 381–382.
orig. ms. Fujinami.

1846

2850 Gaijiryaku 外事略 (Abridged Records of Foreign Affairs), 1846 (弘化 3). jb. 1v.

ms. Ishin.

2851 Gaikō Zasshi 外交雜誌 (Notes on Diplomatic Affaires), 1846 (弘化 3). jb. 1 v.
ms. Ishin.

2852 Guetzlaff, Karl Friedrich August, LM. 郭實獵 (1803–1851)

Kyūi Shōsho Mōze Go-kyō 舊遺詔書摩西五經 Chiu-i chao-shu Mo-hsi wu-ching (The Pentateuch of the Old Testament), Ningpo 華花聖經書房, 1846 (道光 26). cb. 5 vols., 25cm.

cf. Wylie, p. 59.
contents: 創世傳 (Genesis),　出麥西國傳 (Exodus), 利未書 (Leviticus),　戸口冊紀 (Numbers),

復傳律例書 (Deuteronomy).
c. Otani, Tōhoku-Kano.
ms. Tōyō.

2853 Inoue Shun'yō 井上春洋 (1812–1892)
Aboku Chikushi 亞墨竹枝 (Poems on America), 學半堂 1846 (弘化 3). jb. 1v., [2], 2, 9, [1]f., 23cm.
cf. Kaikoku, pp. 59–60.
c. Ayuzawa, Hibiya-Kaga, Okada, Waseda.
ms. Waseda.

2854 Kawakita Kiuemon 川北喜右衛門 (1794–1853)
Harajō Kiji 原城紀事 (Records of the Hara Castle), 1846 (弘化 3). jb. 4 vols.
ms. Jingu.
2855 —— annotated by Muraoka Yoshisuke 村岡良弼 etc., (Shiseki Shūran) Tokyo 觀奕堂, 1883 (明治 16). jb. 8 vols., 19cm.
c. Ebisawa, Nagasaki, Ueno.
2856 —— (Kaitei Shiseki Shūran)
2857 —— (Nagasaki Sōsho, B., v. I)
2858 —— (Kirishitan Bunko, v. IV–V).

2859 Medhurst, Walter Henry, LM. 麥都思 (1796–1857)
Yaso Kōseiden 耶蘇降生傳 *Yeh-su Chiang-sheng chuan* (Life of Christ), Shanghai 1846 (道光 26). cb. 1 v., 191f.
cf. Ozawa, p. 198; Wylie, p. 34.
2860 —— revised by W. Muirhead, LM. 慕維廉, Shanghai 美華書館 1861 (咸豐 11). cb. 1 v., 88f.
2861 —— Shanghai 美華書館 1869 (同治 8). cb. 1 v.
c. Tōdai-Nanki.
2862 —— Shanghai 美華書館, 1870 (同治 9). cb. 1 v., 60f., 25cm.
c. Ebisawa, Kichu, Kompira, Naikaku, Otani, Tenri, Tōdai-Nanki, Yoshida.

2863 Medhurst, Walter Henry, LM. 麥都思 (1796–1857)
Yasokyō-ryaku 耶蘇敎略 *Yeh-su chiao lüeh* (Outline of Christianity), Shanghai 1846 (道光 26). cb. 1 v., 36f.
cf. Ozawa, p. 199; Wylie, p. 33–34.
2864 —— Shanghai 1851 (道光 31). cb. 1 v., 31f.
2865 —— revised by Joseph Edkins, LM. 艾廸謹, Shanghai 1858 (咸豐 8). cb. 1 v. 32f.
c. Seikado.
2866 —— Shanghai 墨海書館, 1862 (同治 1). cb. 1 v., 31f., 21cm.
c. Tenri.
2867 —— Hongkong 英華書館, 1867 (同治 6). cb. 1 v., 19f., 20cm.
c. Doshisha-Niishima, Naikaku, Otani, Tōdai-Nanki.

2868 —— Shanghai 美華書館, 1868 (同治 7). cb. 1 v., 27f., 16cm.
c. Hatano, Saba.
2869 —— Shanghai 美華書館, 1872 (同治 11). cb. 1 v., 27f., 16cm.
c. Saba.
2870 —— Shanghai 美華書館, 1928 (民國 17). cb. 1 v., 1, 27f., 17cm.
c. Tenri.
2871 —— Yokohama 倫敦聖敎書類會社, [1879, 明治 12?] jb. 1 v., 17f., 19cm.
cf Ozawa, p 209.
c. Aoyama, Kichu, Saba.
2872 —— Yokohama 倫敦聖敎書類會社, 1886 (明治 19). wb. 1 v., 23p., 19cm.
c. Aoyama, Saba, Tenri.
2873 —— Yokohama 倫敦聖敎書類會社, 1888 (明治 21). wb. 1 v., 23p., 19cm.
c. Aoyama.

2874 Ōsawa Teijirō 大澤貞次郎
Kirishitan Yashikizu 切支丹屋敷圖 (Map of the Jail for Christians). 1846 (弘化 3). 1 sheet.
ms. Tōhoku-Kano.
See also nos. 952–953, 2273.

2875 Tsutsui Masanori 筒井政憲 (1778–1859)
Tsutsui Masanori Jōshinsho 筒井政憲上申書 (Memorial of Tsutsui Masanori), 1846 (弘化 3). jb. 1 v.
2876 *Isen Uchiharai Fukko Gohyōgi 異船打拂復古御評議 (Conference for Reinstating the exclusion of Foreigners).
2877 —— abridged (Dai-Nippon Ishin Shiryō, Series I, v. I).

2878 Utagawa Yōan 宇田川榕菴 (1798–1846)
Ratengo Kai 羅甸語解 (Interpretation of Latin). jb. 1 v.
orig. ms. Okamura.

1847

2879 Aizawa Seishi 會澤正志 (1782–1863)
Kagaku Jigen 下學邇言 (Essays), [n. p.], 1847 (弘化 4). jb. 3 vols., 26cm.
c. Iwase, Kariya, Kichu (v. III only), Tōhoku-Kano, Ueno, Waseda.
2880 —— Ibarakiken 會澤善, 1892 (明治 35). jb. 1 v., 97, 7, [1]f., 23cm.
c. Ebisawa, Hibiya-Inoue, Kokugakuin, Sonkeikaku, Ueno.
2881 —— (Kinnō Bunko, v. L).
2882 —— (Kokumin Dōtoku Sōsho).
2883 —— (Mitogaku Taikei, v. II).

2884 —— (Nippon Tetsugaku Zensho, v. V).

2885 —— abridged (Nippon Keizai Sō-sho, v. XXXIV).

2886 —— abridged (Nippon Keizai Taiten, v. LII).

2887 —— abridged (Haja Sōsho, v. I).

2888 —— abridged (Yūtoku Zenshū).

2889 Culberton, Michael Simpson, PN. 克陛存 (1819–1862)
Yosefu Genkō Zenden 若瑟言行全傳 *Jo-se yen-hsing chüan-chuan* (Life of Joseph), Ningpo 1847 (道光 27). cb. 1 v., 27f.
cf. Wylie, p. 147.

2890 * Yosefu Genkō Zenden 約瑟言行全傳 *Yo-se yen-hsing chüan-chuan*, Shanghai 美華書館, 1861 (咸豐 11). cb. 1 v., [1], 26f., 24cm.
c. Aoyama, Otani.

2891 Koga Dōan 古賀侗菴 (1788–1847)
Kaibō Shiron 海防私論 (Private Opinions on Coastal Defense) by Koga Dōan and Shionoya Tōin 鹽谷宏陰. jb. 1v.
ms. Hibiya-Kondo.

2892 Koga Dōan 古賀侗菴 (1788–1847)
Orosu Kibun 俄羅斯紀聞 (Notes on Russia). jb. 40 vols.
orig. ms. Waseda.
ms. Daitokyu, Shoryobu.

2893 Koga Dōan 古賀侗庵 (1788–1847)
Taisei Rokuwa 泰西錄話 (Stories of the West). jb. 1 v.
ms. Ebisawa.

2894 —— (Kinji Kaikoku Hitsudokusho, v. VI).

2895 —— (Kaibō Igi, v. XXXVIII).

2896 —— (Heikan Issō, v. VIII).

2897 —— (Nippon Kaibō Shiryō Sōsho, v. II).

2898 Koga Dōan 古賀侗庵 (1788–1847)
Yōkenki 甕涓記 (Essays). jb. 2 vols.
note: Revision of the *Sōzokuki* by Hayashi Razan (See nos. 783–785).
cf. Shimmura-Namban I, p. 112.

2899 McCartee, Divie Bethune, PN. 培端 (1820–1900)
Ahen Rokukai 鴉牙六戒 *Yaya liu-chieh* (Six warnings against Opium), Ningpo, 1847 (道光 27). cb. 1 v., 7f.
cf. Ozawa, p. 229; Wylie, p. 136.

2900 * Kampan Ahenkai 官板鴉片戒 (Official Press, Warnings against Opium), Edo [Tokyo], 老皂館, [1864?]. jb. 1 v., 6f., 18cm.
c. Ueno-Shirai.

2901 McCartee, Divie Bethune, PN. 培端 (1820–1900)
Shinri Sanjikyō 眞理三字經 *Chen-li San-tzu-ching* (Three Character Classic of the Truth), Shanghai 美華書館, 1861 (咸豐 11). 2nd ed. cb. 1 v., 7f., 17cm.
c. Taisho.

2902 —— tr. into Japanese by C. Carrothers PN. 嘉魯日耳士, Tokyo [1873?]. jb. 1 v.
ms. Otani.

2903 McCartee, Divie Bethune, PN. 培端 (1820–1900)
Shinri Sanjikyō Chūshaku 眞理三字經註釋 *Chen-li San-tzu-ching chu-shih* (Commentary on the *Shinri Sanjikyō*), Ningpo 華花聖經書房, 1847 (道光 27). cb. 1 v.
note: This is a commented ed. of Medhurst's *Sanjikyō*. (See nos. 2426–39). The first ed. was published with the title of "Sanjikyō Shinzō Chūkai" 三字經新增註解 *San-tzu-ching hsin-tseng chu-chieh* Ningpo. 1846.
cf. Wylie, p. 136.

2904 —— Ningpo 華花聖經書房, 1863 (同治 2). cb. 1 v., 16f., 18cm.
c. Otani.

2905 —— Shanghai 美華書館, 1867 (同治 6). cb. 1 v.

2906 —— Shanghai 美華書館, 1871 (同治 10). cb. 1 v., 11 f., 19cm.
c. Doshisha.

2907 Miyamoto Shigetoshi 宮本重利
Kōkai Fūhansō 江海風帆草 (Essay), [1847?]. jb. 1v.
ms. Ueno.

2908 —— (Zokuzoku Gunsho Ruijū, v. IX).

2909 * Kōkai Fūhanki 江海風帆記. jb. 1 v.
ms. Hibiya-Kondo.

2910 Oyamada Tomokiyo 小山田與清 (1783–1847)
Matsunoya Hikki 松屋筆記 (Essays). jb. 120 vols.
cf. Waseda Daigaku Toshokan Geppō, v. IV, Tokyo 1951.
cf. Kokushi, p. 295.
ms. Ueno (vv. XVII-XXXVI, XLI, XLIV lacked).

2911 —— pr. by the Kokusho Kankōkai 圖書刊行會, Tokyo 1909 (明治 42). wb. 3 vols.

2912 —— (Nippon Keizai Sosho, v. XXXIV).

2913 —— (Nippon Keizai Taiten, v. LII).

2914 Satō Nobuhiro 佐藤信淵 (1769–1850)

Bōkai Yoron 防海餘論 (Treatise on Coastal Defence) 1847 (弘化 4). jb. 1 v.

2915 —— (Satō Shin'en Kagaku Taiyō).

2916 —— (Satō Shin'en Kagaku Zenshū, v. III).

2917 —— (Satō Shin'en Bugakushū, v. I).

2918 Satō Nobuhiro 佐藤信淵 (1769–1850)

Suitō Hiroku 垂統秘録 (Secret Opinion of World Policy), 1847 (弘化 4). jb. 2 vols.

2919 —— annotated by Oda Kanshi 織田完之, Tokyo 1878 (明治 11).

2920 —— (Satō Shin'en Kagaku Taiyō).

2921 —— (Satō Shin'en Kagaku Zenshū, v. II).

2922 —— (Nippon Keizai Taiten, v. XVIII).

2923 —— (Dai-Nippon Shisō Zenshū, v. VIII).

2924 —— (Kokugaku Taikei, v. XII).

2925 —— (Sekai Dai-shisō Zenshū, v. LIV)

2926 —— (Kinsei Shakai Keizai Gakusetsu Taikei, v. III).

2927 —— (Satō Shin'en Bugakushū, v. I).

2928 Shibukawa Kagesuke 澁川景佑 (1787–1856)

Enkyō Chōken Tebikigusa 遠鏡町見手引草 (General Survey Mensuration Using a Telescope), 1847 (弘化 4). jb. 4 vols.

ms. Tōhoku-Kano.

1848

2929 Gouvea, de Alexandre 湯亞立山 (–1808)

Mokusō Shishō 默想指掌 Mo-hsiang Chih-ch'ang (Manual of Meditations), [n.p.], 1848 (道光 28). cb. 1 v., 59f., 16cm.

c. Aoyama, Tenri.

2930 Asaka Gonsai 安積艮齋 (1791–1860)

Yōgai Kiryaku 洋外紀略 (Brief History of European Countries), 1848 (嘉永 1). jb. 3 vols.

cf. Kaikoku, p. 425.

ms. Ebisawa, Hibiya, Hibiya-Kondo, Keio, Kyoto, Kyudai, Nagasaki-Fuji, Naikaku, Nichidai-Hayashi, Oda, Tōhoku-Kano, Ueno.

2931 —— (Kaibō Igi, Second Series).

2932 Asaka Gonsai 安積艮齋 (1791–1860)

Gyojūsaku 禦戎策 (Plan of Coastal Defence). jb. 1 v.

ms. Ishin

2933 —— (Kaibō Igi v. IV).

2934 —— (Nippon Kaibō Shiryō Sōsho, v. II).

2935 Lowrie, Walter Macon, PN. 婁理華 (1819–1847)

Yasokyō Ryakuron 耶蘇教略論 Yeh-su-chiao Lüeh-lun (Outline of Christianity), Ningpo 1848 (道光 28). cb. 1 v., 4f.

cf. Ozawa, p. 199; Wylie, p. 131.

2936 * Yasokyo Ryakukai 耶蘇教略解, Tokyo 米國聖教書類會社, 1882 (明治 15). wb. 1 v., 2, [1], 22p., 18cm.

c. Hatano, Kichu.

2936b —— Tokyo 米國聖教書類會社, 1888 (明治 21). wb. 1 v., 22p., 19cm.

c. Aoyama.

2937 McCartee, Divie Bethune, PN. 培端 (1820–1900)

Reikon Sōron 靈魂總論 Ling-hun Chung-lun (On the Soul), Ningpo 1848 (道光 28). cb. 1 v., 3f.

cf. Ozawa, p. 190; Wylie, p. 137.

2938 —— Shanghai 美華書館, 1863 (同治 2). cb. 1 v., 5f., 19cm.

c. Tenri.

2939 —— Shanghai 美華書館, 1867 (同治 6). cb. 1 v., 3f., 16cm.

c. Jinshu, Otani, Saba.

2940 McCartee, Divie Bethune, PN. 培端 (1820–1900)

Shinsō Sankō 信操三綱 Hsin-tsao San-kang (Three Important Texts), Ningpo [n.d.]. cb. 1 v., 16f.

contents: Shinkyō Chūshaku 信經註釋 Hsin-ching chu-shih (Explanation of the Apostles' Creed), Ningpo, 1848 (道光 28).
Shu-Kitōbun Kukai 主祈禱文句解 Chu ch'i-tao-wen chü-chieh (Explanation of the Lord's Prayer).
Shinshin Jukkai Shakugi 眞神十誡釋義 Chen-shen Shih-chieh shih-yi (Explanation of the Ten Commandments).

cf. Ozawa, p. 194; Wylie, p. 137.
c. Taisho.

2941 —— [n.p.], 1860 (咸豊 10). cb. 1 v., 13f., 19cm.

c. Tenri.

2942 —— Shanghai 1861 (咸豊 11). cb. 1 v., 22f.

2943 —— Shanghai 美華書館, 1866 (同治 5). cb. 1 v., [1], 3, [1], 2, [1], 4f., 18cm.

c. Otani.

2944 McCartee, Divie Bethune, PN. 麥嘉締 (1820–1900)

Shinzō Seisho Setsukai 新增聖書節解 Hsin-tseng Sheng-shu Chieh-chieh (Commentary on the Testament, enlarged), Ningpo

1848 (道光 28). cb. 2 vols.

note: Revised and enlarged ed. of W. Milne, LM. 米憐, *Seisho Setsukai* 聖書節解, Malacca 1825. See Wylie, p. 19.
cf. Ozawa, p. 195; Wylie, p. 136.

2945 McCartee, Divie Bethune, PN. 麥嘉締 (1820–1900)
Zai'nin Tokusha no Hō 罪人得赦之法 *Tsui-jen te-sho chih-fa* (Method of Getting Forgiveness), Ningpo 1848 (道光 28). 1fold.
cf. Ozawa, p. 201; Wylie, pp. 136–137.

2946 Medhurst, Walter Henry, LM. 麥都思 (1796–1857)
Ron Fukushin no Ri 論復新之理 *Lun fu-hsin chih li* (Discourse on Renovation), Ningpo 1848 (道光 28). cb. 1 v., 4f.
cf. Ozawa, p. 191; Wylie, p. 33.
note: See also, nos. 3236–39.

2947 —— Shanghai 美華館, 1862 (同治 1). cb. 1v., 8f., 16cm.
c. Otani.

2948 —— Shanghai 美華館, 1872 (同治 11). cb. 1 v.
c. Jishu.

2949 Mitsukuri Gempo 箕作阮甫 (1799–1863)
Taisei Daijisaku 大西大事策 (Great Events in European History), 1848 (嘉永 1). jb. 7 vols., 25cm.
note: Contains notes about the Old Testament in Vol. II.
cf. Kaikoku, pp. 430–433.

2950 Muze Kōshi 無是公子
Yōgai Tsūran 洋外通覧 (General History of European Countries), [n.p.], 1848 (嘉永 1). jb. 3 vols., 27cm.
cf. Kaikoku, pp. 425–427.
c. Naikaku, Seishin, Tōhoku-Kano, Ueno, Waseda.

2951 Ortiz, Thomas 白多瑪
Shishū Ryakui 四終略意 *Szu-chung Lüeh-yi* (Instruction in the Four Novissimas), 1848 (道光 28). cb. 1 v.
c. Tōyō.

2952 Saitō Chikudō 齋藤竹堂 (1815–1852)
Banshi 蕃史 (World History), 1848 (嘉永 1). jb. 2 vols.
cf. Kaikoku, pp. 425–427.
ms. Jingu, Kyoto, Naikaku, Oda, Sukeno, Tōhoku.

2953 —— Tokyo 1882 (明治 15). jb. 2 vols., 23cm.
c. Ebisawa.

2954 Yamaga Sosui 山鹿素水
Kaibi Sūgen 海備芻言 (Essentials of Coastal Defense). jb. 1 v.

ms. Hibiya-Kondo.

2955 —— (Kaibō Igi v. IX).
2956 —— (Nippon Kaibō Shiryō Sōsho, v. II).

2957 Yamaga Sosui 山鹿素水
Kaibi Zensaku 海備全策 (Complete Plan of Coastal Defense), 1848 (嘉永 1). jb. 7 vols.
ms. Gakushuin, Hibiya-Kondo, Ueno.

2958 —— (Nippon Kaibō Shiryō Sōsho, v. I).

2959 Yamamura Shōei 山村昌永 (1770–1807)
Seiyō Zakki 西洋雑記 (Notes on Western History), Edo [Tokyo], 文苑閣, 1848 (嘉永 1). jb. 4 vols., 26cm.
note: Western History beginning with Genesis and calling the Nativity of Christ the significant revolution affecting the whole world.
cf. Iwasaki Katsumi, "Yamamura Saisuke no Choyaku to sono Seiyōchishiki no Gensen ni tsuite" (*Rekishi Chiri*, v. LXXVII, n. 4), Tokyo 1941; Ebisawa-Namban, pp. 329–337; Kokushi, pp. 165–166.
c. Akioka, Ayuzawa, Ebisawa, Hibiya-Kondo, Kariya, Saba, Sukeno, Tōhoku-Kano, Ueno, Waseda. Naikaku, Waseda-Ogura.

2960 —— Edo [Tokyo], 1866 (慶應 2). jb. 4 vols., 26cm.
c. Kyodai, Uchida.

2961 * Seiyō Zakki Zoku 西洋雑記續 (Continuation of the Seiyō Zakki). jb. 2 vols.
cf. Kaikoku, p. 416.
ms. Otsuki, Shokokan.

1869

2962 Abe Rampo 安部蘭甫
Shin'u Shōshiki 新宇小識 (The New World) tr. by R. Abe, [n.p.], 1849 (嘉永 2). jb. 6 vols.
note: Human georgraphy of America.
cf. Kaikoku, pp. 119–120.
c. Kyodai, Ueno.

2963 Aizawa Seishi 會澤正志 (1781–1863)
Ryōganko 兩眼考 (Essays), 1849 (嘉永 2). jb. 2 vols.
ms. Sonkeikaku, Ueno, Waseda.

2964 Aizawa Seishi 會澤正志 (1782–1863)
Sangan Yokō 三眼餘考 (Essay Against Christianity), 1849 (嘉永 2). jb. 1 v.
ms. Sonkeikaku.

2965 —— (Sokkyohen, v. XIII).
2966 —— (Nippon Shisō Tōsō Shiryō, v. X).
2967 —— (Kirishitan Shiryō).

2968 —— abridged (Haja Sōsho, v. I).

2969 Akai Tōkai 赤井東海 (1787–1862)
Kaibōron 海防論 (Treatise on Coastal Defense), 1849 (嘉永 2). jb. 1 v.
ms. Kobekeidai, Waseda.

2970 —— (Nippon Kaibō Shiryō Sōsho, v. II).

2971 The Committee of the Presbyterian Mission at Ningpo.
Yasokyō Yōri Mondō 耶蘇教要理問答 *Yeh-su-chiao yao-li wen-ta* (Christian Catechism), Ningpo 1849 (道光 29). cb. 1 v., 24f., 19cm.
cf. Ozawa, p. 199.
c. Otani, Taisho.

2972 * Yasokyō Yōri Dai-mondō 耶蘇教要理大問答 *Yeh-su-chiao yao-li Ta-wen-ta*, Shanghai 美華書館, 1866 (同治 5). cb. 1v., 61f., 23cm.
note: revised ed. of the above.
c. Aoyama, ICU, Naikaku, Seikado, Waseda.

2973 —— Shanghai 美華書館, 1866 (同治 5). cb. 1 v., 2, 18f., 24cm.
c. Doshisha-Niishima, Kichu, Otani.

2974 Happer, Andrew Patton, PN. 哈巴安德 (1818–1894)
Temmon Mondō 天文問答 *T'ien-wen wen-ta* (Dialogue on Astronomy), Ningpo 1849 (道光 29). cb. 1 v., 36f.
cf. Ozawa, p. 197; Wylie, pp. 145, 201.

2975 —— revised by J. Doolittle, ABC., 盧公明, Fuchow 1854 (咸豊 4), cb. 1 v., 23f.

2976 Lowrie, Walter Macon, PN. 婁理華 (1819–1847)
Ruka Fukuin Chūshaku 路加福音註釋 *Lu-chia fu-yin chu-shih* (Commentary of the Gospel according to St. Luke), [n. p.], 1849 (道光 29). cb. 1 v., 78f.
cf. Ozawa, p. 191; Wylie, p. 131.

2977 McCartee, Divie Bethune, PN. 培端 (1820–1900)
Kitō Nyūmon Yōketsu 祈禱入門要訣 *Ch'i-tao ju-men yao-chüeh*, or Kitō Shinshin Nyūmon Yōketsu 祈禱眞神入門要訣 *Ch'i-tao Chen-shen ju-men yao-chüeh* (Manual of Prayer), Ningpo 1849 (道光 29). cb. 1 v., 24f.
cf. Ozawa, p. 191; Wylie, p. 131.

2978 —— Shanghai 美華書館, 1863 (同治 2). cb. 1 v., 1, 2, 27f., 18cm.
c. Kichu, Otani.

2979 —— Shanghai 美華書館, 1871 (同治 10). cb. 1 v., 3, 2, 26f., 20cm.
c. Doshisha-Niishima, Naikaku.

2980 McCartee, Divie Bethune, PN. 麥

嘉締 (1820–1900)
Yasokyō Yōketsu 耶蘇教要訣 *Yeh-su-chiao yao-chüeh* (Fundamental Truths of Christianity), Ningpo, 1849 (道光 29). cb. 1v. 16f.
cf. Wylie, p. 138.

2981 * Yasokyō Yōshi 耶蘇教要旨 *Yeh-su-chiao yao-chih*, revised ed., Ningpo, 1860 (咸豊 10). cb. 1 v., 15f.

2982 —— Shanghai 美華書館, 1868 (同治 7). cb. 1v., 8f., 16cm.
c. ICU, Yoshida.

2983 Mineta Fūkō 嶺田楓江 (1817–1883)
Kaigai Shinwa 海外新話 (New Story about Foreign Countries), 嶺田氏, 1849 (嘉永 2). jb. 5 vols., 26cm.
cf. Asahi, p. 83; Kaikoku, pp. 319–320.
c. Hibiya-Kondo, Ishin, Kyudai-Bunka, Nagasaki, Nichidai-Ueda, Seishin, Tōyō-Fujita, Ueno.
ms. Naikaku.

2984 Mineta Fūkō 嶺田楓江 (1817–1883)
Kaigai Shinwa Shūi 海外新話拾遺 (Supplement to the *Kaigai Shinwa*), 嶺田氏, 1849 (嘉永 2). jb. 5 vols., 26cm.
c. Hibiya-Kondo, Iwase, Nagasaki-Isahaya, Okada.

2985 Mineta Fūkō 嶺田楓江 (1817–1883)
Igirisukoku Kiryaku 英吉利國紀略 (Short Notes on England). jb. 1 v.
note: Extract from the *Kaigai Shinwa*, v. I. (See n. 2983).
cf. Kaikoku, pp. 402–403.
ms. Iwase, Otsuki.

2986 Nagayama Kan 長山貫
Seiyō Shōshi 西洋小史 (Short History of the Western World), 1849 (嘉永 2). jb.
note: Western history beginning with Genesis. Not published.
cf. Kaikoku, pp. 422–425.
ms. Ikeda, Otsuki, Mitsukuri.

2987 Nakabayashi Shigemasa 中林成昌
Kon'yo Ichi Zushiki 坤輿位置圖式 (Illustrated Geography of the World) Edo [Tokyo], 1849 (嘉永 2). jb. 1 v.
cf. Shinto, p. 33.
c. Jinshu.

2988 Tsurumine Shigenobu 鶴峯戊申 (1786–1859)
Naimitsu Tōmonroku 内密答問録 (Secret Dialogues), 1849 (嘉永 2). jb. 1 v.
ms. Gakushuin, Ueno.

2989 —— (Kaibō Igō, v. XXXI).

2990 * Naimitsu Mondōsho 内密問答書 (Secret Dialogues). jb. 1 v.
ms. Hibiya.

2991 Tsurumine Hikoichirō 鶴峯彦一郎 (1786–1859)

Kaibō Mondōroku 海防問答録 (Dialogue on Coastal Defense). jb. 1 v.

ms. Ishin.

1850

2992 Aizawa Seishi 會澤正志 (1781–1863)

Yūhiron 雄飛論 (Treatise on the Great Work), 1850 (嘉永 3) jb. 4 vols.

note: Jap. translation of the *Shinron* (n. 2770).

2993 —— (Gōitsu Sōsho).

2994 —— abridged (Haja Sōsho, v. I).

2995 Guetzlaff, Karl Friedrich Augustus, LM. 郭實獵 (1803–1851)

Bankoku Kōkanroku 萬國鋼鑑録 *Wan-kuo Kang-chien-lu* (Universal History) by K.F. Gützlaff and D.B. McCartee, PN. 培端, Ningpo 1850 (道光 30). cb. 1 v., 266f.

note: Original edition by Rev. Gützlaff was published under the title of *Kokon Bankoku Kōkan* 古今萬國鋼鑑 at Singapore in 1838.

cf. Wylie, pp. 60, 137.

2996 * Bankoku Kōkanroku Wage 萬国鋼鑑録和解 (Japanese Translation of the Bankoku Kōkanroku), tr. by Ōtsuki Seishi 大槻誠之 and Watanabe 渡部, Tokyo 1874 (明治 7). jb. 4 vols.

c. Naikaku.

2997 * Kokon Bankoku Kōkanroku 古今萬國鋼鑑録 (Old and New History of the World), construed from Chinese into Jap. by Ōtsuki Seishi 大槻誠之, Tokyo 青山清吉, 1874 (明治 7). jb. 4 vols.

c. Kyōto, Ōsaka.

2998 Guetzlaff, Karl Friedrich, Augustus, LM. 郭實獵 (1803–1851)

Seikei no Shi 聖經之史 *Sheng-ching chih-shih* (History of the Scriptures). [n.p.], [n.d.]. cb. 1 v., 41f.

cf. Wylie, p. 63.

2999 —— revised ed., by F. Genähr, RM. 葉納清, Hongkong 1850 (道光 30). cb. 1 v., 77f.

cf. Wylie, p. 162.

3000 * Seikei Shiki Satsuyō 聖經史記撮要 *Sheng-ching shih-chi ts'o-yao*, new ed., by F. Genähr, [n.p.], 1861 (咸豊 11). cb. 1 v., 43, 34f., 26cm.

c. Doshisha-Nishima, Seikado.

3001 Jo Keiyu 徐繼畬 *Hsu Chi-yu*

Eikan Shiryaku 瀛環志略 *Ying-huan chih-lüeh* (Outline of Foreign Countries). 紅杏山房, 1850 (道光 30). cb. 5 vols.

cf. Wylie, p. 168; Kaikoku, pp. 160–161.

c. Ayuzawa, Hibiya.

3002 —— Peking 總理衛門, 1866 (同治 5). cb. 6 vols.

c. Tōyō-Fujita.

3003 —— construed from Chinese into Jap. by Inoue Shunyō 井上春洋, Edo [Tokyo]. 1861 (文久 1). jb. 10 vols., 10cm.

c. Ayuzawa, Hibiya-Kondō, Okada, Kyōto, Seishin, Tenri, Ueno, Waseda.

3004 —— tr. into Jap. by Hirai Tadashi 平井正, Tokyo 1874 (明治 7). jb. 6 vols.

c. Uchida.

3005 Shin'itsu 眞逸

Kaibō Gungi Jo 海防群議序 (Preface to a Treatise on Coastal Defense), 1850 (嘉永 3). jb. 1 v.

ms. Hibiya-Kondō.

3006 Kurozawa Okinamaro 黒澤翁満 (1795–1859)

Ijin Kyōfuden 異人恐怖傳 (Dread of Foreigners), [n.p.], 1850 (嘉永 3). jb. 3 vols., 26cm.

contents: v I–II Ijin Kyōfuden, viz. Kaempfer's *Sakokuron* 鎖國論, tr. by Shitsuki Tadao 志筑忠雄 (See no. 2123).
III. Ijinkyōfuden o Kokusuru Ron 刻異人恐怖傳論 by Kurozawa Okinamaro.

c. Hibiya-Kaga, Kariya, Kyūdai-Bunka, Jingū, Nagasaki, Okada, Tōhoku-Kanō, Waseda.

3007 —— (Bummei Genryū Sōso, v. III).

3008 Milne, William Charles, LM. 美魏奈 (1815–1863)

Fukuin Kōkun 福音廣訓 *Fu-yin kuang-hsün* (Sermons on the Gospels), Shanghai 1850 (道光 30). cb. 1 v., 30f.

cf. Wylie, pp. 19, 124.

note: Revised ed. of his father W. Milne's *Gōkun Gojūnisoku,* Malacca, 1824 (n. 2492).

3009 —— Hongkong 1861 (咸豊 11). cb. 1 v., [3], 25f.

3010 —— Hongkong, 1867 (同治 6). cb. 1 v., [3], 25f.

c. Seikado, Tōhoku.

3011 Nagai Soku 永井則

Taisei Sansai Seimō 泰西三才正蒙 (Western Knowledge on the Universe), Chikuzen 崋如樓, 1850 (嘉永 3). jb. 3 vols., 27cm.

cf. Kaikoku, pp. 60–61.

c. Ayuzawa, Imoto, Ueno, Waseda.

3012 Saitō Setsudō 齋藤拙堂 (1797–1865)

Kagai Iden 海外異傳 (Strange News of Foreign Countries), Edo [Tokyo] 須原屋, 1850 (嘉永 3). jb. 1 v., 3, 2, 14, 3f., 23cm.

c. Fujita, Ishin, Kokugakuin, Kyūdai, Naikaku, Nichidai-Hayashi, Okada, Tōdai-Nanki, Ueno.

ms. Hibiya-Kondō.

3013 Saitō Yukinari 齋藤幸成 (1804–1878)

Bukō Nempyō 武江年表 (Chronological Table of the History of Edo), Edo [Tokyo] 須原屋, 1850 (嘉永 3). jb. 12 vols., 26cm.
cf. Kokushi, p. 270.
c. Hibiya, Keiō, Naikaku, Nichidai-Mukasa, Tenri, Tōdai-Nanki.

3014 —— Tokyo 我自刊我, 1882 (明治 15). jb. 2 vols., 23cm.
c. Tenri, Waseda.

3015 —— (Edo Sōsho, v. XII).

3016 ——- revised by Asakura Musei 朝倉無聲, Tokyo 1912 (大正 1).

3017 Sakuma Zōzan 佐久間象山 (1811–1864)

Jōsho 上書 (Memorial), 1850 (嘉永 3). jb. 1 v.
cf. Kokushi, p. 115.

3018 —— (Nippon Keizai Taiten, v. XLVI).

3019 —— (Dai-Nippon Shisō Zenshū, v. VII).

3020 —— (Zōzan Zenshū, v. II).

3021 —— (Kinsei Shakai Keizai Gakusetsu Taikei, v. X).

3022 Sakuma Zōzan 佐久間象山 (1811–1864)

Kaibō Kempakusho 海防建白書 (Written Memorial on Coastal Defense). jb. 1 v.
cf. Asahi, p. 52.
orig. ms. K. Ishigaki.
ms. Kanazawa-Kadō.

3023 —— (Kinsei Shakai Keizai Gakusetsu Taikei, v. X).

3024 —— (Zōzan Zenshū, v. II).

3025 Sakuma Zōzan 佐久間象山 (1811–1864)

Seikenroku 省諐録 (Essay). jb. 1 v.

3026 —— Tokyo 集遠樓, 1871 (明治 4). jb. 1 v., 2, 45f., 26cm.
c. Hibiya, Tōhoku-Kanō.

3027 —— (Sentetsu Chosaku Kokumin Dōtoku, v. II).

3028 —— (Zōzan Zenshū, v. I).

3029 —— (Nippon Kokushi Zensho).

3030 —— (Kinsei Shakai Keizai Gakusetsu Taikei, v. X).

3031 —— abridged (Dai-Nippon Shisō Zenshū, v. XVII).

3032 Satō Nobuhiro 佐藤信淵 (1769–1850)

Donkai Chōkiron 呑海肇基論 (On a Postive Policy). jb.

3033 —— (Kaibō Igi, v. IX).

3034 —— (Nippon Kaibō Shiryō Sōsho, v. II).

3035 Satō Nobuhiro 佐藤信淵 (1769–1850)

Gyobu Shogen 禦侮儲言 (Opinion on Foreign Contempt). jb. 3 vols.
ms. Hibiya-Kondō.

3036 —— (Satō Shin'en Bugakushū, v. I).

3037 * Gyokai Shogen 禦海儲言 (Opinion on Foreign Defense). jb. 1 v.
ms. Hibiya-Kondo

3038 —— (Ishin Shiryō).

3039 Satō Nobuhiro 佐藤信淵 (1769–1850)

Kaikoku Yōron 開國要論 (Treatise on Opening the Country).

3040 —— (Satō Shin'en Kagaku Zenshū).

3041 Satō Nobuhiro 佐藤信淵 (1769–1850)

Satō Genkai-ki 佐藤元海記 (Notes of Satō Genkai).

3042 —— (Kaibō Igi, v. VI).

3043 —— (Nippon Kaibō Shiryō Sōsho, v. II).

3044 Shioda Jun'an 鹽田順庵 (1805–1871)

Kaibō Igi 海防彙議 (Treatise on Coastal Defense). 1850 (嘉永 3). jb. 45 vols.
cf. Tenri-Jap. II. pp, 98–100.
contents: v. I. Tōmon Jissaku 答問十策 by Aoki Teien 青木定遠.
II. Bōkai Bigen 防海微言 by Kamei Akira 亀井昱.
III. Kenkin Bichū 献芹微衷 by Matsumoto Tokizō 松本斗機藏.
IV. Kaikō Sessaku 海寇窃策 by Kuroda Rōkō 黒田老侯.
Gyojūsaku 禦戎策 by Aaska Yūsuke 安積雄助.
V. Satō Akai Nisei Gi 佐藤赤井二生議.
VI. Bojutsu Yumemonogatari 戊戌夢物語 by Takano Chōei 高野長英.
Dō Hyō 同評.
Yume Yume Monogatari 夢々物語.
Satō Genkai-Ki 佐藤元海記.
VIII. Kaibōsaku 海防策 by Saitō Tokuzō 齋藤徳藏.
Shinkiron 慎機論 by Watanabe Noboru 渡邊登.
VIII. Chūkai Shigi 籌海私議 by Shionoya Kōzō 鹽谷宕陰.
IX. Kaibi Sūgen 海備芻言 by Yamaga Sosui 山鹿素水.
Donkai Chōkiron 呑海肇基論 by Satō Genkai 佐藤元海.
Kaibō Setsukai 海防説階.
XVIII. Keisei Hisaku 經世秘策 by Honda Saburōuemon 本田三郎右衛門.
Oranda Kokumitsu 和蘭告密 tr. by Shibukawa Rokuzō 澁川六藏.
XIX. Rinsen Okugi 憐疝臆議 by Toryū Koji 屠龍居士.
XXV. Bōshun Wakumon 防春或問 by Shionoya Kōzō 鹽谷宕陰.
XXVII–XXX. Kaibō Biron 海防備論 by Fujimori

107

Kyōsuke 藤森恭助.

XXXI. Yasō Dokugo 野叟獨語 by Sugita Gempaku 杉田玄白.

XXXIII. Kaibō Shisaku 海防私策 by Hagura Geki 羽倉外記.

Kenkin Bichū 献芹微衷 by Ōtsuki Heiji 大槻平次.

XXXV. Naimitsu Tōmonroku 内密答問録 by Tsurumine Hikoichirō 鶴峯彦一郎.

XXXVIII. Ri Fujitsui 釐不恤緯 by Habu Kumagorō 土生熊五郎.

Taisei Rokuwa 泰西録話 by Koga Dōan 古賀侗菴.

XLIII. Matsumoto Tokizō Jōsho 松本斗機蔵上書. Oranda Hōkan, Hyōmin Gosō Igirisu Morrisson-sen Ichijō Shōyaku 和蘭寶函, 漂民護送英吉利モルリツソン船一條抄譯.

XLIV. Gi Kyokuron Jiji Fūji 擬極論時事封事 by Koga Akira 古賀昱.

ms. Hibiya-Kondō, Ikeda, Iwase, Ishin, Jingū, Sonkeikaku, Tenri, Ueno, Waseda, Yutoku.

3045 —— (Nippon Kaibō Shiryō Sōsho, vv. IV–VI).

3046 Shuck, Jehu Lewis, ABF. 淑士人 (–1863)
Shinshin Sōron 眞神總論 Chen-shen Tsung-lun (Discourse on the True God), Shanghai, 1850 (道光 30). cb. 1 v., 4f.
cf. Ozawa, p. 194; Wylie, p. 92.
note: See also nos. 3331–33.

1851

3047 Bunyan, John (1628–1688)
Kōkaku Keirekiden 行客經歷傳 Hsin-k'o Ching-li-chuan (Pilgrim's Progress), tr. by William Muirhead, LM. 慕維廉, Shanghai, 1851 (咸豊 1). cb. 1 v., 13f.
cf. Ozawa, p. 240; Wylie, p. 168.

3048 Hobson, Benjamin, LM. 合信 (1816–1873)
Zentai Shinron 全體新論 Chüan-t'i hsin-lun (New Discourse of Physiology), Canton 惠愛醫局, 1851 (咸豊 1). cb. 1 v., 99f.
cf. Ebisawa Arimichi, "Bakumatsu ni okeru Kirisutokyō Kagakusho no Shuppan" (Kirisutokyō Shigaku, v. I), Yokohama 1951; Ozawa, pp. 201, 212, 293–299; Wylie, p. 126.

3049 —— Shanghai 墨海書館, 1851 (咸豊 1). cb. 1 v., 2, 1, 1, 2, 3, 71f., 25cm.
c. Ueno.

3050 —— (Kaizansenkan Sōsho, v. CXIX–CXX).

3051 —— Edo [Tokyo] 二書堂, 1857 (安政 4). jb. 2 vols., 25cm.
c. Kariya, Keiō, Kichū, Kompira, Kyōdai, Kyūdai-Ganka, Narita, Nichidai-Ueda, Ōsaka, Shinken, Tōdai-Nanki, Tōhoku-Kanō.

3052 —— Edo [Tokyo] 越智, 1857 (安政 4). jb. 2 vols., 26cm.
c. Ebisawa, Kyōdai-Fujikawa, Kyōdai-Hōi, Gakushūin, Yoshida.

3053 * Zentai Shinron Ryakuge 全體新論

略解 (Jap. translation of the Zentai Shinron), tr. by Takagi Kumasaburō 高木熊三郎, Osaka 文榮堂, 1874 (明治 7). jb. 4 vols., 18cm.
c. Ebisawa, Kompira.

3054 * Zentai Shinron Yakuge 全體新論譯解 (Japanese Translation of the Zentai Shinron), tr. by Ishiguro Atsushi 石黒厚, Tokyo 静觀堂, 1874 (明治 7). jb. 3 vols., 23cm.
c. Ebisawa, Kyōdai, Kyōdai-Fujikawa, Tōhoku-Kanō.

3055 —— Tokyo, 1876 (明治 9).
cf. Nakamura Kyūshirō 中山久四郎, "Kinsei Shina no Nippon Bunka ni oyoboshitaru Seiryoku Eikyō" (Shigaku Zasshi, v. XXV, n. 10), Tōkyō 1914.

3056 *Zentai Shinron Zukai 全體新論圖解 (Illustrations for the Zentai Shinron), [n.p.], [1856?]. jb. 1 v., 26cm.
cf. Ozawa, p. 212.

3057 * Tsūzoku Zentai Shinron 通俗全體新論 (Popular Zentai Shinron), compiled by Matsui Koretoshi 松井惟利, Tokyo, 1878 (明治 11). jb. 1 v.
cf. Ozawa, p. 213.

Manjirō's Tales of Far Away Lands

3058 Hyōryū Manjirō Kichōdan 漂流萬次郎歸朝談 (Manjirō's Tales upon Returning from Abroad). jb. 1 v.

3059 —— (Ikoku Hyōryū Kidanshū).

3060 * Manjirō Hyōryū Kiji 萬次郎漂流記事 (Notes on the Return of Manjirō). jb. 1 v.
ms. Naikaku.

3061 * Nansenjin Kichō Kiji 難船人歸朝記事, or Manjirō Zatsuwa 萬次郎雜話 (Notes on the Return of a Shipwrecked Sailor or Manjirō's Tales). jb. 2 vols.
ms. Hibiya-Kondō.

3062 Taikyo Dōjin 太虚道人
Manjirōdan Wage Funabanashi 萬次郎譚和解船話 (Manjirō's Tales). jb. 2 vols.

3063 —— (Hyōryūki Sōsho, vv. LXXI–LXXII).

3064 * Tosa no Kuni Hakatagōri Nakahama-mura Gyojin Manjirō Ikoku Tadayoi no Shidai Tosho Jitsuroku 土佐國博多郡中濱村漁人萬次郎異國漂之次第圖書實録 (True Record of the Return of Manjirō of Tosa). jb. 1 v.
ms. Hibiya-Kondō.

3065 * Tosa no Kuni Manjirō Ikoku

Monogatari 土佐國萬次郎異國物語 (Man-jiro's Tales of Foreign Countries).
3066 —— (Hyōryūki Sōsho, v. LXXVII).

3067 Yoshida Seiyo 吉田正譽
Hyōkyaku Danki 漂客談奇 (Tales of a Shipwrecked Sailor). jb. 1 v.
ms. Hibiya-Kondō, Naikaku, Sonkeikaku.
3068 —— (Hyōryū Kidan Zenshū).
3069 —— (Hyōryūki Sōsho, vv. LXV-LXIX).

3070 McCartee, Divie Bethune, PN. 培端 (1820–1900)
Sambishi 讚美詩 *Tsan-mei shih* (Hymnal), Ningpo, 1851 (咸豊 1). cb. 1 v. 16f.
cf. Ozawa, p. 191; Wylie, p. 138.

3071 McCartee, Divie Bethune, PN. 培端 (1820–1900)
Shogakuhen 初學篇 *Ch'u-hsüeh-p'ien* (Instruction on the Bible), Ningpo, 1851 (咸豊 1). cb. 3 vols.
cf. Wylie, p. 138.

3072 Milne, William Charles, LM. 美魏奈 (1815–1863)
Shindō Nyūmon 眞道入門 *Chen-tao Ju-men* (Introduction to the True Doctrine) Shanghai, 1851 (咸豊 1). cb. 1 v. 17f.
cf. Wylie, p. 124.
3073 —— Hongkong, 1851 (咸豊 1). cb. 1 v., 19f.
3073b —— Hongkong 英華書院, 1867 (同治 6). cb. 1 v., 19f., 16cm.
c. Saba.
3074 —— Shanghai 美華書館, 1870 (同治 9). cb. 1 v., 18f., 25cm.
c. Kichū.

3075 Mitsukuri Gempo 箕作阮甫 (1799–1863)
Hakkō Tsūshi 八紘通誌 (World Geography), [Edo] 天竺樓, 1851 (嘉永 4). jb. 6 vols., 27cm.
cf. Kaikoku, pp. 178–189, 321; Asahi, p. 26.
orig. ms. S. Kure.
c. Kariya, Kyōto, Waseda.

3076 Sha Seikō 謝清高 *Hsieh Ch'ing-Kao*
Kairoku 海録 *Hai-lu*, 1851 (咸豊 1).
note: This edition is not known to the compiler. Specifically outlawed in Japan.
3077 —— 1870 (同治 9). cb. 2 vols.
c. Tōyō-Fujita.

3078 Shinozaki Shōchiku 篠崎小竹 (1781–1851)
Chōya Zakki 朝野雜記 (Miscellany on the Government and the People). jb. 1 v.
ms. Tōdai, Ueno.

3079 Sugita Genzui 杉田玄瑞 (1818–1889)
Chigaku Seisō 地學正宗 (True Theories of Geography) tr. by Sugita Genzui, [n.p.] 天眞樓, 1851 (嘉永 4). jb. 7 vols.
cf. Kaikoku, pp. 120–122.
c. Ayuzawa, Tōhoku-Kanō.
3080 —— 1883 (明治 16). jb. 7 vols.
c. Waseda.

3081 Yamazaki Shiken 山崎士謙
Roshia Shiryaku 魯西亞史略 (Outline of Russian History), [n.p.], 1851 (嘉永 4). jb. 2 vols., 27cm.
cf. Kaikoku, p. 394.
note: Revised ed. of Maeno's *Roshia Hongi* (n. 2032).
c. Kyōto, Tōhoku-Kanō.

1852

3082 Albrand, Bp. 斯徳範
Seikyō Rishō 聖敎理證 *Sheng-chiao Li-cheng* (Catholic Apologetics), tr. into Chinese by Bp. Albrand, Lazarist, [Shanghai], 1852 (咸豊 2). cb. 1 v.
cf. Jo, pp. 124–125; Laures, p. 149.
c. Jingū, Seikadō.
3083 —— Shanghai, 1884 (光緒 10). cb. 1 v.
3084 —— Shanghai, 1898 (光緒 24). cb. 1 v., 42f.
3085 —— Shanghai, 1923 (民國 12). 10th ed., wb. 1 v., 6, 8, 86p., 19cm.
c. Ebisawa, Tōhoku.
3086 —— Peking, 1924 (民國 13). cb. 1 v., 6, 78f., 17cm.
c. Tōhoku.
3087 —— Peking 遣使會印書館, 1937 (民國 26). wb. 1 v., 98p., 19cm.
c. Tenri.
3088 —— tr. into Jap., [Yokohama, 1873 (明治 6)]. jb. 1 v., 44f., 24cm.
cf. Ebisawa Arimichi, "Kirishitan Tenseki Kenkyū Yoroku" (*Seishin Studies*, v. III), Tōkyō 1953; Laures, n. 84.
c. Ebisawa, Yanagiya.
phot. Sophia.
3089 —— Yokohama 1876 (明治 9). wb. 1v., [4], 60, 77p., 21cm.
cf. Laures, n. 89.
c. Ebisawa, Junshin, Ōura, Nagasaki, Seishin, Sophia.
3090 —— Osaka? 1880 (明治 13). wb. 1v., [3], 21, 27f., 22cm.
cf. Laures, n. 111; Streit-X, p. 377.
c. Kichu, Sophia.
3091 —— Tokyo? 1882 (明治 15). jb. 1 v., 53p., 23cm.
c. Aoyama, Ebisawa, Kansei, Kichu, Nagasaki, Sophia.

3092 Bosscha, Johannes (1797–1874)
Seishiryaku 西史略 (An Outline History of West) tr. by Banji Sanjin 蟠坭散人, 1852 (嘉永 5). jb. 5 vols.
cf. Kaikoku, pp. 445–446.
orig. Title: *Schets der Algemeene Geschiedenis en van die des Vaderlands,* Amsterdam 1838.
note: The translator is unknown. Not published.
ms. Ikeda, T. Okubo, Shoryobu.

3093 Edkins, Joseph, LM. 艾約瑟 (1823–1905)
Chūsei Tsūsho 中西通書 *Chung-hsi t'ung-shu* (A Chinese Western Almanac) edited by J. Edkins and Alexander Wylie, 1852 (咸豊 2).
cf. Ozawa, p. 198; Wylie, pp. 188–189.
3094 *Kayō Wagō Tsūsho 華洋和合通書 *Hua-yang ho-ho t'ung-shu* (Chinese and Western concord Almanac), 1853–65 (咸豊 3–同治4).
note: Changed title of the above.

3095 Happer, Andrew Patton, PN. 哈巴安德 (1818–1894)
Kyūyaku Shiki Jōmon 舊約史記條門 *Chiu-yüeh Shih-chi T'iao-wen* (Questions on the History of the Old Testament), Ningpo 1852 (咸豊 2). cb. 1 v., 82f.
cf. Ozawa, pp. 188–189, Wylie, p. 145.
3096 —— Shanghai 1860 (咸豊 10). cb. 1 v.
3097 —— Shanghai 美華書館, 1864 (同治 3). cb. 1 v., 57f., 25cm.
c. ICU, Ōtani.
3098 —— Shanghai, 1875 (光緒 1). cb. 1v.
c. Saba.

3099 Happer, Andrew Patton, PN. 哈巴安德 (1818–1894)
Shinyaku Shiki Mondō 新約史記問答 *Hsin-yüeh Shih-chi Wen-ta* (Dialogue on the Chronicle of the New Testament), Canton 1852 (咸豊 2). cb. 1 v., 43f.
cf. Ozawa, p. 195; Wylie, p. 145.
3100 —— Shanghai 1864 (同治 3). cb. 1 v., 17f.
3101 —— Shanghai 1874 (同治 13). cb. 1v., [1], 1, 15f., 24cm.
c. Kichu.

3102 Hoashi Banri 帆足萬里 (1778–1852)
Tōsempuron 東潜夫論 (Essay on Politics). jb. 3 vols.
cf. Kokushi, p. 220.
c. Sonkeikaku.
3103 —— (Nippon Keizai Taiten, v. XXXVIII).
3104 —— (Nippon Bunko, v. I).

3105 —— (Hoashi Banri Zenshū, v. I).
3106 Hotei Shunjin 穂亭主人
Seiyō Gakuka Yakujutsu Mokuroku 西洋學家譯述目録 (List of Translations by the Masters of Western Learning), [n.p.], 1852 (嘉永 5). jb. 1 v., 9, 39f., 8×19cm.
cf. Kaikoku, pp. 62–63; Tenri-Jap. II, p. 2.
c. Hibiya-Morohashi, Keiō-Kōda, Seishin, Tenri, Tōhoku-Kanō, Waseda.
3107 —— facs. repr. by the Shōundō 松雲堂, Tokyo 1926 (大正 15).
3108 —— (Bummei Genryū Sōsho, v. III).

3109 Ichikawa Gengo 市川弦五
Kaigan Biyō 海岸備用 (Coastal Defense), Kyoto 陵霄園, 1852 (嘉永 5). jb. 5 vols., 26cm.
c. Hibiya-Kondō.
3110 —— (Nippon Kaibō Shiryō Sōsho, v. VIII).

3111 McCartee, Divie Bethune, PN. 培端 (1820–1900)
Kai-Kaishin Yaso Setsuryaku 改悔信耶蘇說略 *Kai-hui-hsin Yeh-su shuo-lüeh* (Brief Discourse on Repentance), Ningpo 1852 (咸豊 2). cb. 1 v., 8f.
note: The original ed. was published under the title *Kaikai Setsuryaku* 悔改説略 *Hui-kai Sho-lüeh,* Ningpo, 1847.
cf. Ozawa, p. 187–; Wylie, p. 136.
3112 —— Shanghai, 1860 (咸豊 10). cb. 1 v., 9f., 19cm.
c. Tenri.
3113 —— Shanghai 美華書館, 1861 (咸豊 11). 3rd ed. cb. 1 v., 9f., 13cm.
c. Ōtani.
3114 —— Shanghai 美華書館, 1868 (同治 7). cb. 1 v.
c. Naikaku.

1853

3115 Ban'i Bōeki Ranshō 蕃夷貿易濫觴 (Beginnings of Foreign Trade), 1853 (嘉永 6). jb. 1 v.
ms. Naikaku.

3116 Bunyan, John 約翰本文 (1628–1688)
Tenro Rekitei 天路歴程 *T'ien-lu Li-ch'eng* (Pilgrim's Progress), tr. into Chinese by William Chalmers Burns, PCE., 賓, Amoy, 1853 (咸豊 3). cb. 5 vols.
cf. Ozawa, pp. 197, 241–244; Saeki-Shincho, pp. 495–503; Wylie, p. 175.
3117 —— Hongkong, 1856 (咸豊 6). cb. 1 v.
3118 —— revised by W. Milne, Shanghai

墨海書館, 1856 (咸豊 6). cb. 1 v., [1], 12, 11, 12, 14, 13, 3f., 21cm.
c. Ōtani.

3119 —— revised by the American Methodist Episcopal Mission, Fuchow, 1857 (咸豊 7). cb. 1 v.

3120 —— Shanghai 1858 (咸豊 8). cb. 1 v.
c. Aoi.

3121 —— Shanghai, 1862 (同治 1). cb. 1 v., 63f.

3122 —— new ed., Hongkong, 1863 (同治 2). cb. 1 v.

3123 —— Shanghai 美華書館, 1865 (同治 4). cb. 1 v., 55f.

3124 —— Shanghai 美華書館, 1869 (同治 8). cb. 1 v., 2, 49f., 20cm.
c. Ebisawa, Kompira, Naikaku, Ōsaka, Ōtani, Saba, Tōhoku-Kanō, Yoshida.

3125 —— mandarin language, Peking, 1865 (同治 4). cb. 1 v.

3126 —— dialect language (土話), Yang-ch'eng 羊城惠師禮堂, 1871 (同治 10). cb. 2 vols., 24cm.
c. ICU, Tōhoku.

3127 —— dialect language (土話), (different ed.), Yang-ch'eng 羊城惠師禮堂, 1871 (同治 10). cb. 2 vols., 22cm.
c. Tōhoku.

3128 —— mandarin language, Shanghai 美華書館, 1872 (同治 11). cb. 1 v., 1, 19, 17, 18, 22, 20f., 24cm.
c. Seikadō, Tōhoku-Kanō.

3129 —— Hongkong 中華印務總局, 1873 (同治 12). cb. 1 v., 1, 65f., 20cm.
c. Kichū, Saba.

3130 —— Peking 小書會眞寶堂, 1883 (光緒 9). cb. 1 v., 103f., 15pl., 25cm.
c. Tōhoku.

3131 * Iyaku Tenro Rekitei 意譯天路歷程 (Free Translation of the *Tenro Rekitei*), tr. by Satō Kihō 佐藤喜峰, Tokyo 十字屋書舗, 1879 (明治 12). jb. 1 v., 3, [2], 173f., 23cm.
note: Original translation by Murakami Shunkichi 村上俊吉, in the *Shichi-ichi Zappō* 七一雜報, 1876–1877.
cf. Ozawa, pp. 244–246.
c. Aoyama, Doshisha-Niishima, Kichū, Saba, Sophia, Ueno, Yoshida.

3132 —— Tokyo 十字屋書舗, 1881 (明治 14). 2nd ed. jb. 1 v., 3, [1], 1, 173f., 23cm.
c. Aoyama, Ebisawa, Kichū, Naikaku, Saba.
note: See Pt. II, about the translation from the original text by W. J. White.

3133 Culbertson, Michael Simpson, PN. 克陛存 (1819–)
Iria Genkōden 以利亞言行傳 *Y-li-ya Yen-hsing-chuan* (Life of Elija), Ningpo, 1853 (咸豊 3). cb. 1 v., 23f.

cf. Ozawa, p. 186; Wylie, p. 147.
3134 —— Shanghai 美華書館, 1861 (咸豊 11). cb. 1 v., 2, 18f., 25cm.
c. ICU, Otani.

3135 Fujimori Kōan 藤森弘庵 (1799–1862)
Kaibō Biron 海防備論 (Treatise on Coastal Defense), 1853 (嘉永 6). jb. 1 v.
ms. Hibiya-Kondō, Iwase, Tōhoku-Kanō, Ueno.

3136 —— (Kaibō Igi, vv. XXVII–XXX).

3137 —— (Ishin Shiryō).

3138 —— (Hokō Tōka Ibun).

3139 —— (Nippon Kaibō Shiryō Sōsho, v. I).

3140 Fujimori Taiga 藤森大雅 (1799–1862)
Kaibō Shisaku 海防私策 (Private Plans of Coastal Defense). jb. 1 v.
ms. Hibiya-Kondō, Ishin.

3141 Fujimori Taiga 藤森大雅 (1799–1862)
Kyōkō Shinron 恐惶新論 (New National Defense). jb. 2 vols.
ms. Tenri.

3142 * Kōsei Kyūkō Shinron 校正恐惶新論 (Revised *Kyōkō Shinron*), [n.p.], 1860 (萬延 1). jb. 2 vols., 23cm.
c. Kichū, Tenri, Waseda.

3143 Happer, Andrew Patton, PN. 哈巴安德 (1818–1894)
Matai Fukuinsho Mondō 馬太福音書問答 *Ma-t'ai Fu-yin-shu Wen-ta* (Dialogue on the Gospel according to St. Matthew), Canton 1853 (咸豊 3). cb. 1 v., 176f.
cf. Wylie, p. 145.

3144 —— Shanghai 美華書館, 1864 (同治 3). cb. 1 v., 58f., 25cm.
c. Naikaku, Ōtani, Seikadō.

3145 —— Shanghai 美華書館, 1874 (同治 13). cb. 1 v., [1], 58f., 23cm.
c. Aoyama.

3146 Happer, Andrew Patton, PN. 哈巴安德 (1818–1894)
Yōgaku Shijikyō 幼學四字經 *Yu-hsüeh Ssu-tze-ching* (Four Character Book for Youth), Canton 1853 (咸豊 3). cb. 1v., 20f., 22cm.
cf. Wylie, p. 145.
c. Tōhoku.

3147 Hayashi Fukusai 林復齋 (1800–1859)
Tsūkō Ichiran 通航一覧 (Historical Documents concerning Transportation between Japan and other Countries), 1853

(嘉永 6). jb. 345 vols.
cf. Kaikoku, pp. 66–67; Kokushi, pp. 207–208.
orig. ms. Naikaku.
ms. Nichidai-Ueda.

3148 —— pr. by the Kokusho Kankōkai 國書刊行會, Tokyo 1912–1913. (大正 1–2). w.b. 8 vols.

3149 * Tsūkō Ichiran Shō, Namban Sōkatsubu 通航一覧抄, 南蠻總括部 jb. 1 v.
ms. Nagasaki.

3150 Ihaku Jōmonki 異舶乘聞記 (Reports of Travel on a Foreign Ship), 1853 (嘉永 6). jb. 1 v.
ms. Rikkyō.

3151 Ikokusen Toraiki 異國船渡來記 (Record of the Arrival of Foreign Boats), 1853 (嘉永 6). jb. 1 v.
ms. Hibiya-Kondō, Gakushūin.

3152 Jijimusai 時々夢斉
Kaigai Jimbutsu Shōden 海外人物小傳 (Short Biography of Famous Foreign People), Edo [Tokyo] 萬邦樓, 1853 (嘉永 6). jb. 5 vols., 27cm.
cf Kaikoku, pp. 179–180, 455.
c. Kichū.

3153 Kakusei Dōjin 覺世道人
Sakokuron Fubi 鎖國論附尾 (Addition to the *Sakokuron*), compiled by Kakusei Dōjin, [n.p.], 1853 (嘉永 6). jb. 1 v., [1], 17f., 26cm.
note: Reprint of the *Oranda Hōkan*, *Nippon no Bu* (n. 2621).
c. Ebisawa, Naikaku.
ms. Kanazawa-Kadō.

3154 Kinsei Hyōryūdan 近世漂流談 (Tales of Recent Shipwrecked Sailors), 1853 (嘉永 6). jb. 1 v.
ms. Jingū.

3155 Macgowan, Daniel Jerome, ABF. 瑪高温 (1814–1893)
Kōkai Kinshin 航海金針 *Hang-hai Chin-chen* (Golden Art on Cyclones), 愛華堂, 1853 (咸豊 3). cb. 1 v., [31]f., 1 map., 26cm.
cf. Wylie, p. 133.
c. Ueno.

3156 —— Edo [Tokyo], 岡田屋, 1857 (安政 4). jb. 1 v., [1], 8, 10, 8f., 5 pl., map., 26cm.
cf. Ozawa, p. 220; Kaikoku, pp. 155–156.
c. Gakushiin, Hibiya-Kondō, Kadō, Kyūdai-Butsuri, Naikaku, Okada, Tōhoku-Kano, Waseda.

3157 —— (Kaiji Shiryō Sōsho, v. VI).

3158 McCartee, Divie Bethune, PN. 麥嘉締 (1820–1900)
Shinri Ichi 眞理易知 *Chen-li yi-chih* (Plain Introduction to the Truth), Ningpo, 1853 (咸豊 3). cb. 1 v., 16f.

cf. Ozawa, p. 194; Wylie, p. 138.

3159 —— Shanghai 美華書館, 1862 (同治 1). cb. 1 v., 21f., 16cm.
c. Aoyama.

3160 —— Fuhchow, 1863 (同治 2). revised by C. Hartwell, ABC. cb. 1 v., 14f.
cf. Ozawa, p. 194; Wylie, pp. 221–222.

3161 —— Shanghai 美華書館, 1872 (同治 11). cb. 1 v., 17f., 16cm.
c. ICU, Kichū.
ms. Aoyama.

3162 —— tr. into Jap. by James C. Hepburn, PN., [Yokohama], [1867]. jb. 1 v., 39f., 23cm.
c. ICU, Kichū, Meiji, Ōtani, Saba, Sophia, Tōdai-Nanki, Tokyōshin, Waseda.
ms. Waseda.
See also Pt. II on the Jap. ed.

3163 Mitsukuri Gempo 箕作阮甫 (1799–1863)
Tsūshi Hachizai Shokugen 通誌八材飭元 (State of Affairs in the United States of America), 1853 (嘉永 6). jb. 3 vols.
note: Vol. II contains notes about the Catholic missions in China.
orig. ms. Mitsukuri.

3164 The Morrison Education Society
Kaji Kanchin 遐邇貫珍 *Hsia-erh Kuan-chen* (Monthly Magazine), Hongkong 1853–56 (咸豊 3–6).
cf. Wylie, p. 120.
ms. Narita, Waseda.

3165 Muirhead, William, LM. 慕維廉 (1822–1900)
Chiri Zenshi 地理全志 *Ti-li Ch'üan-chih* (Outline of Geography), Shanghai 1853–54 (咸豊 3–4). cb. 15 vols.
cf. Ozawa, pp. 197, 286–291; Kaikoku, p. 156; Wylie, p. 168.

3166 —— (Shōhōkosai Yoshi Sōshō).

3167 —— (Seigaku Taisei, v. III).

3168 —— construed from Chinese into Japanese by Shionoya Tōin 鹽谷宏陰, Edo [Tokyo] 爽快堂, 1859 (安政 6). jb. 10 vols., 26cm.
cf. Ozawa, p. 230; Kaikoku, pp. 156–158, 324.
c. Ayuzawa, Gakushūin, Jingū, Kyūdai, Naikaku, Oda, Ueno, Waseda, Yoshida.

3169 * Chigaku Zenshi Jōhen 地學全志上篇 construed from Chinese into Japanese by Iwase Senshū 巖瀨蟾州, Edo [Tokyo], 山城屋, 1859 (安政 6). jb. 5 vols.
c. Okada.

3170 * Zōtei Wayaku Chiri Zenshi 增訂和譯地理全志 (Japanese Translation of the *Chiri Zenshi*), tr. by Abe Hirokuni 阿部弘國, Tokyo 1874 (明治 7). jb. 10 vols., 23cm.
c. Gakushūin, Ueno.

3171 Saitō Chikudō 齋藤竹堂 (1815–1852)

Gaikoku Eishi 外國詠史 (Poem on Foreign History), Edo [Tokyo] 梅花深處, 1853 (嘉永 6). jb. 1 v., [2], [7]f., 23cm.

c. Ebisawa.

3172 Sakuma Zōzan 佐久間象山 (1811–1864)

Kyūmu Jūji 急務十事 (Ten Articles on Urgent Bussiness) 1853 (嘉永 6). jb. 1 v.

3173 —— (Zōzan Zenshū, v. I).

3174 Shibata Shūzō 新發田収藏 (1820–1859)

Kakkoku Shoryō Bankoku Chimei Shōran 各國所領萬國地名捷覽 (World Dictionary of Place Names), 1853 (嘉永 6). jb. 1 v., 52f., 16cm.

c. Ayuzawa, Hibiya.

3175 Takashima Shūhan 高島秋帆 (1798–1866)

Takashima Kihei Jōsho 高島喜平上書 (Memorials of Takashima Kihei), 1853 (嘉永 6). jb. 1 v.

cf. Kokushi, p. 193.

3176 —— (Nippon Keizai Taiten, v. XVLI).

3177 Tokugawa Nariaki 徳川齋昭 (1800–1860)

Kaibō Guson 海防愚存, or Suifukō Kaibōsaku Jukkajō 水府公海防策十ケ條 (Private Plan of Coastal Defense, or Ten Articles of the Coastal Defense Plan of Suifukō, Lord of Mito-han), 1853 (嘉永 6). jb. 1 v.

ms. Hibiya-Kondō, Nagasaki.

3178 Toryū Koji 眉龍居士

Rinsen Okugi 鄰疝臆議 (Private Opinions), 1853 (嘉永 6). jb. 1 v.

ms. Sonkeikaku, Tōhoku-Kanō.

3179 —— (Kaibō Igi, v. XIX).

3180 —— (Nippon Kaibō Shiryō Sōsho, v. II).

3181 * Rinsen Okugi Jukkajō On-kotae 憐疝臆議十ケ條御答 (Responce to Ten Articles of the *Rinsen Okugi*). jb. 1 v.

ms. Tenri.

3182 Toyota Ryō 豊田亮 (1805–1864)

Seikai Zensho Gasshūkoku-kō 靖海全書合衆國考 (Notes on the United States), [n.p.], 1853 (嘉永 6). jb. 1 v., 79f., 27cm.

cf. Kaikoku, pp. 68, 409.

c. Ayuzawa, Iwase, Naikaku.

3183 Wylie, Alexander, LM. 偉烈亞力 (1815–1887)

Sūgaku Keimō 數學啓蒙 *Shu-hsüeh Ch'i-meng* (Compendium of Arithmetic), Shanghai, 1853 (咸豊 3). cb. 1 v., 127f.

cf. Ozawa, p. 272; Wylie, p. 173.

c. Jingū.

3184 —— 1886 (光緒 12). cb. 2 vols.

c. Waseda-Ogura.

3185 —— (Kokon Sangaku Sōsho).

3186 —— (Zoku Seigaku Taisei, v. I).

3187 —— Edo [Tokyo] 陸軍所, 1853 (嘉永 6). jb. 1 v., 1, 51, 55, 17, 1f., 23cm.

c. Kanazawa-Kado, Naikaku, Tōhoku-Kanō, Waseda.

1854

3188 Aiko Gyosō 靄湖漁叟

Kaigai Ibun 海外異聞 or Amerika Shinwa 亞墨利加新話 (News of America) [n.p.] 青峽園, 1854 (嘉永 7). jb. 5 vols., 26cm.

cf. Kaikoku, pp. 59, 322.

c. Hibiya, Hibiya-Kondō, Iwase, Jingū, Kariya, Kyūdai-Bunka.

ms. Naikaku.

3189 Yu Shinsei 兪秦生 *Yü Chin-sheng*

Jumbi Zuimonroku 盾鼻隨聞録 *Tun-pi Sui-wen-lu* (Recollection) 1854 (咸豊 4). cb. 2 vols.

c. Tōyō-Fujita.

ms. Sophia, Tōhoku-Kanō, Ueno.

3190 Gouvea, Alexandre de, SJ. 湯亜立山 (–1808)

Seikyō Nikka 聖教日課 *Sheng-chiao Jih-k'o* (Daily Prayers) approved by Bp. Alexandre de Gouvea, Peking 始胎大堂, 1854 (咸豊 4). cb. 1 v., 156, 86f., 15cm.

c. Nagasaki, Naikaku, Tenri.

3191 Ikoku Ochibakago 異國落葉籠 (Miscellaneous Notes on Foreign Countries), [n.p.], 1854 (嘉永 7). jb. 1 v.

c. Hibiya-Kondō, Yokohama City Office.

3192 Ishizuka Yutaka 石塚豊

Kaigai Hyōryū Nendaiki 海外漂流年代記 (Chronological List of Shipwrecked Sailors), 大和屋, 1854 (嘉永 7). jb. 2 f., 37 × 103cm.

c. Hibiya-Kondō, Naikaku, Sonkeikaku, Tōdai-Nanki, Ueno.

3193 —— (Kaiji Shiryō Sōsho, v. XIII).

3194 Jōzan 錠山

Kita Meriken Gasshūkoku-kō 北米利堅合衆國考 (An Account of North America), [1854?]. jb. 1 v.

cf. Kaikoku, pp. 71, 407.

ms. Ayuzawa, Naikaku, Tohoku-Kano.

3195 —— (Shun'urō Sōsho).

3196 Kōyama Gendaiyu 向山源太夫
Setsuban Nempyō 接蠻年表(Chronological Table of the Arrival of Foreigners) compiled by Gūdō Shoshi 偶堂處士, jb. 2 vols.
cf. Asahi, p. 80.
ms. Iwase.

3197 Kyūyaku Zensho 舊約全書 *Chiu-yüeh Ch'üan-shu* (Complete Books of the Old Testament), Shanghai 墨海書館, 1854 (咸豐 4). wb. 1 v., 20cm.
c. Tōhoku.

3198 —— Hongkong, 1855 (咸豐 5). cb. 2 vols., 20cm.
c. Keiō, Tōhoku.

3199 —— Shanghai 墨海書館, 1858 (咸豐 8). cb. 3 vols., 21cm.
c. Aoyama, Kichu, Tenri, Waseda, Yoshida.

3199b —— Shanghai 墨海書館, 1859 (咸豐 9). cb. 3 vols., 23cm.
c. Aoi, Doshisha, Yutoku.

3200 —— Hongkong, 1861 (咸豐 11). cb. 3 vols.
c. Seikadō.

3201 —— Shanghai 美華書館, 1863 (同治 2). cb. 3 vols., 24cm.
c. Kobejo, Tōhoku.

3202 —— Shanghai 美華書館, 1863-4 (同治 2-3). cb. 4 vols., 30cm.
c. ICU, JBS, Kichu, Kobejo Ōtani, Rikkyō, Seikadō, Tōhoku, Tokyoshin, Yoshida.

3203 —— Shanghai 美華書館, 1864 (同治 3). cb. 6 vols., 15cm.
c. Tenri.

3204 —— Hongkong 英華書院, 1864-5 (同治 3-4). cb. 7 vols., 27cm.
c. Tenri, Tōhoku, Tokyoshin.

3205 —— Shanghai 美華書館, 1865 (同治 4). wb. 3 vols., 14cm.
c. Dōshisha, Gakushūin, Kompira, Narita, Waseda, Yoshida.

3206 —— Hongkong 英華書院, 1865-6 (同治 4-5). cb. 3 vols., 27cm.
c. Tenri.

3206b —— Hongkong 英華書院, 1866-67 (同治 5-6). cb. 3 vols., 20cm.
c. Yoshida.

3207 —— Shanghai 美華書館, 1868 (同治 7). cb. 3 vols., 18cm.
c. Aoyama, Ōtani.

3207b —— Peking 美華書院, 1874 (同治 13). cb. 3 vols.
c. Tokyoshin.

3208 —— Shanghai 美華書院, 1875(光緒 1). cb. 1 v., 833f.
c. Tokyoshin.

3208b —— Shanghai 美華書館, 1880 (光緒 6). cb. 3 vols.
c. Kansei.

3209 —— Shanghai 墨海書館, 1889 (光緒 15). cb. 2 vols., 21cm.
c. Kōbejo.

3210 * Kunten Kyūyaku Zensho 訓點舊約全書 (Complete Books of the Old Testament), construed from Chinese into Jap., Yokohama 米國聖書會社, 1883 (明治 16). wb. 2 vols., 20cm.
c. Dōshisha, Hibiya-Ichimura, Kichū, Kōbejo, Tōdai, Tokyoshin, Waseda, Yoshida

3211 —— Yokohama 大英國聖書會社, 1883 (明治 16). wb. 3 vols., 20cm.
c. Aoi, Kansei, Yoshida.

3211b —— Yokohama 北英國聖書會社, 1883 (明治 16). wb. 3 vols., 20cm.
c. JBS, Tokyoshin (v. II only).
note: See Pt. II on other editions in Japan.

3212 Macgowan, Daniel Jerome, ABF. 馮高温 (1814–1893)
Chūgai Shimpō 中外新報 *Chung-wai Shin-pao* (Chinese and Foreign Gazette), edited by D. J. Macgowan and Elias B. Inslee, PN. 應思理, Hongkong 1854 (道光 24).
note: Issued semi-monthly.
cf. Ozawa, p. 198; Wylie, p. 133.

3213 —— Edo [Tokyo] 萬屋, 1858–59 (安政 5–萬延 1), jb. 13 vols.
cf. Ozawa, pp. 216, 220.
c. Naikaku, Ueno.

3214 Martin, William Alexander Parsons, PN. 丁韙良 (1827–1916)
Tendō Sogen 天道溯原 *T'ien-tao Suo-yüan* (Evidences of Christianity), Ningpo 1854 (咸豐 4). cb. 3 vols.
cf. Ozawa, p. 196; Saeki-Shinchō, pp. 503–515; Wylie, pp. 204–205; Yoshida Tora 吉田寅, "Tendō Sogen to sono Fukyū" (*Shichō*, n. 61), Tōkyō 1956.

3215 —— revised ed., Ningpo 1858 (咸豐 8). cb. 3 vols.

3216 —— Ningpo 1860 (咸豐 10). cb. 1 v., 10, 22, 40, 46f., 25cm.
c. Aoi.

3217 —— Shanghai 美華書館, 1867 (同治 6). cb. 1 v., [6], 4, 116f., 24cm.
c. ICU, Keiō, Ōtani, Toyo.
ms. Ōtani.

3218 —— Shanghai 美華書館, 1869 (同治 8). cb. 1 v., [5], 3, 48f., 20cm.
c. Aoyama, Doshisha, Ebisawa, Hatano, Kichū, Jinshu, Naikaku, Narita, Ōsaka, Seikadō, Sophia, Taishō, Tenri, Tōhoku-Kanō, Waseda, Yoshida.

3219 —— Shanghai 美華書館, 1872 (同治 11). cb. 1 v.
c. Nagasaki.

3220 —— Peking 華北書會, 1887 (光緒 13). cb. 1v., 4, 3, 2, 70f., 20cm.
c. Doshisha-Niishima.

3221 —— Shanghai 美華書館, 1899 (光緒 25). cb. 1 v., 1, 16, 27, 30f., 21cm.
ms. Tokyoiku.

3222 —— Shanghai 美華書館, 1917 (民國 6). cb. 1 v., 2, 3, 6, 16, 22, 30, 6f., 20cm.
c. Kichū.

3223 * Kunten Tendō Sogen 訓點天道溯原 (Tendō Sogen, construed from Chinese into Japanese), [by Nakamura Masanao 中村正直], Tokyo 敬虔社, [n.d.]. jb. 3 vols., 24cm.

cf. Ozawa, p. 225.

c. Aoyama, Dōshisha-Niishima, Yoshida.

3224 —— Tokyo 山田俊藏, 1875 (明治 8). jb. 3 vols., 24cm.

c. Aoyama, Ebisawa, Kichū, Tanaka, Tōdai, To-kyoiku, Ueno, Waseda, Yoshida.

3225 —— Tokyo 山田俊藏, 1877 (明治 10). jb. 1 v., [6], 112f., 24cm.

c. Aoyama, Ebisawa, Hatano, Hibiya-Kaga, Kana-zawa-Kadō, Keiō, Kichū, Kyūdai-Butsuri, Tenri, Tōyō, Yoshida.

3226 —— Yokohama 倫敦聖教書類會社, 1880 (明治 13). jb. 1 v., [4], 81f., 22cm.

c. Hatano, Kansei, Kompira, Rikkyō, Tōhoku-Sūgaku, Tokyoshin, Waseda, Yoshida.

3227 —— Yokohama 倫敦聖教書類會社, 1881 (明治 14). jb. 1 v., [4], 81f., 22cm.

c. Aoyama, Ebisawa, Dōshisha-Niishima, Hatano, ICU, Gakushūin, Keiō, Kichu, Nagasaki, Narita, Oda, Taishō, Tenri, Yoshida.

3228 —— Yokohama 倫敦聖教書類會社, 1882 (明治 15). jb. 1 v., [4], 81f., 23cm.

c. Yoshida.

3229 —— Yokohama 倫敦聖教書類會社, 1886 (明治 19). jb. 1 v., [4], 81f., 23cm.

c. Aoyama, Dōshisha, Murakami, Tenri, Tokyoshin.

3230 —— Yokohama 倫敦聖教書類會社, 1886 (明治 19). wb. 1 v., [8], 161p., 20cm.

c. Yoshida.

3231 —— Yokohama 倫敦聖教書類會社, 1887 (明治 20). wb. 1 v., [8], 161p., 20cm.

c. Aoyama, Ebisawa, Dōshisha, Kōbejo, Tenri, Tōdai-Nanki, Yoshida.

3232 —— Yokohama 倫敦聖教書類會社, 1889 (明治 22). wb. 1 v., [8], 161p., 19cm.

c. Dōshisha, Hatano, Tenri.

3233 —— Yokohama 倫敦聖教書類會社, 1896 (明治 29). wb. 1v., [8], 161p., 19cm.

c. Tenri.

See also Pt. II. on the Japanese translations.

3234 * Tendō Sogen Chokkai 天道溯原直解 T'ien-tao Suo-yüan Chih-chieh (Exposition of the Tendō Sogen), by J. S. Burdon 包爾騰, [n.p.], 1870 (同治 9). cb. 1 v., 5, 15, 21, 30f., 24cm.

c. Seikadō.

3234b —— Peking 華北書會, 1883 (光緒 9). cb. 1 v., 27, 40, 57f., 23cm.

c. Saba.

3235 —— Shanghai 美華書館, 1890 (光緒 16). cb. 1 v., 5, 15, 21, 30f., 26cm.

c. Tōyō.

3236 Medhurst, Walter Henry, LM. 麥都思 (1796–1857)

Tenchijinron 天地人論 T'ien-ti-jen-lun (Heaven, Earth and Man), Shanghai 1850

(道光 30). cb. 1 v., 9f.

cf. Wylie, p. 33.

note: Revised ed. of his Ron Fukushin no Ri 論復新之理, Lun fu-hsin Chih-li, nos. 2946–48.

3237 —— Shanghai 1854 (咸豊 4). cb. 1 v.

3238 —— Shanghai 1855 (咸豊 5). cb. 1 v.

3239 —— Hongkong 1869 (同治 8). cb. 1 v.

c. Tōhoku.

3240 Medhurst, Walter Henry, LM. 麥都思 (1796–1857)

Yakaku Monnanki 野客問難記 Yeh-k'o Wen-nan chi (Customs among the Chinese), Shanghai 1854 (咸豊 4). cb. 1 v., 7f.

cf. Wylie, p. 28.

note: The original edition was entitled Shin Min Sōbo no Ron 清明掃墓之論, Ting-Ming Sao-mu chih lun, Batavia 1826.

3241 —— Shanghai 1863 (同治 2). cb. 1 v.

3242 Miyazaki Narumi 宮崎成身

Kempō Ruishū 憲法類集 (Classified Collection of Laws), 1854 (安政 1). jb. 15 vols.

cf. Kokushi, p. 88.

ms. Naikaku.

3243 Nagata Nankei 永田南溪

Kaigai Jimbutsushū 海外人物輯 (Well Known Foreign People), compiled by N. Nagata, Edo [Tokyo], 1854 (嘉永 7). jb. 2 vols.

cf. Kaikoku, pp. 336–338.

c. Okada, Waseda.

3244 Nelson, Robert, PE. 孫

Kyūyakusho Sōseiki 舊約書創世記 Chiu-yüeh-shu Ch'uang-shih-chi (Genesis), Shang-hai 1854 (咸豊 4). wb. 1 v., 94p.

cf. Wylie, p. 213.

3245 —— Hongkong 1873 (同治 12). cb. 1v.

c. Tōhoku.

3246 —— 1886 (光緒 12). cb. 1 v.

c. Tōhoku.

3247 Nagasaki-kō e Igirisu Gunsen Torai Shokan Wage narabini Mizuno Chikugono-Kami Ōsetsu 長崎港江英吉利軍船渡來書翰和解並水野筑後守應接 (Notes on the Arrival of English Warships), 1854 (安政 1). jb. 1 v.

ms. Hibiya-Kondō.

3248 Seki Ransai 關 蘭齋

Kaisei Kaigai Shotō Zusetsu 改正海外諸島圖說 (Illustrations of Foreign Islands, revised), Edo [Tokyo] 弘道軒, 1854 (嘉永 7). jb. 1 v., 18cm.

note: Quotes the Kon'yo Gaiki (See n. 1321).

cf. Kaikoku, pp. 338–339.

ms. Hibiya-Kondō.

3249 Smith, George, CE. 四美

Yaso Seikyō Tōkokubun 耶蘇聖教禱告文 Yeh-su Sheng-chiao Tao-kao-wen (Christian

Prayers), Hongkong 聖保羅書院, 1854 (咸豊
4). cb. 1 v., 21f., 26cm.
cf. Wylie, p. 142.
c. Ōtani.

3250　Taylor, Charles M.D., MEF. 戴
Yaso Rairekiden 耶蘇來歷傳 *Yeh-su Lai-li-chuan* (Life of Jesus Christ), Ningpo, 1854
(咸豊 4). cb. 1 v., 164f.
cf. Ozawa, p. 200; Wylie, p. 193.

3251　Tokugawa Nariaki 德川齋昭 (1800–1860)
Keizankō Kempaku 景山公建白 (Written
Memorials of Prince Keizan Nariaki Toku-gawa, Lord of Mito), [Edo] 1854 (嘉永 7).
jb. 1 v., 43f., 28cm.
note: Contains a memorial and another note about
excluding foreigners and Christianity.
c. Ebisawa, Ishin, Kompira.
ms. Kyūdai-Ogino.

3252　Tsuda Masamichi 津田正路
Ikoku Ōrai Ryakufu 異國往來略譜 (Short
Chronology of Foreign Intercourse), 1854
(安政 1). jb. 3 vols.
cf. Asahi, p. 80.
ms. Naikaku, Kōbe Keidai, Ueno.

3253　Yokoi Shōnan 橫井小楠 (1809–1869)
Iryo Ōsetsu Taii 夷虜應接大意 (Outline
on the Reception of Foreigners), 1854 (安
政 1). jb. 1 v.
3254　—— (Shōnan Ikō).

3255　Yoshida Shōin 吉田松蔭 (1830–1859)
Kaikoroku 回顧録 or Sangatsu Nijūshichi
Yoru no Ki 三月二十七夜記 (Account of the
night of the 27th, Third Month), 1854
(安政 1). jb. 1 v.
note: This was the night that Yoshida had planned
to escape abroad but was captured.
3256　—— (Dai-Nippon Shisō Zenshū,
v. XVII).

1855

3257　Aizawa Seishi 會澤正志 (1782–1863)
Bugyosaku 侮禦策 (Policy against Foreign
Contempt), 1855 (安政 2). jb. 1 v.

3258　Bettelheim, Bernard John, LNM.
伯德令 (1811–1870)
Pōro Ki Rōmajin-sho 保羅寄羅馬人書 *Pao-lo chi Lo-ma-jen shu* (The Epistle of St. Paul
to the Romans), Hongkong 1855 (咸豊 5).
wb. 1 v., 38f., 24cm.
c. Ichikawa, Tenri.

3259　Bettelheim, Bernard John, LNM.
伯德令 (1811–1870)
Rukaden Fukuinsho 路加傳福音書 (The
Gospel according to St. Luke), Hongkong
1855 (咸豊 5). cb. 1 v. 93f., 29cm.
cf. Ueda, pp. 1–2; Toyoda, p. 678.
c. Daitokyū, Tenri, Tōyō, Ueda (destroyed).
3260　—— Hongkong 1858. cb. 1 v., 99f.,
30cm.
cf. Ozawa, p. 191; Kadowaki, pp. 8–10; Toyoda,
pp. 678–7681.
c. Aoyama, Dōshisha-Shingaku, Ōsaka, Ōtani, Ten-ri, Tōhoku.
3261　—— Wien, Adolf Holzhauzen 阿度
留布保流都方前, 1873. wb. 1 v., 86f., 18cm.
cf. Kadowaki, p. 9.
c. Aoyama, Seikadō, Sophia, Tanaka, Tenri.

3262　Bettelheim, Bernard John, LNM.
伯德令 (1811–1870)
Seisa Genkōroku 聖差言行録 (The Acts),
Hongkong 1855 (咸豊 5). wb. 1 v., 90f.,
30cm.
cf. Kadowaki, p. 9.
c. Tenri.
3263　* Shitogyōden 使徒行傳, repr. by A.
Pfizmaier, Wien 1874. wb. 1 v., 83f., 18 cm.
c. Aoyama, Seikadō, Tenri, Tokyōshin.

3264　Bettelheim, Bernard John, LNM.
伯德令 (1811–1870)
Yohaneden Fukuinsho 約翰傳福音書 (The
Gospel according to St. John), Hongkong
1855 (咸豊 5). cb. 1 v., 66f., 30cm.
cf. Kadowaki, pp. 7–10; Ueda, p. 2.
c. Tanaka, Tenri.
3265　—— Hongkong 1858. jb. 1 v.
3266　—— Wien, Adolf Holzhauzen 阿度
留布保流都方前, 1873. wb. 1 v., 65f., 18cm.
c. Aoyama, Dōshisha-Shingaku, JBS, Seikadō,
Tokyoshin.

3267　カラメール
Shinyaku Gasshūkoku Shōshi 新譯合衆國
小誌 (Brief History of the U.S.A.), tr. by
Kozeki Takahiko 小關高彦, Edo [Tokyo],
知芳堂 1855 (安政 2). jb. 2 vols.
cf. Kaikoku, pp. 409–410.
c. Ayuzawa, Kyōto, Naikaku.

3268　Chōnen 超然 (1792–1868)
Gohō Shōhin 護法小品 (Short Apology
for Buddhism), 華雲閣 1855 (安政 2). jb.
1 v., 16f., 23cm.
c. Ōtani.

3269　Crawford, Tarleton P. SBS. 高茅丕
Sanshinshi 讚神詩 *Tsan-Shen-shih* (Hymn
in Praise of God), Shanghai 1855 (咸豊 5).
cb. 1 v.
cf. Ozawa, p. 207; Wylie, p. 214.

3270 Fujimori Kōan 藤森弘庵 (1799–1862)

Shin Seidan 新政談 (New Discourse on Politics), 1855 (安政 2). jb. 5 vols.

cf. Kokushi, p. 153.

3271 —— (Nippon Keizai Taiten, v. XLV).

3272 Hamberg, Theodore 戴文光 (– 1854)

Yaso Shinto Juku Sōron 耶蘇信徒受苦總論 *Yeh-su Hsin-t'u Shou-k'u tsung-lun* (General Account of the Christian Martyrs), [n.p.], 1855 (咸豐 5). cb. 1 v., 44f., 26cm.

cf. Wylie, p. 160.

c. Ōtani, Seikadō.

3273 Hobson, Benjamin, LM. 合信 (1816–1873)

Hakubutsu Shimpen 博物新篇 *Po-wu Hsin-p'ien* (New Book of Natural History), Canton, 1855 (咸豐 5). cb. 1 v. 132f.

cf. Ozawa, p. 186; Wylie, pp. 126–127.

c. Shinken, Tōhoku-Kanō.

3274 —— Edo [Tokyo] 1864 (元治 1). jb. 3 vols., 25cm.

cf. Ozawa, p. 213.

c. Iwase, Naikaku, Tenri, Tōdai-Nanki, Yokoshidai-Igaku, Yoshida.

3275 —— Tokyo 福田氏, 1872 (明治 5). jb. 3 vols., 26cm.

c. Imoto, Jingū, Narita, Shinken, Waseda-Ogura, Yoshida.

3276 —— Tokyo 福田氏, 1874 (明治 7). jb. 3 vols., 26cm.

c. Gakushiin, Naikaku, Tōhoku-Kanō.

3277 * Bettō Hakubutsu Shimpen 鼇頭 博物新篇 (*Hakubutsu Shimpen*, Noted), annotated by Komuro Seiichi 小室誠一, Tokyo 柳絮書屋, 1876 (明治 9). jb. 3 vols., 26cm.

cf. Ozawa, p. 214.

c. Jingū, Kompira, Naikaku, Nichidai-Ueda, Ueno.

3278 * Hakubutsu Shimpen Chūkai 博物新篇註解 (*Hakubutsu Shimpen* with Notes), by Fukuda Keigyō 福田敬業, Tokyo 1876 (明治 9). jb. 4 vols.

c. Jingū, Naikaku.

3279 * Hakubutsu Shimpen Engi 博物新篇演義 (Notes on the *Hakubutsu Shimpen*) by Horino Ryōhei 堀野良平, 1876 (明治 9).

3280 * Hakubutsu Shimpen Kibun 博物新篇記聞 (Notes on the *Hakubutsu Shimpen*) by Ishizaka Kensō 石坂堅壮 and Kanzaki Yūrin 神崎有隣, 1875 (明治 8). jb. 3 vols.

c. Kompira.

3281 * Hakubutsu Shimpen Kōgi 博物新篇講義 (Lecture on the *Hakubutsu Shimpen*) by Kondō Keizō 近藤圭造, Tokyo 1876 (明治 9). jb. 4 vols.

c. Tōdai-Kyōiku.

3282 * Hakubutsu Shimpen Yakuge 博物新篇譯解 (Translation of the *Hakubutsu Shimpen*) by Ōmori Shūzō 大森秀三, Tokyo 菊翠居, 1868–70 (明治 1–3). jb. 5 vols., 18cm.

c. Keiō, Kichū, Okada, Sonkeikaku.

3283 —— Tokyo 青山書店, 1874 (明治 7). jb. 5 vols., 18cm.

c. Kichu, Kyōdai-Fujikawa, Narita.

3284 * Hyōchū Hakubutsu Shimpen 標註博物新篇 (*Hakubutsu Shimpen*, Noted), noted by Ajiro Ryōsuke 安代良輔, Tokyo 三府樓, 1877 (明治 10). jb. 3 vols.

c. Kompira, Naikaku.

3285 * Kampan Hakubutsu Shimpen 官板博物新篇 (Official Edition of the *Hakubutsu Shimpen*), construed from Chinese into Jap. by Kaiseijo 開成所, Edo [Tokyo] 老皂館, [n.d.]. jb. 3 vols., 26cm.

c. Ueno.

3286 Hongkong Cathedral

Tenshukyō Sōshū 天主教奏摺 *T'ien-chu-chiao Tsou che* (Memorials from the Catholic Church), Hongkong 天主堂, 1855 (咸豐 5). cb. 1 v., 20f.

c. Hibiya-Ichimura.

3287 Kunitomo Kojurō 國友戸十郎

Kunitomo Hōkan Kenyoroku 國朝砲煩權興録 (Report on Guns in Japan), 1855 (安政 2). jb. 1 v.

3288 Nagasaki Bugyō Todokegaki 長崎奉行届書 (Documents of the Magistrate [*Bugyō*] of Nagasaki) 1855 (安政 2). jb. 1 v.

ms. Sophia.

3289 オツトモンヱセ

Oranda Nempyō 倭蘭年表 (Chronological Table according to a Dutch Book), tr. by Kaizan Mukaishi 魁山無懐子, [n.p.], 1855 (安政 2). jb. 2 vols., 26cm.

cf. Kaikoku, p. 383.

c. Ueno.

3290 —— (Bummei Genryū Sōsho, v. III).

3291 Oshida Shimotsuke-no-kami 押田下野守

Isen Torai Nempyō 異船渡來年表 (Chronology of the Arrivals of Foreign Ships). 1855 (安政 2). jb. 14 vols.

ms. Ueno.

3292 Ōtsuki Seiban 大槻西盤 (1818–1857)

Ensei Kiryaku 遠西紀略 (Short History of Europe), [n.p.], 1855 (安政 2). jb. 2 vols., 27cm.

cf. Kaikoku, pp. 427–428.

c. Kyōto, Oda, Okada, Naikaku, Seishin.

3293 Quarterman, John Winn, PN. 赴
德明 (1821–)

Seikei Zuki 聖經圖記 *Sheng-ching t'u chi*
(Illustrated Stories from the Holy Bible),
Ningpo, 1855 (咸豊 5). cb. 1 v., 1, 38f.,
25cm.

cf. Ozawa, p. 192; Wylie, p. 159.

c. Dōshisha, Hatano, Kichū, Kōbejo, Naikaku, Seikadō, Taishō, Tenri, Tōdai-Nanki, Tōhoku-Kanō.

3294 —— [n.p.], 1894 (光緒 20). cb. 1 v.,
[1], 38f., 25cm.

c. Aoyama, Dōshisha-Niishima, Tenri.

3295 * Keimō Seikei Zuki 啓蒙聖經圖記,
construed from Chinese into Jap. by
Mineta Fūkō 嶺田楓江, [1864?]. jb. 2 vols.

cf. Asahi, p. 103.

orig. ms. Minetas.

3296 Seimiya Hidekata 清宮秀堅 (1809–
1879)

Shinsen Nempyō 新撰年表 (New Chronological Table), [n.p.], 1855 (安政 2). jb.
1 v., [9], 45, [1]f., 27cm.

cf. Kaikoku, pp. 456–457.

note: Chronological table from the time of Adam
and Eve.

c. T. Ōkubo.

3297 Shinyaku Zensho 新約全書 *Hsin-
yüeh Ch'üan-shu* (New Testament), Hongkong, 1855 (咸豊 5). cb. 1 v., 240f., 21cm.

cf. Wylie, p. 35.

c. Keiō, Tōhoku.

3298 —— Shanghai 墨海書館, 1858 (咸豊
8). cb. 1 v., 147f., 21cm.

c. Aoyama, Yūtoku.

3299 —— Shanghai 墨海書館, 1858 (咸豊
8). cb. 4 vols.

c. Waseda.

3300 —— Ningpo 華花印書館, 1859 (咸豊
9). cb. 1 v., 25cm.

c. Aoi, Tōhoku-Kanō.

3301 —— Shanghai 墨海書館, 1861 (咸豊
11). cb. 3 vols., 21cm.

c. Yoshida.

3302 —— Shanghai 美華書館, 1863 (同治
2). cb. 1 v., [1], 253f., 28cm.

c. Aoyama, ICU, Jingū, Ōtani, Tōhoku, Waseda,
Yoshida.

3303 —— Shanghai 美華書館, 1864 (同治
3). wb. 1 v., 2, 384p., 14cm.

c. Aoyama, Dōshisha, Ebisawa, Gakushūin, Kompira, Naikaku, Tenri, Waseda.

3304 —— Hongkong 英華書院, 1865–66
(同治 4–5). cb. 3 vols., 27cm.

c. Tenri.

3305 —— Hongkong 英華書院, 1866 (同治
5). cb. 2 vols., 30cm.

c. Rikkyō, Tōhoku, Tokyoshin.

3305b —— Hongkong 英華書院, 1866 (同治
5), cb. 1 v., 104, 92f., 19cm.

c. Yoshida.

3306 —— Shanghai 美華書局, 1866 (同治
5). cb. 1 v., [1], 185f., 17cm.

c. ICU, JBS, Kyōdai, Ōtani, Tenri, Tohoku, Tokyoshin, Yoshida.

3307 —— Shanghai 美華書館, 1869 (同治
8). cb. 1 v., [3], 144f., 19cm.

c. JBS, Kichū.

3308 —— Shanghai 美華書館, 1869 (同治
8). cb. 2 vols., 18cm.

c. Aoyama, Dōshisha, Hatano, Kōbejo, Seikadō,
Tenri, Yoshida.

3309 —— in the mandarin dialect, Shanghai 美華書局, 1872 (同治 11). cb. 1 v., 304f.,
18cm.

c. Kichū.

3310 —— in the mandarin dialect, Peking 東交民巷耶蘇堂, 1872 (同治 11). cb. 5 vols.,
26cm.

c. Rikkyō.

3310b —— Hongkong 英華書院, 1873 (同治
12). cb. 1 v., 187f., 20cm.

c. Yoshida.

3311 —— Shanghai 美華書館, 1875 (光緒
1). cb. 1 v., 175f., 16cm.

c. Yoshida.

3312 —— Shanghai 申報館, 1880 (光緒 6).
cb. 1 v., 175f., 17cm.

c. Aoyama, Kansei.

3313 —— in the mandarin dialect, [n.
p.]., 1883 (光緒 9). cb. 2 vols., 23cm.

c. Tōhoku.

3314 —— Shanghai 美華書館, 1884 (光緒
10). cb. 2 vols.

c. Kansei.

3315 —— Shanghai 墨海書館, 1887 (光緒
13). cb. 1 v., 205f., 23cm.

c. Ueda (destroyed).

3316 —— Fuhchow 英華書局, 1895 (光緒
21). cb. 1 v., [1], 113f., 19cm.

c. Kichū.

3317 —— Shanghai 美華書局, 1898 (光緒
24). cb. 1 v., 27cm.

note: Each books bound in one volume.

c. Tōhoku.

3317b —— in the mandarin dialect, [n.p.].,
聖書公會, 1902 (光緒 28). cb. 1 v., [1], 548p.,
19cm.

c. JBS.

3318 —— Shanghai 米國聖經書局, 1903 (光
緒 29). wb. 1 v., 664p., 21cm.

c. Aoyama.

3319 * Kunten Shinyaku Zensho 訓點新
約全書 (New Testament construed from
Chinese into Jap.), Yokohama 米國聖書會社,
1879 (明治 12). wb. 1 v., [2], 586p., 20cm.

c. Aoyama, Tokyoshin, Yoshida.

See also Pt. II on other Jap. editions.

3320 Stronach, John, LM. 施敦力
(1810–1879)

Yasokyō Wakumon 耶蘇教或問 *Yeh-su-chiao Huo-wen* (Questions about Christian Doctrine), Shanghai, 1855 (咸豊 5). cb. 1 v., 81f.
cf. Ozawa, p. 199; Wylie, p. 106.
ms. Ueno.

3321 —— Hongkong 英華書院, 1863 (同治 2). cb. 1 v., 35f.

3322 —— Hongkong 英華書院, 1869 (同治 8). cb. 1 v., 37f., 20cm.
c. Aoyama, Hatano, Kichū, Tōhoku, Waseda, Yoshida.

3323 —— Hongkong 英華書院, 1871 (同治 10). cb. 1 v.
c. Seikadō, Tōdai-Nanki, Waseda.

3324 Tokugawa Akitake 徳川昭武 (1853–1910)
Sokkyohen 息距篇 (Collections of Anti-Christian Books), jb. 20 vols.
cf. Shimmura-Namban I, pp. 395–397; Tenri-Jap. II, p. 86.
contents: v. I. Hōrei 法令 (Laws) 1546–1830.
  II–VII. Jijitsu 事實 (Documents) 1529–1829.
  IX. Haiya 排耶. Razanbunshū 羅山文集, Kirishitan Monogatari 切支丹物語.
  X. Kirishitan Raichō Jikki 切支丹來朝實記.
  XI–XII. Tembun Batsuroku 天文末録.
  XIII. Sangan Yokō 三眼餘考 by Aizawa Seishi 會澤正志.
  XIV. Samidareshō 五月雨抄 by Miura Baien 三浦梅園.
  XV. Ha-Kirishitan 破吉利支丹 by Suzuki Shōsan 鈴木正三, Ha-Daiusu 破提宇子 by Fukan Fabian 不干ハビアン.
  XVI. Hai-Kirishitan 排吉利支丹, Taiji Jashūron 對治邪執論 by Sessō 雪窓, Edo Monogatari 江戸物語.
  XVII–XVIII. Yaso Seibatsuki 耶蘇征伐記.
  XIX–XX. Shimabara Shimatsuki 島原始末記.
orig. ms. Shōkōkan.
ms. Naikaku, Tenri (vv. I–VIII only), Tōdai, Waseda.
phot. Sophia.

3325 Tsurumine Shigenobu 鶴峯戌申 (1788–1859)
Meriken Shinshi 米利幹新誌 (New Treatise on America), Edo [Tokyo], 春日樓, 1855 (安政 2). jb. 5 vols., 26cm.
cf. Kaikoku, pp. 72–73.
c. Ayuzawa, Kyūdai-Bunka, Rikkyō.
ms. Hibiya-Kondō, Kyōto.

3326 Uehara Masakuni 上原昌邦
Fūsetsugaki 風說書 (Report on Foreign Countries), 1855 (安政 2). jb. 1 v.
cf. Asahi, p. 43.
ms. Hakodate.

1856

3327 Ajiro Hironori 足代弘訓 (1784–1856)
Kirishitan Jikki 切支丹實記 (The Facts about Christianity). jb. 1 v.
orig. ms. Iwase.

3328 Ajiro Hironori 足代弘訓 (1784–1856)
Kirishitan no Koto 切支丹の事 (On Christianity). jb. 1 v.
ms. Iwase.

3329 Cobbold, Robert Henry, CE. 哥伯播義
Shōgaku Seishū 小學正宗 *Hsiao-hsüeh Cheng-tsung* (Instruction on the True Religion), Shanghai 1856 (咸豊 6). cb. 1 v., 1, 29f., 20cm.
cf. Ozawa, p. 196; Wylie, p. 183.
c. ICU, Kichū, Ōtani.

3330 Cumming, Seneca, ABC. 簡明 (1817–1856)
Shindō Sōron 眞道總論 *Chen-tao Tsung-lun* (Introduction to the True Way), Fuhchow, 1856 (咸豊 6) cb. 1 v. 6f.
cf. Ozawa, p. 194; Wylie, p. 179.

3331 Cumming, Seneca, ABC. 簡明 (1817–1856)
Shinshin Sōron 眞神總論 *Chen-shen Tsung-lun* (Discourse on the True God), Fuhchow 1856 (咸豊 6). cb. 1 v., 6f.
cf. Wylie, p. 179.
note: Revised ed. of no. 3046.

3332 —— Shanghai 美華書館, 1863 (同治 2). cb. 1 v., 7f., 16cm.
c. Ōtani.

3333 —— 1868 (同治 7). cb. 1 v., 5f., 16cm.
c. Saba.

3334 Genaehr, Ferdinand, RM. 葉納清 (—1864)
Byōshuku Mondō 廟祝問答 *Miao-chu wen-ta* (Dialogue with an Idol Keeper), Hongkong, 1856 (咸豊 6). cb. 1 v.
cf. Wylie, p. 162.

3335 —— Hongkong 英華書院, 1871 (同治 10). cb. 1 v., 8f., 19cm.
c. Naikaku, Saba.

3336 —— Yang-ch'eng 羊城小書會, 1889 (光緒 15). cb. 1 v., 16f., 21cm.
c. Tōhoku.

3337 —— tr. into Jap. by John H. Ballagh, RCA. and Okuno Masatsuna 奥野昌綱, Yokohama, [n.d.]. jb. 2 vols., 23cm.
c. Aoyama, Ebisawa, Kichū.

3338 —— (Meiji Bunka Zenshū, v. XI).

3339 —— Yokohama, [n.d.]. jb. 1 v., 31f., 19cm.
c. Aoyama, Ebisawa, Kichu, Kadowaki, Kōbejo, Tokyoshin, Yoshida.

3340 —— Yokohama 倫敦聖教書類會社, 1879 (明治 12).

3341 —— Yokohama 倫敦聖教書類會社, 1882 (明治 15). wb. 1 v., 60p., 19cm.
c. Aoyama, Kichu, Tenri.

3342 —— Yokohama 倫敦聖教書類會社, 1884 (明治 17). wb. 1 v., 50p., 19cm.
c. Aoyama, Kichu.

3343 —— Yokohama 倫敦聖教書類會社, 1885 (明治 18). wb. 1 v., 50p., 19cm.
c. Aoyama, Waseda.

3344 —— Yokohama 倫敦聖教書類會社, 1888 (明治 21). wb. 1 v.
c. Kadowaki.

3345 —— Tokyo 奥野昌綱, 1890 (明治 23). wb. 1v., 41p., 18cm.
c. Dōshisha, Tanaka.

3346 —— Tokyo 基督教書類會社, 1898 (明治 31). wb. 1 v., 41p., 21cm.
c. Kōbejo.

3347 Gesshō 月性 (1817–1858)
Buppō Gokokuron 佛法護國論 (Defense of Japan by Buddhism), [n.p.], 1856 (安政 3). jb. 1 v. 19f., 26cm.
c. Aoyama, Ebisawa, Kyōto, Ueno.

3348 —— [n.p.], [n.d.]. jb. 1 v., 15f., 17cm.
c. Hibiya-Inoue.

The Trip of Hikozō and Sentarō to America, 1850–1856

3349 Banshūjin Beikoku Hyōryū Shimatsu 播州人米國漂流始末 (History of the Ship of Harima drifting to America). jb. 1 v.

3350 —— (Ikoku Hyōryū Kidanshū).

3351 Hori Hiroaki 堀熙明 (1825–1864)
Eiryokumaru Hyōryū Kidan 榮力丸漂流奇談 (Strange Tales of Eiryokumau and how it drifted about), 1856 (安政 3). jb. 2 vols.
note: Contains the record of Sentarō 仙太郎 and Joseph Hikozō 彦藏.
ms. Kyōdai-Kokushi,

3352 —— (Kaihyō Sōsho, v. III).

3353 Hobson, Benjamin, LM. 合信 (1816–1873)
Shihen 詩篇 Shih-p'ien (Hymns), Canton, [1856?]. 1 sheet.
cf. Ozawa, p. 193; Wylie, p. 127.

3354 Keith, Caroline Phebe, PE. 吉 (1827–   )
Kyōri Jitsuroku 享利實録 Heng-li Shih-lu (Henry and his Bearer), Shanghai 1856 (咸豊 6). cb. 1 v., 35f.
cf. Wylie, p. 212.

3355 —— Shanghai 1867 (同治 6). cb. 1 v.
c. Saba.

3356 Keith, Cleveland, PE., 吉 (1827–)
Shitogyōden 使徒行傳 Shih-t'u hsing-chuan (The Acts), tr. by C. Keith, Shanghai 1856 (咸豊 6). cb. 1 v., 60f.
cf. Ozawa, p. 195; Wylie, p. 211.

3357 Legge, James, LM. 理雅各 (1815–1897)
Chikan Keimō Jukuka 智環啓蒙熟課 Chih-huan Ch'i-meng Shu-k'o (Textbook of Western Learning), Hongkong 英華書院, 1856 (咸豊 6). cb. 1 v., 56f., 19cm.
note: The whole book has Christian flavor, especially lessons 192–200 which are completely Christian. The English text is given at the top of the page, and under it the Chinese translation.
cf. Ozawa, pp. 135–156, 217–219; Cordier-Sinica, col. 1687; Wylie, p. 120.

3358 —— Hongkong 英華書院, 1858 (咸豊 7). cb. 1 v., 55f., 19cm.
note: The Chinese title page lists the date of publication as the Seventh Year of Hsien Feng (咸豊), but the title page of the English part places the date at 1858.
c. Aoyama, Jinshū.

3359 —— Canton 1859 (咸豊 9). cb. 1 v., 51f.
note: Without the English text.

3360 —— Hongkong 英華書院, 1864 (同治 3). cb. 1 v., 4, 51f., 20cm.
c. Yoshida.

3361 * Honkoku Chikan Keimō Jukuka 飜刻智環啓蒙熟課 (The Chikan Keimo Jukuka construed from Chinese into Japanese) by Yanagawa Shunzō 柳河春三, Edo [Tokyo] 開物社, 1866 (慶應 2). jb. 1 v., [2], 51f., 19cm.
note: Based on the press of Hongkong, 1864.
cf. Ozawa, p. 217; Kaikoku, p. 163.
c. Ebisawa, Hatano, Ishin, Kyūdai-Butsuri, Okada, Sonkeikaku, Waseda, Yoshida.

3362 —— different ed. jb. 1 v., 23cm.
c. Ozawa.

3363 * Chikan Keimō 智環啓蒙, Numazu 沼津學校, 1870 (明治 3). jb. 1 v., [1], 48f., 18cm.
note: Based on the Hongkong edition of 1858, but excludes lessons 192–200 which concern Christianity.
c. Hatano.

3364 —— Kagoshima 鹿児島藩, 1870 (明治 3). jb. 1 v., 51f., 25cm.

3365 —— [n.p.], [n.d.]. jb. 1 v., 23cm.
cf. Ozawa, p. 218.

3366 —— construed from Chinese into Japanese by Kondō Makoto 近藤眞琴, Tokyo 攻玉社, 1877 (明治 10). wb. 1 v.
c. Ozawa.

3367 * Keimō Chie no Wa 啓蒙智恵乃環 (Japanese Translation of the *Chikan Keimō Jukuka*) tr. by Uryū Tora 瓜生寅, Tokyo 和泉屋, 1872 (明治 5). jb. 3 vols. 19cm.
note: Based on the Hongkong edition of 1864.
c. Ozawa, Saba, Tenri, Yoshida.

3368 —— Tokyo 和泉屋, 1873 (明治 6). jb. 3 vols., 19cm.
c. Ebisawa.

3369 —— Tokyo 和泉屋, 1874 (明治 7), 3rd ed. jb. 1 v., 2, 32, 37, 24f., 19cm.
c. Yoshida.

3370 —— Tokyo 和泉屋, 1874 (明治 7), 5th ed. jb. 3 vols., 19cm.
c. Kichu, Ozawa.

3371 —— Tokyo 和泉屋, 1875 (明治 8). jb. 3 vols., 19cm.
c. Ozawa.

3372 * Chikan Keimō Wage 智環啓蒙和解 (Japanese Translation of the *Chikan Keimō Jukuka*) by Hirose Wataru 廣瀬渡, and Nagata Tomonori 長田知儀, Kanazawa 石川縣學校, 1873 (明治 6). jb. 3 vols., 18cm.
cf. Ozawa, p. 219.
c. Ebisawa, Hatano, Kanazawa-Ujiie, Okada, Ozawa.

3373 * Chikan Keimō Zukai 智環啓蒙圖解 (Illustration of the *Chikan Keimō Jukuka*), compiled by Hashizume Kan'ichi 橋爪貫一, Tokyo 1872 (明治 5). jb. 1 v.
c. Murakami.

3374 * Jōtō Shōgaku Keimō Chie no Wa 上等小學啓蒙智恵乃環 (Textbook of the Higher Elementary Course, the *Chikan Keimō Jukuka*), by Uryū Tora 瓜生寅, Tokyo 1876 (明治 9). jb. 3 vols.
cf. Meiji Bunka Zenshū, v. XV, Tokyo 1929, p. 240.

3375 McCartee Divie Bethune, PN. 培端 (1820–1990)
Reikon-hen 靈魂篇 *Ling-hun-p'ien* (On the Soul), Ningpo, 1856 (咸豊 6). cb. 1 v., 26f.
cf. Wylie, p. 137 ; Ozawa, p. 190.

3376 —— Shanghai 美華書館, 1862 (同治 1). cb. 1 v., 36f., 18cm.
c. ICU, Ōtani.

3377 —— Shanghai 美華書館, 1868 (同治 7). cb. 1 v., 32f., 16cm.
note: Limited ed. of 100 copies.
c. Waseda.

3378 —— Shanghai 美華書館, 1872 (同治 11). cb. 1 v., 32f., 16cm.
c. Aoyama, Naikaku, Seikado, Yoshida.

3379 —— tr. into Jap. by Kiryū Issaku 霧生一作, Tokyo 1887 (明治 20). wb. 1 v., 3, [1], 85p., 19cm.
c. Aoyama.

3380 —— [Kiriu's translation] 2nd ed., [n.p.] 春祥堂, [n.d.]. wb. 1 v., 85p., 19cm.
c. Aoyama.

3381 McCartee, Divie Bethune, PN. 培端 (1820–1900)
Reikon Ki Yu Shintairon 靈魂貴於身體論 *Ling-hun kui-yü Shen-t'i-lun* (Treatise on the Worth of the Soul), Ningpo, [n.d.]. cb. 1 v., 4f.
cf. Wylie, p. 137.

3382 —— Shanghai 美華書館, 1862 (同治 1). 11th ed., cb. 1 v., 6f., 17cm.
c. Ōtani.

3383 —— Shanghai 美華書館, 1867 (同治 6). cb. 1 v.
c. Jinshu.

3384 Muirhead, William, LM. 慕維廉 (1822–1900)
Dai–Eikokushi 大英國志 *Ta-ying-ko-chih* (History of Great Britain), Shanghai 墨海書館, 1856 (咸豊 6). cb. 2 vols., 28cm.
cf. Ozawa, p. 230; Wylie, p. 169.
c. Hibiya-Inoue, Yoshida.

3385 —— (Goshū Rekkoku Shi-i).

3386 —— (Seigaku Taisei, v. IV).

3387 * Wakun Eikokushi 和訓英國志 construed from Chinese into Japanese, Nagato 温知社, 1861 (文久 1). jb. 8 vols., 23cm.
c. Kariya, Kyōto, Okada, Waseda.

3388 —— [n.p.] 和泉屋, 1861 (文久 1). jb. 8 vols., 26cm.

3389 Muirhead, William, LM. 慕維廉 (1822–1900)
Raishū Yaso 來就耶蘇 *Lai-chiu Yeh-su* (Come to Jesus), Shanghai, 1856 (咸豊 6). cb. 1 v. 34p.
cf. Wylie, p. 168.

3390 —— Shanghai 1861 (咸豊 11). cb. 1 v., 30f.

3391 —— Hongkong 1863 (同治 2). cb. 1 v., 27f.

3392 —— Nagasaki 長田屋, 1856 (安政 3). jb. 1 v., 35f., 23cm.
c. Ueda (destroyed).

3393 Muirhead, William, LM. 慕維廉 (1822–1900)
Tenjin Idō 天人異同, *T'ien-jen Yi-t'ung* (Analogy of Natural and Revealed Religion), Hongkong 英華書院, 1856 (咸豊 6). cb. 1 v., 6f., 20cm.
cf. Wylie, p. 169.
c. Ōtani.

3394 McCartee, Divie Bethune, PN. 培端 (1820–1900)

Seikei Ruisho 聖經類書, *Sheng-ching Lei-shu* (Collection of Scripture), Ningpo 華花聖經書房, 1856 (咸豊 6). cb. 2 vols.
cf. Wylie, p. 139; Ozawa, p. 192.
c. Naikaku.

3395 Ōtsuki Seiban 大槻西盤 (1818–1857)
Seiyō Nempyō 西洋年表 (Chronological Table of Western World History), 1856 (安政 3). jb. 1 v.
cf. Kaikoku, p. 456.
orig. ms. Ōtsuki.

3396 Reiyū 靈遊
Gohō Sakushin 護法策進, (Buddhist Apology against Western Learning and Christianity), [n.p.], 1856 (安政 3). jb. 1 v., 4, 11f., 26cm.
c. Ebisawa, Tōhoku-Kanō.

3397 Way, Richard Quarterman, PN. 褘理哲 (1819–1895)
Chikyū-setsu-ryaku 地球說略 *Ti-ch'iu Shuo lüeh* (Outline of World Geography), Ningpo 華花聖經書房, 1856 (咸豊 6). cb. 1 v. 114f., 6 maps, 25cm.
note: The original of this was published with the title *Chikyū Zusetsu* 地球圖説 *Ti-ch'iu t'u-shuo,* Ningpo 1848.
cf. Ozawa, pp. 197, 291–293; Kaikoku, pp. 158–159; Wylie, p. 140.
c. Seikadō, Shinken, Tenri, Yoshida.
3398 —— (Shōhōkosai Yochi Sōshō).
3399 —— construed from Chinese into Japanese by Mitsukuri Gempo 箕作阮甫, Edo [Tokyo] 老皁館, 1860 (萬延 1). jb. 3 vols., 26 cm.
cf. Ozawa, p. 291; Kaikoku, pp. 158–160, 325.
c. Ebisawa, Naikaku, Hibiya-Kondō, Keiō, Okada, Tenri, Tōdai-Nanki, Tōkyō Kagaku Museum, Tōhoku-Kanō, Ueno, Waseda, Yoshida.
3400 —— Edo [Tokyo] 萬屋, 1864 (元治 1). jb. 3 vols., 26cm.
c. Naikaku, Ueno, Waseda.
3401 —— Tokyo 萬屋, 1871 (明治 4). jb. 3 vols., 25cm.
c. Ebisawa.
3402 —— Tokyo, 1874 (明治 7). jb. 3 vols. 25cm.
cf. Osatake, p. 58.
3403 * Chikyūsetsu-ryaku Soshō 地球説略疏證 (A Treatise on the *Chikyū-setsu-ryaku*), by Mitsukuri Gempo 箕作阮甫. jb. 1 v., 43f., 23cm.
cf. Kaikoku, p. 361.
orig. ms. Mitsukuri.
3404 * Chikyūsetsu-ryaku Wage 地球説略和解 (Japanese Translation of the *Chikyū-setsu-ryaku*), tr. by Akazawa Tsunemichi 赤澤常道, Tokyo 甘泉堂, 1874 (明治 7). jb.

5 vols., 23cm.
cf. Kaikoku, p. 159.
c. Ayuzawa, Naikaku.
3405 * Chikyūsetsu-ryaku Yakuge 地球説略譯解 (Japanese Translation of the *Chikyū-setsu-ryaku*), tr. by Fukuda Keigyō 福田敬業, Tokyo 寶集堂, 1875 (明治 8). jb. 4 vols., 19cm.
cf. Kaikoku, pp. 159–160.
c. Naikaku.

3406 Way, Richard Quarterman, PN. 褘理哲 (1819–1895)
Yaso Monto Kinshin 耶蘇門徒金針 *Yeh-su men-t'u Chin-chen* (The Disciple's Guide), Ningpo, 1856 (咸豊 6). cb. 1 v., 27f.
cf. Ozawa, p. 200; Wylie, p. 140.
3407 —— 1871 (同治 10). cb. 1v.
c. Naikaku.

3408 Yamazaki Yoshinari 山崎美成 (1797–1856)
Kairoku 海録 (Memorandum). jb. 20 vols.
3409 —— pr. by the Kokusho Kankōkai 國書刊行會, Tokyo 1915 (大正 4).

1857

3410 Abe Masahiro 阿部正弘 (1819–1857)
Kaikyū Kiji 懐舊紀事 (Recollections).
cf. Kokushi, p. 43.
3411 * Abe Masahiro Jiseki 阿部正弘事蹟 (Life of Abe Masahiro) compiled by Hamano Shōkichi 濱野章吉, Tokyo 1899 (明治 32). wb. 1 v.

3412 Aizawa Seishi 會澤正忘 (1782–1863)
Gai Kōben 豈好辯 (Ideas which I cannot Suppress), Edo [Tokyo] 玉巖堂, 1857 (安政 4). jb. 1 v., 24, (3)f., 26cm.
cf. Tokushige-Seishin, p. 515.
c. Dōshisha, Ebisawa, Kichū, Jingū, Ryūkoku, Seishin, Tōdai-Nanki, Ueno.
3413 —— (Rinchi Sōsho, Gaihen).
3414 —— (Nippon Jurin Sōsho, v. IV).

3415 Defoe, Daniel (1660–1731)
Hyōkō Kiji 漂荒紀事 (Robinson Crusoe, Part I), tr. by Kuroda Kikuro 黒田鞠廬, 1857 (安政 4). jb. 3 vols.
cf. Shimmura-Namban I, pp. 514–515; Toyota-Eigaku, pp. 621–629.
ms. Shōkōkan, Waseda.
3416 —— (Bummei Genryū Sōsho, v. I).
3417 * Robinson Hyōkō Kiryaku 魯敏遜漂行紀略 (Abridged Translation of Robinson Crusoe), tr. by Yokoyama Yoshikiyo 横山由清, 瓊華書院, 1857 (安政 4). jb. 1 v., 15, 3f., 19cm.

cf. Shimmura-Namban I, pp. 516–518, 546–549.

c. Hibiya-Kondō, Narita, Okada, Seishin, Waseda.

3418 —— repr., Tokyo 1925 (大正 14). jb. 1 v.

3419 Edkins, Joseph, LM. 艾約瑟 (1823–1905)

Shakkyō Shōbyū 釋教正謬 *Shih-chiao Cheng-niu* (Criticism of Buddhism), Shanghai, 1857–59 (咸豊 7–9). cb. 2 vols.

cf. Wylie, p. 188; Ebisawa Arimichi, "Shakkyō Shōbyū to sono Hankyō" (*Shien*, v. XIII, n, 2), Tōkyō 1940.

3420 —— Hongkong 英華書院, 1866 (同治 5). 2nd ed., cb. 1 v., 26f., 20cm.

c. Ebisawa, Hatano, Jingū, Tōdai-Nanki. ms. Waseda.

3421 —— Hongkong 英華書院, 1868 (同治 7). cb. 1 v., 26f., 20cm.

c. Dōshisha, Kompira, Saba, Seikadō, Tōdai-Nanki, Ueno, Waseda. ms. Kichū.

3422 —— [Kyoto], [1869?], jb. 2 vols., 19cm.

note: Limited to 100 copies.

c. Aoyama, Ebisawa, ICU, Keiō-Koda, Kichū.

3423 —— [Kyoto], [1870?]. jb. 2 vols., 23cm.

note: Limited to 100 copies.

c. Ebisawa, Ōtani, Ryūkoku, Sophia.

3424 —— Yang-ch'eng 羊城小書會, 1878 (光緒 4). cb. 1 v., 46f., 21cm.

c. Yoshida.

3425 * Shakkyō Shōbyū Shoha 釋教正謬初破 (First Criticism of the *Shakkyō Shōbyū*) by Kiyū Dōjin 杞憂道人, [Tokyo] 三縁山, 1868 (慶應 4). jb. 2 vols., 27cm.

note: contains the original text.

c. Ebisawa, Narita, Sophia, Taisho, Tenri, Waseda.

3426 —— [different ed.] 有志中, 1868 (慶應 4). jb. 2 vols., 27cm.

c. Ryūkoku, Seishin.

3427 —— (Nippon Shisō Tōsō Shiryō, v. X).

3428 —— abridged (Haja Sōsho, v. II).

3429 * Shakkyō Shōbyū Shoha narabini Saiha 釋教正謬初破並再破 (First and Second Criticism of the *Shakyō Shōbyū*), by Kiyū Dōjin 杞憂道人, [Tokyo] 三縁山, 1873 (明治 6). jb. 3 vols., 23cm.

note: Contains the original text.

c. Aoyama, Ebisawa, Hatano, Kyūdai, Narita, Ōtani, Sophia, Sukeno, Tōhoku, Waseda, Yoshida.

See also Pt. II, on the other critic works by Buddhists.

3430 Edkins Joseph, LM. 艾約瑟 (1823–1905)

Shokubutsugaku 植物學 *Chih-wu-hsüeh* (Botany) by J. Edkins and Alexander Williamson, LM., 韋廉臣, Shanghai 墨海書館, 1857 (咸豊 7). cb. 1 v., 1, 2, 10, 5, 14, 10, 16, 14, 11, 18f., 23cm.

cf. Wylie, p. 239; Makino Tomitarō (*Toshokan Zasshi*, v. XXXI, n. 5).

c. Iwase, Jingū, Ueno-Shirai.

3431 —— Shanghai, 1859 (咸豊 9). cb. 1v., 101f.

3432 —— (Seigaku Keimō).

3433 —— annotated by Imai Sen 今井潜, Kyoto, 1868 (慶應 4). jb. 3 vols.

c. Ueno, Waseda-Hanabusa.

3434 * Honkoku Shokubutsugaku 翻刻植物學, construed from Chinese into Jap. by Kimura Kahei 木村嘉平, Edo [Tokyo] 川越屋, 1867 (慶應 3). jb. 3 vols., 27cm.

cf. Ozawa, p. 234; Makino Tomitarō (*Toshokan Zasshi*, v. XXXI, n. 5).

c. Keiō, Odagiri, Okada, Tōhoku-Kanō, Yoshida, Ueno.

3435 * Shokubutsugaku Keimō 植物學啓蒙 (Introduction to Botany), Shanghai, 1886 (光緒 12). cb. 1 v.

c. Kyūdai.

3436 * Shokubutsugaku Shōyaku 植物學抄譯, (Abridged translation from the *Shokubutsugaku*), tr. by Tawara Tōki 田原陶猗, Tokyo 天野芳次郎, 1875 (明治 8). jb. 5 vols.

c. Ueno-Shirai.

3437 * Shokubutsugaku Yakuge 植物學譯解 (Translation of the *Shokubutsugaku*), tr. by Abe Tametō 阿部爲任, Tokyo 1875 (明治 8). jb. 3 vols.

3438 Hattori Masayo 服部政世

Gaikan Biyoroku 外患備豫録 (Defense against Foreign Troubles), 1857 (安政 4). jb. 1 v.

cf. Tenri-Jap. II, p. 97. ms. Tenri.

3439 Hobson, Benjamin, LM. 合信 (1816–1873)

Sei-i Ryakuron 西醫略論 *Hsi-yi lüeh-lun* (Outline of Western Medicine), Shanghai 仁済醫館, 1857 (咸豊 7). cb. 1 v., 2, 1, 3, 47, 94, 18f., 28cm.

cf. Ebisawa Arimichi, "Bakumatsu ni okeru Kirisutokyō Kagakusho no Shuppan" (*Kirisutokyō Shigaku*, v. I), Yokohama 1951; Wylie, p. 127.

c. Ebisawa, Ikeda, Kyōdai-Fujikawa, Ueno.

3440 —— Edo [Tokyo] 桃樹園, 1858 (安政 5). jb. 4 vols., 24cm.

c. Hibiya, Kyōdai-Fujikawa.

3441 —— Edo [Tokyo] 老皂館, 1859 (安政 5 晩冬) jb. 4 vols., 26cm.

c. Shinken, Yokohama Shidai, Yoshida, Kyōdai-Fujikawa (v. IV missed).

3442 —— construed from Chinese into

Japanese by Uchida Kaichi 内田嘉一, Tokyo 1874 (明治 7). jb. 1 v.
3443 * Sei-i Ryakuron Yakuge 西醫略論譯解 (Japanese Translation of the *Sei-i Ryakuron*) tr. by Yamamoto Yoshitoshi 山本義俊, Tokyo 江島喜兵衛 1877 (明治 10). jb. 3 vols. 19cm.
cf. Ozawa, p. 214.
c. Ueno.

3444 Keith, Caroline, Phebe, PE. 吉 (1827–)
Mōdōkun 蒙童訓 *Meng-t'ung-hsün* (Instruction for Children), Shanghai 1857 (咸豐 7). cb. 1 v., 35, 26, 26f., 24cm.
cf. Ozawa, p. 189; Wylie, p. 213.
c. Ōtani.

3445 Legge, James, LM. 理雅各 (1815–1897)
Aburahamu Kiryaku 亞伯拉罕紀略 *Ya-po-la-han Chi-lüeh* (Brief History of Abraham), Hongkong, 1857 (咸豐 7). cb. 1 v.
cf. Wylie, p. 120.
3436 —— Hongkong 1862 (同治 1). cb. 1 v., 26f.
3447 —— Hongkong 英華書館, 1870 (同治 9). cb. 1 v., [2], 24f., 16cm.
c. Kichū.

3448 McCartee, Divie Bethune, PN. 培端 (1820–1900)
Yasokyō Reigen 耶蘇教例言 *Yeh-su-chiao Lieh-yen* (Instruction in Christianity), Ningpo [n.d.]. cb. 1 v., 7f.
cf. Ozawa, p. 199; Wylie, p. 137.
3449 —— Ningpo 1857 (咸豐 7). cb. 1 v., 4f.
3450 —— Shanghai 美華書館, 1862 (同治 1). 11th ed. cb. 1 v., 11f., 17cm.
c. Ōtani.
3451 —— Shanghai 美華書館, 1868 (同治 7). cb. 1 v., 27f., 16cm.
c. Saba.
3452 —— Shanghai 美華書館, 1872 (同治 11). cb. 1 v., 27f., 16cm.
c. Saba.
3453 —— Shanghai 美華書館, 1928 (民國 17). cb. 1 v., 1, 27f., 17cm.
3454 * Iesukyo Reigen 耶蘇教例言 (Japanese Translation of the *Yasokyō Reigen*), Yokohama 倫敦聖教書類會社, 1880 (明治 13). jb. 1 v.
3455 —— Yokohama 倫敦聖教書類會社, 1885 (明治 18), wb. 1 v., 8p., 19cm.
c. Ebisawa.
3456 —— Yokohama 倫敦聖教書類會社, 1886 (明治 19). wb. 1 v., 8p. 18cm.
c. Aoyama.

3457 Nevius, John Livingstone, PN. 倪維思 (1829–1893)
Tenro Shi'nan 天路指南 *T'ien-lu Chih-nan* (Guide to Heaven), Ningpo 1857 (咸豐 7). cb. 1 v., 73f.
cf. Ozawa, p. 197; Wylie, p. 224.
3458 —— Shanghai, [n.d.]. wb. 1 v., 191p., 15cm.
c. Tenri.
3459 —— Shanghai 1861 (咸豐 11). cb. 1 v., 2, 2, [1], 85, 7f., 25cm.
c. ICU, Ōtani, Seikadō.
3460 —— Shanghai 美華書館, 1874 (同治 13). cb. 1 v., 84f., 25cm.
c. Dōshisha, Saba.
3461 —— tr. into Japanese by Nakata Michinosuke 中田道之助, Tokyo 米國聖教書類會社, 1884 (明治 17). wb. 1 v., [8], 185p., 21cm.
cf. Ozawa, p. 231.
c. Aoyama, Dōshisha, Ebisawa, Kōbejo, Saba, Tokyoshin, Yoshida.

3462 Ōhashi Totsuan 大橋訥庵 (1816–1862)
Byakuja Shōgen 闢邪小言 (Treatise against Christianity), Edo [Tokyo] 思誠塾, 1857 (安政 4). jb. 4 vols., 27cm.
c. Aoyama, Dōshisha, Ebisawa, Hibiya-Inoue, Ishin, Ikeda, Kariya, Keiō, Kichū, Kyūdai, Ryūkoku, Sophia, Okada, Tanaka, Tenri, Tōhoku, Waseda, Yoshida.
3463 —— Tokyo 至文堂, 1938 (昭和 15).
3464 —— (Meiji Bunka Zenshū, v. XV).
3465 —— abridged (Haja Sōsho, v. I).

3466 Kubo Sueshige 久保季滋 (1830–1886)
Doku Byakuja Shōgen 讀闢邪小言 (Impression of the *Byakuja Shōgen*). jb. 1 v.
ms. Jinshu,

3467 Okabe Suruga-no-Kami 岡部駿河守
Hizen no Kuni Urakami-mura Hyakushō-domo Ishū Shinkō itashisoro Ikken no Gi ni tsuki mōshiagesoro Kakitsuke 肥前國浦上村百姓共異宗信仰致候一件之儀に付申上候書付 (Report on the Discovery of Hidden Christians in Urakami), 1857 (安政 4). jb. 1 v.
ms. Ebisawa, Nagasaki.
3468 —— pr. by Urakawa Wasaburō 浦川和三郎, in *Kirishitan no Fukkatsu*, v. I, Tokyo 1927 (昭和 2), pp. 280–292.
3469 Okabe Suruga-no-kami 岡部駿河守
Hizen no Kuni Urakami-mura Hyakushō-domo Ishū Shinkō itashisoro Ikken Oshioki Ukagai tatematsurisoro Kakitsuke 肥前國浦上村百姓共異宗信仰致候一件御仕置奉伺候書付

(Report on the Discovery of Hidden Christians in Urakami), 1857 (安政 4). jb. 1 v.

ms. Ebisawa, Nagasaki.

3470 —— pr. by Urakawa Wasaburō 浦川和三郎, in *Kirishitan no Fukkatsu,* v. I., Tokyo 1927 (昭和 2), pp. 292–297.

3471 Wylie, Alexander, LM. 偉烈亞力 (1815–1887)

Rikugō Sōdan 六合叢談 *Liu-ho Ts'ung-t'an* (Monthly Periodical, *Stories of the World*), Shanghai 墨海書館, 1857–58 (咸豊 7–8). 21cm.

cf. Ozawa, pp. 190, 273; Wylie, p. 173.

3472 * Kampan Rikugō Sōdan 官板六合叢談 (Official Press, *Rikugō Sōdan*), Edo [Tokyo] 1864 (元治 1). jb. 16 vols., 23cm.

cf. Ozawa, p. 236.

c. Ebisawa, Ishin, Okada, Tōhoku-Kanō, Ueno.

3473 Yoshida Shōin 吉田松蔭 (1830–1859)

Gaiban Tsūryaku 外蕃通略 (Correspondence with Foreign Countries), [n.p.], 1857 (安政 4). jb. 1 v., 2, 21f., 29cm.

c. Ebisawa, Hibiya-Kondō, Kanazawa-Kadō, Tōhoku-Kanō, Tōdai-Nanki.

3474 —— Tokyo, 1894 (明治 27). wb. 1 v., [3], 1, 19, 1p., 24cm.

c. Ebisawa.

3475 —— (Yoshida Shōin Zenshū, v. VIII).

1858

3476 Gamō Kumpei 蒲生君平 (1768–1813)

Fujutsui 不恤緯 (Treatise on Coastal Defense), [n.p.], 1858 (安政 5). jb. 1 v., 3, 32f., 19cm.

cf. Kokushi, p. 271.

c. Ebisawa, Hibiya, Hibiya-Kondō, Hibiya-Morobashi, Kanazawa-Kadō, Tōdai-Nanki, Waseda.

3477 —— (Gamō Kumpei Zenshū).

3478 —— (Nippon Kokusui Zensho).

3479 —— (Kokumin Dōtoku Sōsho).

3480 Hobson, Benjamin, LM. 合信 (1816–1873)

Fuei Shinsetsu 婦嬰新說 *Fu-ying hsin-shuo* (A New Treatise on Obstetrics), Shanghai 仁濟醫館, 1858 (咸豊 8). cb. 2 vols., 26cm.

cf. Ozawa, p. 215; Wylie, p. 127.

c. Gakushūin, Ikeda, Shinken, Ueno.

3481 —— Edo [Tokyo] 老皂館, [1859?]. jb. 2 vols., 26cm.

c. Fujimoto, Kyōdai-Fujikawa, Tōhoku-Kanō, Ueno.

3482 * Wayaku Fuei Shinsetsu 和譯婦嬰新說 (Japanese Translation of the *Fuei Shinsetsu*), tr. by Hirose Genshū 廣瀬元周, Tokyo 文明書樓, 1874 (明治 7). jb. 3 vols., 23cm.

c. Ueno.

3483 Hobson, Benjamin, LM. 合信 (1816–1873)

Naika Shinsetsu 內科新說 *Nei-k'o hsin-shuo* (New Practices in Internal Medicine), Shanghai 仁濟醫館, 1858 (咸豊 8). cb. 1., 2, 2, 2, 72, 45f., 25cm.

cf. Ozawa, p. 215; Wylie, pp. 127–128.

c. Iwase, Kyodai, Ueno.

3484 —— Edo [Tokyo] 老皂館, 1859 (安政 6). jb. 3 vols. 26cm.

c. Hibiya, Ikeda, Kyodai-Fujikawa, Shinken, Yokohamashidai-Igaku, Yoshida, Ueno.

3485 —— Edo [Tokyo] 須原屋, 1860 (安政 7). jb. 3 vols. 26cm.

c. Ebisawa, Kyūdai.

3486 Ikokusen Torai Nikki Hikae 異國船渡來日記控 (Notes on the Arrivals of Foreign Ships), 1858 (安政 5). jb. 1 v.

ms. Sophia.

3487 Martin, Samuel Newell D., PN. 孟子元

Tendō Kyōyō 天道鏡要 *T'ien-tao Ching-yao* (Summary of Scriptural Truth), Ningpo 華花聖經書房, 1858 (咸豊 8). cb. 1 v., 9 7f.

cf. Wylie, p. 204.

ms. Yoshida.

3488 Martin, William Alexander Parsons, PN. 丁韙良 (1827–1916)

Pōro Suikun 保羅垂訓 *Pao-lo Ch'ui-hsün* (St. Paul's Discourse at Athens), Ningpo, [1858]. cb. 1 v.

cf. Ozawa, pp. 189–190; Wylie, p. 205.

3489 —— Ningpo, 1859 (咸豊 9). 2nd ed., cb. 1 v.

3490 —— Shanghai, 1861 (咸豊 11). 3rd ed., cb. 1 v.

3491 Martin, William Alexander Parsons, PN. 丁韙良 (1827–1916)

San'yōroku 三要錄 *San-yao-lu* (The Three Principles), Ningpo 華花印書房, 1858 (咸豊 8). cb. 1 v., 22f., 24cm.

cf. Ozawa, p. 191; Wylie, p. 205.

3492 —— Ningpo 華花印書房, 1859 (咸豊 9). cb. 1 v., 1, 27f., 19cm.

c. Aoyama, Ōtani, Saba, Seikadō.

3493 —— Shanghai 美華書館, 1869 (同治 8). cb. 1 v., 1, 30f., 17cm.

c. Ebisawa, ICU, Hatano, Naikaku, Yoshida.

3494 * San'yōmon 三要文, tr. into Jap. by James C. Hepburn, PN. and Okuno

Masatsuna 奧野昌綱, Yokohama [1872?]. jb.
1 v., 5f., 16cm.
c. Saitō, Waseda-Ōkuma.
phot. Saba.

3495 —— repr. and phot., annotated by
Ozawa Saburō 小澤三郎, in *Bakumatsu Meiji
Yasokyōshi Kenkyū*, Tokyo 1944 (昭和 19).
pp. 358–360.

3496 —— repr. and annotated by Saba
Wataru 佐波亘, in *Uemura Masahisa to sono
Jidai*, v. IV, Tokyo 1938 (昭和 13).

3497 Martin, William Alexander P.,
PN. 丁韙良 (1827–1916)
Yudōden 喩道傳 *Yü-tao-chuan* (Religious
Allegories), Ningpo 華花印書房, 1858 (咸豊
8). cb. 1 v., [3], 1, 44f., 20cm.
cf. Ozawa, p. 201; Yoshida Tora, Yudōden to sono
Setsuwa (*Kirisutokyō Shigaku,*, v. VIII), Yokohama 1958, pp. 28–35; Wylie, p. 205.
c. Ōtani.

3498 —— Shanghai 1863. 2nd ed. cb. 1 v.
3499 —— Shanghai 美華書館, 1869 (同治
8). cb. 1 v. [4], 31f., 17cm.
c. Ebisawa, Hatano, ICU, Kompira, Naikaku,
Seikadō, Waseda, Yoshida.

3500 * Yudōden-kai 喩道傳解 (Translation of the *Yudōden*) tr. by C. Carrothers
PN. 嘉魯日耳士, Tokyo 1875 (明治 8). jb. 1 v.
cf. Ozawa, p. 224.

3501 * Kanzen Yudōden 勸善喩道傳 (The
Way of Virtue, the *Yudōden*), construed
from Chinese into Japanese by Watanabe
On 渡部温, Tokyo 稻田佐兵衛, 1877 (明治
10). jb. 1 v., 39f., 22cm.
cf. Ozawa, p. 224.
c. Aoyama, Kagoshima, Naikaku, Seikadō, Waseda.

3502 Mori Shōmon 森正門
Katsuenhyō 割圓表 (Table of Trigonometrical Functions), [Edo] 勝村治右衛門, 1858
(安政 5). jb. 3 vols., 26cm.
c. Gakushiin, Tōhoku-Sūgaku, Ueno, Waseda-
Ogura.

3503 Muirhead, William, LM. 慕維廉
(1822–1900)
Sanshu Shiika 讚主詩歌 *Tsan-chu Shih-ko*
(Hymns of Praise), Shanghai, 1858 (咸豊
8). cb. 1 v., 38f.
cf. Wylie, p. 170.

3504 * Yaso Sanka 耶蘇讚歌 *Yeh-su Tsan-
ko*, revised ed., Shanghai, [1858]. cb. 1 v.

3505 Nijhoff, Isaak Anne (1795–1865)
Taisei Shiryaku 泰西史略 (A Brief History
of Europe), tr. by Tezuka Ritsuzō 手塚律藏,
Edo [Tokyo] 又新堂, 1858 (安政 5). jb.
3 vols., 27cm.
orig. title: *Kort Overzigt der Algemeene Geschiedenis,*
1823.

cf. Kaikoku, pp. 447–449.
c. Kansei, Ueno.

3506 Shōkokukō Monjo 照國公文書
(Documents of Prince Shōkoku).
cf. Kokushi, pp. 140–141.
note: Documents of Shimazu Nariakira 島津齋彬
(1809–1858) written in 1845–1858; contains
several documents on Rev. Bettelheim and More-
ton.
orig. ms. Shimazu.

3507 —— compiled and published by 島
津家臨時編纂所, Kagoshima, 1910 (明治 43).
2 vols.

3508 —— abridged repr. (Dai-Nippon
Ishin Shiryō, Series II, v. I).

3509 * Shimazu Nariakira Monjo 島津
齋彬文書, compiled by its Kankōkai 刊行會,
Tokyo 1959 (昭和 34). wb. 2 vols.

3510 Wylie, Alexander, LM. 偉烈亞力
(1815–1889)
Jūgaku Sensetsu 重學淺說 *Chung-hsüeh
Ch'ien-shuo* (Popular Treatise on Mechanics),
Shanghai 墨海書館, 1858 (咸豊 8). cb. 1 v.,
14f., 21cm.
cf. Ozawa, pp. 236, 273; Wylie, p. 173.
c. Gakushiin, Odagiri, Ōtani, Tōhoku-Kanō.

3511 —— (Rikugō Sōdan, v. XVI).
3512 —— (Seigaku Shūzon, v. II).
3513 —— construed from Chinese into
Jap. by Arai Kōri 荒井公履, Edo [Tokyo],
1860 (萬延 1). jb. 1 v.
c. Naikaku, Waseda-Ogura.

3514 Yochi Kiryaku 輿地紀略 (Outline
of World Geography), edited by Itō
Keisuke 伊藤圭介, Nagoya 花綵書屋, 1858
(安政 5). jb. 1 v.
orig. title: *Geographisch Zakboekje voor de Nederlandsche
Jeugd, of Korte Beschrijving des Geheelen Aardrijks,*
Leiden 1829. 11th ed.
c. Keiō, Odaka.

Treatise of Foreign Affairs in the Middle of the XIX Century

3515 Abokushi Sōkō 亞墨史草稿 (Draft
Manuscript on the History of America),
jb. 1 v., 19f.
note: Translator is not known.
cf. Kaikoku, p. 410.
orig. ms. The Mitsukuris.

3516 Aizawa Seishi 會澤正志 (1782–
1863)
Byakujahen 闢邪篇 (Treatise against
Christianity).
cf. Tokushige-Seishin, pp. 315–516.

3517 Aizawa Seishi 會澤正志 (1782–
1863)

Kyūmon Ihan 及門遺範 (Essays on Confucianism), [n.p.], [n.d.]. jb. 1 v., 3, 17f., 15cm.

note: Limited edition of 100 copies.
c. Hibiya-Kaga, Hibiya-Ichimura.

3518 —— (Yūkoku Zenshū).
3519 —— (Bushidō Sōsho, v. II).
3520 —— (Kinsei Juka Shiryō, v. II).
3521 —— (Nippon Jurin Sōsho, v. II).

3522 Aizawa Seishi 會澤正志 (1782–1863)
Sokuja Bikō 息邪備考 (Essays against Christianity). jb. 1 v.
3523 * Sokuja Manroku 息邪漫録, 1852 (嘉永 5). jb. 1 v.

ms. Jinshu, Naikaku, Ueno.

3524 Ban'i Hiroku 蠻夷秘録 (Secret Records about Foreigners). jb. 1 v.

ms. Sonkeikaku.

3525 Bankokuden 萬國傳 (History of the World). jb. 1 v.

ms. Naikaku.

3526 Bansen Fūsetsugaki 蠻船風説書 (Report on Foreign Ships).
3527 —— (Chūko Sōsho, v. LXXXVIII).

3528 Bansen Nyūshi Yuraiki 蕃船入津由來記 (History of the Arrival of Foreign Ships). jb. 1 v.

ms. Iwase.

3529 Bansen Torai Kikigaki 蠻船渡來聞書 (Recollection of the Arrival of Foreign Ships).
3530 —— (Hōsai Nisshō, Koshū).

3531 Bosscha, Johannes (1797–1874)
Kyokusei Shiei 極西史影 (Western History), tr. by Mitsukuri Gempo 箕作阮甫, jb. 5 vols.

note: Translation from Bosscha's *Schets der Algemeene Geschiedenis en van die des Vaderlands,* Amsterdam, 1838.
cf. Kaikoku, pp. 433–440; Rangaku, p. 31.
orig. ms. Ueno.

3532 Enkai Kiyū 沿海杞憂 (Imaginery Fears about Invasion).

ms. Ishin.

3533 Fujimori Taiga 藤森大雅 (1799–1862)
Amerika Sōki 亞米利加總記 (American History and Geography), tr. by Fujimori Taiga. jb. 1 v.

c. Rikkyō.

3534 Furanki Amerika Toraiki 佛朗機亞墨利加來記 (Arrival of the French and Americans). jb. 1 v.

ms. Iwase.

3535 Gaikokujin Ōsetsuki 外國人應接記 (Report the Foreigners' Reception).
3536 —— (Nagasaki Sōsho, A., v. III).

3537 Gaikokusen Toraiki 外國船渡來記 (Notes on the Arrivals of Foreign Ships). jb. 1 v.

ms. Shiryō.

3538 Gaikō Zassan 外交雜纂 (Diplomatic Notes).

ms. Tōhoku-Kanō.

3539 Gasshūkoku Nempyō 合衆國年表 (Chronology of the History of the United States, 1776–1853). jb. 1 v.

ms. Sonkeikaku.

3540 Gasshūkoku Toraiki 合衆國渡來記 (On the Arrival of the Americans). jb. 1 v.

ms. Jingū.

3541 Habu Kumagorō 土生熊五郎
Kaibō Rokuron 海防六論 (Six Plans of Coastal Defence). jb. 1 v.

ms. Ishin.

3542 Habu Kumagorō 土生熊五郎
Rifujutsui narabini Sempakukō 蕶不恤緯並船舶考 (Essays on Coastal Defense and Ships). jb. 1 v.

ms. Hibiya-Kondō.

3543 —— (Kaibō Igi, v. XXXVIII).
3544 —— (Nippon Kaibō Shiryō Sōsho, v. II).
3545 —— (Nippon Keizai Sōsho, v. XII).
3546 —— (Nippon Keizai Taiten, v. XX).

3547 Hagura Geki 羽倉外記
Kaibō Shisaku 海防私策 (Private Plan for Coastal Defense). jb. 1 v.

ms. Hibiya-Kondō.

3548 —— (Kaibō Igi, v. XXXIII).
3549 —— (Nippon Kaibō Shiryō Sōsho, v. II).

3550 Ichimada Ki 一萬田 希
Kaibō Kigen 海防危言 (Outspoken Advice on Coastal Defense). jb. 1 v.

ms. Ishin.

3551 Ikei Zatsuroku 夷警雜録 (Miscellaneous Records on National Defense).
3552 —— (Nanyō Sōsho).

3553 Ikoku-Kankei Zakki 異國關係雜記 (Miscellaneous Notes on Foreign Countries). jb. 1 v.

ms. Hakodate.

3554 Ikoku Kibun 異國紀聞 (Notes on Foreign Countries). jb. 1 v.

ms. Naikaku.

3555 —— (Gaikoku Sōsho).

3556 Ikoku Ōrai narabini Hyōryū Nempyō 異國往來並漂流年表 (Chronology of the Dates of Foreign Intercourse and the Arrival of Shipwrecked Sailors), [n.p.], [n.d.]. 1 fold., 37 × 112cm.
c. Ueno.
ms. Waseda.

3557 Ikoku Ōrai narabini Hyōryū Nempyō 2 hen 異國往來並漂流年表二篇 (Second Series of the *Ikoku Ōrai* narabini Hyōryū Nempyō), Edo [Tokyo] 千松堂, [n.d.]. 1 fold.
c. Hibiya-Kaga, Hokudai.

3558 Ikokusen Nendaiki 異國船年代記 (Dates of the Arrivals of Foreign Ships). 1 fold., 18cm.
c. Hibiya-Kondō.

3559 Ikokusen Shokoku Nyūkōki 異國船諸國入港記 (Notes on the Arrivals of Foreign Ships).
3560 —— (Nanyō Sōsho).

3561 Ikokusen Torai narabini Hyōryū-jin Shūsho 異國船渡來並漂流人集書 (Collected Notes on Foreign Intercourse and the Arrival of Shipwrecked Sailors). jb. 1 v.
ms. Kyōto.

3562 Ikokusen Torai Shimatsu 異國船渡來始末 (History of the Arrival of Foreign Ships). jb. 1 v.
ms. Kanazawa-Ujiie.

3563 Ikokusen Torai Tomegaki 異國船渡來留書 (Notes of the Arrival of Foreign Ships). jb. 1 v.
ms. Hibiya-Kondō.

3564 Isen Jijitsu Kibun Shūi 異船事實記聞拾遺 (True Description of Foreign Intercourse). jb. 26 vols.
ms. ICU.

3565 Kaibō Hibunshū 海防秘聞集 (Secret News of Coastal Defense). jb. 1 v.
ms. Ishin.

3566 Kaibō Shimpen 海防新編 (New Treatise on Coastal Defense). jb. 4 vols.
3567 —— (Chūkō Sosho, vv. LXIV-LXVII).

3568 Kaibō Shūroku 海防輯録 (Collective Records on Coastal Defense). jb. 1 v.
ms. Ishin.

3569 Kaigai Ibunshū 海外異聞集 (Collection of Strange Accounts of Foreign Countries).
c. Tōhoku-Kanō.

3570 Kaihen Bōgyo Shikō 海邊防禦私考 (Private Opinion on Coastal Defense). jb. 1 v.
ms. Sonkeikaku.
3571 —— (Nippon Kaibō Shiryō Sōsho, v. II).

3572 Kaikō Sessaku 海寇竊策 fu. Matsumoto Tokizō Jōshin Kiroku 附, 松本斗機藏上申記録, Kenkin Bichū 献芹微衷 (Private Opinion on Coastal Defense).
ms. Sonkeikaku.
3573 —— (Kaibō Igi, v. IV).
3574 —— (Nipon Kaibō Shiryō Sōsho, v. II).

3575 Karitsu Gaishi 華律外史
Bankoku Tokai Nendaiki 萬國渡海年代記 (Chronicle of the History of World Navigation), [Edo] 五守堂, [n.d.]. jb. 1 v., 26f., 2pl., 15cm.
c. Daitokyu, Hibiya, Hibiya-Kondō, Jingū, Tōdai-Nanki.
3576 —— (Kaiji Shiryō Sōsho, v. XIII).
3577 * Bankoku Torai Nempyō 萬國渡來年表 (Chronology of Arrivals of Representatives of the Foreign Countries). jb. 1 v.
ms. Gakushūin.

3578 Kinji Kaikoku Hitsudokusho 近時海國必讀書 (Books Indispensable at the Present for the Sea-Girt Land). jb. 10 vols.
contents: v. I. Seiyō-jin Nippon Kiji 西洋人日本紀事, tr. by Takahashi Kageyasu 高橋景保.
II. Oranda Kiryaku 和蘭紀略 by Shibukawa Rokuzō 澀川六藏.
III. Hokusui Kiyu 北陲杞憂 by Tōyō Konsō 東洋鯤叟.
Seibu Kiji 西俤紀事 by Tōyō Konsō 東洋鯤叟.
IV. Angeriajin Seijōshi 諳厄利亞人性情志 tr. by Yoshio Gi 吉雄宜.
VI. Taisei Rokuwa 泰西録話 by Koga Dōan 古賀侗庵.
Seiyō Shoi Ryakuhyō 西洋諸夷略表.
VII. Shinkiron 慎機論 by Watanabe Noboru 渡邊登.
Kyokuron Jiji Fuji 極論時事封事 by Koga Seiri 古賀精里.
VIII. Bōkaisaku 防海策 by Satō Hyakuyū 佐藤百佑.
IX. Jōsho 上書 by Matsumoto Tokizō 松本斗機藏.
Kaibō Gosaku 海防五策 by Saitō Seiken 齋藤正謙.

3579 —— (Nippon Kaibō Shiryō Sōsho, v. III).

3580 Kyōhō Zakki 徼報雜記 (Notes on the Arrival of Foregners since the Tempo Era). jb. 20 vols.
ms. Sonkeikaku.

128

3581 Matsudaira Shungaku 松平春嶽 (1828–1890)

Gōdōhaku Nyūsō Hiki 合同舶入相秘記 (Secret Record of the Arrival of American Ships).

3582 —— (Matsudaira Shungaku Zenshū, vv. II–III).

3583 Matsumoto Tokizō 松本斗機藏

Kenkin Bichū 献芹微衷 (Memorial on Diplomatic Problems). jb. 1 v.

ms. Ishin, Jingū, Sonkeikaku, Tōhoku-Kanō.

3584 —— (Kaidō Sessaku).

3585 —— (Kaibō Igi, v. III).

3586 —— (Nippon Bunko, v. X).

3587 —— (Nippon Kaibō Shiryō Sōsho, v. II).

3588 Matsumoto Tokizō 松本斗機藏

Matsumoto Tokizō Jōsho 松本斗機藏上書 (Memorials of Matsumoto Tokizō).

3588b —— (Heikan Issō v. VIII).

3589 —— (Kaibō Igi, v. XLIII).

3590 —— (Kinji Kaikoku Hitsudokusho, v. IX).

3591 —— (Nippon Kaibō Sōsho, v. II).

3592 —— (Ikoku Hyōryū Kidanshū, Appendix).

3593 Mitsukuri Gempo 箕作阮甫 (1799–1863)

Kyokusei Zashi Benshō 極西眡史辯證 (Treatise on Western History). jb. 1 v.

cf. Kaikoku, p. 444.

orig. ms. Mitsukuris.

3594 Mitsukuri Gempo 箕作阮甫 (1799–1863)

Seishi Geden 西史外傳 (Biographies of Distinguished Men in Western History), jb. 2 vols.

note: not printed.

cf. Kaikoku, pp. 452–453.

orig. ms. Mitsukuris.

ms. Otsuki, Shōkōkan.

3595 Mitsukuri Gempo 箕作阮甫 (1799–1863)

Taisei Shunjū 大西春秋 (World History), tr. by Mitsukuri Gempo. jb. 1 v., 116f., 23cm.

note: The original text is *Kort Bedrip der Algemeene Historie,* but its author is unknown.

cf. Kaikoku, pp. 442–443.

orig. ms. Mitsukuris.

3596 Miyata Bin 宮田 敏

Kaibō Sūgen 海防芻言 (Essence of Coastal Defense). jb. 1 v.

orig. ms. Ishin.

3597 Nagayama Chōen 長山樗園

Kaibō Shigi 海防私議 (Private Opinion on Coastal Defense). jb. 1 v.

ms. Ishin, Okada, Yūtoku.

3598 —— (Nippon Kaibō Shiryō Sōsho, v. VIII).

3599 Nakamura Zenkin 仲村善筠

Gaikoku Tsushinshi 外國通信志 (International Correspondences). jb. 9 vols.

ms. Naikaku, Tōhoku.

3600 Nakane Shishitsu 中根師質 (1807–1877)

Sakumu Kiji 昨夢紀事 (Life of Matsudaira Yoshinaga 松平慶永).

cf. Kokushi, p. 115.

3601 —— Tokyo 1896 (明治 29). wb. 2 vols.

3602 —— pr. by the Nippon Shiseki Kyōkai 日本史籍協會, Tokyo. wb. 4 vols.

3603 Narushima Ryōjō 成島良讓 (1803–1854)

Kaikeiroku 海警録 (Records of Coastal Defense). jb. 2 vols.

ms. Naikaku, Sonkeikaku.

3604 Nippon Kaibō-kō 日本海防考 (Treatise on the Coastal Defense of Japan).

3605 —— (Nippon Kaibō Shiryō Sōsho, v. III).

3606 Nonoguchi Takamasa 野々口隆正 (1792–1871)

Gyojū Mondō 馭戎問答 (Dialogue on Coastal Defense). jb. 1 v.

cf. Shintō-Kaidai, pp. 24–25.

ms. Ebisawa, Jingū, Waseda.

3607 —— (Nippon Kokushi Zensho, v. XIV).

3608 Ōhashi Totsuan 大橋訥庵 (1816–1862)

Kaei Zuihitsu 嘉永随筆 (Essays during the Kaei Era). jb. 1 v.

3609 —— (Nippon Keizai Taiten, v. XLVI).

3610 Okada Hōsai 岡田蓬齋

Hokō Tōka Ibun 浦港十日彙聞 (News of the Uraga Port during Perry's Visit).

ms. Tohoku.

3611 Rai Shishun 賴子春 (1825–1859)

Nan'yō Seiyō Kakukoku Kyōmonhyō 南洋西洋各國教門表 (List of the Denominations of Christianity in Southern and Western Countries).

3612 Rōmō Sanjin 聾盲山人

Kaikei Nempyō 海警年表 (Chronological

Table of the History of Coastal Defense).
3613 —— (Ishin-Shiryō).
3614 Ryūban Tsūsho 流蕃通書 (Record of Shipwrecked Sailors). jb. 1 v.
ms. Iwase, Kyūdai-Bunka, Okada.

3615 Saitō Seiken 齋藤正謙 (1797–1865)
Chigaku Kyoyō 地學擧要 (A Summary Geography). jb. 2 vols.
note: Taken from the Jesuits' works in China. Not published.
cf. Kaikoku, pp. 68–69.
ms. Ayuzawa.

3616 Saitō Seiken 齋藤正謙 (1797–1865)
Kaibō Gosaku 海防五策 (Five Plans of Coast Defence). jb. 1 v.
ms. Jingū.
3617 —— (Kinji Kaikoku Hitsudokusho, v. IX).
3618 —— (Nippon Kaibō Shiryō Sōsho, v. II).
3619 * Kaibōsaku 海防策 (Plans of Coastal Defense). jb. 1 v.
ms. Hibiya-Kondō, Ishin, Shiryō, Tōdai-Nanki, Tōhoku-Kanō.
3620 —— (Kaibō Igi, v. VII).
3621 —— (Hokō Tōka Ibun).
3622 —— (Nippon Kaibō Shiryō Sōsho, v. II).
3623 —— (Haja Sōsho, v. I).

3624 Saitō Seiken 齋藤正謙 (1797–1865)
Tekkensai Yūken Shomoku 鐵研齋輶軒書目 (Catalogue of Saitō's Private Collection), [Edo], [n.d.]. jb. 1 v., 21f.
c. Keio-Koda, Waseda.
3625 —— (Bummei Genryū Sōsho, v. III).

3626 Seiban On-toriatsukai Jikki 西蕃御取扱實記 (Records of the Treatment of the Western Barbarians). jb. 1 v.
ms. Tohoku-Kanō.

3627 Seichin Yōran 西鎮要覧 (Handbook of National Defense). jb. 1 v.
ms. Ueno.

3628 Seiō Kiji 西歐紀事 (Notes on Intercourse between Europe and Japan since the Keichō Era). jb. 7 vols.
ms. Sonkeikaku.

3629 Seishi Ki'nen 西史紀年 (Chronicle of the History of the West). jb. 1 v.
ms. Tōdai-Nanki.

3630 Shionoya Kōzō 鹽谷甲藏 (1809–1867)
Bōshun Wakumon 防春或問 (Introduction to Coastal Defense). jb. 1 v.

ms. Nagasaki-Fuji, Tōhoku-Kanō.
3631 —— (Kaibō Igi, v. XXV).
3632 —— (Nippon Kaibō Shiryō Sōsho, v. II).
3633 * Kaibō Wakumon 海防或問 jb. 1 v.
ms. Hibiya-Kondō.

3634 Shionoya Kōzō 鹽谷甲藏 (1809–1867)
Chūkai Shigi 籌海私議 (Private Opinion on Coastal Defense). jb. 1 v.
ms. Waseda.
3635 —— (Kaibō Igi, v. VIII).
3636 —— (Nippon Kaibō Shiryo Sōsho, v. II).

3637 Tazan no Ishi 他山之石 (Lessons from Western Learning), [Edo], [n.p.]. jb. 5 vols., 27cm.
cf. Kaikoku, pp. 162–163.
contents: v. IV. Kōmō Ban'i Igirisu Kōryaku 紅毛番夷噗咭唎考略 Hung-mao-fan-yi Ying-chi-li K'ao-lüeh by Ō Buntai 汪文泰 Wang Wen-t'ai.
V. Chikyū Zusetsu 地球圖説 by Michel Benoit, SJ. 蔣友仁.
c. Kyōdai, Naikaku.

3638 Tessō Dōjin 徹桑道人
Kaihyō Ibun 海表異聞 (Records of Foreign Relations). jb. 79 vols.
cf. Ebisawa Arimichi, Tempō 15 nen Ryūfutsu kankei Nippon Shiryō (ICU Asian Cultural Studies, v. I), Tōkyō 1958, pp. 62–64.
ms. Dōshisha.

3639 Tezuka Ritsuzō 手塚律藏 (1823–1878)
Kaibō Kokoroegusa 海防心得草 (Principles of Coastal Defense). jb. 1 v.
ms. Hibiya-Kondō.

3640 Tōyō Konsō 東洋鯤叟
Seibu Kiji 西侮記事 (Contempt of the Western World).
jb. 1 v.
3641 —— (Kinji Kaikoku Histsudokusho, v. III).
3642 —— (Nippon Kaibō Shiryō Sōsho, v. II).

3643 Tsūkō Jihyō 通航事表 (Chronological Table of the History of Trade). jb. 1 v.
ms. Naikaku.

3644 Yōchōroku 庸懲録 (Chastisement). jb. 1v.
note: Abridged manuscript of the Nagasakishi (n. 1842).
ms. Tōhoku.

3645 Yōgai Zatsuroku 洋外雜録 (Notes on Foreign Countries). jb. 8 vols.
ms. Sonkeikaku.

3646 Yōiki 洋夷記 (Notes on Foreigners).
jb. 1v.
ms. Naikaku.

3647 Yoshida 吉田
Kaikei Mōgen 海警妄言 (Private Opinion
on Coastal Defense).

3648 —— (Nippon Kaibō Shiryō Sōsho,
v. VII).

131

Appendix

Alphabetical List of Collectanea

(The owners are mentioned only for collectanea of manuscripts and the Chinese collectanea)

Amakusagun Shiryō 天草郡史料, compiled and published by the Amakusagun Kyōiku-kai 天草郡教育會, 1913–1914 (大正 2–3). wb. 2 vols.

Anzai Sōsho 安齋叢書, A., jb. 27 vols.
ms. Ueno.

Anzai Sōsho 安齋叢書, B., jb. 30 vols.
ms. Tōyō-Iwasaki, Ueno.

Arai Hakuseki Zenshū 新井白石全集, compiled and published by the Kokusho Kan-kōkai 國書刊行會, Tokyo, 1905–1909 (明治 38–42). wb. 6 vols.

Baien Zenshū 梅園全集, compiled and published by the Baienkai 梅園會, Tokyo 弘道館, 1912 (明治 45). wb. 2 vols.

Baishi Sōsho Shūyō 梅氏叢書輯要 *Mei-shih Ts'ung-shu chi-yao*, compiled by Bai Kokusei 梅穀成 *Mei Ku-ch'eng*, [Shanghai], 1761 (乾隆 26). cb. 24 vols.
See the present volume, nos. 1879–1881.

Bakumatsu Gaikoku Kankei Monjo 幕末外國關係文書, compiled and published by the Shiryō Hensanjo 史料編纂所, Tokyo, 1910–1955 (明治 43–昭和 30). wb. 30 vols.

Bakumatsu Ishin Gaikō Kankei Shiryō 幕末維新外交關係史料, compiled by the Ishin Shigakukai 維新史學會, Tokyo 財政經濟學會, 1943– (昭和 18–). wb. 6 vols.

Bansui Zonkyō 盤水存響, compiled and published by Ōtsuki Shigeo 大槻茂雄, Tokyo, 1912–1914 (大正 1–3). wb. 3 vols.

Ban'yū Bunko 萬有文庫, compiled and published by the Ban'yū Bunko Kankōkai 萬有文庫刊行會, Tokyo, 1926–1927 (大正 15–昭和 2). wb. 36 vols.

Banzan Zenshū 蕃山全集, compiled by Masamune Atsuo 正宗敦夫, Tokyo 蕃山全集刊行會, 1940–1943 (昭和 15–18). wb. 6 vols.

Bokkai Kinko 墨海金壺 *Mo-hai Chin-hu*, compiled by Chō Kaihō 張海鵬 *Chang Hai-p'eng* Shanghai 博古齋, 1921 (民國 10). cb. 160 vols.
c. ICU, Kyōdai-Bungakubu.

Bōsō Bunko 房總文庫, compiled and published by the Bōsō Bunko Kankōkai 房總文庫刊行會, Chiba 1930–1931 (昭和 5–6). wb. 4 vols.

Buhen Sōsho 武邊叢書 A., compiled by Ban Nobutomo 伴信友. jb. 10 vols.
ms. Ueno.

—— (Shiseki Shūran).

Buhen Sōsho 武邊叢書 B., compiled by Ban Nobutomo 伴信友. jb. 46 vols.
ms. Shoryobu.

Bummei Genryū Sōsho 文明源流叢書, compiled and published by the Kokusho Kankōkai 國書刊行會, Tokyo, 1913–1914 (大正 2–3). wb. 3 vols.

Bummei Tōzenshi 文明東漸史, compiled by Fujita Mokichi 藤田茂吉, Tokyo 1884 (明治 17). wb. 1 v.

—— Tokyo 聚芳閣, 1926 (大正 15).

Bunsenrō Sōsho 文選樓叢書 *Wen-hsüan-lou ts'ung-shu*, compiled by Gen Kyō 阮亨 *Yüan Heng,* 1842 (道光 22). cb. 72 vols.
c. Naikaku, Tōyō.

Bushidō Sōsho 武士道叢書, compiled by Inoue Tetsujirō 井上哲次郎 and Arima Suke-masa 有馬祐政, Tokyo 博文館, 1905 (明治 38). wb. 4 vols.

Byakuja Kankenroku 關邪管見録, compiled by Kiyū Dōjin 杞憂道人, [n.p.], 1861 (文久 1). jb. 2 vols.
See Pt. II.

Byakujashū 關邪集 *P'i-hsieh-chi*, compiled by Shō Shisei 鐘始聲 *Chung Shih-sheng*, [n.p.], [n.d.]. cb. 2 vols.
See present volume, nos. 1253–1254.

Chintei Sōsho 椿亭叢書. jb. 31 vols.
ms. Shōryōbu.

Chōfū Irin 朝風意林, compiled by Tsutsumi Chōfū 堤朝風. jb. 4 vols.
ms. Ueno.

Chōkai Sōsho 鳥海叢書, compiled by Tori-umi Jūzaburō 鳥海重三郎, jb. 22 vols.
ms. Ueno.

Chūko Sōsho 中古叢書. jb. 150 vols.
ms. Ueno.

Chūsei Sangaku Shishu 中西算學四種 *Chung-hsi Suan-hsüeh Szu-chung*, compiled by Ri Zenran 李善蘭 *Li Shan-lan*, Seoul 朝鮮總督府. cb. 1 v.
c. Gakushiin.

Chūsei Sangaku Shūyō 中西算學集要 *Chung-hsi Suan-hsüeh chi-yao,* compiled by Shu Ki 朱熙 *Chu Hsi* and Shū Bin'ei 周敏英 *Chou Min-ying,* Seoul 朝鮮總督府, 1881 (光緒 7). cb. 6 vols.
c. Gakushiin, Waseda-Ogura.

Chūsei Sangaku Taisei 中西算學大成 *Chung-hsi Suan-hsüeh Ta-ch'eng,* compiled by Chin Iki 陳維祺 *Chen Wei-chi,* 1889 (光緒 15). cb. 20 vols.
c. Keiō, Tōhoku-Kanō, Waseda-Ogura.

Dai-Nippon Bukkyō Zensho 大日本佛教全書, compiled by Takakusu Junjirō 高楠順次郎 and Mochizuki Shinkyō 望月信享, Tokyo 佛教全書刊行會, 1912 (大正 1). wb. 161 vols.

Dai-Nippon Fūkyō Sōsho 大日本風敎叢書, compiled by Hori Shigeyuki 堀成之, Tokyo 大日本風敎叢書刊行會, 1917–1921 (大正 6–10). wb. 12 vols.

Dai-Nippon Ishin Shiryō 大日本維新史料, compiled and published by the Ishin Shiryō Hensan Jimukyoku 維新史料編纂事務局, Tokyo, 1939– (昭和 14–). wb. 19 vols.

Dai-Nippon Kokiroku 大日本古記録, compiled by the Shiryō Hensanjo 史料編纂所, 1952– (昭和 27–). wb. 18 vols.

Dai-Nippon Komonjo, Bakumatsu Gaikoku Kankei Monjo 大日本古文書, 幕末外國關係文書, compiled and published by the Shiryō Hensanjo 史料編纂所, Tokyo, 1910–1955 (明治 43–昭和 30). wb. 30 vols.

Dai-Nippon Shiryō 大日本史料, compiled and published by the Shiryō Hensanjo 史料編纂所, Tokyo, 1902– (明治 35–). wb. 128 vols.

Dai-Nippon Shisō Zenshū 大日本思想全集, compiled and published by the Dai-Nippon Shisō Zenshū Kankōkai 大日本思想全集刊行會, Tokyo, 1931–35 (昭和 6–10). wb. 18 vols.

Date Kashi Sōdan 伊達家史叢談, compiled by Date Kunimune 伊達邦宗, Tokyo, 1920–1921 (大正 9–10). jb. 15 vols.
ms. Seishin.

Dōgen Seisui 道原精粹 *Tao-yuan Ching-ts'ui,* compiled by Valentin Garnier 倪懷倫, [n.p.], 1887 (光緒 13). cb. 7 vols.
c. Nagasaki (vv. I–III only), Tenri.

Edo Monogatari 江戸物語, compiled by the Edo Bungaku Kenkyūkai 江戸文學研究會, 1927 (昭和 2). wb. 1 v.

Edo no Omokage 江戸の面影, compiled by the Edo Bungaku Kenkyūkai 江戸文學研究會, 1915 (大正 4). wb. 1 v.

Edo Sōsho 江戸叢書, compiled and published by the Edo Sōsho Kankōkai 江戸叢書刊行會, Tokyo, 1916–1917 (大正 5–6). wb. 2 vols.

Ekiken Zenshū 益軒全集, compiled and published by the Ekikenkai 益軒會, Tokyo, 1910–1911 (明治 43–44). wb. 8 vols.

Ekisai Hitsuroku 惕齋筆録, compiled by Nakamura Ekisai 中村惕斉. jb.
ms. Ueno.

Enseki Jusshu 燕石十種, compiled by Iwamoto Sashichi 岩本佐七, 1863 (文久 3). jb. 60 vols.
ms. Gakushūin, Naikaku, Ueno.
—— published by the Kokusho Kankōkai 國書刊行會, Tokyo, 1907 (明治 40). wb. 3 vols.

Futokui 不得已 *Pu-te-yi,* compiled by Yō Kōsen 楊光先 *Yang Kuang-hsien.*
See the present volume, nos. 1267–1268.

Gaikoku Sōsho 外國叢書.
ms. Waseda.

Gajikanga-sho 我自刊我書 published by Hokiyama Kageo 甫喜山景雄, Tokyo, 1880–1884 (明治 13–17). jb. 127 vols.

Gakukai Ruihen 學海類編 *Hsüeh-hai Lei-p'ien,* compiled by Sō Yō 曹溶 *Ts'ao Yung,* 1831 (道光 11). cb. 299 vols.
c. Naikaku, Shinken, Tōyō.
—— Shanghai 商務印書館, (民國 9) cb. 120 vols.
c. Kyōdai-Bungakubu.

Gakuritsu Zensho 樂律全書 *Yüeh-lü Chüan-shu,* cb. 48 vols.
c. Seikadō, Shinken, Tōhoku, Tōyō-Fujita.

Gamō Kumpei Zenshū 蒲生君平全集, compiled by Okabe Seiichi 岡部精一 and Mishima Yoshitarō 三島吉太郎. Tokyo, 1911 (明治 44). wb. 1 v.

Geien Kunka 藝苑捃華 *Yi-yuen Chün-hua.*
c. Tōyō.

Geikai Shujin 藝海珠塵 *Yi-hai Chu-ch'en,* compiled by Go Seiran 呉省蘭 *Wu Sheng-lan,* 南滙聴彝堂, [n.d.]. cb. 64 vols.
c. Iwase, Kyōdai, Kyōdai-Bungakubu, Kyūdai, Naikaku, Seikadō, Shinken, Tōhoku-Kanō, Tōyō-Fujita, Ueno.

Gōitsu Sōsho 合一叢書. jb. 6 vols.
ms. Naikaku.

Gojiryaku 五事略, Tokyo 國文社, 1883 (明治 16). jb. 2 vols.
See the present volume, nos. 1677–1684.

Goshū Rekkoku Shii 五州列國志彙 *Wu-chou Lieh-kuo-chih hui,* compiled by Bin Suishō 閔萃祥 *Min Tsui-hsiang,* 1902 (光緒 28). cb. 32 vols.
c. Waseda.

Gunsho Ruijū 群書類從, compiled by Hanawa Hokiichi 塙保己一, Edo [Tokyo], 1819- . (文政 2-). jb. 666 vols.
—— published by the Keizai Zasshisha 經濟雜誌社, Tokyo 1893–94 (明治 26–29). wb. 21 vols.

Gyokuchō Sōsho 玉晁叢書, compiled by Kodera Gyokuchō 小寺玉晁. jb. 244 vols.
ms. Waseda.

Haja Sōsho 破邪叢書, compiled by Kanzaki Issaku 神崎一作, Tokyo 哲學書院, 1893 (明治 26). wb. 2 vols.

Hakusekiran 白石爛, by Arai Hakuseki 新井白石. jb. 14 vols.
ms. Naikaku (vv. VIII, XI and XII lacked).

Hakusekishi 白石子, by Arai Hakuseki 新井白石. jb. 9 vols.
ms. Naikaku.

Hakuseki Sōsho 白石叢書 A., by Arai Hakuseki 新井白石. jb. 17 vols.
ms. Shoryōbu.

Hakuseki Sōsho 白石叢書 B., by Arai Hakuseki 新井白石. jb. 11 vols.
ms. Nichidai-Ueda.

Hakuseki Sōsho 白石叢書 C., by Arai Hakuseki 新井白石. jb. 28 vols.
ms. Naikaku.

Hakuseki Sōsho 白石叢書 D., by Arai Hakuseki 新井白石. jb. 40 vols.
ms. Tōhoku-Kanō.

Hayashi Razan Bunshū 林羅山文集, compiled by Kyōto Shisekikai 京都史蹟會, Osaka 弘文社, 1930 (昭和 5). jb. 2 vols.

Hayashi Shihei Zenshū 林子平全集, compiled by Yamamoto Gyō 山本饒, Tokyo 生活社, 1943–1946 (昭和 18–21). wb. 3 vols.

Heikan Issō 弊函一掃. jb. 12 vols.
ms. Ueno.

Heion Moji Shiryō Sōsho 拼音文字資料叢書 *P'in-yin Wen-tzu Tzu-liao Ts'ung-shu,* compiled and published by the Moji Kaikaku Shuppansha 文字改革出版社, Peking, 1957 (民國 46). wb.
c. Seishin (not complete).

Heikija Kijitsu 劈邪紀實 *P'i-hsieh chi-shih,* compiled by Tenka Daiichi Shōshin no Hito 天下第一傷心之人 *T'ien-hsia ti-yi shang-hsin chih jen,* [n.p.], 1871 (同治 10). cb. 3 vols.
c. Tenri.

Higo Bunken Sōsho 肥後文献叢書, compiled by Mutō Itsuo 武藤嚴男 and etc., Tokyo 隆文館, 1909–1910 (明治 42–43). wb. 7 vols.

Hikki Shōsetsu Taikan 筆記小說大觀 *Pi-chi Hsiao-shuo Ta-kuan,* Peking 進步書局, cb. 324 vols.
c. Waseda.

Hirado Matsūrake Shiryō 平戶松浦家史料, compiled and published by Kyoto Daigaku Bungakubu Kokushi Kenkyūshitsu 京都大學文學部國史研究室, Kyoto 1951 (昭和 26). wb. 1 v.

Hirata Atsutane Zenshū 平田篤胤全集, compiled by Hirata Moritane 平田盛胤 and Miki Ioe 三木五百枝, Tokyo 平田學會, 1911–1918 (明治 44–大正 7). wb. 15 vols.

Hoashi Banri Zenshū 帆足萬里全集, compiled by Toshimitsu Magotarō 利光孫太郎, Ōita 帆足記念圖書館, 1926 (大正 15). wb. 2 vols.

Hōgandō Hikyū 寶顏堂秘笈 *Pao-yen-t'ang Mi-chieh,* compiled by Chin Keiju 陳繼儒 *Ch'en Chi-ju,* 1606–1620 (萬曆 34–泰昌 1). cb. 53 vols.
c. ICU, Keiō, Waseda.

Hokumon Sōsho 北門叢書, compiled by Ōtomo Kisaku 大友喜作, Sapporo 北光書房, 1943- (昭和 18-). wb. 6 vols.

Hyakka Setsurin 百家說林, compiled by Imaizumi Teisuke 今泉定介 and Hatakeyama Ken 畠山健, Tokyo, 1890–92 (明治 23–25). wb. 10 vols.
—— Tokyo 吉川弘文館, 1905–06 (明治 38–39). wb. 7 vols.

Hyakka Zuihitsu 百家隨筆, compiled and published by the Kokusho Kankōkai 國書刊行會, Tokyo, 1917–1918 (大正 6–7). wb. 3 vols.

Hyakumantō 百萬塔, compiled by Nakane Shuku 中根淑, Tokyo 金港堂, 1892 (明治 25). jb. 22 vols.

Hyōryū Kidan Zenshū 漂流奇談全集, compiled by Ishii Kendō 石井研堂, in the Zoku Teikoku Bunko 續帝國文庫, Tokyo 1900 (明治 33). wb. 1 v.

Hyōryūki Sōsho 漂流記叢書. jb.
ms. Ueno.

Ikoku Hyōryū Kidanshū 異國漂流奇談集, jb.
ms. Waseda.

Ikoku Hyōryū Kidanshū 異國漂流奇譚集, compiled by Ishii Kendō 石井研堂, Tokyo 福永書店, 1927 (昭和 2). wb. 1 v.

Ikoku Sōsho 異國叢書, compiled and published by the Shun'nansha 駿南社, Tokyo, 1929 (昭和 4). wb. 13 vols.

Irō Monogatari 遺老物語, compiled by Kusakabe Kagehira 日下部景衡, 1703 (元禄 16). 20 vols.
ms. Ueno.

Ishimoda Monjo 石母田文書.
ms. Tenri.

Ishin Shiryō 維新史料, compiled by the Yashidai 野史臺, Tokyo, 1877–1886 (明治 10–19). jb. 182 vols.

Jo Buntei-kō-shū 徐文定公集 *Hsü Wen-ting kung chi,* compiled and published by the Catholic Church of Shanghai, Shanghai 慈母堂, 1896 (光緒 22). cb. 4 vols.
c. Toyo.
—— revised and enlarged, Shanghai 徐家滙天主堂, 1933 (民國 22). cb. 8 vols.
c. ICU.

Joken Isho 如見遺書, compiled by Nishikawa Tadasuke 西川忠亮, Nagasaki 1898–1907 (明治 31–40). jb. 18 vols.

Kaga Noto Kyōdo Tosho Sōkan 加賀能登郷土圖書叢刊, published by the Ishikawaken Toshokan Kyōkai 石川縣圖書館協會, Kanazawa 1931–1941 (昭和 6–17). wb. 55 vols.

Kaibō Igi 海防彙議, compiled by Shioda Jun'an 鹽田順庵. jb. 45 vols.
See the present volume, nos. 3044–3045.

Kaihyō Ibun 海表異聞, compiled by Tessō Dojin 徹桑土人. jb. 79 vols.
See the present volume, n. 3638.

Kaihyō Sōsho 海表叢書, compiled by Shimmura Izuru 新村出, Kyoto 更生閣, 1927–1928 (昭和 2–3). wb. 6 vols.
* Namban Kōmō Shiryō 南蠻紅毛史料, 2nd ed. of the *Kaihyō Sōsho,* Kyoto 更生閣, 1930 (昭和 5). wb. 2 vols.

Kaiji Shiryō Sōsho 海事史料叢書, compiled by Sumita Shōichi 住田正一, Tokyo 巖松堂, 1929–1931 (昭和 4–6). 20 vols.

Kaishoku 海色, compiled and published by the Nagasaki Bunken Kankōkai 長崎文献刊行會, Nagasaki 1934–1936 (昭和 9–11). wb. 4 vols.

Kaitei Shiseki Shūran 改訂史籍集覧, revised by Kondō Keizō 近藤圭三, Tokyo 近藤活版所, 1900–1905 (明治 33–35). wb. 33 vols.

Kaizansenkan Sōsho 海山仙館叢書 *Hai-shan-hsien-kuan Ts'ung-shu,* compiled by Han Shisei 潘仕成 *P'an Shih-ch'eng,* Peking 1845–51 (道光 25–31). cb. 120 vols.
c. Keiō, Kyōdai, Kyūdai-Bunka, Hibiya-Ichimura, Osakadai, Seikadō, Shinken, Tōhoku-Hayashi, Tōyō, Tōyō-Fujita (v. VI–X missing), Ueno, Waseda-Ogura.

Kakyōroku 可恐録, compiled by Kato Nantei 加藤南汀, 1816 (文化 13). jb. 1 v.
ms. Tenri.
See the present volume, n. 2331.

Kansai Henchosho 攤齋編著書, compiled by Kimura Masakoto 木村正辭. jb. 88 vols.
ms. Tōyō-Iwasaki.

Kan'utei Sōsho 甘雨亭叢書, compiled by Itakura Katsuaki 板倉勝明, Edo [Tokyo], 1845–1856 (弘化 2–安政 3). jb. 56 vols.

Kazan Zenshū 華山全集, compiled by Suzuki Seisetsu 鈴木清節, Tokyo 華山叢書出版會, 1941 (昭和 16). wb. 1 v.

Kibi Gunsho Shūsei 吉備群書集成, compiled by Tanaka Seiichi 田中誠一, Okayama 吉備群書集成刊行會, 1919–1932 (大正 10–昭和 7). wb. 10 vols.

Kichō Tosho Eihon Kankōkai Sōsho 貴重圖書影本刊行會叢書, compiled and published by the Kichō Tosho Eihon Kankōkai 貴重圖書影本刊行會, Tokyo, 1930– (昭和 5–). jb.

Kieiken Sōsho 喜咏軒叢書 *Hsi-yung-hsüan Ts'ung-shu,* compiled by Tō Shō 陶湘 *T'ao Hsiang,* 1926–1931 (民國 15–20). cb. 42 vols.
c. Kyōdai-Bungakubu.

Kimurake Monjo 木村家文書. jb. 39 vols.
ms. Hokudai.

Kindai Nippon Bungaku Taikei 近代日本文學大系, compiled and published by the Kokumin Tosho Kabushiki Kaisha 國民圖書株式會社, Tokyo 1926–1928 (大正 15–昭和 3). wb. 25 vols.

Kinji Kaikoku Hitsudokusho 近時海國必讀書. jb. 10 vols.
See the present volume, nos. 3578–79.

Kinko Bungei Onchi Sōsho 近古文藝温知叢書, compiled by Kishigami Misao 岸上操, Tokyo 博文館, 1891–1892 (明治 24–25). wb. 12 vols.

Kinnō Bunko 勤王文庫, compiled by Arima Sukemasa 有馬祐政, Tokyo 1919–21 (大正 8–10). wb. 6 vols.

Kinsei Bungei Sōsho 近世文藝叢書, published by the Kokusho Kankōkai 國書刊行會, Tokyo, 1910–1912 (明治 43–45). wb. 12 vols.

Kinsei Chihō Keizai Shiryō 近世地方經濟史料, compiled by Ono Takeo 小野武夫, Tokyo 近世地方經濟史料刊行會, 1931–1932 (昭和 6–7). wb. 10 vols.

Kinsei Jitsuroku Zensho 近世實錄全書, complied and published by the Waseda Daigaku Shuppambu 早稲田大學出版部, Tokyo, 1917 (大正 6). wb. 20 vols.
—— Tokyo, 1928 (昭和 3). wb. 20 vols.

Kinsei Jurin Shiryō 近世儒林史料, compiled by Seki Giichirō 關儀一郎, Tokyo 東洋圖書刊行會, 1942–43 (昭和 17–18). wb. 2 vols.

Kinsei Shakai Keizai Gakusetsu Taikei 近世社會經濟學說大系, published by Seibundō-Shinkōsha 誠文堂新光社, Tokyo, 1935–1937 (昭和 10–12). wb. 18 vosl.

Kirishitan Bunko 吉利支丹文庫 A., compiled by Hiyane Antei 比屋根安定, Tokyo 警醒社, 1926–1927 (大正 15–昭和 2). wb. 5 vols.

Kirishitan Bunko 切支丹文庫 B., compiled by Ebisawa Arimichi 海老澤有道, Tokyo 聖心女子大學カトリック文化研究所, 1955– (昭和 30–). wb.

Kirishitan Shiryō 吉利支丹史料, compiled and published by the Tōhō Shoin 東方書院, Tokyo 1932 (昭和 7). wb. 1 v.

Kirishitan Shiryōshū 吉利支丹史料集, compiled by Nagayama Tokihide 永山時英, Nagasaki 藤木博英社, 1926 (大正 15). wb. 1 v.

Kirishitan Sōsho 吉利支丹叢書, published by the Osaka Mainichi Press 大阪毎日新聞社, Osaka, 1928–1929 (昭和 3–4). jb. 18 vols.

Kisho Fukuseikai Sōsho 稀書複製會叢書, published by Yoneyamadō 米山堂, Tokyo, 1918–1940 (大正 7–昭和 15). jb. 438 vols.

Kōchō Hanzoku Yochi Sōsho 皇朝藩屬輿地叢書 Huang-ch'ao fan-shu Yü-ti Ts'ung-shu, compiled by Ō Haigyō 黃沛翹 Huan P'ei-ch'iao, 1903 (光緒 29). cb. 48 vols.
c. Tōyō, Waseda.

Kōgaku Sōsho 皇學叢書, compiled by Mozume Takami 物集高見, Tokyo 廣文庫刊行會, 1927–31 (昭和 2–6). wb. 12 vols.

Kō Hakuseki Sōsho 廣白石叢書, by Arai Hakuseki 新井白石. jb. 22 vols.
ms. Waseda.

Kōhikyū 廣秘笈 Kuang-mi-chi, compiled by Chin Keiju 陳繼儒 Ch'en Chi-ju, 1615 (萬曆 43). cb. 52 vols.
c. Naikaku, Tōhoku.

Kō Hyakusen Gakukai 廣百川學海 Kuang Pai-ch'uan-hsüeh-hai, compiled by Hyō Kahin 馮可賓 Feng K'o-pin. cb. 16 vols.
c. Naikaku, Seikadō, Tenri, Tōyō, Ueno, Waseda.

Kojitsu Sōsho 故實叢書, compiled by Imaizumi Teisuke 今泉定介, Tokyo, 1899–1906 (明治 32–39). jb. 168 vols. and 12 folds.
—— Zōtei Kojitsu Sōsho 增訂故實叢書, revised by Sekine Masanao 關根正直 and etc., Tokyo 吉川弘文館, 1928– (昭和 3–). wb. 42 vols.

Kōkaishū 江海集. jb. 1v.
See the present volume, n. 2613.

Kokon Sangaku Sōsho 古今算學叢書 Ku-chin Suan-hsüeh Ts'ung-shu, compiled by Ryū Taku 劉鐸 Liu Tuo, Peking 算學書局, 1898 (光緒 24). cb. 30 vols.
c. Tōhoku-Sugaku, Tōyō, Waseda-Ogura.

Kokugaku Kihon Sōsho 國學基本叢書 Kuo-hsüeh chi-pen Ts'ung-shu, Shanghai 商務印書館, 1936 (民國 25). wb.
c. ICU, Seishin (not complete).

Kokugaku Taikei 國學大系, compiled and published by the Chiheisha 地平社, Tokyo, 1943–1944 (昭和 18–19). wb. 12 vols.

Kokumin Dōtoku Sōsho 國民道德叢書, compiled and published by the Hakubunkan 博文館, 1912 (明治 45). wb. 3 vols.

Kokumin Shisō Sōsho 國民思想叢書, compiled and published by the Daitō Shuppansha 大東出版社, Tokyo, 1931–1932 (昭和 6–7). wb. 12 vols.

Kokushi Sōsho 國史叢書, compiled by Kurokawa Mamichi 黑川眞道 and Yano Tarō 矢野太郎, Tokyo 國史研究會, 1914–1917 (大正 3–6). wb. 51 vols.

Kokushi Taikei 國史大系, compiled and published by the Keizai Zasshisha 經濟雜誌社, Tokyo, 1897–1901 (明治 30–34). wb. 17 vols.

—— Shintei Zōho Kokushi Taikei 新訂増補 國史大系, compiled by Kuroita Katsumi 黒板勝美, Tokyo 吉川弘文館, 1928– (昭和 3–). wb.

Kōnan Seizōkyoku Yakusho Ikoku 江南製造局譯書彙刻 *Chiang-nan Chih-tsao-chü Yi-shu hui-k'o*, cb.

Kondō Seisai Zenshū 近藤正齋全集, compiled and published by the Kokusho Kankōkai 國書刊行會, Tokyo 1905–1906 (明治 38–39). wb. 3 vols.

Koshindō Sōsho 古心堂叢書, compiled by Koga Akira 古賀煜. jb. 98 vols.
   ms. Shoryobu.

Kōshin Keikai 皇清經解 *Huang-Ch'ing ching-chieh,* compiled by Gen Moku 嚴杰 *Yen Chieh,* Canton 學海堂, 1829 (道光 9). cb. 400 vols.
   c. Hibiya-Ichimura, Hibiya-Morobashi, ICU, Naikaku, Tōyō-Fujita.
—— Peking 1860 (咸豐 10). cb. 316 vols.
   c. Gakushiin, Keiō, Kyūdai, Nichidai-Hayashi, Seikadō, Shinken, Tōhoku-Kanō, Tōyō, Ueno, Waseda.

Kyōrin Sōsho 杏林叢書, compiled and published by Tohōdō 吐鳳堂, Tokyo, 1922–1926 (大正 11–15). wb. 5 vols.

Kyōto Sōsho 京都叢書, compiiled and published by the Kyōto Sōsho Kankōkai 京都叢書刊行會, Kyoto, 1914–1916 (大正 3–5). wb. 6 vols.

Kyūshū Shiryō Sōsho 九州史料叢書, compiled by the Kyūshū Bunkashi Kenkyūjo 九州文化史研究所, published by the Kyūshū Shiryō Kankōkai 九州史料刊行會, Fukuoka, 1955– (昭和 30–). wb. 11 vols.

Matsudaira Shungaku Zenshū 松平春嶽全集, compiled by Ashida Ijin 芦田伊人, Tokyo 松平春嶽全集編纂刊行會, 1939–1942 (昭和 14–17). wb. 3 vols.

Matsumiya Kanzan-shū 松宮觀山集, compiled by the Kokumin Seishin Bunka Kenkyūjo 國民精神文化研究所, Tokyo 1935–1941 (昭和 10–16). wb. 4 vols.

Matsunoya Sōsho 松屋叢書, jb. 30 vols.
   ms. Ueno.

Meiji Bungaka Zenshū 明治文化全集, compiled by Yoshino Sakuzō 吉野作造, Tokyo 日本評論社, 1927–1930 (昭和 2–5). wb. 24 vols.

Minchō Hajashū 明朝破邪集, compiled by Jo Shōji 徐昌治, edited by Tokugawa Nari-aki 徳川齋昭, Edo [Tokyo] 水戸藩, 1855 (安政 2). jb. 8 vols.
   See the present volume, n. 907.

Misonoya 三十輻, compiled and published by the Kokusho Kankōki 國書刊行會, Tokyo, 1917 (大正 6). wb. 4 vols.

Mitogaku Taikei 水戸學大系, compiled by Takasu Yoshijirō 高須芳次郎, Tokyo 井田書店, 1940 (昭和 15). wb. 8 vols.

Mitogaku Zenshū 水戸學全集, compiled by Takasu Yoshijirō 高須芳次郎, Tokyo 日東書院, 1923–1924 (大正 12–13). wb. 6 vols.

Nagasaki Ikyō 長崎遺響, compiled Shiba Hideo 柴秀夫, Tokyo 双林社, 1943 (昭和 18). wb. 1 v.

Nagasaki Sōsho 長崎叢書, A., compiled and published by the Nagasaki Komonjo Shuppankai 長崎古文書出版會, Nagasaki 1894 (明治 37). jb. 9 vols.

Nagasaki Sōsho 長崎叢書, B., compiled and published by Nagasaki Shiyakusho 長崎市役所, Nagasaki 1926– (大正 15–). wb. 4 vols.

Namban Bunshū 南蠻文集, compiled by Naganuma Kenkai 長沼賢海, Tokyo 春陽堂, 1929 (昭和 4). wb. 1 v.

Nambanki Bunsen 南蠻紀文選, compiled by Mishima Saiji 三島才二, Tokyo 聚芳閣, 1926 (大正 15). wb. 1 v.

Nan'yō Sōsho 南陽叢書. jb. 92 vols.
   ms. Shoryobu.

Nippon Bunko 日本文庫, compiled by Naitō Chisō 内藤耻叟, Tokyo 博文館, 1891–92 (明治 24–25). wb. 12 vols.

Nippon Ijin Genkō Shiryō 日本偉人言行資料, compiled by Hotta Kusuzō 堀田璋左右 and Kawakami Tasuke 川上多助, Tokyo 國史研究會, 1915–1917 (大正 4–6). wb. 23 vols.

Nippon Jurin Sōsho 日本儒林叢書, compiled by Seki Giichirō 關儀一郎, Tokyo 東洋圖書刊行會, 1927–37 (昭和 2–12). wb. 13 vols.

Nippon Kaibō Shiryō Sōsho 日本海防史料叢書, compiled by Sumita Shōichi 住田正一, Tokyo 1932 (昭和 7). wb. 10 vols.
—— 2nd ed., Tokyo 東洋堂, 1943–44 (昭和 18–19). wb. 2 vols.

Nippon Kagaku Koten Zensho 日本科學古典全書, compiled by Saegusa Hakuon 三枝博音, Tokyo 朝日新聞社, 1942–1946 (昭和 17–21). wb. 7 vols.

Nippon Keizai Sōsho 日本經濟叢書, compiled by Talimoto Seiichi 瀧本誠一, Tokyo 日本經濟叢書刊行會, 1914–1917 (大正 3–6). wb. 36 vols.

Nippon Keizai Taiten 日本經濟大典, compiled by Takimoto Seiichi 瀧本誠一, Tokyo 啓明社, 1928–1930 (昭和 3–5). wb. 54 vols.

Nippon Kokusui Zensho 日本國粹全書, compiled and published by the Nippon Kokusui Zensho Kankōkai 日本國粹全書刊行會, Tokyo 1915–17 (大正 4–6). wb. 24 vols.

Nippon Koten Zensho 日本古典全書, compiled and published by the Asahi Shimbunsha 朝日新聞社, Tokyo, 1947– (昭和 22–). wb. 100 vols.

Nippon Koten Zenshū 日本古典全集, compiled by Masamune Atsuo 正宗敦夫, Tokyo 古典全書刊行會, 1926–44 (大正 15–昭和 19). wb. 264 vols.

Nippon Kyōiku Bunko 日本教育文庫, compiled and published by Dōbunkan 同文館, Tokyo, 1910–1911 (明治 43–44). wb. 12 vols.

Nippon Kyōikushi Shiryō 日本教育史資料, compiled and published by the Mombushō Sōmukyoku 文部省總務局, Tokyo, 1890 (明治 23). wb. 9 vols.

Nippon Rekishi Bunko 日本歴史文庫, compiled by Kurokawa Mamichi 黒川眞道, Tokyo 集文館, 1911–12 (明治 44–45). wb. 20 vols.

Nippon Rinri Ihen 日本倫理彙編, compiled by Inoue Tetsujirō 井上哲次郎 and Kanie Yoshimaru 蟹江義丸, Tokyo 育成會, 1901–1903 (明治 34–36).wb. 10 vols.

Nippon Sangyō Shiryō Taikei 日本産業資料大系, compiled by Takimoto Seiichi 瀧本誠一 and Mukai Shikamatsu 向井鹿松, Tokyo 中外商業新報社, 1926–1927 (大正 15–昭和 2). wb. 12 vols.

Nippon Shisō Tōsō Shiryō 日本思想闘争史料, compiled by Washio Junkei 鷲尾順敬, Tokyo 東方書院, 1930–1931 (昭和 5–6). wb. 10 vols.

Nippon Tetsugaku Shisō Zensho 日本哲學思想全書, compiled by Saegusa Hakuon 三枝博音, Tokyo 平凡社, 1955–1956 (昭和 30–31). wb. 20 vols.

Nippon Tetsugaku Zensho 日本哲學全書, compiled by Saegusa Hakuon 三枝博音, Tokyo 第一書房, 1936–1937 (昭和 11–12). wb. 12 vols.

Nippon Zuihitsu Taisei 日本隨筆大成, compiled and published by the Yoshikawa Kōbunkan 吉川弘文館, Tokyo 1927–1931 (昭和 2–6). wb. 41 vols.

Nippon Zuihitsu Zenshū 日本隨筆全集, compiled and published by the Kokumin Tosho Kabushiki Kaisha 國民圖書株式會社, Tokyo 1927–1930 (昭和 2–5). wb. 20 vols.

Nyofukyūsai Sōsho 如不及齋叢書, compiled by Fujimori Taiga 藤森大雅, 1789 (寛政 1). jb. 4 vols.
ms. Hibiya-Morobashi, ICU.

Ōen Sōsho 櫻園叢書, compiled by Majima Ōen 眞島櫻園. jb. 75 vols.
ms. Ueno.

Ōitaken Kyōdo Shiryō Shūsei 大分縣郷土史料集成, compiled by Kakimoto Tokio 垣本言雄, Oita 大分縣郷土史料集成刊行會, 1938–1940 (昭和 13–15). wb. 3 vols.

Ōitaken Shiryō 大分縣史料, compiled and published by the Ōitaken Shiryō Kankōkai 大分縣史料刊行會, Ōita

Okinagusa 翁草, compiled by Kanzawa Teikan 神澤貞幹, jb. 98 vols.
See the present volume, nos. 2058–62.

Ōkōchike Kiroku 大河内家記録.
ms. Shiryō.

Orosu Kibun 俄羅斯紀聞, compiled by Koga-Dōan 古賀侗庵. jb. 40 vols.
See the present volume n. 2892.

Oshie no Sono 教の園, compiled by Saeki Yūgi 佐伯有義, Tokyo 青山堂, 1891 (明治 24). wb. 2 vols.

Ōshuku Zakki 鶯宿雑記, compiled by Komai Jōson 駒井乗邨. jb. 536 vols.
ms. Ueno.

Reisai Sōsho 麗齋叢書. jb. 40 vols.
ms. Ueno.

Rekidai Shōsetsu Ihen 歴代小説彙編 Li-tai Hsiao-shuo Hui-pien.
c. Toyo.

Rekizan Zensho 曆算全書 Li-suan Ch'üanshu, by Bai Buntei 梅文鼎 Mei Wen-ting, Peking, 1723 (雍正 1). cb. 32 vols.
See the present volume, nos. 1644–1647.

Renjō Sōsho 連城叢書, compiled by Kodera Gyokuchō 小寺玉晁. jb. 8 vols.
ms. Ueno.

Rinchi Sōsho 輪池叢書, compiled by Yashiro Hirokata 屋代弘賢. jb. 43 vols.
ms. Ueno.

Ritsureki Engen 律曆淵源 *Lü-li yüan-yüan*. Peking, 1724–30 (雍正 2–8). cb.
c. Miyagi, Naikaku, Seikadō.

Ritsuri Sensei Zassho 栗里先生雜著, compiled by the Yoshikawa Kōbunkan 吉川弘文館, Tokyo, 1901 (明治 34). wb. 3 vols.

Rokumeikan Sōsho 鹿鳴館叢書, compiled by Hagiwara Yutaka 萩原裕, Tokyo 金港堂, 1891 (明治 24). wb. 1 v.

Rokumusai Zensho 六無齋全書, Tokyo 同求社, 1882 (明治 15). jb. 4 vols.

Ryūi Hisho 龍威秘書, *Lung-wei mi-shu*, compiled by Ma Shunryō 馬俊良 *Ma Chün-liang*, 石門 大酉山房, 1794 (乾隆 59). cb. 80 vols.
c. Gakushiin, Kyōdai-Bungakubu, Naikaku, Seikadō, Ueno, Waseda.
—— 世徳堂, [n.d.]. cb. 80 vols.
c. Tōyō-Fujita.

Sanrin Keizaiseki 山林經濟籍 *Shan-lin ching-chi chi*, compiled by To Honshun 屠本畯 *Tu Pen-chün*. cb. 12 vols.
c. Naikaku.
ms. Naikaku.

Sappan Sōsho 薩藩叢書, compiled by the Sappan Sōsho Kankōkai 薩藩叢書刊行會, Kagoshima 1906 (明治 39). wb. 2 vols.

Satō Shin'en Bugakushū 佐藤信淵武學集, compiled and published by the Nippon Bugaku Kenkyūjo 日本武學研究所, Tokyo 1942 (昭和 17). wb. 3 vols.

Satō Shin'en Kagaku Zenshū 佐藤信淵家學全集, compiled by Takimoto Seiichi 瀧本誠一, Tokyo 1925–29 (大正 14–昭和 4). wb. 3 vols.

Seichō Hajashū 聖朝破邪集 *Sheng-ch'ao P'o-hsieh-chi*, compiled by Jo Shōji 徐昌治 *Hsü ch'ang-chih*, Peking 1640 (崇禎 12). cb. 8 vols.
See the present volume, n. 906.

Seigaku Keimō 西學啓蒙 *Hsi-hsüeh ch'i-meng*, compiled by Joseph Edkins, LM. 艾約瑟, 1896 (光緒 22). cb. 16 vols.
c. Waseda.

Seigaku Shūzon 西學輯存 *Hsi-hsüeh Chi-ts'un*, Shanghai 1889–1890 (光緒 15–16). cb. 6 vols.
c. Waseda-Ogura.

Seigaku Taisei 西學大成 *Hsi-hsüeh Ta-ch'eng*, compiled by Son Ukan 孫迂翰 *Sun Yü-han*. Shanghai 醉六堂, 1895 (光緒 21). cb. 12 vols.
c. Waseda-Ogura (vv. IX–XII lacked).

Seihō Zatsuwa 西邦雜話.
See the present volume, n. 1296.

Seika Bunshū 惺窩文集, by Fujiwara Seika 藤原惺窩. Tokyo 國民精神文化研究所, 1939 (昭和 14). wb. 2 vol.s

Seisakudō Sōsho 成簀堂叢書, compiled and published by Tokutomi Sohō 徳富蘇峯, Tokyo 民友社, 1913–1923 (大正 2–12). jb. 24 vols.

Seishōdō Sōsho 青照堂叢書 *Ch'ing-chao-t'ang Ts'ung-shu*, compiled by Ri Genshun 李元春 *Li Yüan-ch'un*, 1835 (道光 15).
c. Seikadō, Tōyō.

Seiyūdō Sōsho 静幽堂叢書. jb. 68 vols.
ms. Shoryōbu.

Seiyō Shimpō Rekisho 西洋新法曆書 *Hsi-yang Hsin-fa Li-shu*, compiled by Jo Kōkei 徐光啓 *Hsü Kuang-chi* and etc., Peking 1645 (順治 2). cb. 100 vols.
See the present volume, n. 983.

Sekai Daishisō Zenshū 世界大思想全集, compiled and published by the Shunjūsha 春秋社, Tokyo 1927–29 (昭和 2–4). wb. 126 vols.

Sekiinken Sōsho 惜陰軒叢書 *Hsi-yin-hsüan Ts'ung-shu*, compiled by Ri Shakurei 李錫齡 *Li Hsi-ling*, Ch'angsha 1896 (光緒 22). cb. 100 vols.
c. Tōyō-Fujita.

Sendai Hansō Seiseki 仙臺藩祖成蹟, compiled by Shimoiizaka Hideji 下飯坂秀治 and Tanno Eiji 丹野英治, Sendai 1884 (明治 17). jb. 5 vols.

Sendai Sōsho 仙臺叢書 A., compiled and published by the Sendai Sōsho Shuppankyōkai 仙臺叢書出版協會, Sendai 1893 (明治 26). wb. 6 vols.
Sendai Sōsho 仙臺叢書 B., compiled and published by the Sendai Shōsho Kankōkai 仙臺叢書刊行會, Sendai 1922–1926 (大正 11–15). wb. 16 vols.

Senshū Sōsho 泉州叢書, compiled by Terada Hyōjirō 寺田兵次郎, 1914–1917 (大正 3–6). wb. 5 vols.

Sesshūsai Sōsho 拙修齋叢書, compiled by Nakanishi Chūzō 中西忠藏, jb.
ms. Waseda.

Setsurei 說鈴 *Shuo-ling*, compiled by Go Shimpō 吳震方 *Wu Chen-fang*, 1702 (康熙 41). cb. 24 vols.

c. Gakushiin, Keiō, Naikaku, Seikadō, Shinken, Tōhoku-Kanō, Tōyō, Tōyō-Fujita, Ueno, Waseda.

Settsuchōsho 攝津徵書. jb. 110 vols.
ms. Ueno.

Shikai 指海 *Chih hai,* compiled by Sen Kiso 錢熙祚 *Ch'ien Hsi-tso,* Peking, [n.d.].
c. Tōyō.

Shin-hyakka Setsurin, Shokuzanjin Zenshū 新百家說林蜀山人全集, by Ota Nampo 太田南畝, Tokyo 吉川弘文館, 1907–08 (明治 40–41). wb. 6 vols.

Shinobazu Sōsho 不忍叢書, compiled by Yashiro Hirokata 屋代弘賢, jb. 16 vols.
ms. Ueno.

Shinshū Zensho 眞宗全書, compiled and published by the Zōkyō Shoin 藏經書院, 1913–1916 (大正 2–5). wb. 74 vols.

Shintō Sōsetsu 神道叢說, compiled by Yamamoto Shinya 山本信哉, Tokyo 國書刊行會, 1911 (明治 44). wb. 1 v.

Shintō Sōsho 神道叢書, compiled by Nakajima Hiromitsu 中島博光 and Ōmiya Heima 大宮兵馬, Tokyo 1896–1898 (明治 29–31). wb. 8 vols.

Shinyaku Nippon Bungaku Sōsho 新譯日本文學叢書, compiled and published by the Naigai Shoseki Kabushiki Kaisha 内外書籍株式會社, Tokyo 1922–32 (大正 11–昭和 7). wb. 24 vols.

Shiseki Shūran 史籍集覽, compiled by Kondō Heizō 近藤瓶藏, Tokyo 觀奕堂, 1881–1885 (明治 14–18). jb. 468 vols.

Shiseki Zassan 史籍雜纂, compiled and published by the Kokusho Kankōkai 國書刊行會, Tokyo 1911–1912 (明治 44–45). wb. 5 vols.

Shōdai Sōsho 昭代叢書 *Chao-tai Ts'ung-shu,* compiled by Chō Chō 張潮 *Chang Ch'ao,* [n.d.]. cb. 12 vols.
c. Naikaku, Tōhoku-Kanō, Waseda.
—— Wuchiang 世楷堂, 1833 (道光 13). cb. 160 vols.
c. Gakushūin, ICU, Kyōdai-Bungakubu.

Shōhōkosai Yochi Sōshō 小方壺齋輿地叢鈔 *Hsiao-fang-hu-tsai Yü-ti ts'ung-ch'ao,* 1891 (光緒 17). cb. 64 vols.
c. Hibiya-Ichimura, Keiō, Kyōdai, Tōyō, Tōyō-Fujita, Waseda.

Shōnan Ikō 小楠遺稿, compiled by Yokoi Tokio 橫井時雄, Tokyo 民友社, 1889 (明治 22). wb. 1 v.

Shōsho 抄書. jb. 14 vols.
ms. Gakushūin.

Shun'urō Sōsho 春雨樓叢書. jb. 32 vols.
ms. Ueno.

Shūyō Bunko 修養文庫, compiled by Arima Sukemasa 有馬祐政, Tokyo 修養文庫刊行會, 1919–1922 (大正 8–11). wb. 6 vols.

Shuzankaku Sōsho 守山閣叢書 *Shou-shan-ko Ts'ung-shu,* compiled by Sen Kiso 錢熙祚 *Ch'ien Hsi-tso,* Sung-kiang 1844 (道光 24). cb.
c. ICU, Imoto, Kyōdai-Bungakubu, Kyūdai, Shinken, Tōhoku-Kanō, Seikadō, Tōyō.
—— Peking, 1889 (光緒 15). cb. 100 vols.
c. Gakushūin, Tōyō-Fujita.

Sokkyohen 息距篇, compiled by Tokugawa Akitake 徳川昭武. jb. 20 vols.
See the present volume, n. 3324.

Sōsho Shūsei 叢書集成.
c. Kyōdai.

Sūbun Sōsho 崇文叢書, compiled and published by the Sūbunin 崇文院, Tokyo, 1926–1932 (大正 15–昭和 7). jb. 124 vos.

Sūri Seiun 數理精蘊 *Shu-li ching-yün,* compiled by Seiso 聖祖 *Sheng-chu,* Peking 1722 (康熙 61). cb. 37 vols.
See the present volume, nos. 1648–52.

Takano Chōei Zenshū 高野長英全集, compiled by Takano Chōun 高野長運, Tokyo 高野長英全集刊行會, 1930–31 (昭和 5–6). wb. 4 vols.

Tanshi Sōsho 覃思叢書, compiled by Hanai Ikkō 花井一好, 1879 (明治 12). jb. 35 vols.
ms. Sonkeikaku.

Tazan no Ishi 他山之石, [n.p.], [n.d.]. jb. 5 vols.
See the present volume, n. 3637.

Teishi Bokuen 程氏墨苑 *Ch'eng-shih Mo-yüan* by Tei Kumbō 程君房 *Ch'eng Chün-fang,* [n.p.], [n.d.]. cb. 2 vols.
c. Seikadō, Tōkyō Geijutsu Daigaku, Tōyō.

Tengaku Shokan 天學初函 *T'ien-hsüeh Ch'u-han,* compiled by Ri Shisō 李之藻 *Li Chih-tsao,* Peking 1629 (崇禎 2). cb.
See the present volume, n. 641.

Tenkōrō Sōsho 天香樓叢書, compiled by Takenaka Kunika 竹中邦香. Tokyo 1882 (明治 15). jb. 6 vols.

Tenkyō Goten 天教五典
ms. Shokokan.

Tokugawa-jidai Shōgyō Sōsho 徳川時代商業叢書, compiled and published by the Kokusho Kankōkai 國書刊行會, Tokyo 1913–1914 (大正 2–3). wb. 3 vols.

Tokugawa Kinreikō 徳川禁令考, compiled by Kikuchi Shunsuke 菊地駿助, Tokyo 司法省, 1888–1895 (明治 21–28). jb. 46 vols.
—— Tokyo 吉川弘文館, 1931–1932 (昭和 6–7). wb. 12 vols.

Tōyō Bunko Ronsō 東洋文庫論叢, compiled and published by the Tōyō Bunko 東洋文庫 (Oriental Lib.), Tokyo 1925– (大正 14–).

Tsūzoku Nippon Zenshi 通俗日本全史, compiled by the Weseda Daigaku Henshū-bu 早稲田大學編輯部, Tokyo 早稲田大學出版部, 1912–1913 (大正 1–2). wb. 20 vols.

Wasan Zenshū 和算全集, compiled and published by the Koten Sūgaku Shoin 古典數學書院, Tokyo 1933–1938 (昭和 8–13). jb. 193 vols.

Yasokyō Sōsho 耶蘇教叢書. jb.
See the present volume, nos. 2048–2050.

Yōchō Sōsho 庸懲叢書. jb. 2 vols.
ms. Ueno.

Yōkyō Shichishu 洋教七種
ms. Jinshu.

Yoshida Shōin Zenshū 吉田松陰全集, compiled by the Yamaguchiken Kyōikukai 山口縣教育會, Tokyo 岩波書店, 1934–1936 (昭和 9–11). wb. 10 vols.

Yūhōdō Bunko 有朋堂文庫, compiled by Tsukamoto Tetsuzō 塚本哲三, Tokyo 有朋堂, 1914–1918 (大正 3–7). wb. 120 vols.

Yūkoku Zenshū 幽谷全集, by Fujita Yū-koku 藤田幽谷. Compiled by Kikuchi Ken-jirō 菊地謙二郎, Tokyo 1935 (昭和 10). wb. 1 v.

Yūsō Nenroku 莠草年録, compiled by Takano Takesada 高野武貞. jb. 209 vols.
ms. Ueno.

Zoku Gunsho Ruijū 續群書類從, compiled by Hanawa Hokiichi 塙保己一, Edo [Tokyo], jb. 1000 vols.
—— Tokyo 經濟雜誌社, 1893–94 (明治 26–27). wb. 19 vols.
—— Tokyo 經濟雜誌社, 1902–12 (明治 35–45). wb. 19 vols.

—— 續群書類從完成會, 1923–28 (大正 12–昭和 3). wb. 33 vols.

Zoku Hakuseki Sōsho 續白石叢書 C., by Arai Hakuseki 新井白石. jb. 22 vols., ms. Naikaku.

Zoku Hakuseki Sōsho 續白石叢書 D., by Arai Hakuseki 新井白石. jb. 50 vols. ms. Tōhoku-Kanō.

Zoku Kokumin Bunko 續國民文庫, compiled and published by the Kokumin Bunko Kankōkai 國民文庫刊行會, Tokyo, 1912–13 (明治 45–大正 2). wb. 18 vols.

Zoku Kokushi Taikei 續國史大系, compiled and published by the Keizai Zasshi-sha 經濟雜誌社, Tokyo 1902–04 (明治 35–37). wb. 15 vols.

Zoku Nippon Keizai Sōsho 續日本經濟叢書, compiled by Takimoto Seiichi 瀧本誠一, Tokyo 大鐙閣, 1923 (大正 12). wb. 3 vols.

Zoku Seigaku Taisei 續西學大成 Hsü Hsi-hsüeh Ta-ch'eng, 1897 (光緒 23). cb. 16 vols.
c. Waseda-Ogura.

Zoku Seppu 續說郛 Hsü Shuo-fu, compiled by Tō Tei 陶珽 T'ao T'ing, 1646 (順治 3). cb. 46 vols.
c. Gakushiin, Hibiya-Ichimura, Iwasaki, Keiō, Kyūdai, Naikaku, Seikadō, Shinken, Tōyō, Ueno, Waseda.

Zoku Shiseki Shūran 續史籍集覧, compiled by Kondō Heizō 近藤瓶藏, Tokyo, 1893–1898 (明治 26–31). jb. 70 vols.

Zoku Teikoku Bunko 續帝國文庫, compiled and published by the Hakubunkan 博文館, Tokyo, 1899–1903 (明治 32–36). wb. 50 vols.

Zokuzoku Gunsho Ruijū 續々群書類從, compiled by the Kokusho Kankōkai 國書刊行會, Tokyo 1906–1909 (明治 39–42). wb. 16 vols.

Zonsai Sōsho 存採叢書, compiled by Kondō Keizō 近藤圭造, Tokyo 1880–1887 (明治 13–20). jb. 132 vols.

Zōzan Zenshū 象山全集, compiled by the Shinano Kyōikukai 信濃教育會, Nagano 信濃毎日新聞社, 1934–1935 (昭和 9–10). wb. 5 vols.

Zuihitsu Bungaku Senshū 隨筆文學選集, compiled by Kususe Jun 楠瀬淳, Tokyo 書齋社, 1927 (昭和 2). wb. 12 vols.

INDEX

Figures in Roman and Italic styles indicate pagenations

(a) Title

147

151

156

Yohane Jō-chū-ge-sho	2607–08	Yü-tao-chuan	3497–501
Yōiki	3646		
Yōkenki	2898	Zai'nin Tokusha no Hō	2945
Yōmei Sambi	1373	Zappitsushō	174
Yosefu Genkō Zenden	2889–90	Zeigo	1986–88
Yo-se Yen-hsin Chüan-chuan	2890	Zen-aku Hō Ryakusetsu	1302–03
Yōshū Fushi	1386–88	Zensei Fukujū Seiro	1157–61
Yōzō Kaikuron	2727–36	Zenshin Isshi	1412
Yüan-ching-shuo	650–53	Zentai Shinron	3048–52
Yüan-hsi Ch'i-ch'i T'u-shuo Lu-tsui	623–25	Zentai Shinron Ryakuge	3053
Yüan-hsüeh-chi	282–83	Zentai Shinron Yakuge	3054–55
Yüan-tao P'i-hsieh shuo	1253, 1259–61	Zentai Shinron Zukai	3056
Yü-ch'u Hsin-chih	1483–87	Zesshō Dōbunki	492
Yudōden	3497–99	Zesshō Dōbunki Shūyō	493
Yudōden-kai	3500	Zezusu no Kumi Reigarasu no Koto	470–71
Yüeh-li Li-chih	680–81	Zōho Kai Tsūshōkō	1528–34
Yüeh-ling Kuang-i	190–92	Zōho Sengaikyō Kōchū	1984
Yüeh-lü Ch'üan-shu	*133*	Zoku Amerika Sōki	2746
Yūhiron	2992–94	Zokubun Kaitei	414–18
Yu-hsüeh Ch'ien-chieh Wen-ta	2342–43	Zoku Kon'yō Manroku	1899–901
Yu-hsüeh Ssu-tze-ching	3146	Zokushū Raichō Jikki	1133
Yume Monogatari	2613, 2640–55, 3044	Zoku Zenrin Kokuhōki	1601–03
Yume Monogatari-hyō	2613, 2614–18, 3044	Zōtei Kōyoki	1410–11
Yume Monogatari Ruishū	2681	Zōtei Wayaku Chiri Zenshi	3170
Yume no Shiro	2388–92	Zue Ransetsu Sansai Kikan	2236
Yume Yume Monogatari	2613, 2624–29, 3044	Zuhō Sambushū	1488

(b) Author, Translator, Compiler and Others

Abe Hirokuni	2701, 3170	1709–16, 1717–20, 1721–30, *134, 136, 141*	
Abe Masahiro	3410–11	Arai Kōri	3513
Abe Rampo	2962	Arai Rempei	1487
Abe Shinzō	159	Arai Yoshimichi	1693
Abe Tametō	3437	Araki Ibyōe	xvii
Adam Schall → Schall von Bell		Araki Kōtarō	xvii
Aikansha → Guetzlaff		Araki Murahide	1585
Aiko Gyosō	3188	Araki Sai	2755
Aizawa Seishi 2122, 2491, 2710–21, 2770–81,		Arima Harunobu	352–60
2879–88, 2963, 2964–68, 2992–94, 3257, 3324,		Arima Seiho	2089
3412–14, 3516, 3517–21, 3522–23		Arima Sukemasa	*132, 136, 140*
Ajiro Hironori	3327, 3328	Arisaka Takamichi	2070
Ajiro Yoshisuke	3284	Aristotle	636
Akai Tōkai	2691–93, 2969–70, 3044	Asahi Shimbunsha	xvii, *138*
Akamatsu Renjō	1256	Asai Ryōi	1269–71, 1428–30
Akamatsu Sokuyō	2234–35	Asaka Gonsai	2930–31, 2932-34, 3044
Akazawa Tsunemichi	3404	Asaka Tampaku	1709
Akioka Takejirō	xiii, 2112	Asakura Kagehira	1560–62
Albrand	3082–91	Asakura Musei	3016
Aleni, Guiglio 505–06, 541–47, 548–55, 618–21,		Ashida Ijin	*137*
627–35, 641, 644–46, 659–60, 723–26, 930–36,		Aurel, J.C.	xvii
937–43, 966–67, 996–98, 1134–35, 1136–39, 2191		Ayuzawa Shintarō xiii, xvii, 206b, 225, 1556, 2121	
Almeida, Luis de	24		
Amakusagun Kyōikukai	*132*	Baba Teiyu	2498
Amakusa Shirō	1286, 1787	Bachiene, W.A.	2511
Amano Nobukage	1747–52	Bahr, Florian	1911–12
American Methodist Episcopal Mission	3119	Bai Buntei 1634–35, 1636–39, 1644–47, 1879–81,	
Anesaki Masaharu xvii, 70, 77, 134, 260, 296,		*138*	
522, 639, 678, 714, 2044–45		Baienkai	*132*
Aochi Ei → Aochi Rinsō		Bai Kokusei	1882–83, *132*
Aochi Rinsō 2184, 2498, 2506–07, 2511, 2572		Bai Tan → McCartee	
Aōdō Denzen	2266	Baku Katei → McCartee	
Aoki Kon'yō	1776–79, 1891–901	Baku Toshi → Medhurst	
Aoki Teien	2146–53, 3044	Ballagh, John H.	3337
Aoyama Gakuin Majima Ki'nen Toshokan		Banji Sanjin	3092
	xiii, xvii,	Ban Nobutomo	*132*
Arai Hakuseki 207, 1495–97, 1535–39, 1540,		Ban Saikoku → Varo	
1541, 1542, 1543–52, 1553–54, 1555–56, 1567–71,		Banyū Bunko Kankōkai	*132*
1590–99, 1604–04, 1654–69, 1672–76, 1677–84,		Banzan Zenshū Kankōkai	
1685–87, 1688–91, 1692–702, 1703–07, 1708,		Barreto, Manoel	74

163

(c) Subjects

The Committee on Asian Cultural Studies

International Christian University

Director	Dr. Hachiro Yuasa
Associate Director	Mrs. Kiyo Takeda Cho
Associate Director	Dr. Roy A. Miller
Secretary	Maurice E. Troyer

*   *   *   *

The following colleagues have assisted in checking the List language-wise.

Dr. Norman N. M. Sun	Chinese language
Dr. Henry Henne	European languages
Mr. John F. Howes	English language

Miss Tane Takahashi was consulted on library matters.